The Special Relationship between West Germany and Israel

Written under the auspices of the
Center for International Affairs, Harvard University

The Special Relationship between West Germany and Israel

LILY GARDNER FELDMAN
Associate Professor of Political Science, Tufts University

Boston
GEORGE ALLEN & UNWIN
London   Sydney

© Lily Gardner Feldman, 1984.
This book is copyright under the Berne Convention. No reproduction without permission. All rights reserved.

Allen & Unwin, Inc.,
Fifty Cross Street, Winchester, Mass 01890, USA

George Allen & Unwin (Publishers) Ltd,
40 Museum Street, London WC1A 1LU, UK

George Allen & Unwin (Publishers) Ltd,
Park Lane, Hemel Hempstead, Herts HP2 4TE, UK

George Allen & Unwin Australia Pty Ltd,
8 Napier Street, North Sydney, NSW 2060, Australia

First published in 1984.
Second impression 1985.

Library of Congress Cataloging in Publication Data

Feldman, Lily Gardner.
  The special relationship between West Germany and Israel.
1. Germany (West)—Relations—Israel. 2. Israel—
Relations—Germany (West) 3. Near East—History—
20th century. 4. Israel—Politics and government—1948-
I. Title.
DD258.85.I75F45 1984   303.4′8243′05694   84-6168
ISBN 0-04-327068-9

British Library Cataloguing in Publication Data

Feldman, Lily Gardner
  The special relationship between West
Germany and Israel.
1. Germany (West)—Foreign relations—
Israel 2. Germany—Foreign relations—
1945- 3. Israel—Foreign relations—
Germany (West)
I. Title
327.4305694   DD258.85.I75
ISBN 0-04-327068-9

Set in 10 on 11 point Times by
Mathematical Composition Setters Ltd,
7 Ivy Street, Salisbury, Wiltshire, UK
and printed in Great Britain by
Blackmore Press, Shaftesbury, Dorset

Contents

Foreword	*page* xi
Acknowledgements	xv
Glossary	xvii
Introduction	1
PART ONE FOUNDATIONS	**11**
1 History	13
2 Psychology	32
3 Mutual Needs	49
PART TWO OPERATION	**87**
4 Economic Relations	89
5 The 'Special' Special Relationship: Military Affairs	122
6 Exchanges in Science, Technology and Youth	142
7 Political Support	157
8 An Overview of German–Arab Relations	194
PART THREE ENDURANCE	**213**
9 The Maintenance of the Special Relationship	215
PART FOUR THEORY AND CONCLUSIONS	**245**
10 Special Relationships and International Relations Theory	247
11 A Theoretical Framework for Special Relationships	261
12 Conclusion	273
List of Interviews	289
List of Correspondence	293
Bibliography	295
Index	323

To my parents and my husband – models of hard work and perseverance

Foreword

This book underwent its final updating at the beginning of 1982 and wherever possible data for 1980 and 1981 were included. Some events of significance for German-Israeli relations have occurred since that time but none changes the basic argument regarding the resilience of ties: West Germany maintains its sympathy and preference for Israel while trying to improve its links with the moderate elements of the Arab World.

The Israeli invasion of Lebanon in June 1982 met with widespread disapproval and West Germany was among the critics. Yet, as often, its views were tempered. Within the European Economic Community immediate words were strong as the Ten announced on June 9, 1982 that they 'vigorously condemn the new invasion of Lebanon [which] constitutes a flagrant violation of international law and of the most basic humanitarian principles' (Commission of the European Communities, 1982b, p. 79). Action was limited, however, by the end of June to a deferment of the signature of the second EEC-Israeli Financial Protocol (the first was concluded in 1977) and to a postponement of the next Co-operation Council meeting (ibid., p. 80). The measures were lifted just a year later. The June 1982 decision, considered too soft by the Arabs, was pushed by West Germany as an alternative to France's proposal for tough economic sanctions (*Süddeutsche Zeitung*, July 9, 1982) and was in line with Foreign Minister Genscher's promise (made during his visit to Israel at the beginning of June) of German reticence and moderation on the Middle East (*Der Spiegel*, June 7, 1982). At home Germany continued its caution for a while in public statements but by mid-August the harshness of Chancellor Schmidt's earlier pronouncements (particularly 1979 and 1981) on Israeli policy returned. 'Settling conflicting motives and interests with bombs and missiles', he said 'cannot be reconciled with human dignity' (*Boston Globe*, August 15, 1982).

EEC and Bonn criticism sharpened even further in September 1982 with the refugee camp massacre in Lebanon. The Community expressed 'profound shock and revulsion', demanded the immediate withdrawal of Israeli forces from West Beirut, reiterated its Venice resolution of 1980 and called for the mutual recognition of all parties involved (Commission of the European Communities, 1982c, p. 53). No new measures, however, were taken against Israel.

Criticism was also apparent within German society but again the pattern was inconsistent. The German press continued its basic disapproval of Israeli policies with magazines like *Der Spiegel* featuring Israel as a military state capable of initiating nuclear war (*Der Spiegel*, July 19, 1982) and calling for an end to the special relationship (ibid., August 16, 1982). Israel's friends took a different tack with groups like the German-

Israeli Parliamentary Association eschewing public condemnation and preferring, in a letter to its Knesset counterparts, the quiet warning that Israel's actions could be a roadblock to peace. CDU and SPD members of the Foreign Affairs Committee of the Bundestag blocked a planned resolution on Lebanon because it was too critical of Israel, and SPD deputy Norbert Gansel noted: 'We are always a little biased in favour of Israel' (ibid., June 28, 1982).

The critical reaction of German society to Israeli behavior in Lebanon revealed a growing impatience with Israeli policies on the general Middle East conflict. A February 1983 poll of the Institut für Demoskopie indicated that 52 percent of those surveyed sympathized with the following statement: 'We should not place our good relations with Israel above all else. The Arab countries are important for our oil needs. Therefore, we should not become enemies of these countries on Israel's account'. Only 18 percent agreed with the opposing statement that 'Still today it is important for the Federal Republic to attend to its especially friendly relationship with Israel. We have brought on ourselves too much guilt concerning the Jews'; 30 percent was undecided (Institut für Demoskopie, 1983, p. 648). Such answers, however, did not suggest a clear preference for the Arabs over Israel, for, indeed, in the event of a war between the two sides, 19 percent of respondents supported Israel and only 15 percent the Arabs. Again the number of undecided was high at 51 percent (ibid.). This two-pronged attitude of criticism and support of Israel was echoed in responses concerning the Palestinian question in February 1983 when 51 percent believed the Palestinians should have their own state (13 percent said it was too great a danger for Israel and 36 percent was undecided) but 36 percent said the Palestine Liberation Organization should not be recognized (27 percent said it should and 37 percent were undecided) (ibid., p. 652). Public opinion regarding Israel and the Middle East, then, is in transformation but its significance is unclear. For the future of relations, the shift will be most dramatic if it is registered largely among young people and is accompanied by changes in institutional ties. It was too early in the spring of 1983 to have an accurate picture of either dimension.

By the spring of 1983 a new government was installed in Bonn and from the beginning it was clear that special attention would be paid to the friendship with Israel. Chancellor Kohl was criticized by the SPD for backing away from the EEC policy on the Middle East and for leaning towards the American position on the Palestinians (Deutscher Bundestag und Bundesrat, November 25, 1982, p. 8023). He was attacked also for pursuing a contradictory policy on the Middle East. Contradiction occurred in part because of the choice of the two new ministers of state in the Foreign Office. Alois Mertes (CDU) stressed the 'special quality' of German-Israeli relations (*Deutschland-Berichte,* May 1983), while Jürgen Möllemann (FDP) was well known for his sympathies towards the Arab and Palestinian positions. Despite different emphases within his government, Kohl's priorities were obvious in his announcement soon after entering office that he would visit Israel, an act Chancellor Schmidt had declined in order to express dissatisfaction with Israeli policies. Moreover, in his inaugural address of May 4, 1983 Kohl underlined the principle of the specialness regarding Israel:

> Our policy in the Middle East is based on respect for the legitimate interests of all peoples and countries in the region, some of them in conflict with one another. In addition, we are particularly attached to Israel and we support Israel's right to live in freedom and security. We will intensify our friendly relations with Israel and we will expand our traditional friendship with the Arab world. Together with the United States and our European partners, we will help to bring about a settlement of the Middle East conflict. Our policy on the Middle East is based on Israel's right to existence, the right of the Palestinian people to self-determination and the principle of mutual renunciation of force. (*Bulletin,* May 25, 1983)

The special relationship, though not in name, was intact publicly and German policy towards the Middle East would be as much a function of relations with the USA as with the EEC. The Palestinians would not be forgotten but the interlocuteurs for peace would be the old Arab friends who hold political and economic importance for West Germany. The essentially moral commitment to Israel would be accompanied by a pragmatic attitude towards the Arab World.

The balancing-act between morality and pragmatism has been reflected in acceptance by Kohl of the SPD's May 1982 new guidelines for the export of weapons. West Germany will retain a restrictive arms export policy but the old criterion of 'areas of tension' has been abolished and export will be guided by the vaguer term 'national interest' (*The Economist,* May 8, 1982; Philipp, 1982; *Der Spiegel,* May 10, 1982). The formal possibility of German weapons for Saudi Arabia now exists, but the new German government has not leapt to finalize an agreement despite lobbying efforts from the German arms industry. Pressure from both Israel and Saudi Arabia has been fierce (*Der Spiegel,* June 20, 1983). A decision in Saudi Arabia's favour will not damage the relationship between West Germany and Israel, for the new arms export guidelines equally permit Israel to be a recipient and there could be compensation for Israel in this or some other policy area if West Germany concludes a deal with the Saudis.

Chancellor Kohl emphasized in his trip to Israel in January 1984 that on the question of arms to Saudi Arabia he was 'very conscious of our special responsibility for the security of Israel'. It was Prime Minister Begin's resignation and not choice that caused Kohl's mission to Israel to fall after his visit to the Arab World. Yet the delay did not dilute the special position Israel held for Kohl. Like his predecessors Brandt and

Schmidt, Kohl refrained from using the term 'special relationship' but, as in his inaugural address, it was apparent that from the German perspective ties were marked by friendship, preference and resilience:

> Our relations were founded by Adenauer and Ben-Gurion and built up in decades of effort and with considerable goodwill. They now form a dense network of ties and contacts in a large number of sectors. No other country in Europe – and this is a little known fact – has as many ties of partnership with Israel as the Federal Republic of Germany. In accordance with my own convictions I will personally advocate the preservation and further expansion of this very close relationship. Our special relationship based on the past has been increasingly normalized as the younger generation replaces the old. This relationship – and this is something I wish to underscore – rests on a specific moral foundation. Based on this responsibility we strongly advocate secure and recognized borders for Israel. (Auswärtiges Amt, January 29, 1984)

Germany still assigns great importance to its partnership with Israel, and Israel continues to view West Germany as its avenue to Europe. After leaving Germany in 1981, Ambassador Meroz became the director-general of the West European Division of the Israeli Ministry for Foreign Affairs. Prime Minister Shamir has stressed the economic and political significance of the Federal Republic within Europe as Ben-Gurion did in the 1950s. But pragmatism dominates for neither Israel nor West Germany as Shamir reminded Kohl in January 1984: 'It is extremely important that the German people and its leaders do not forget the past' (*Washington Post,* January 25, 1984). Publicly, West Germany and Israel continue to complain about each other, but they place limits on their open disputes and elsewhere preference is still very much the order of the day.

Acknowledgements

The data for this book were acquired from more than 180 elite interviews conducted in person and through correspondence in West Germany and in Israel during 1973–5 and 1979–80. In addition, documentary evidence was collected from archives in London, Bonn, Cologne, Hamburg, Jerusalem and Tel Aviv.

The number of people I wish to thank is large: past and present officials of most ministries in West Germany and in Israel involved in the special relationship who gave both their time and knowledge; the staffs of the Wiener Library, the Orient-Institut, the Germania Judaica, the Presse- und Informationsamt and the Bundestag, and the libraries of the Hebrew University, Tel Aviv University and the University of Bonn. Their familiarity with the subject-matter and their experience with pertinent detail were invaluable. And I want to thank the various individuals and groups who have sustained German-Israeli relations since the early 1950s. Their enthusiasm made my task considerably easier.

I cannot acknowledge everyone who helped me in West Germany and Israel because discussions often were confidential. In addition to those who granted me formal interviews (listed at the end of the book), I want to express appreciation to Otto Küster, Erich Lüth, Edeltraut Scholtz and Klaus Schütz in Germany, and Asher Ben-Natan, Fanny Ginor, Felix Shinnar and Leni Yahil in Israel for their generous help and warm hospitality. I also wish to thank Professor Karl Kaiser, Dr Gebhardt von Walther and the library and press archivists of the Deutsche Gesellschaft für Auswärtige Politik in Bonn for extending me the use of their facilities, and for providing a home for the conduct of research in West Germany. I appreciate too the help given by Susan Boyd, the head of the Press Library at the Royal Institute of International Affairs in London, and other members of her staff.

The Deutscher Akademischer Austauschdienst supported two months of pre-dissertation research in West Germany, through the Council on European Studies, so that I could explore the study's feasibility. Subsequently, the DAAD funded a year of full-time research in the Federal Republic. Dr Martin Peretz generously supported two months of research in Israel. Tufts University provided a summer faculty fellowship and research expenses for data collection for parts of the work. Without their encouragement and generous financial assistance, this book would not have been possible.

Various people have read all or parts of the book at different times and I am grateful for their insights: David Abraham, Yehudith Auerbach, Asher Ben-Natan, Lincoln P. Bloomfield, Seyom Brown, Mordechai Gazit, Sol Gittleman, Manfred Götemaker, Guido Goldman, William E.

Griffith, Peter Katzenstein, R. Gerald Livingston, Roger Morgan, Martin Newhouse, Joseph Nye, John Odell, Rob Paarlberg, Klaus Schütz and Janice Stein. In addition, I thank Dov Ronen for translations from Hebrew. All of them have influenced this book, although I alone am responsible for the interpretations and whatever errors remain.

For typing the manuscript, I wish to thank Stephanie Newburgh and Susan Swain, and also Kay Bierwiler and Margo Blake. Finally, my greatest debt is to my husband, Elliot J. Feldman; throughout the preparation of this book, which often has imposed separation and concentration, he has challenged me intellectually and sustained me spiritually. His generosity and patience have been unlimited. I could not have written this book without him.

Glossary

Act for the Control of Weapons of War	Kriegswaffenkontrollgesetz
Africa Association	Afrika-Verein
Agrarian League	Bund der Landwirte
Agreement for the Avoidance of Double Taxation	Abkommen zur Vermeidung der Doppelbesteuerung beim Einkommen und der Gewerbesteuer
Agreement on Co-operation in Scientific Research and Technological Development	Abkommen über Zusammenarbeit in der wissenschaftlichen Forschung und technologischen Entwicklung
Antisemitic Correspondent	Antisemitische Korrespondenz
Antisemitic People's Party	Antisemitische Volkspartei
Association for Defence against Antisemitism	Verein zur Abwehr des Antisemitismus
Association of National Jews	Verband Nationaldeutscher Juden
Association of National Research Centres of the Federal Republic of Germany	Arbeitsgemeinschaft der Grossforschungseinrichtungen der Bundesrepublik Deutschland
Basic Law	Grundgesetz
Central Association of German Citizens of Jewish Faith	Centralverein deutscher Staatsbürger jüdischen Glaubens
Central Council of Jews in Germany	Zentralrat der Juden in Deutschland
Central Youth Association	Studentische Zentralstelle
Centre Party	Zentrum
Christian Democratic Union	Christlich-Demokratische Union
Christian Socialist Union	Christlich-Soziale Union
Christian Social Workers' Party	Christlichsoziale Arbeiterpartei
Credit Bank for Reconstruction	Kreditbank für Wiederaufbau
Extra Parliamentary Opposition	Ausserparlamentarische Opposition
Federal Armed Forces Academy	Hochschule der Bundeswehr
Federal Association of German Industry	Bundesverband der deutschen Industrie
Federal Indemnification Law	Bundesentschädigungsgesetz
Federal Ministry for Economic Co-operation	Bundesministerium für wirtschaftliche Zusammenarbeit
Federal Ministry for Economics	Bundesministerium für Wirtschaft
Federal Ministry for Education and Science	Bundesministerium für Bildung und Wissenschaft
Federal Ministry for Research and Technology	Bundesministerium für Forschung und Technologie
Federal Ministry for Youth, Family and Health	Bundesministerium für Jugend, Familie und Gesundheit
Federal Ministry of Defence	Bundesministerium der Verteidigung
Federal Ministry of Finance	Bundesministerium der Finanzen
Federal Ministry of the Interior	Bundesministerium des Innern
Federal Ministry of Justice	Bundesministerium der Justiz

xviii *Glossary*

Federal Office for Industry and Allied Trades	*Bundesamt für gewerbliche Wirtschaft*
Federal Republic of Germany	*Bundesrepublik Deutschland*
Federal Restitution Law	*Bundesrückerstattungsgesetz*
Federal Statistical Office	*Statistisches Bundesamt*
Federal Supplementing Law for the Indemnification of Victims of National Socialist Persecution	*Bundesergänzungsgesetz für die Entschädigung der Opfer der nationalsozialistischen Verfolgung*
Federation of the German Jews	*Verband der deutschen Juden*
Final Amendment of the Indemnification Law	*Bundesentschädigungsgesetz-Schlussgesetz*
Foreign Office	*Auswärtiges Amt*
Foreign Trade Act	*Aussenwirtschaftsgesetz*
Foreign Trade Ordinance	*Aussenwirtschaftsverordnung*
Franco-German Youth Office	*Deutsch-Französisches Jugendwerk*
Franco-German Youth Plan	*Deutsch-Französisches Jugendplan*
Free Democratic Party	*Freie Demokratische Partei*
Friends of the Hebrew University	*Freunde der Hebräischen Universität*
German Academic Exchange	*Deutscher Akademischer Austauschdienst*
German Antisemitic Alliance	*Deutsche Antisemitische Vereinigung*
German Conservative Party	*Deutschkonservative Partei*
German Democratic Party	*Deutsche Demokratische Partei*
German Democratic Republic	*Deutsche Demokratische Republik*
German Federation of Salaried Commercial Employees	*Deutscher Handlungsgehilfen Verband*
German Federation of Trade Unions	*Deutscher Gewerkschaftsbund*
German-Israeli Committee for Scientific and Technological Co-operation	*Deutsch-Israelisches Komitee für wissenschaftliche und technologische Zusammenarbeit*
German-Israeli Parliamentary Association	*Deutsch-Israelische Parlamentariergruppe*
German-Israeli Society	*Deutsch-Israelische Gesellschaft*
German-Israeli Study Groups	*Deutsch-Israelische Studiengruppen*
German-Israelite Community League	*Deutsch-Israelitischer Gemeindebund*
German National People's Party	*Deutschnationale Volkspartei*
German Oriental Institute	*Deutsches Orient-Institut*
German Party	*Deutsche Partei*
German People's Union	*Deutscher Volksverein*
German Social Party	*Deutschsoziale Partei*
German Society for Economic Relations with Israel	*Deutsche Gesellschaft zur Förderung der Wirtschaftsbeziehungen mit Israel*
German Tax Law for the Protection of Investments in Developing Countries	*Entwicklungsländer-Steuergesetz*
League of Antisemites	*Antisemiten-Liga*
Mixed Commission of Experts	*Gemischter Fachausschuss*
Mixed Economic Commission	*Gemischte Wirtschaftskommission*
National Democratic Party of Germany	*Nationaldemokratische Partei Deutschlands*

National Socialist German Workers' Party	*Nationalsozialistische Deutsche Arbeiterpartei*
Near and Middle East Association	*Nah- und Mittelostverein*
Pan-German League	*Alldeutscher Verband*
Peace with Israel Movement	*Aktion Friede mit Israel*
Press and Information Office of the Federal Government	*Presse- und Informationsamt der Bundesregierung*
Protocol Office of the German Parliament	*Deutscher Bundestag, Protokoll*
Reform Unions	*Reformvereine*
Sign of Atonement Movement	*Aktion Sühnezeichen*
Social Democratic Party of Germany	*Sozialdemokratische Partei Deutschlands*
Social Reich Party	*Soziale Reichspartei*
Socialist Education Organization	*Sozialistische Bildungsgemeinschaft*
Socialist Student Federation	*Sozialistische Studentenbund*
Societies for Christian-Jewish Co-operation	*Gesellschaften für christlich-jüdische Zusammenarbeit*
Society for Scientific Co-operation with Tel Aviv University	*Gesellschaft zur Förderung der wissenschaftlichen Zusammenarbeit mit der Universität Tel Aviv*
Treaty on the Encouragement and Reciprocal Protection of Investments	*Vertrag über die Förderung und den gegenseitigen Schutz von Kapitalanlagen*
Zionist Federation of Germany	*Zionistische Vereinigung für Deutschland*

Introduction

It is difficult to imagine a less likely bilateral relationship of friendship and mutual support after the Second World War than one between West Germany and Israel. Germans were desperate to put their recent past far behind them, and Jews settling in Israel were fleeing the Europe defined for more than a decade by Germany. Germany wanted to forget a past that Jews refused to forget.

West Germany and Israel did not exist as states before 1948. Both sought to establish legitimacy in the family of nations. For West Germany, the greatest need was to persuade the world that there was no similarity between the new German state and its predecessor; for Israel, the greatest need was the financial means to absorb an impoverished, starved and dispossessed population of Holocaust survivors. And so, in one of history's greatest ironies, West Germany looked to Israel for the Nazi victims to acknowledge the moral acceptability of the successor state, and Israel looked to West Germany as the lone industrial state with both the means and the will to provide a measure of economic security.

Since 1952 the relationship between West Germany and Israel has blossomed over a broad field of policy issues critical for Israel's survival. What began as a reparations and restitution agreement quickly spread into other economic arrangements including economic aid, trade and investment. Through 1965 Israel received more unilateral transfers from Germany than from any other country. Thereafter Germany was the only country other than the USA to provide significant unilateral transfers.

Since 1966 West Germany has given more development aid per capita to Israel than to any other recipient. By the 1970s West Germany and the USA were the only two countries to grant Israel capital aid. West Germany has been one of Israel's main sponsors in the European Economic Community and is credited with facilitating the current preferential trade agreement between Israel and Europe. Defence ties have spanned the course of relations between West Germany and Israel, involving arms transfers through 1965 and exchanges of information on weapons technology ever since. Collaboration in broader areas of science and technology also have constituted a mainstay of the relationship and West Germany has contributed large sums of money to Israel's scientific programmes.

At specific times and in particular policy areas other countries have loomed larger for Israel than the Federal Republic of Germany. The military relationship with France in the 1950s or the military and economic relationship with the USA since 1967 are examples. Yet no country has matched the Federal Republic for the consistency of support over three decades. It is the story of that support, largely unknown, that is related here.

Much of West German-Israeli relations has unfolded behind closed doors while more publicly visible diplomacy has captured attention. Since 1967 the content of diplomatic statements has diverged from the quality and quantity of policy ties, rendering a misleading impression of overall relations. West German-Israeli relations exposed in public pronouncements seemed to be dominated by disagreement on the Arab-Israeli-Palestinian problem, as exemplified in the bitter exchange between Prime Minister Menachem Begin and Chancellor Helmut Schmidt in May 1981. That public impression, however, is incomplete and often wrong because it interprets what leaders say for what they do. This book reveals, often for the first time, the intricacies of the German-Israeli policy relationship in a setting of extensive and complicated ties between German and Israeli societies and individuals.

The German-Israeli friendship that developed out of mutual and simultaneous needs for recognition and support might easily be seen as unique, for the circumstances of the Holocaust certainly have no parallel. Nevertheless, the relationship between West Germany and Israel does bear the characteristics of bilateral relations between other nation-state pairs. The story warrants telling for its own sake, but the task of the analyst of international relations is also to interpret patterns in relations and to determine whether generalizations can be made that will acknowledge but not be limited by uniqueness. Hence, the remarkable character of West German-Israeli relations demands theoretical as well as substantive attention. A friendly relationship between obvious enemies is intrinsically interesting because many observers of international relations are concerned with conflict resolution. This particular relationship may be valued also for its theoretical potential in defining a category of bilateral relations.

I began this book with separate interests that converged. I had studied and I had lived in Germany. As a European, I understood that Germany was the decisive force in the formation of a peaceful continent, and I had been drawn as an area specialist to the fashioning of a European community. My interest in Germany was matched by the conviction that the world peace that had depended on Europe in the first half of the twentieth century would depend on the Middle East in the second half. I developed, therefore, a substantive interest in these two regions.

Israel, as the orphan of Europe, had come to expect European support in the 1950s and 1960s. After the Yom Kippur War in 1973, however, Arab pressure on Europe through the control of oil encouraged European countries to take the Arab side in conflicts with Israel. Nevertheless, the Arab countries won less sympathy than they had expected. As the French and the British leaned towards the Arabs, the Germans resisted and stood by Israel. To the extent that the future of the industrial world was linked to European relations in the Middle East (the chronologically consecutive volatile centres), it revolved around West Germany's relations with Israel. My substantive regional interests acquired a focus.

The third and decisive interest that converged to produce this study was theoretical. West German-Israeli relations frequently were called 'special', and although definitions rarely were offered, consistent meanings were implied. However, many other countries during the 1970s began claiming special relations with one another. Given the unique origins of West German-Israeli relations, I wondered whether the reference to them as special could be applied equally to other bilateral examples. Could many bilateral relationships be special, and could 'special' in this context mean the same thing? Was 'special' a casual diplomatic and journalistic term, or was its use among officials and journalists deliberate? Was the problem, in short, merely semantic, or was there an implicit category of bilateral international relations whose identity might have lasting theoretical value for the study of the essential building-blocks of the international system?

The popularity of references to special relationships concentrated mostly in the Middle East. In a television interview on October 28, 1973 West German Foreign Minister Walter Scheel said, 'Our relationship is of a special nature not only to Israel, but also to the Arab world' (*Frankfurter Allgemeine Zeitung*, October 28, 1973). Walter Laqueur wrote of the same period: 'The Dutch asked the French to intervene on their behalf [over the Arab oil boycott of Holland]. But to jeopardize their special relationship with the blackmailers was about the last thing Paris wanted' (1974, p. 244). The European Community as a whole soon used the term also. On Arab insistence the first meeting of the Euro-Arab Dialogue between the European Community and the Arab League, held in Cairo in June 1975, stipulated in its joint communiqué: 'Both sides agreed that the Euro-Arab Dialogue is the product of a joint political will, that emerged at the highest level with a view to establishing a special relationship between the two sides' (European Communities, 1975).

Special relationships, although most frequently identified in the Middle East, were not confined to relations with Europe. The Shah of Iran, on American television, staked his claim to a 'special relationship' with the USA, and in November 1975 an American assistant secretary of state endorsed the claim by declaring that the relationship with Iran was 'a very special one' (*Department of State Bulletin*, 1975, p. 864). King Faisal affirmed *Newsweek* editor Arnaud de Borchgrave's description of relations between the United States and Saudi Arabia in 1974 in like terms:

> *de Borchgrave*: Saudi Arabia and the U.S. now have a 'special relationship' which is being institutionalized in all fields from defense to finance and technology — and which has been compared to the special

relationship the U.S. had with Britain during and after World War II.
King Faisal: ...We believe the special relationship is in the interest of both countries and the entire Arab world. (*Newsweek*, 1974, p. 41)

King Khaled adopted the same characterization of relations as his brother; in June 1977, Saudi Arabia bought four pages of *Newsweek* to proclaim its special relationship with the USA. Garrick Utley of NBC News on September 4, 1979 endorsed the idea from the American side.

'Special relationships' obviously referred to the Muslim world, but as in the German-Israeli case they could refer to partnership with Israel. Secretary of State Henry Kissinger in 1975 said: 'And it is, of course, clear that there has been a special relationship between Israel and the United States' (USIS, 1975, p. 15). The next administration concurred in May 1977 when, during a press conference, President Carter stated: 'We have a special relationship with Israel' (*Weekly Compilation of Presidential Documents*, 1977, p. 706). And Israeli Prime Minister Yitzhak Rabin already had acknowledged this idea during his visit to Washington earlier that year when he noted that Israel was 'strengthened and encouraged by the special relationship that has long marked the ties between our two peoples' (The White House, 1977, p.3).

Beyond the Middle East the term was used in many other contexts before and after the Yom Kippur War: 'special relationship' was used to describe, for example, ties between Great Britain and the USA; West Germany and the USA; Japan and the USA; Canada and the USA; West Germany and France; France and Algeria; West and East Germany; West Germany and Poland; and the Soviet Union and Cuba.

One concept seemed to underlie the frequent reference to special relationships. Everyone using the term seemed to see close friendship and co-operation framed in the pursuit of preferential policies. However, in a world apparently dominated by conflict it was not obvious to me that so many bilateral relations could be characterized by expressions of mutual preference. Could all the relationships cited indeed be special? Or was the only common feature in these cases the persistent failure of observers to define terms or to use terms systematically?

An obvious reason for the absence of definition was the brevity with which journalists are forced to write or with which politicians and government officials are obliged to speak. However, this professional constraint does not excuse scholars whose task is the elucidation of concepts. Yet the plight of this term was not unusual. Other terms had suffered the same fate during other decades.

Realism, with its vague concepts of 'power', 'balance of power' and the 'national interest', was the vogue in the 1950s. 'Integration' and 'linkage politics' dominated much of the writing in international relations during the 1960s, and whereas these concepts provided a new analytical approach, they sustained the old problems of ambiguous language: 'integrationists' often were unsure whether integration referred to a process or a terminal condition, or both, and 'linkage' analysts linked so many issues that they were unable to suggest what was not linked. The early 1970s, moreover, saw 'transnationalism' introduced so pervasively that Samuel P. Huntington said it 'achieved popularity at the price of precision' (Huntington, 1973, p. 334). Its companion, 'interdependence', shared the problem. The term 'special relationship' endured with its forerunners in popularity the flaw of ambiguity, but in one vital respect it stood alone: 'realism', 'integration', 'linkage', 'transnationalism' and 'interdependence' all arose from an extensive literature which, even if not always successful, tried to give content to these concepts. There is no body of literature to explicate the 'special relationship'.

The effort to derive meaning from the term 'special relationship' is no mere exercise in semantics, for the consequences of the imprecise and often careless use of the term itself can be far-reaching. Ambiguity is often the intention of diplomacy, but the generation of unwarranted expectations through the deceptive characterization of bilateral relations courts many risks. Nations constantly seek assurances of where they stand with other nations. If relationships are 'special', they plainly cannot be 'special' with everyone. Already concern has developed in the Middle East as nations in conflict inquire as to who has 'special relations' with whom. A mistaken belief in undying support could precipitate catastrophic consequences, and the equivocal use of the term 'special relationship' could make a substantial contribution to the catastrophe. Disasters may not be the products of mere words, yet we invariably understand the emergence of disasters through words and through an understanding of what words are meant to represent. The use of the term 'special relationship' has been intentional in the international arena and comprehension of what officials have meant to communicate is therefore essential.

The term 'special relationship' did mean something, and it had policy implications that related to the content and nature of bilateral relations in general. Most of the characterizations of special relationships referred to bilateral ties between states, which reminded me that despite the multilateral emphases of many theories, bilateralism remains the foundation of international relations. Some of the most popular concepts of the last two decades in international relations tend to diminish the importance of the nation state; their emphases fall on combinations of states, subunits of government and non-governmental actors. Attaching importance to other actors was indeed overdue, but fundamental transactions in the international system do continue between pairs of central governments.

The growing number of references to special relations by government officials seemed to signal a more general consciousness respecting bilateral ties. Bilateralism has been an essential feature of North–South relations, for example, despite the multilateralism of fora, players and deliberations. For both the North and the South, *sauve qui peut* has proved stronger than *esprit de corps* (Pinder, 1977; Bissell, 1980; Levy, 1980; Maull, 1980b; ul Haq, 1980; Ward, 1980), and bilateralism has become a more central, conscious element of policy planning within the North. In a major foreign policy statement in early 1981 Canadian Secretary of State for External Affairs Mark MacGuigan ushered in a general policy of bilateralism:

> I think an important feature of the Eighties is the growing preeminence of government-to-government relationships in international economic decision-making. For an increasing number of countries in the world, significant economic exchanges and co-operation are the bond for solid political relationships between the countries concerned. And the world of the Eighties will undoubtedly see an increase in these state-to-state relationships. Canada is compelled to examine very carefully how we will respond to systematically developing the kind of political partnerships which our development requires...we must pursue more concentrated bilateralism. (MacGuigan, 1981, p. 1)

Raymond Vernon had decried this kind of bilateralism as it affects the West's relations with the Soviet Union, arguing that it is detrimental to the pursuit of collective Western interests and permits Soviet manipulation. But he fears the process of bilateralism cannot be reversed: 'The individual states of Western Europe and Japan are already tied up in so many complex deals with the U.S.S.R. ...that the world may well have reached the point at which a cooperative effort is beyond the collective capabilities of the advanced industrial nations' (Vernon, 1979, p. 1051).

Whether bilateralism is good or evil, there can be no mistaking its importance. The concept of the special relationship resurrects the significance of relations between central governments while according appropriate attention to transnational actors. Bilateral relations may take many forms, but special relations do appear to be a legitimate category among many possible bilateral arrangements. My theoretical and substantive interests thus came together and now were fastened to German-Israeli relations. I began to mine the secondary literature on this case, and on other bilateral cases examined in the language of special relationships.

The German-Israeli relationship enjoyed but modest attention in German and almost none in English. Despite some useful descriptions of the relations between the two countries, there was essentially no analysis. To observers of this relationship the case was 'of' nothing but a unique partnership. Nor was the use of 'special relationship' in some studies, particularly Anglo-American relations, of much more help. The descriptions of other bilateral relations called 'special' often bore remarkable resemblance to the casual preliminary observations I made of the German-Israeli case, but no analyst had cast any case in the context of any other. No generalizations were offered, no careful definitions and no systematic analytical categories.

I decided in view of the convergence of theoretical and substantive interests, and a preliminary reading of three bodies of literature – on German-Israeli relations, on other bilateral relations called 'special' and on theories of international relations – to use the special relationship as an analytical window on to bilateral relations in general, and on to the critical case of German-Israeli relations in particular. The task then became twofold: (1) to develop understanding of special relations which are an increasingly important category of the essential building-block of international affairs, bilateral relations; and (2) to produce a thorough examination of a case, German-Israeli relations, whose past and future determine larger sets of relations.

This book is a first step in the formulation of a general theory of bilateral international relations. It centres on the special relationship but is suggestive of other types of bilateral ties. However, all the cases considered here are examples of the special relationship. A more comprehensive theory embracing the range of bilateral relations must await the systematic analysis of other detailed cases. Moreover, even the four cases to be considered (US relations with Great Britain, Canada and West Germany, and German-Israeli relations) have not proved sufficient to elaborate fully a theoretical framework for special relationships. It is still not possible, for example, to distinguish which factors are most important in creating or terminating a special relationship, nor is it possible to specify which policy areas are the most central to the conduct of the relationship. In part, these difficulties arise from the complexity of special relations and the linkage of issues, but they also arise because the number of cases here remains small.

Even with additional cases, some features of special relations may not be subject to reliable measurement. For example, I will argue that certain conditions are essential for the creation of a special relationship. These conditions, including an historical intertwining, an intensity of relations and a psychological resonance between peoples, may be understood in the context of the case, but it is harder to specify how intense, or how much history, or how vital the psychological response must be for relations to be special. Measurement in this book, then, is something of a compromise between Karl Deutsch and Stanley Hoffmann, between the so-called 'scientific' and 'traditional' approaches. Certain transactions are quantifiable, especially in the policy arena, but other important factors require the acceptance of ambiguity and dependence on judgement and even intuition.

The book begins with the West German-Israeli case and traces the bilateral relationship through three stages: foundations, operation and endurance. Chapters 1–3 concern the creation of West German-Israeli relations (history, psychological resonance and mutual need); Chapters 4–7 examine the operation of the relationship – and the essential evidence that it is special – by focusing on a number of policy areas (economics, defence, science and technology, youth exchange and international diplomacy). In Chapter 8 I consider the most important pressures of the international system on West German-Israeli friendship by assessing German–Arab relations. Chapter 9 then is devoted to the endurance of relations, despite such pressures, through active maintenance by both partners.

Any bilateral relationship comes into being and operates for a time. Some are maintained actively and some are not. Some therefore endure, while others terminate. A special relationship deviates from the norm in every phase. The features that make West German-Israeli relations special will be apparent in the next nine chapters, and the details of the relationship are presented with an implicit theoretical framework.

'Theory' is used here in Eckstein's sense (1975, p. 86), residing somewhere between 'soft theory' ('any mental construct that orders phenomena or inquiry into them') and 'hard theory' ('statements like those characteristic of contemporary theoretical physics'). Although the study began in 1974, the building of theory offered in this book conforms to the later ideas of Eckstein, elaborated by George (1979). The concept of the special relationship and the framework to guide the detailed study of German-Israeli relations were developed from the scant literature on the term itself and from other theories that might bear on this type of relationship (Eckstein, 1975, pp. 91, 99; George, 1979, pp. 54–5). The concept is made explicit in Chapter 10, after the case has been presented, so that the full weight of the example can contribute to an appreciation of the theory. The preliminary theoretical construct was embellished and refined from the 'crucial case' (Eckstein, 1975, pp. 83, 91, 94, 100, 104, 110–23; George, 1979, pp. 46–7, 51–3, 55), and is offered in detail in Chapter 11. The elaborated framework then was applied (Chapter 12) in a limited sense to other cases to demonstrate its validity beyond the initial cases and the major single test (Eckstein, 1975, p. 105). This analytical method is consistent with the one employed by Robert Dahl (1966) in *Political Oppositions in Western Democracies*, where he offered a theoretical framework in part on the basis of cases already fully elaborated.

The order of the book, then, does not follow strictly the order of the intellectual inquiry. Although I began with a preliminary theoretical construct before full investigation of the German-Israeli case, the book begins with the case. It is easier, I think, for the reader to appreciate the weakness of extant theories in international relations to explain German-Israeli relations after the details of this case are known. Hence, although the preliminary theoretical construct may appear to come after the case, it did guide data collection and dictated the order of presentation for the rest of the book. The refined theoretical framework (Chapter 11) resulted

Introduction 9

from the case and from integration of applicable extant theories in international relations (Chapter 10).

Because the presentation of the case results from a theoretical framework, the terms of the theory are used throughout the book. I refer to the West German-Israeli relationship as special, even as I am proving that this nomenclature is justified. I hope the reader will agree, when finally matching the evidence to the framework, that this judgement is correct.

In sum, I have examined German-Israeli relations as the substantive fulcrum of relations between Europe and the Middle East and as a case of a theoretical category of bilateral relations in the international system. A theoretical idea guided the empirical investigation; the empirical results in turn helped elaborate and refine the theory. Finally, I took the product of the single case effort and began testing it on observable data in other cases in international relations. I hope, in the process of formulating this theory, to have improved our understanding of both Germany and Israel, and of Europe and the Middle East.

Part One

FOUNDATIONS

Relations between West Germany and Israel did not begin with the creation of the two states. The special relationship that developed between the two states was built on the foundations of a complex relationship between the two peoples. We could retreat a great distance into history to observe and assess this relationship, but it is probably most useful to choose an historical departure-point that involves at least one state. The founding of the Second German Reich in 1871 provides an appropriate beginning, especially because Bismarck's conquest of the German states coincided with the completion of legal emancipation for the Jews.

The historical relationship between Germans and Jews is altogether unusual and significant. In the period through 1939 it was characterized by a high degree of mutual preoccupation. It developed between 1939 and 1945 into an obsession between two peoples inscribed with unparalleled psychological and physical consequences. Both periods involved emotions and perceptions of morality whose expression developed psychological responses. Germans and Jews underwent peculiar psychological responses with respect to each other. Historical intertwining, intensity of relations and psychological responsiveness are the building-blocks, the foundations, of the special relationship between West Germany and Israel.

The historical and intense features of a special relationship are transitory. The psychological relationship that emerges from them, however, must endure if the special relationship is to endure. It comprises the continuity: it develops through the historical intertwining and period of intensity; it is the final product of them. It is also an essential feature in the maintenance of the special relationship, the linchpin between past and present. This psychological feature, therefore, will be important not only here in our appreciation of the foundation of a special relationship, but also later when the factors that maintain the relationship are analysed.

Historical and psychological factors are necessary preconditions for the evolution of a special relationship. The existence of mutual and simultaneous need is essential for the translation of these preconditions into an operational relationship manifested in policy.

1
History

HISTORICAL INTERTWINING, 1871–1938

THE SECOND REICH

The existence of the 'Jewish question' in the Second Reich testifies to the mutual consciousness of Germans and Jews[1] in their individual searches for identity. Jacob Toury locates the 'Jewish question' 'at the crossroads between old and new Jewry and between traditional Jew-hatred and new extreme antisemitism' (1966b, p. 106), a crossroad reached with the completion of legal emancipation for Jews at the beginning of the Second Reich.[2]

Why was there a 'Jewish question'? Why were Jews, only 1·25 per cent of the total population in 1871 and slightly less than 1 per cent in 1910 (Schorsch, 1972, p. 13), considered different from all other minorities? Reinhard Rürup's answer is persuasive. He points to a consolidation of emancipation insufficient to withstand challenge in a crisis, yet sufficient enough to be the object of envy and blame (1975, pp. 16–20).[3]

Continuity or discontinuity? Whether the particular antisemitic formulation of the 'Jewish question' in the Second Reich contributed to the antisemitism of the Third Reich is the theme in most studies of German-Jewish relations during Wilhelmine Germany. There are three interpretations, and they mirror the central controversy of German historiography. One school argues that German history is one of constant and continuous themes; a second school contends that German history is characterized by ruptures that divide periods and themes; the third interpretation is a compromise of the two main views. The existence and durability of mutual awareness are necessary conditions of historical intertwining; discontinuity in German-Jewish relations would cast doubt, therefore, on the special relationship.

The chief proponent of the discontinuity approach to German-Jewish relations is Peter Gay (1968, 1978). Gay, like other interpreters, characterizes National Socialist antisemitism as unparalleled evil, recognizes anti-Jewish and antisemitic behaviour in the Second Reich and acknowledges opposition to antisemitism in Imperial Germany. He differs from other analysts over the question of the significance of the 'Jewish question' during the Second Reich and its consequences for later

National Socialist patterns. He sees antisemitism as 'one, but only one, manifestation' of 'the forces of political paranoia', emphasizing the 'eccentric' nature of racial antisemitism and noting that popular antisemitism, while not dissipated, had declined after the 1890s. Gay argues that for an increasing number of Germans the 'Jewish question' lost vibrancy at the same time that emancipation enabled Jews to perceive themselves as Jewish Germans rather than as German Jews. Hence, Gay doubts the determinism that designates the Second Reich as 'a pestilential breeding ground for the Third': 'To say that the Third Reich was grounded in the German past is true enough; to say that it was the inescapable result of that past, the only fruit that the German tree would grow, is false' (Gay, 1978, pp. 8–9, 17–19, 94–5).

A second school agrees with Gay's observation that antisemitic political parties failed during the Second Reich, but historians such as Massing (1949), Pulzer (1964) and Tal (1975) see an increase in popular antisemitic and anti-Jewish sentiment. They emphasize the incomplete nature of emancipation to argue that the 'Jewish question' retained its potency for Germans and for Jews. The outward appearance after the 1890s of a decline in formal, organized political antisemitism masked other developments. Massing, Pulzer and Tal perceive an evolutionary, if not absolutely linear, path from the broader political and social thought of the Second Reich to the specific political and social action of the Third. Massing explains:

> Measured in terms of the number of their adherents, organizational strength, or political representation, the pre-Hitler anti-Semites never achieved the status of major political parties. But their significance cannot be judged by such criteria alone. They kept alive and disseminated anti-Semitism throughout German culture. They formulated the racist ideology long before the Nazis came into existence and helped pave the way for a political alliance of social forces that proved fatal to the German Republic and disastrous to the world. (Massing, 1949, pp. xvi–xvii)

Cultural and intellectual historians, such as Fritz Stern (1963) and George Mosse (1964, 1970), are the most unequivocal exponents of the continuity argument. Their work differs from Massing, Tal and Pulzer mainly in focus: the latter group concentrates on antisemitism in political parties and organizations, whereas Stern and Mosse concentrate on culture and broader political and social questions. In their view emancipation was by no means total and the 'Jewish question' persisted. Germans considered Jews outsiders by virtue of culture, ethnicity, religion, ideology and ethical values. Popular and political antisemitism provided the foundation for the excesses of the Third Reich. The direct link is made, for example, in Mosse's discussion of Volkish thought. He argues that 'This nationalism is the soil from which National Socialism took much of its nourishment and whose ideology Adolf Hitler used in his struggle for power' (Mosse, 1970, p. 21).

Richard S. Levy seeks to find a compromise between the continuity and discontinuity positions. He consciously dissociates himself from the continuity arguments by asserting the relative insignificance of the Jewish problem for most Germans, yet he notes the widespread nature of anti-Jewish sentiment (as opposed to purposeful antisemitism); he sees an indirect link between the minority of revolutionary antisemites (who opposed but ceded ground to the parliamentary solutions of the conventional antisemites) and the practices and philosophy of the Nazis (Levy, 1975, pp. 1–7, 145, 264–5).

The weight of other scholarship, and recent critical reviews of Gay's work (Loewenberg, 1979; Klein, 1980), render discontinuity the least cogent of the three views on German-Jewish relations in the Wilhelmine period and thereafter.[4] Stern and Mosse, Massing, Pulzer and Tal all expose the pervasiveness, diversity and complexity of a German consciousness that Jews were a group, thereby demonstrating that the Jewish preoccupation with being 'German' was matched by a continuity of German hostility towards Jews.

German views on the 'Jewish question' Even if emancipation had been complete, the 'Jewish question' would not have faded away because the role of Jews in the Second Reich was embedded in larger issues. As Fritz Stern has noted, 'The history of Germans and Jews in the post-emancipation period is a central aspect in the process of Germany's modernisation' (1975, p. 79).

Jews could not escape the German gaze; they served as mirrors to liberals and as obstacles to conservative and clerical elements.[5] Liberals pondered the 'Jewish question' as a reflection of the state's success on the issues of liberalism, secularization and nationality (Tal, 1975, pp. 34, 78, 82, 87, 119); conservatives and clerical groups saw Jews as the personification of all that was bad in the Second Reich: liberalism, capitalism and materialism (Stern, 1963, pp. xiii, xix; Mosse, 1964, ch. 7, 1970, pp. 4, 8, 20). Reinhard Rürup summarizes the sentiment: 'When the exponents of Prussian conservatism and political catholicism, the antisemitic critics of culture and the popular agitators moaned about "Jewish rule", they looked upon it by and large as merely the ultimate incarnation of the liberal-capitalist system that was the real target of their wrath' (1975, p. 23). Jews stood in the way of the nationalism espoused by various conservative elements. They were deemed 'an unreliable element from the national point of view' (Tal, 1975, p. 293).

On the political spectrum from liberals to conservatives attitudes towards Jews ranged from belief in emancipation and equality to open antisemitism. What liberals and conservatives had in common, however, was the goal of removing a separate Jewish identity, 'the elimination of the Jews as a discernible and effective corporate entity on German soil' (Cohen, 1975, p. xv).

German liberals sponsored emancipation and fought those who tried to rescind it.[6] They reacted instantly to the 1880 Antisemitic Petition (to turn back emancipation), issuing public statements and forming groups to battle political antisemitism; a decade later they established the Association for Defence against Antisemitism (Tal, 1975, pp. 48–51; Levy, 1975, ch. 6).

The petition of 1880 generally is considered the 'first *organized* effort of the anti-Semites' (Levy, 1975, p. 131; emphasis added). But it was neither the first nor the last expression of anti-Jewish sentiment. The central difference, which informs much of the scholarly disagreement, is between political, organized antisemitism and the tacit, more informal, social antisemitism. Let us consider them separately.

(1) *Organized antisemitism* There were various manifestations of organized political antisemitism: Marr's League of Antisemites founded in 1879, Stoecker's Berlin Movement and his Christian Social Workers' Party, Henrici's Social Reich Party (in 1880, according to Levy, the first openly antisemitic political party), the creation in 1881 by Liebermann and Förster of the German People's Union, the first International Antisemitic Congress in Dresden in 1882, the German Antisemitic Alliance and the various antisemitic Reform Unions which also sprang up in the 1880s. These organizational developments were accompanied by antisemitic newspapers such as the *Antisemitic Correspondent* and pamphlets such as those by Marr and Glagau.[7]

Two political parties emerged by the end of the 1880s with antisemitism as their *raison d'être*, Liebermann's German Social Party and Böckel's Antisemitic People's Party.[8] Throughout their existence these parties failed to pass any unequivocally anti-Jewish measure in the Reichstag (Levy, 1975, p. 1),[9] and after 1896 organized political antisemitism declined. However, by then it had been incorporated into legitimate political discourse. Moreover, while it lasted, the movement attracted support from large sections of the *Mittelstand* – what Levy has defined as 'small shopkeepers, clerks, self-employed artisans, technicians, petty civil servants, primary and secondary school teachers, and the less successful or wealthy practitioners of law, journalism, and medicine' – and significant numbers from the peasantry (1975, pp. 18–19, 55, 59; Massing, 1949, pp. 10–12, 209).

The antisemitic parties hoped to widen their base of support through links with other parties and political organizations that already had displayed antisemitism. The Conservative Party seriously flirted with the idea of a political alliance and *Kreuzzeitung*, its 'ultrarightist organ', had been the fount of antisemitic press denunciations beginning with the economic depression of 1873 (Levy, 1975, pp. 13–14, ch. 3; Tal, 1975, ch. 3). The Centre Party was less willing to entertain the idea of political co-operation with the antisemites, but its right-wing Catholic newspaper *Germania* was with *Kreuzzeitung* at the forefront of antisemitic journalism in the mid-1870s. The farmers' Agrarian League, the German Federation of Salaried Commercial Employees and the professionals' Pan-German League all had connections with the antisemitic parties and at times preached antisemitism themselves (Levy, 1975, pp. 3–4, 87–9, 127–9; Tal, 1975, pp. 129–32; Massing, 1949, pp. 138–43).

The antisemitic parties were unable to establish a consistent and effective organizational link with any of these entities. Nevertheless, these political parties and the various political organizations of similar views were important in Imperial Germany for their propagation of informal antisemitism and anti-Jewish thought.

(2) *Informal hostility towards Jews* There were many demonstrations of informal antisemitism and anti-Jewishness and they took many forms.[10] Hostility towards Jews was expressed in newspapers, in intellectual works, in popular literature, in various Volkish writings and movements and in educational institutions. The 'contribution' of Treitschke, a professor at the University of Berlin, to the antisemitism of Imperial universities is noteworthy: it was his phrase, 'the Jews are our misfortune', that the Nazis took as their own. Jews were refused entry to certain hotels and resorts and to some institutions of higher learning (Stern, 1963, pp. xi–xxx; Mosse, 1964, chs 8–12, 1970, chs 2–3; Levy, 1975, pp. 68–9, 163–4).

In all of this activity the state played a crucial contradictory role as opponent of popular organized antisemitism but perpetrator of informal discrimination:

> [Its authority] was strong enough in Imperial Germany to keep down the rowdy brand of antisemitism and restrict the freedom of manoeuvre of the extremist racists. On the other hand, the state itself aided and abetted the latent antisemitism of ever wider middle-class circles by subjecting the Jews to increasingly open discrimination in the army, the administrative civil service and the judiciary. (Rürup, 1975, p. 25)

(3) *The roots of antisemitism* Antisemitism and general antipathy towards Jews possessed political and social roots. It was channelled politically and socially. It also had important origins and consequent manifestation in economic, religious and racial attitudes.

In the 1870s the antisemitism of Stoecker and Glagau was based on the economic argument that Jews had caused the financial crash of 1873 and the resultant economic perturbations. In the 1880s and 1890s there followed the racial antisemitism of Dühring, Marr, Fritsch and Lange among others, an antisemitism that was often anti-Christian in the sense of denying the Christian principle that Jews were still 'eligible for salvation' (Massing, 1949, chs 6–7; Levy, 1975, pp. 11–18; Tal, 1975, ch. 5). Hence, by the turn of the century the questions raised about Jews touched German life in every sphere. Although visible preoccupation declined in some formal respects, informally the disease of antisemitism seemed to spread.

Jewish views on the 'Jewish question' In a variety of ways a cross-section of citizens in Imperial Germany turned their minds to Jews: 'The Jews never ceased to be a "problem" or "question" to Germans, and Jewishness, accordingly, soon became an obsessive problem to the Jews themselves' (Cohen, 1975, p. xvi). The Jews of the Second Reich became as obsessed with their relationship to Germany as Germans had become involved in defining themselves by contrasts with Jews.

Scholars disagree over the degree to which Jews contributed through assimilation to their own later demise under National Socialism (Arendt, 1966; Schorsch, 1972; Bolkosky, 1975; Scholem, 1976). They agree, however, that with emancipation the 'Jewish question' became crucial for Jews themselves:

> That process [of emancipation] set off the most revolutionary event in German-Jewish history: the transformation of the ghetto Jew into the European Jew of modern times. At the same time it created the most difficult problem of the Diaspora: the problem of the intellectual, psychological, religious and political self-questioning of the Jew in his confrontation with the intellectual, psychological, religious and political powers of his environment. (Stern-Taeubler, 1970, p. 3)

The Jewish community was 'split into recognizable divisions', as Fritz Stern notes, 'varying with economic and social status, and marked by different views on political and religious issues, and especially on the problems of Jewish destiny itself' (1977a, p. 136).

The common search for identity *vis-à-vis* Germans did not yield common outcomes. Between the founding of the Second Reich and the outbreak of the First World War German Jewry underwent such significant changes in self-identity and in attitudes towards Germany that one eminent commentator has referred to the period as 'unparalleled' in the history of the Jewish diaspora (Rosenblüth, 1976, p. 549). These changes were associated with German politics and the specific issues of antisemitism. To the legal grant of emancipation and the subsequent efforts to reverse it Jews offered four responses: (i) integration (used here to refer to the retention of Jewish heritage and a diluted form of religious identity coupled with a denial of any Jewish nation and an identification with the German nation); (ii) orthodoxy (identification with Judaism in religious and national terms); (iii) Zionism (separate Jewish nationhood ultimately through emigration); and (iv) assimilation (the stricter use of the term is employed here to mean the total surrender of separate Jewish identity either through a legal declaration of disaffiliation or the extreme of conversion and baptism).[11] These responses varied in emphasis according to the dominant pressures of the overall German environment.

(1) *The first phase* When German Jews began their quest for self-identification during the 'liberal era' of 1871–8, the liberal majority, under relentless pressure from Germans to assimilate, chose integration (Schorsch, 1972, pp. 12–21; Tal, 1975, pp. 291–4; Greive, 1975, pp. 37–43). According to the theological scholar Greive, identification with the German liberal state and nation was consistent for liberal Jews with their religion of reason; moreover, their religious identity persisted in a weak form as *Konfession*, a denominational category. Most Jews were reluctant to flaunt their Jewishness through organizational structures; the German-Israelite Community League waited many years before finding broad support. Organizational coherence was prevented, too, by the profound divergence of religious outlook between the reform and orthodox elements of German Jewry (Schorsch, 1972, ch. 1).[12]

Whereas reform Jews clearly disavowed the concept of Jewish nationhood and peoplehood, orthodox Jews were not as categorical. They were unwilling to deny in Judaism what Greive has called a 'comprehensive, in a vague sense national character' (1975, p. 40). The two groups shared support for the liberal parties (Toury, 1966a, pp. 131–53), but political consensus broke down with the onset of antisemitism at the end of the 1870s and Bismarck's move towards conservatism. Among orthodox Jews, there was a perceptible shift towards the Centre Party which, in representing a religious minority, provided some common ground. The liberal majority found increasing agreement with the progressive left (Toury, 1966a, p. 275).

(2) *The second phase* Only after the second wave of antisemitism, beginning in 1891 with charges against German Jewry of ritual murder in Xanten, did attitudes towards identity of both wings of Judaism appear to sharpen. The Conservatives adopted an antisemitic plank in 1892; in the 1893 Reichstag elections the antisemitic parties won sixteen seats and 3·4 per cent of the votes, their greatest success. Jews then left their 'silent reliance on progressive Christians' (Levy, 1975, p. 156) in favour of solutions that distinguished them more from Germans.

The Central Association of German Citizens of Jewish Faith was created in 1893 and 'heralded a turning point in the prolonged "identity crisis" of German Jewry' (Schorsch, 1972, p. 1; Reinharz, 1975, ch. 2; Ragins, 1980, ch. 3). The very existence and vitality of the organization in the Second Reich challenges, according to Schorsch, Hannah Arendt's argument that Jewish leadership historically was naïve, submissive and thereby an accessory to its undoing in the Third Reich. The leadership and supporters of the Centralverein were essentially Jews of the integrationist school. Facing a new wave of antisemitism they were ready to espouse through public, institutionalized channels their belief in a dual identification on the one hand with German society, state and nation, and the other with their own religious and cultural heritage.

The Centralverein boasted in 1903 that it represented some 100,000

German Jews through individual and corporate membership. By 1916 this number had doubled (Schorsch, 1972, p. 119).[13] The organization used the courts, the printed word and public statements to combat antisemitism and to defend the rights of all branches of Judaism. In addition to countering antisemitic charges, the Centralverein increasingly promoted the strengthening of Jewish identity and self-respect. Judaism was now clearly more than a denominational category for integrationist Jews.

(3) *Zionism* The Centralverein sought political neutrality and, accordingly, was publicly passive towards Zionism. However, the Centralverein adopted at its national convention in 1913 a resolution separating itself from 'the Zionist who denies any feeling of German nationality, who feels himself a guest among a host people and nationally only a Jew' (quoted in Schorsch, 1972, p. 179). The divergence among Jews became public.

Theodor Herzl's secular Zionism, with its idea of establishing a national home in Palestine, at first found little receptivity among German Jews. They supported the movement more out of sympathy for Jews in Eastern Europe than as a response to antisemitism, and adherents were not infrequently East European Jews residing in Germany (Schorsch, 1972, pp. 183–91). After 1900, however, 'the turn to Zionism ... represented an intensely personal reaction to the circumstances of Jewish life in the Second Reich' (Schorsch, 1972, p. 192). The Zionist Federation of Germany grew from 2,200 in 1901 to 9,000 by 1914 (Poppel, 1977, p. 33).

Liberals divorced themselves from the Jewish nationalism of the Zionists, but for orthodox Jews, who displayed only a 'civic loyalty' to the German state, there was some affinity with the Zionist notion of a separate national consciousness. The distinction between the liberal and orthodox positions on Zionism has been described by Greive:

> And just as the *Centralverein* was the creation and the rallying point above all of liberal Judaism, in particular the moderate liberalism of the largest Jewish communities, so the pre-Zionist and subsequently Zionist circles – to the limited extent that the weight of German Jews in this movement counted at all beside that of the Jewish immigrants from Eastern Europe – derived their strength chiefly from Orthodoxy in the narrow sense. (Greive, 1975, p. 43)

Zionism was never a major movement in Germany, but it did represent one solution for Jews to the problem of their interaction with Germans (Reinharz, 1975, chs 3 and 4; Poppel, 1977, ch. 6; Ragins, 1980, chs 4 and 5).

(4) *Assimilation* Both liberal and orthodox Jews, despite their other differences, wanted to halt the stream of defections from Judaism that

seemed to coincide with the increasing economic and social discrimination against Jews at the turn of the century. Disaffiliation and conversion rates grew as a means to obviate exclusion (Schorsch, 1972, p. 138). The pace of intermarriage also had quickened (Massing, 1949, p. 106). Apostasy was castigated publicly by both the Centralverein and the organs of orthodoxy.

The continuation of antisemitism By the end of the nineteenth century other Jewish organizations had appeared to complement the Centralverein. The Federation of the German Jews, the most important, had over 250,000 members within a year of its establishment in 1904. Their representatives met in conference biennially. The Verband sought to defend Jews as a group, whereas the Centralverein had concentrated on individual rights. The main targets of Verband activity were governmental discrimination and contentious Protestant scholarship on Judaism.

The Verband, according to Schorsch, mirrored the prewar decade in Germany: 'The cruder forms of German anti-Semitism had slowly subsided; the efforts of the *Verband* were directed against the institutions that nourished the pervasive anti-Jewish sentiment that remained' (1972, p. 162). According to Levy, antisemitic parties 'had declined into virtual insignificance', but antisemitism persisted: 'On the eve of war, anti-Jewish sentiment was widespread in German life.' And the source of antisemitism was constant: 'The groups in German society most likely to politicize their anti-Semitism were still the *Mittelstand* and elements of the German right' (Levy, 1975, p. 259).

The institutionalization of anti-Jewish feelings was part of the process of institutionalizing Volkish thought. Mosse explains how 'Educators, students, and a multitude of such groups attempted to implement the Volkish ideology as a part of the social and national character of the German nation' (1964, p. 151). He singles out the youth movement or Wandervögel. The Volkish hostility towards Jews on the part of the Wandervögel had its adult counterpart in the Pan-German League, which Mosse considers 'the most important of the organizations that advocated a program based on various Volkish precepts [before the First World War]' (1964, p. 219). The revival of a glorious German nation was one of its primary aims.

THE FIRST WORLD WAR

The First World War tested national loyalty. The historian Werner Mosse has noted that, whatever their political persuasion, Jews rushed to defend the Fatherland at the outbreak of the war (Mosse, 1971, p. 14).[14] Nearly one out of every six Jews fought for Germany in the First World War. Robert Weltsch, one of the most eminent chroniclers and analysts of German Jewry, writing from the field of battle in 1916, describes how Jews were at pains to underscore to the Germans their nationalism:

> We ourselves praise our fallen 'heroes', and serious men occupy themselves with organizing childish depictions and drawings of Jewish heroic deeds, in order to prove the 'heroism' and 'patriotism' of Jews and to refute the antisemitic and stupid invective of the Germans. (Weltsch, 1972, p. 6)

Yet, as George Mosse points out, Jews did not support the war with the same consistency as Germans: '[The] persistence of ethical attitudes, of a refusal to join in the symphony of hate and the deification of the nation, separated some important Jews from most Germans' (1977, p. 15). Even though Jews served in large numbers and adopted German and Christian attitudes towards death and war, the notion of being separate remained.

Despite the general patriotism of German Jews, a new wave of antisemitism and anti-Jewish thinking appeared both at the front and at home during the war and in the defeat and revolution that followed (Weltsch, 1971; Mosse, 1971; Friedländer, 1971; Jochmann, 1971). It was stimulated, according to Saul Friedländer, first, by the contact of German soldiers during the war, and of the general public after the war, with Polish Jews. Germans thought their negative stereotypes of uncivilized, odd people engaged in usurious activity to be confirmed. Antisemitism resulted, too, from Jewish participation in war industries, for Germans perceived Jewish profit from German suffering. Germans interpreted active Jewish contributions to the war effort as cowardice, a view little relieved, from their perspective, by Jewish political and ideological views in which Germans saw pacifism, defeatism, revolution and treason. They criticized especially the liberal 'Jewish press', the thoughts of the political journalist Maximilian Harden, the actions of extreme leftists like Rosa Luxembourg and Hugo Haase (Friedländer, 1971, p. 34), and the views of a host of mainstream socialist journalists and officials.

Weltsch points out that Jews were particularly disconcerted by the revival of antisemitism because they had perceived its retreat immediately before the war and they anticipated integration into German society, finally, at the end of the war (1971, pp. 615–16). For Weltsch, as for other distinguished observers of this period, the socialist-inspired July 1917 Peace Resolution of the German Reichstag marked a turning-point after which much of the German population, spearheaded by the nationalists and rightists, began unremittingly to blame the Jews for Germany's fate, regarding them as traitors (1971, p. 618). The 'stab in the back' theory arose in this atmosphere.

German antisemitic and anti-Jewish expressions caused integrationist Jews to reaffirm an identity that sought to combine patriotism with

Jewish heritage. Thus, the Centralverein continued to believe that both full emancipation and full integration were possible. Zionists, by contrast, reconfirmed their belief in a non-German option, and the orthodox leadership advised its members to refrain from political involvement altogether. Hence, internal differences within Judaism and Jewishness persisted (Reichmann, 1971, pp. 511–24, 548, 559–70; Jochmann, 1971, pp. 409–10, 424; Angress, 1971, p. 148), but all seemed to believe that antipathy towards Jews was a passing problem that could be solved in the framework of German law and the German state.

WEIMAR

Old and new antisemitism The birth of the Republic was accompanied by antisemitism.[15] For the nationalists (largely in the German National People's Party), Jews were the progenitors of the despised 'Weimar system':

> Preuss shaped the constitution; the major German press was ruled by Jews; Jews were ministers: Haase, Landsberg, Hilferding ... Jews were members of the commission of inquiry into the wartime defeat ... In antisemitic propaganda, Weimar was a regime for and of Jews. (Friedländer, 1971, pp. 56–7)

Walther Rathenau, as Minister for Reconstruction and later Minister of Foreign Affairs, personified for the nationalists the pervasive Jewish influence and the Jewish danger. The majority of Jews in Weimar either coalesced around the left-liberal German Democratic Party, the 'flagbearer' of republican ideology, or could be found among the ranks of the Social Democrats[16] or the extreme left (Angress, 1971). To nationalists they symbolized the flaws of the Republic, so again the 'Jewish question' was embedded in the larger issue of Germany's fate as a polity and as a society. Once more, Jews were blamed for political and economic upheaval.

The nationalists hated Rathenau, the most visible member of the German Democratic Party, for his policy of compliance on reparations and for Rapallo. He was murdered in 1922 by right-wing nationalists who justified the assassination as a response to their fear of a worldwide Jewish conspiracy (symbolized in part by Russian revolutionaries) and a Jewish corruption and contamination of the Aryan race. Other acts of anti-Jewish hostility and antisemitism, including the desecration of synagogues and the verbal and physical harassment of Jews, preceded Rathenau's assassination and followed it.

Increasingly beliefs in a Jewish conspiracy were woven into the fabric of German society. The German Federation of Salaried Commercial Employees, the Pan-German League, the Agrarian League and the youth movement reinvigorated their Volkish thought by transmitting antisemitism from the old Germany to the new. The newest organization, the National Socialist German Workers' Party, registered its antisemitism early on in the life of the Republic. The full meaning of its views came after the Great Crash of 1929 and success in the Reichstag elections of 1930 (Barbu, 1966).

Jewish reactions to German antisemitism The initial threat against the Republic subsided with a period of relative political and economic stability in the period 1924–8. Organized political antisemitism was then confined largely to rightist nationalist parties and organizations, and the 'Jewish question' was not an integral part of the agenda. There remained among the wider public a prevalent anti-Jewish disposition, but the status of Jews was improved significantly over their position in Wilhelmine Germany. For the majority of Jews, Weimar, at least until 1929, meant substantial progress: Jews perceived themselves emancipated politically, socially and psychologically (Mosse, 1966, p. 12).

For most individual Jews, the 'Jewish question' did not seem important, but the Centralverein continued to take it seriously and the minority orthodox movement continued its advocacy of non-involvement in the political and public life of the Republic.[17] Assimilation through disaffiliation and conversion persisted, but it still involved a minority.[18] Zionism attracted new adherents, particularly among the young, and received governmental assistance (Nicosia, 1979), but it too reached relatively few Jews (Loewenstein, 1966, p. 352; Poppel, 1977, pp. 33, 161–7). Members of a new right-wing group, the Association of National Jews, aspired to be 'German nationals in the way the political right understood the term' (Reichmann, 1966, p. 517), but the organization was of marginal significance for Jews. For some, the radical left continued to offer a resolution of the 'Jewish question' as a 'by-product of socialism' (Reichmann, 1971, p. 513).

All these groups were addressing the 'Jewish question', but only the Centralverein was tackling antisemitism head-on through publications, meetings and the courts. Already in 1928 the Centralverein identified the spread of Nazi activity and warned against its consequences. And by the end of the 1920s Jews were endangered by economic and political threats to the Republic:

> The world economic crisis of 1929 led to a new wave of antisemitism in Germany. This found its political expression in a movement which ... threatened German Jewry in unimagined ways. While antisemitism had been widespread in the past and often had been used by other political groups for their own purposes, only with the growing national socialist movement was it converted into a mortal danger for Jews. The major electoral success of the National Socialists in 1930 was a huge blow which forced Jews to undergo a profound self-appraisal. (Paucker, 1966, p. 406)

After the Reichstag elections, the Centralverein expanded its role as the main Jewish defence organization, adding a major propaganda offensive of its own against the mounting verbal and physical abuse of the Nazis, and joining with political parties of the centre and left to fight anti-semitism and defend the Republic.

When the National Socialists took power in 1933, the 'liberal' era incontrovertibly ended. Jews emancipated by liberalism remained its staunchest supporters, and when liberalism was defeated, the destiny of the Jews was in the balance as never before. The 'Jewish question' no longer was enmeshed in wider issues. It soon became the central issue.

THE THIRD REICH, 1933-8

The 'Jewish question' had been for sixty years a preoccupation of Germans and Jews. The preoccupation, now institutionalized, became an obsession. The events leading to *Kristallnacht* (the Night of the Broken Glass) reveal the separation, humiliation and finally the active persecution of the German Jews.[19]

Institutionalized antisemitism Hermann Göring declared the Jews traitors in March 1933. Their ouster from public life, the first of the important Nazi actions against them, began immediately. Less than one month later Julius Streicher imposed an anti-Jewish boycott by declaring in the *Völkischer Beobachter*:

> The same Jew who plunged the German people into the blood-letting of the World War, and who committed on it the crime of the November Revolution... is now engaged in stabbing Germany...in the back ...Millions of Germans longed to see the day on which the German people would be shaken up in its entirety to recognize at last the world enemy in the Jew ...At 10:00 A.M....1 April, the defensive action of the German people against the Jewish world criminal will begin. (Quoted in Levin, 1968, p. 43)

Legislation soon followed to eliminate Jews from all professional and public life in Germany. Jews were purged from universities, and judicial decisions formally separated Jews as non-Aryans from the Aryan Germans. 'Mixed' marriages were annulled; children were awarded to Aryans.

The Nuremberg Laws spread the attack against all Jews in September 1935 by moving from separation and humiliation to ban and persecution. Government policy continued to legitimize violence already occurring against Jews. Through the Law Respecting Reich Citizenship Jews were declared officially non-German. The Law for the Protection of German Blood and German Honour prohibited marriage and sexual relations between Germans and Jews.

Kristallnacht – November 9-11, 1938 – established maximum physical abuse of the Jews as a new norm. Allegedly a reaction to the murder of a German diplomat in Paris by a young Jew (who was avenging the deportation of his parents from Germany to Poland), Germans across the country indulged in 'spontaneous' outrages orchestrated by Joseph Goebbels. Nora Levin has called *Kristallnacht* 'an orgy of arson, property destruction and murder of Jews on a scale not yet experienced in Hitler Germany' (1968, p. 80). For Robert Weltsch, 1938 signified 'the end of the period of independence' for Jews. Preoccupation turned into obsession, and independence was replaced with extinction. Weltsch, in fact, apprehended the German preoccupation with Jews in 1933, long before many of his compatriots: 'Now the Jewish question is such a popular topic that every small child, every school boy, and the man on the street has no other topic of conversation. On April 1, 1933, all Jews in Germany were marked with the stamp "Jew"' (1972, p. 25).

The Jewish attempt to resist Jewish responses to German challenges never had been monolithic, and this pattern did not change in the period 1933–8. The responses built gradually:

> The National Socialist accession to power sent tremors throughout this Jewish population from right to left. On the one hand, panic and flight, despair and suicide. On the other, steadfastness and solidarity, courage and a stubborn will to resist. (Dawidowicz, 1975, p. 172)

Jews of all political and religious shades again were forced by Germans to confront the issue of their identity as Germans and as Jews. The Centralverein tried to unify a Jewish defence against persecution, but after the Nuremberg Laws, 'as the community became even more impoverished by Nazi oppression, even more enfeebled by emigration' (Dawidowicz, 1975, p. 195), its energies appeared spent. Its mission inevitably changed:

> Of the type of active resistance required against the established Nazi regime the official Jewish organisations...were...constitutionally incapable. They had often waged a vigorous fight against the Nazi danger before the fall of the Republic but exposed as they now were, and under a repressive dictatorship, they could not join a conspiratorial resistance. Their task was to defend a minimum of Jewish rights in retreat, to construct and reconstruct Jewish life in an interim period and to organise the emigration from Germany. (Weltsch, 1970, p. 143)

Active resistance did not disappear completely, but it was confined to small groups of young people involved with one of the workers' parties or with Zionist organizations (Eschwege, 1970).[20]

INTENSITY, 1939-45

National Socialism separated Jews from Germans, but their separate existence did not separate their destinies. And with the invasion of Poland in September 1939, the fate of Jews in many other countries became tied to the fate of the German Jews. It is difficult to imagine relations between peoples more intense than relations between Germans and Jews from 1938 until the end of the Second World War. During this period German policy towards Jews (and others, including gypsies, Jehovah's Witnesses, the disabled, and so on) assumed unparalleled forms of brutality.

Policy evolved from forced emigration in 1939 to the enactment of the 'Final Solution' in 1941, which was implemented until 1945. There is no exact figure for the number of Jews killed by the National Socialists because documentary evidence is incomplete; still, there is a general agreement on 6 million victims. A precise number, for our purposes, is unimportant; the sheer magnitude, even according to the most conservative estimates, indicates the Nazis' pathological obsession with Jewry.

Table 1.1 *Estimated Number of Jews Killed in the Holocaust*

Country	Estimated pre-Final Solution population	Estimated Jewish population annihilated (number)	(%)
Poland	3,300,000	3,000,000	90
Baltic countries	253,000	228,000	90
Germany/Austria	240,000	210,000	90
Protectorate	90,000	80,000	89
Slovakia	90,000	75,000	83
Greece	70,000	54,000	77
The Netherlands	140,000	105,000	75
Hungary	650,000	450,000	70
SSR White Russia	375,000	245,000	65
SSR Ukraine	1,500,000	900,000	60
Belgium	65,000	40,000	60
Yugoslavia	43,000	26,000	60
Rumania	600,000	300,000	50
Norway	1,800	900	50
France	350,000	90,000	26
Bulgaria	64,000	14,000	22
Italy	40,000	8,000	20
Luxembourg	5,000	1,000	20
Russia (RSFSR)	975,000	107,000	11
Denmark	8,000	—	—
Finland	2,000	—	—
Total	8,861,800	5,933,900	67

Source: Dawidowicz, 1975, p. 403.

As for the Jew, every minutia of his life, including the taking of it, was determined by the National Socialists. Once Hitler had chosen his course, the obsession was inescapably mutual.

It is difficult to identify the most important events of the Holocaust, since the tragedy was so massive and widespread. Nevertheless, it may be useful to etch the enormity and the pervasiveness of the Nazi obsession inside and outside Germany by noting the location and extent of the destruction of Jews, as formulated by Dawidowicz, in Table 1.1.

THE MAKING OF A SPECIAL RELATIONSHIP

The Final Solution testifies to the obsession of Germans with Jews. Its antecedents and consequences meant that German-Jewish relations would be marked by something indelible. Special relationships can be the product of intense relations, whether in positive alliance or in extraordinary blood-letting. They may also emerge from long periods of historical intertwining, of peoples as well as of states. The special relationship between West Germany and Israel was founded on both historical intertwining and extraordinarily intense interaction. The mutual experiences yielded a psychological response among the two peoples which fostered the special relationship, and later maintained it. But as much as relations between Germans and Jews were marked by deep tragedy, they were also characterized, at one time, by mutual benefit.

The relationship between Germany and its Jews from 1871 until 1945 involved a gradual intensification of antagonism, particularly in the hostility expressed by Germans. Yet there were also positive elements before 1933. The antagonism inevitably led to hostility between the peoples and states in the era after the Second World War; the positive elements, the common traditions, later contributed to new co-operation. The special relationship was not the product, after all, of wholly negative experiences.

COMMON TRADITIONS

Germans may have felt threatened by a Jewish presence in aspects of German public life, but for Jews this participation represented the positive side of German-Jewish relations. The number of Jews in German activities was small, but the achievements and influence of some Jews indicate that two peoples shared more than geography.

German public life includes public adminstration and politics, journalism and literature, theatre and film, music and fine arts, academic research and teaching (Lowenthal, 1966, p. 53), and involvement in the economy. Discussion of this public life includes the activities of those who were Jews in name only and those who recognized themselves as

Jews of one kind or another. Frederic Grunfeld has crystallized the common heritage of all Jews and Germans:

> For well over a half century the confluence of these two intellectual traditions, the German and the Jewish, produced such an outpouring of literature, music and ideas that, had it not been for its infamous finale, the cultural historians would now be writing of it as a golden age second only to the Italian Renaissance. It was a time of great poets and painters, of composers, philosophers, scholars, critics; of Expressionism, Dadaism and a new sense of compassion in the arts. (Grunfeld, 1979, p. 1)

Vitality and accomplishment were also apparent outside the arts. Some Jews in the German polity and society have become famous personalities. Mention of a sample will enrich Grunfeld's observation.

Jewish contributions to the development of German society predate 1871 as much as does antisemitism. This earlier period includes Moses Hess, Johann Jacoby, Ferdinand Lassalle, Karl Marx, Heinrich Heine, Moses Mendelssohn and Jacques Offenbach. During the Second Reich and Weimar a parade of Jews crossed the German national and international stages and helped to forge a joint German-Jewish heritage.[21] Ludwig Bamberger, Eduard Lasker, Hugo Heimann, Rudolf Hilferding, Otto Landsberg, Julius Moses and Gustav Stolper distinguished themselves in politics. In government service Hugo Preuss, Albert Ballin, Gerson von Bleichröder and Walther Rathenau stand out. Ballin, Bleichröder, and Rathenau or their families strengthened German economic development, as did the industrial and financial leadership of Goldschmidt-Rothschild, Rothschild, Mendelssohn-Bartholdy, Oppenheim, Friedländer-Fuld, Simon and Warburg.

Jews enriched the spectrum of German culture: in theatre Siegfried Jacobsohn, Max Reinhardt and Kurt Weill; in film Max Ophüls and Fritz Lang; in music Otto Klemperer, Bruno Walter, Gustav Mahler and Arnold Schönberg; in literature Carl Sternheim, Jakob Wasserman, Kurt Tucholsky, Else Lasker-Schüler and Ernst Toller; and in art Max Liebermann.

Germany and the world are indebted to the scientific achievements of Albert Einstein and Fritz Haber, and Jews were eminent in other domains of the academy. Ernst Herzfeld in archaeology and Ernst Cassirer in philosophy exemplify the range of accomplishment among Jews in Germany.

Jews made major contributions to publishing – Mosse and Ullstein – and to the press, as owners, editors, or journalists – *Frankfurter Allgemeine Zeitung*, *Berliner Tagesblatt*, *Vossische Zeitung* and the *Weltbühne*. Thus, Jews could be found across the political-cultural spectrum, but most were progressive and democratic; they believed this course promised them greatest security.

Despite the tragedy of the Holocaust that followed or accompanied these men and women, their intellectual radiance could not be eclipsed. It was the 'heritage that...outlasted the catastrophe' (Adler, 1969, p. 140). This heritage of achievement in Germany, the Jews' own language of Yiddish[22] and the strictly German language and culture shared in the past are intangible spiritual forces that, with the intense mutual experience of the Holocaust, bind Germans and Israelis. Scholarly disputes over the continuity of German-Jewish contact notwithstanding, there can be little doubt that during the course of a century the culture and politics of Germans and Jews built the foundations of a special relationship between Germany and Israel, at once out of triumph and out of tragedy.

NOTES: CHAPTER 1

1 For a variety of articles on the relationship between Germans and Jews in Germany before 1871, see the *Leo Baeck Institute Year Book* beginning with Vol. 1(1955). See also Richarz (1974, 1975) and Liebeschütz and Paucker (1977) for details of emancipation before the Second Reich.
2 More exhaustive analyses of German history's relationship to Jewish history after 1871 may be found in the *Leo Baeck Institute Year Book* and in the Leo Baeck Institute's separate volumes on particular themes (*Schriftenreihe wissenschaftlicher Abhandlungen des Leo Baeck Instituts*), and its *Bulletin*; the bibliographies in its various publications are also of great use. A detailed history of the Second Reich in general is offered by Rosenberg (1964).
3 In-depth studies of emancipation and discrimination during the Second Reich can be found in Toury (1966a), Hamburger (1968) and Mosse (1976).
4 The most comprehensive treatments of different aspects of the Jewish role in the Second Reich and German attitudes towards Jews are presented in Mosse and Paucker (1976), Bronsen (1979) and in the proceedings of the Historians' Convention in Braunschweig in 1974, reproduced in the *Leo Baeck Institute Year Book*, 1975. Other good studies not examined here are reviewed in the Introduction of Levy (1975). A number of the historians involved in this debate are themselves the product of the confrontation between German and Jewish identities.
5 For detailed definitions of 'liberal', 'conservative' and 'clerical' in party political terms, see Massing (1949, chs 1 and 2); Tal (1975, chs 2 and 3). For looser interpretations of the terms, see Stern (1963, Introduction) and Mosse (1970, Introduction).
6 The liberal attitude towards emancipation and antisemitism was not entirely clear-cut; see Tal (1975, chs 1 and 4).
7 The texts of various antisemitic statements during the Second Reich are reproduced in Mendes-Flohr and Reinharz (1980, section VII).
8 For the organizational and titular transformations these parties underwent, see Levy (1975, pp. 65, 109).
9 Levy notes that decline could be witnessed not only in parliamentary seats, but more importantly, in a reduction in party membership and in general dissatisfaction with strategy among growing numbers of political antisemites; see Levy (1975, p.225).
10 Different forms of anti-Jewish hostility – political, philosophical and intellectual – are analysed in Low (1979). He refers also to positive relations between Germans and Jews.
11 On the various Jewish responses, see Reinharz (1975); Scholem (1979); and Ragins (1980).
12 Schorsch distinguishes among the positions of the different parts of orthodoxy (1972).

By the turn of the century, orthodoxy of various kinds embraced only 10–15 per cent of all German Jews.
13 These membership figures represented about one-fifth of German Jews in 1903 and one-third in 1916. In part, the latter increase in proportion was attributable to a declining Jewish birthrate (Schorsch, 1972, pp. 13–14).
14 On the question of German-Jewish relations during the First World War, see the essays in Mosse and Paucker (1971).
15 The interaction between Germans and Jews in Weimar, particularly at the last stage, receives important consideration in the essays in Mosse and Paucker (1966). On Jewish attitudes towards Germans and Germany during the Weimar Republic, see Bolkosky (1975). Eyck provides one of the most definitive studies of the history of Weimar and the fate of the Republic (1970a, 1970b). The Wiener Library bibliography on the period 1918–33 remains one of the best (no. 2, 1964).
16 Support among German Jews for social democracy was growing already at the end of the nineteenth century (Toury, 1966a, p. 275).
17 Bolkosky (1975) reaches his conclusions about German Jews' perceptions through an analysis of various Centralverein publications. His operating assumption is that the organization represented the large majority of German Jews.
18 As Bennathan points out, it is extremely difficult to ascertain precisely the numbers for disaffiliation and conversion. He maintains that the latter occurred much more frequently. Mixed marriages took place more often than either conversion or disaffiliation. In the years 1920–30 on average, according to Bennathan, 17·5 per cent of all Jewish marriages were to non-Jewish partners (1966, p. 96).
19 One of the most comprehensive analyses of the actions of the Nazis against the Jews is Dawidowicz (1975), which Gerson D. Cohen considers 'superseding all others' (1975, p. xv). See the Wiener Library bibliographies on German Jewry (no. 3, 1958, no 6, 1978), which also cover writings on German Jewry appearing before and after the Third Reich. The Wiener Library bibliographies on persecution and resistance under the Nazis (no. 1, 1953, no. 7, 1978b) and on Nazi prejudice (no. 5, 1971) are also invaluable. Bracher's book (1970) on the origins and expressions of National Socialism continues to be one of the most thorough general examinations.
20 Bolkosky suggests there was even less opposition (1975). Eschwege's evidence of resistance is convincing, whereas Bolkosky's psychologizing forty years after the events diminishes the cogency of his otherwise valuable examination of the Centralverein positions during the period 1918–35. For details of the intensive defence effort of the Centralverein in the last phase of the Weimar Republic, see Paucker (1966).
21 The following have been most instructive for details of Jewish contributions to German society after 1871: Prowe-Isenbörger (1962); Lowenthal (1966); Toury (1966a); Hamburger (1968); Tramer (1971); Hamburger (1975); Harris (1975); Kahn (1975); Kesten (1975); Matenko (1975); Williamson (1975); Mosse (1976); Pulzer (1976); Schulin (1976); and Stern (1977b).
22 The number of Jews who actually spoke Yiddish had declined considerably by 1939. None the less, Yiddish did provide an important institutionalized link between German and Jewish cultures. Whether Jews spoke Yiddish or not, throughout Eastern Europe they were often carriers and advocates of German culture and allied themselves with Germans against 'unenlightened' Slavic populations.

2
Psychology

The third element in the foundation of a special relationship, the product of historical intertwining and intense mutual experience (through mutual preoccupation, even obsession, and through common traditions), is the psychological relationship that exists between two peoples prior to the development of the policy relationship between governments.[1]

THE SILENCE

In the period 1945–51 there was a silence in both Germany and Israel about the past. Feelings, whether of horror and guilt on the German side, or of grief and hostility on the Israeli side (Tavor, 1976), simply were not expressed on a large scale or in any public or official way. If this silence meant that there were no feelings, there would also be no special relationship. It is important, then, to analyse the silence, to suggest why it occurred and why it ended dramatically in 1951.

Social scientists need words and actions for analysis. But silence means neither words nor actions. The only available analytic avenue for reaching some understanding of the silence in the period 1945–51 depends upon interpretation. There are some fragmentary survey data, the observations of participants and bystanders, and some scholarly assessment. A few individual Germans did raise their voices before 1951, permitting some interpretation.[2] Mostly there was only silence.

The fact of a general silence in Germany was noted at the time by a variety of sources. For example, the Israeli government referred to the silence in its letter of September 24, 1951 to Erich Lüth commenting on his Peace with Israel Movement:

> Since the end of the last war the Jews all over the world have been waiting for a declaration of the German people and its Government made in the spirit of your call to expiate the crimes of the past. So far only very few Germans have voiced repentance and have urged action on the part of the German Government ... For six years, since the end of the Nazi regime, have the German people and its Government been silent. (Text in Lüth, 1976, pp. 22–3)

The Central Council of Jews in Germany, in its comment on Lüth's call for peace with Israel noted that, 'it is especially pleasing that the Federal Government has also finally proclaimed before world opinion the renunciation by the German people of the crimes of the past and has declared its will to make amends' (*Die Neue Zeitung*, October 9, 1951). Nahum Goldmann, on behalf of the World Jewish Congress, responded on September 14, 1951 to Lüth's call:

> I am sure you understand that the absence of any official or spontaneous stand on Nazi crimes towards Jews, whether on the part of officials or on the part of public opinion in Germany, cannot be comprehended by Jewish public opinion or by decent people the world over. (Quoted in Aktion 'Friede mit Israel', 1951, p. 23)

Jews were waiting for a shattering of the silence, a gesture of atonement.

There are two main explanations for the German silence. There are social-psychological arguments that focus on the individual psyche and attempt to generalize to society or the nation at large, and there are analyses that locate cause in political and economic forces within the general social structure of the Federal Republic. Both deal with the concept of 'mastering the past' (*Aufarbeitung der Vergangenheit*).[3]

SOCIAL-PSYCHOLOGICAL EXPLANATIONS
Germans could not confront their National Socialist past because they were paralysed by guilt, confusion and psychological inadequacy. A divided society discouraged isolated groups from speaking out.

The problem was first articulated in 1952 by the German psychologist Walter Jacobsen. Fifteen years after his report, Alexander and Margarete Mitscherlich, eminent German psychoanalysts, elaborated on the theme and completed the conceptualization of the problem in *The Inability to Mourn. Principles of Collective Behavior*. Most recently, similar explanations have been advanced by Peter Märthesheimer, the key proponent in the German television industry for screening the American film *Holocaust*.

According to Jacobsen and the Mitscherlichs, the psychological inhibitions which produced paralysis were complex (Jacobsen, 1963, pp. 171–7; Mitscherlich and Mitscherlich, 1975, pp. xv–xxviii, 3–68, 297–308), rooted in a neurotic guilt and fear of acknowledging National Socialist tyranny and inhumanity.[4] The Mitscherlichs emphasize that the guilt was particularly debilitating: 'The defense against guilt, shame, and mourning over its losses that is being collectively carried out by the population of postwar Germany confronts us with the same technique of infantile self-protection, although here it is used not against infantile experiences of guilt but against real guilt on a massive scale' (1975, p. 17). Deep-seated fear prevented a healthy resolution of the guilt: 'Unconditional surrender and the occupation of Germany by adversaries who had for many years been utterly ridiculed or represented as devils led to massive fears of reprisal' (Mitscherlich and Mitscherlich, 1975, p. 19).

The avoidance of the 'psychic' self was buttressed by a need to care for 'material' self. In Jacobsen's words:

> Conditions immediately following the collapse of the Hitler regime did not favor rigorous self-examination. Everyone was too preoccupied with pressing problems of 'self' – of how to maintain the most primitive standards of life and overcome dire need. (Jacobsen, 1963, p. 173)

According to the Mitscherlichs, this immediate concern became a permanent preoccupation, at the expense of psychological introspection: 'Since the end of the war the restoration of the economy has been the average German's pet concern' (1975, p. 9). Self-preservation was a psychological and economic imperative.

Whether they had been active participants or they had 'acquiesced silently', after the war Germans reacted to the Nazi trauma in a similar way: they employed psychological defence mechanisms, especially projection and denial. Hitler in particular and the Nazis in general were the target of projected guilt. Denial took various forms, ranging from the contention that Jews simply had not been persecuted or harmed to the proposition that dictatorship was a 'natural phenomenon' over which individual citizens had no control. The only way Germans could account for their idolization of Hitler as a 'good father' was through a denial of both his evil and his death, a line of argument stressed by Märthesheimer (1979a, pp. 11–18).

The combination of these defence mechanisms was powerful enough to obliterate the past for most Germans. 'Together, projection and denial worked to create a painted backdrop masking reality. As a result, retroactive emotional comprehension of the wickedness of those war aims and the destruction they wrought has occurred only sporadically' (Mitscherlich and Mitscherlich, 1975, p. xvi). In Freudian terms Germans had not engaged in 'working through' (*Aufarbeitung*) the horror of National Socialism and the losses it incurred for Germany. For Märthesheimer, this failure amounted to the 'psychopathology of a whole nation', where 'in 1945, these people put their soul on ice' (1979a, p. 13). Psychological avoidance translated into 'political and social immobilism' (Mitscherlich and Mitscherlich, 1975, p. xxv), into 'civic alienism and apathy' (Jacobsen, 1963, p. 175).

The social-psychological explanations for a German desire to bury the past rely on conflict within individuals. The fragmentary survey data available on the immediate postwar period point to the existence of two competing attitudes towards the past which cut through society, however, not through individuals. Between one-quarter and one-third of the respondents in a number of surveys conducted at the time persisted in an expression of anti-democratic, and particularly antisemitic, sentiments, while two-thirds denied even partial responsibility for the emergence of antisemitism (Neumann and Noelle-Neumann, 1967, pp. 186, 189, 191, 192; Merritt and Merritt, 1970, pp. 31, 99, 100, 146–8, 239–40; and 1980, p. 146).[5] Yet nearly two-thirds of the population surveyed by the American military government indicated a feeling that the population as a whole should bear some blame or guilt for Nazi crimes, recognizing that such crimes were committed on a massive scale (Merritt and Merritt, 1970, p. 149). Other apparent contradictions appear. It is clear from this same military government survey conducted in the American zone of occupation in December 1946 that the population, on a variety of measures, tended to accept responsibility for Hitler's crimes; yet this same population was deeply divided over the interpretation of that responsibility.[6] Whereas there was a perception of guilt, there was a persistently negative view of Jews. A full third of the surveyed population in October 1946 clung to a belief in the inferiority of Jews and in the justice of discrimination (ibid., p. 31), and a remarkable 83 per cent of respondents considered German crimes on the same terms as the crimes of other nations (ibid., p. 149). Surveys conducted across the Federal Republic suggest that openly expressed antisemitism actually grew in the period 1949–52 (Neumann and Noelle-Neumann, 1967, p. 186).

The views from the surveys are clear. They do not reflect a whole society too ashamed to speak. Rather, some would never accept the blame (at least 25 per cent) and others perhaps feared the consequences of a divided society. Or that portion of the population which did accept responsibility was psychologically paralysed. Whatever the exact cause, the effect was the same: silence, and burial of the past.

POLITICAL AND ECONOMIC EXPLANATIONS
The alternative explanation to historical amnesia centres on the 'structural continuity of fascism and capitalism' (Huyssen, 1980, p. 121) and can be identified particularly in the work of Theodor Adorno (1977a, pp. 555–72, 1977b, pp. 816–17) and Reinhard Kühnl (1971, pp. 248–71). Both see internal and external reasons for structural endurance, although their emphases are different.

In a lecture in 1959 Adorno criticized the German interpretation of mastering the past which saw 1945 as a *tabula rasa*. He also found incomplete the psychological explanations for this repression of history: 'Forgetting National Socialism can be understood much more as a result of the general social situation than as a result of psychopathology' (1977a, p. 558).

Mastery of the past could occur, according to Adorno, only if the structural determinants of the past were removed. In Germany 'The spell of the past has not been broken purely because the causes [of National

Socialism] endure' (ibid., p. 572). Adorno said, 'Fascism lives on' (ibid., p. 566), and he chided the immaturity of German political and economic forms which 'erase just the [kind of] autonomous subjectivity which the idea of democracy invokes' (ibid., p. 567). In his assessment the 'totalitarian potential' of these political and economic forms was great and democracy, imposed from the outside, had shallow roots. When he repeated his lecture in 1962, Adorno's concern about neo-Nazi organizations and their popular appeal had increased (Adorno, 1977b, pp. 816–17).

A decade later Kühnl endorsed Adorno's diagnosis of the German body politic: the persistence of old and sick organisms prevented health. Kühnl elaborated on the absence of structural change and on the deficiencies of the postwar capitalist economic and political system to effect such change. Yet he also assigned fault for the persistence of antidemocratic tendencies to the failure of the Allies fully to implement denazification.[7] Soon after the war the occupation authorities disbanded the anti-fascist committees, fearing their revolutionary potential, and gradually retreated on their aim of extensive denazification. He blames a Cold War mentality and the power of conservative economic interests within the Allied camp, as well as the form of identifying Nazis, for the Allied reversal on denazification.[8] As a result of Allied policy, 'a large number of officials and judges, teachers and lawyers, professors and publishers, who had "fulfilled faithfully their duty" during the Third Reich, once more occupied influential positions in the state and in society'. The leniency of the Allies extended also to 'leaders of powerful banks and industrial concerns' (Kühnl, 1971, p. 262).

In a situation of unchanging social, political and economic control, Adorno and Kühnl argue, the possibility for introspection with respect to the past is limited, and an expression of repentance is impossible. One of the likely vehicles for such demonstrations of guilt, denazification, actually had been removed by those who conquered the Nazi regime (Herf, 1980, p. 50).

AN END TO THE SILENCE?

The competing interpretations of the silence share one common feature: all perceive beneath silence the presence of powerful emotions, whether of guilt, fear, anger, or antisemitism. Emotions were not expressed, and certainly not in words or deeds of penitence to the Jews or to the new State of Israel before 1951. It might be easy, then, to interpret the silence as the end of the mutual feelings of Germans and Jews. That would be a mistake.

It may be true that Germans never faced directly their past or their relationship to Jews before the televising of *Holocaust* in 1979. Indirectly, however, history has been addressed through ties with Israel. Observers have downplayed this process of interaction between Germans and Israelis in a host of activities and across all social levels, presumably because it is not an overt and direct confrontation with the horrors of National Socialism. Nevertheless, by founding the Peace with Israel Movement Erich Lüth and Rudolf Küstermeier in 1951 did begin to penetrate the psychological barrier separating Germans from Jews that had maintained the silence.

THE GERMAN VIEW

PUBLIC OUTCRY

In his autobiography, *Many Stones Lay along the Path*, Erich Lüth relates the origins of the Peace with Israel Movement:

> In the summer of 1951, 47 states announced that they would end the state of war with Germany ... Only one voice indicated that it would oppose these decisions, [that] of the Israeli Prime Minister David Ben-Gurion ... The founder of the Jewish state...could point to the fact that official postwar Germany had failed to denounce Hitler's war against the Jews ... There was also lacking evidence of concrete change of heart ... The protest of the Israeli Prime Minister rang through the German newspapers at the beginning of August ... I said to Tichatschek [Hamburg correspondent of the American-run *Neue Zeitung*]: 'Now the Federal Chancellor must reply!' But Bonn cloaked itself in a deep silence. It was not even clear whether it was a silence of embarrassment. Three weeks went by and still Bonn did not answer. 'If Adenauer does not speak', I said to Tichatschek, 'then others must speak for him! But who?' (Lüth, 1966, pp. 271–2)

Lüth himself, with Rudolf Küstermeier, spoke for Adenauer. In two newspaper articles which appeared in *Die Neue Zeitung*, the *Telegraf* and *Die Welt*, and during a roundtable discussion on North West German Radio, Lüth and Küstermeier proposed a reconciliation with the Jews and with Israel. On August 31, 1951 Lüth broke the silence:

> What we all can do, the way in which we can all make a beginning, is to speak to the Jews in Germany and in Israel. Neither Israel, which is so terribly afflicted, nor the individual Jew, who in his flight from the Nazi concentration camps suffered a thousand deaths of fear, can utter the first word. We are the ones who must begin! We must say: We ask Israel for peace ... We must set an example, which at the same time should be a sign that we are prepared to wage the struggle against the remnants of antisemitism with the same passion and uprightness with which we will fight any new antisemitism. We must link this call for peace...with an expression of grief for the six million innocent victims and of thanks for the incalculable good which the Jews have

done in the service of mankind and in Germany. (Aktion 'Friede mit Israel', 1951, p. 7)

The statement precipitated a dramatic response from thousands of Germans. It is important, therefore, to contemplate for a moment Lüth's own motivation. His decision to speak out was based on a wealth of emotion which, he says, could no longer be stemmed. He was one of those Germans who, on an individual basis, already had accepted blame for the past (Lüth, 1966, pp. 245–79). In the late 1940s he had begun to work actively for a reconciliation with France. During this period he led discussion groups in Hamburg, trying to find answers for Germany's past treatment of the Jews. In the period 1950–8 (when the Constitutional Court in Karlsruhe ruled on the matter), Erich Lüth questioned whether Veit Harlan, the director of antisemitic propaganda films in the Third Reich, should represent the German film industry after 1945.

Lüth already had expressed his shame. Now he made a full and general public statement. He describes his decision in strictly emotional terms, and there is no reason to doubt the sincerity of his explanation: 'I acted spontaneously on the basis of the situation. Emotionally. And if there was any force at all, it was the force of conscience' (Lüth, 1966, p. 271).

Lüth spoke out on August 31; Küstermeier wrote in *Die Welt* the next day:

> The guilt of the blood of six million dead Jews, which besmirches the German name, cannot be washed away ... World Jewry complains that the Federal Republic as the responsible representative of the German people still has not found a word of reconciliation towards the Jews. Was it really necessary that we should have allowed ourselves to have this additional burden on the German name ... Our cry...goes out not only to our government but also to every one who feels himself responsible for the task of bringing about peace and cooperation between Germany and the Jews...after so much of the most inhuman inhumanity we want to be human, that means upright and honest, understanding, helpful and good. (Aktion 'Friede mit Israel', 1951, pp. 9–10)

Küstermeier had much less cause than the average German to speak of feelings of shame and guilt for he, himself, had been a victim of National Socialism, incarcerated and physically abused over a twelve-year period.[9]

Neither Lüth nor Küstermeier seems able to explain how they chose their moment. Only Ben-Gurion's provocation seems to offer a plausible explanation. In this respect it seems their response was uncalculated and indeed emotional (Lüth, interview, 1975; Küstermeier, interview, 1975). Nor is it clear why the German people reacted in the way they did at that time, except for the provocation of Lüth and Küstermeier in national newspapers and on national radio. They had not responded to the

Federal President, Theodor Heuss, when he had spoken of collective shame in December 1949. People seemed to reject the notion that collectively the 'Germans' should feel guilty or ashamed. Perhaps 'Peace with Israel' allowed people to act as individuals, to come to terms with their conscience on an individual basis. Lüth has explained, somewhat mysteriously, that, 'Somehow the time was suddenly ripe'; whatever the reasons for the response, 'it was like a dam breaking, or an avalanche rushing' (interview, 1975). Küstermeier was similarly overwhelmed: 'I see the importance of the Peace with Israel Movement mainly in the mobilization of public opinion in Germany, particularly among the younger generation, whose reaction was tremendous' (interview, 1975).

Lüth has detailed the response from organizations, groups and individuals (Aktion 'Friede mit Israel', 1951, pp. 11–22; Lüth, 1952, pp. 3–6; Lüth, 1976, pp. 118–39). Newspaper columns and letters to the editors at the time support his claim of an avalanche of response to the call for 'Peace with Israel' (for example, the *Allgemeine Wochenzeitung der Juden in Deutschland*, September 21 and 28, 1951; *Die Welt*, September 10, 1951; *Stuttgarter Zeitung*, September 8, 1951). Many Germans, it seems, wanted to share in the call, wanted to join in the attempt at reconciliation. Meetings, discussions, lectures and rallies across Germany to express sympathy with the Jews and with Israel were all held within the framework of the Peace with Israel Movement.[10]

On the basis of the psychological reaction elicited by the call from Lüth and Küstermeier, Lüth proceeded to suggest other expressions of public sympathy for Israel. He started the Olive Tree Fund, which was to be 'a symbol ... Every person who participated, even the poorest, was to be linked through the planting of these peace trees with that country, which was the last refuge of his Jewish brothers' (Lüth, 1966, p. 277). Whereas the psychological relationship between Germans and Jews in the past had led to an often negative relationship of historical intertwining and intensity, the hope now was expressed that the Federal Republic and Israel would be intertwined in the future on the basis of friendship and peace.

GOVERNMENT RESPONSE

Just one month after the initiation of the Peace with Israel Movement, Konrad Adenauer, as Federal Chancellor, broke the government silence on German-Israeli relations. There is much speculation concerning Adenauer's motives, and there was surely a strong political element. Moreoever, there can be no certainty in linking the government's declaration with the Lüth–Küstermeier appeal which Adenauer never mentioned. Nevertheless, it is also certain that Adenauer's offer of material restitution for the wrongs done Jews during the Third Reich was motivated at least partially by an emotional and psychological response.

Speaking before the Bundestag on September 27, 1951 Adenauer declared:

> The Federal Government and with it the great majority of the German people are aware of the immeasurable suffering that was brought upon the Jews in Germany and the occupied territories during the time of National Socialism...unspeakable crimes have been committed in the name of the German people, calling for moral and material indemnity ... The Federal Government are prepared, jointly with representatives of Jewry and the State of Israel...to bring about a solution of the material indemnity problem, thus easing the way to the spiritual settlement of infinite suffering. They are profoundly convinced that the spirit of true humanity must once again come alive and become fruitful. The Federal Government consider it the chief duty of the German people to serve this spirit with all their strength. (Text in Vogel, 1969, p. 33)

There was general support for Adenauer's statement in the Bundestag. At the close of the session a minute's silence – to end the silence – was observed.

Nahum Goldmann, one of the chief architects of the Luxembourg Agreement, perceived a dramatic importance in the Adenauer statement and the Bundestag response: 'What happened on that day in the German Federal Parliament was a novel departure in political history...the German people...through their authorized representatives, freely and of their own accord acknowledged their guilt of past events and assumed responsibility for them' (quoted in Weymar, 1957, p. 406). Adenauer himself claims that the offer of restitution was motivated by moral concerns. In his memoirs he reports: 'As I stressed many times, I felt our duty to the Jews as a deep moral debt', and 'The treaty with Israel was quite different from a normal treaty between two states. It was based on a pressing moral obligation' (Adenauer, 1968, pp. 145, 153).

Men who knew and worked with Adenauer at the time of the Bundestag statement and the subsequent negotiations agree that perhaps one of Adenauer's primary motives was a sense of moral obligation towards the Jews and the State of Israel, a desire to make amends. For example, Werner Kliesing, who had grown up with Adenauer and later became an important figure in the Christian Democratic Union (CDU), has talked about Adenauer's sense of 'ethical duty' that he said derived from deep religious feelings (interview, 1975). Apparently Adenauer felt awe and respect for Judaism,[11] a view confirmed by both Ludger Westrick, who advised Adenauer on financial and foreign policy aspects of the agreement with Israel (interview, 1975), and Josef Hermann Abs, another chief adviser on economic questions; Abs cites Adenauer's 'moral conviction' (interview, 1975). Ludwig Erhard, then Minister for Economics and later Chancellor, saw Adenauer's motive for the

September 1951 statement 'primarily as a moral question, as it was for every German' (interview, 1975). Adenauer's press secretary, Felix von Eckardt, has referred to the 'moral obligation, which he felt most keenly in the name of the German people, and which led him to deal in this most extraordinary way' (von Eckardt, 1967, p. 200).

Outside Adenauer's own Christian Democratic circle the Social Democrats (Adenauer's most bitter political opponents) echo the view that Adenauer was driven by moral imperatives. For example, Carlo Schmid, an influential spokesman for social democracy in Germany, stated: 'Adenauer had personal reasons for his statement. The moral motive was the strongest: the idea that a great burden lay on the Germans which obliged us morally to say and do something' (interview, 1975). Similarly, Israeli participants in the incipient relationship did not question Adenauer's moral proclamations (Pearlman, 1965, pp. 163, 170; Shinnar, 1967, p. 28).

Adenauer did have political motives, of course, which he himself freely confessed: 'On the one hand there was the force of great *political and moral obligation* to Israel ... On the other hand in economic terms we were not yet capable of paying or giving credit to the desired extent' (1968, p. 138; emphasis added). Political necessity and the capacity to pay will be taken up in Chapter 3. What is important to understand here is that the perception of morality, which was shared by Adenauer, his Christian Democratic supporters and his Social Democratic opponents, was essential in the launching of the special relationship. This moral view is tied, explicitly, to the psychological response, the feelings and emotions, embedded in the German people. The special relationship would last as long as these feelings persisted.

THE ISRAELI VIEW

GOVERNMENT RESPONSE

In many ways the silence in Palestine (later Israel) concerning crimes perpetrated by the Germans is more easily understood than German reticence. The enormity of shame may have silenced the Germans. The magnitude of the grief and hostility clearly silenced the Israelis. According to Menachem Begin, leader of the Israeli Herut Party (and later Prime Minister):

> After the Second World War, there was a resolve among our people not to have contacts with Germans. This decision resulted from our awareness in May 1945 of the enormity of the physical annihilation of our people. After 1948, our resolve was expressed in our passports which were not valid for Germany. (Interview, 1975)

As in Germany, there were only temporary and minor exceptions among Israelis to the silence (Tavor, 1976).[12]

Israel was forced to break the silence. During negotiations between the three Western powers and the Federal Republic on the state of their future relations the Western powers indicated willingness to end the state of war with Germany. Israel feared that such a move might curtail its right, as it was seen, to claim material amends from the Federal Republic. Therefore, a Note was issued to the four powers on January 16, 1951, requesting that Britain, France, the USA and the USSR retain special rights 'to ensure that Germany shall be compelled to meet what the Israeli government considers her obligations to those Jews or their heirs who suffered under the Hitler regime' (*The Times*, January 18, 1951). The Israeli disdain for the Federal Republic was expressed by Israel's refusal to deal with Germany directly.

When the German silence was broken, the force of emotions was strong. Similarly, the full force of Israeli feelings towards Germany was made apparent in a subsequent Note to the Four Powers in March, elaborating on the January message. Again addressed to the four powers and not Germany, the Note eloquently reveals the intensity of Israeli hostility:

> The harm done to the Jewish people by Germany has no parallel in history. There is no precedent for a massacre and despoliation such as those whose victims the Jews of Europe became through the entire German people ... The annihilation of these Jews is one of the saddest chapters in the history of mankind ... A crime so horrifying as this cannot be atoned for by material reparation ... The Jewish people has been reduced by one-third; three out of every four European Jews were killed. No indemnity can make good the destroyed human lives and cultural values, or pay for the tortures and suffering of the men, women and children killed by all the means at the disposal of a bestial imagination ... What can be done is: Payment of damages to the heirs of the victims and the reintegration of the survivors under the conditions of normal existence. The Jews have been killed, and the German people continue to enjoy the fruits of the butcheries and plundering of its leaders of yesterday. To quote the Bible, 'Hast thou killed, and also taken possession?' (Text in Vogel, 1969, pp. 27–30)

David Ben-Gurion reverted to this same Biblical passage some nine months later when the question of direct negotiations with Germany over the issue of reparations had to be faced in the Knesset. The Western powers refused to act as go-betweens in response to the Israeli Note (State of Israel Ministry for Foreign Affairs, 1953, pp. 28–41) and Adenauer's September statement, which posed the question of direct negotiations, forced Israel to confront an issue it preferred to defer.

The decision in favour of direct negotiations unleashed one of the bitterest and most enduring debates in Israel's history. On the basis of a careful study of the decision Michael Brecher writes:

> The Holocaust and the very name, 'Germany' evoked the most powerful feelings of revulsion among Israelis, crossing ideological lines. In fact, no other issue in Israel's foreign policy throughout the period of independence was as explosive as relations with Germany – economic, military, cultural, and diplomatic. (Brecher, 1973, p. 76)

Morality, and the complex emotions that underwrite the perception of it, now broke open a sometimes violent debate within Israel and among world Jewry, just as it set the terms of discussion and decision in Germany. On December 30, 1951 the Cabinet accepted the invitation for direct negotiations. The debate in Israel broke in two directions, divided over competing views of morality. One side argued the moral justice of claims, while opponents contended the obligation to refuse any contact with Germany or Germans.

There were, of course, as in Germany, other considerations, which will be addressed in Chapter 3. What is important here, as on the German side, is the recognition of morality – a psychologically motivated perception – as the focus of debate. The Knesset debates were riveted to the moral issue; public attitudes expressed in the newspapers of the period reinforce such an emphasis,[13] and numerous interviews with officials of the period confirm the importance of morality.[14] There can be no doubt, as we shall later see, that there were expedient considerations in Israel – largely economic – just as there were political considerations in Germany. But there also can be no doubt that morality animated the Israeli debate just as it motivated the German decision to break the long silence.

The Cabinet in Israel agreed to negotiations, apparently, with a view of morality that emphasized a right to reparations. Its view followed largely the position of Hendrik van Dam, the secretary-general of the Central Council of Jews in Germany, who wrote in a position paper requested by the Israeli government in July 1950: 'The moral duty of the German people corresponds to the morally based claim of the Jewish people' (text in Vogel, 1969, p. 22). He urged action. Nahum Goldmann also seems to have influenced the Cabinet view (see Brecher, 1973, pp. 79, 90):

> To deny this right of Jews to restitution, to take the position that we don't want our own property returned to us by the Germans, would be, in my opinion, *absolutely immoral* ... The adoption of such a Quixotic attitude may have, aesthetically, a certain appeal...in terms of reality, it is silly and *morally unjustifiable* ... But we are not dealing ...with a *quid pro quo*. Nobody is saying to the Germans: You pay us; we forgive you. We are promising nothing; we are offering nothing. We are simply claiming what is ours, morally and legally. (Goldmann, 1952, pp. 9, 11; emphasis added)

Goldmann's stress on morality, denying that negotiations would negate Israel's hostility and anger towards Germany, were frequent themes of the Cabinet. For example, in the Knesset session of January 7, 1952 Ben-Gurion referred to Israel's moral duty to insure the return of goods taken from the Jews by the Nazis (*New York Times*, January 8, 1952), and in an interview with Brecher he claimed, 'There was also the moral obligation of Germany to pay for the crimes it had committed' (1973, p. 79). In his memoirs, Ben-Gurion noted:

> If you want the overall reason in a single sentence, it was the final injunction of the inarticulate six million...whose very murder was a ringing cry for Israel to...be strong and prosperous...and so prevent such a disaster from ever again overwhelming the Jewish people ... I was proposing neither forgiveness nor wiping the slate clean when I presented the demand for reparations from West Germany at the Knesset session in January 1952. (Pearlman, 1965, p. 162)

Moshe Sharett, Ben-Gurion's Foreign Minister, reaffirmed the themes of moral duty without forgiveness in the Knesset debate:

> Is it not our sacred duty to rescue whatever is still obtainable, to bring it here and turn it to creative uses? ... And if there is no other way of recovering this property except by negotiation with the heirs of the robbers or the robbers themselves, then it is not merely permissible but our bounden duty to enter such negotiations. (Sharett, 1952a, p. 29)

Sharett indicated that there was no chance of forgetting or forgiving the crimes, for the Federal Republic was considered 'the heir to the reign of blood, violence and destruction which preceded it' (ibid.), and 'there can be no reckoning whatever for the Jewish blood that was shed. This we can only remember for generations' (Sharett, 1952b, p. 14). Ze'ev Scheck, who was Sharett's political secretary from 1953 until 1956, confirmed the sincerity of Sharett's sentiments (interview, 1975).

Felix Shinnar, who was not immediately involved in the December decision but was closely linked to events thereafter (in his capacity as joint head of the Israeli delegation to the reparations negotiations), recalled, 'It was our moral duty...we wanted justice applied' (interviews, 1975). David Horowitz, in raising the issue of reparations, shared Shinnar's memory of a moral motive: 'It was our moral right, against the background of events in Germany, to claim reparations. It was our duty towards those who died and those who remained' (interview, 1975). Yet Horowitz still felt the same animosity towards the Germans. He declined the offer to lead the Israeli delegation to the reparations negotiations because he did not wish to meet with Germans, whom he found repugnant (ibid.). The pervasive view of those who opted for direct negotiations is defined by a perceived moral duty to negotiate directly with Germany because of the hostility and anger they felt towards Germans, not in spite of those feelings.

PUBLIC OUTCRY

When the issue of reparations from Germany was first raised officially in Israel's Notes to the Four Powers, there was no hue-and-cry in Israel. The commitment at that time was to indirect negotiations (Brecher, 1973, p. 76). When complaint did come, Moshe Sharett reminded Israelis of their earlier silence, and noted that when the Knesset had taken up the issue, 'there was no debate on the basic question, whether we are entitled to reparations' (1952b, p. 14). With the decision to negotiate directly, however, the debate exploded.

Perhaps the most violent public demonstration in Israel's history challenged the Cabinet decision outside the Knesset building on January 7, 1952. The police could not manage the insurrection, which was quelled by the army. The demonstrations outside the Knesset, moreover, were matched by acrimony within. Formal opposition came principally from different ends of the political spectrum, from the Herut and Mapam parties.

The intensity of emotion is apparent in newspaper accounts of the January 7 riots:

Police using clubs and tear gas and firing shots into the air dispersed about 2,000 youths attempting to storm the Knesset ... The battle around the Knesset building lasted about an hour. At least 180 people were injured, some seriously. (Associated Press report, January 8, 1952)

A mob of 1,000 adherents of the extreme right-wing Herut Party today stormed through police barricades, set fire to or demolished automobiles, and stoned the Knesset building ... Steel-helmeted policemen, carrying...shields to protect themselves from a shower of stones, fought the mob with tear gas, smoke bombs and nightsticks. Tear gas poured into the building through broken windows. (*New York Times*, January 8, 1952)

A public opinion poll conducted by *Maariv* during the week before the Knesset debate reported 80 per cent of those surveyed to be against negotiations with Germany (*The Times*, January 9, 1952). The issue raised emotions of an intensity sufficient to shatter the unity of a people, turning victims of violence to violence against their fellow victims.

Verbally the violence inside the Knesset matched the tumult outside. Herut's leader, Menachem Begin, asked the Knesset: 'Who ever heard of the son of the murdered going to the murderer to ask for compensation?' (*New York Times*, January 8, 1952). Begin, and those who shared his views, believed it was immoral to negotiate with Germany. He submitted a petition of distinguished rabbis, scholars and poets against negotiations. He called the Prime Minister a 'hooligan', and he has been described himself as debating 'with mounting hysteria':

> Some things are dearer than life. Some things are worse than death. We are willing to leave our families and die. People went to the barricades for lesser things ... I know we will be dragged to concentration camps...but we will die together. (*Jerusalem Post*, January 8, 1952)

Begin did not relent after the Knesset debate, seeking a plebiscite on the question of direct negotiations with Germany. He contended that 'the overwhelming majority of our people are against the revolting abomination of negotiations with Germany and taking blood money from those who murdered millions of our father's children, brothers and sisters' (*New York Times*, January 15, 1952). The *Maariv* poll supports his interpretation of the popular feeling.

Yaacov Haazan presented Mapam's opposition: 'Negotiations mean recognition of a neo-Nazi Government, managed mostly by ex-Nazis, whose Military [Establishment] is already Nazi today' (quoted in Brecher, 1973, p. 92; *Jerusalem Post*, January 8, 1952). The hyperbole on the left, like the hyperbole on the right, was painted in vivid emotions. And there is no evidence that the government occupied the debate's middle ground.

CONCLUSIONS

The Knesset approved the Cabinet decision, 61–50. Direct negotiations opened between the Federal Republic of Germany and the State of Israel in March 1952. The mutual recognition of the two states came after a deafening silence that covered explosive feelings produced by a complex and intense historical relationship. Those feelings did explode, bearing witness to the misleading quality of the silence. The negotiations over reparations would proceed in the framework of the domestic debates that preceded them, constantly emphasizing perceptions of morality. Yet despite this emphasis, a different reality would also pervade the negotiations: Israel and Germany needed each other.

The special relationship between the states of West Germany and Israel began with direct negotiations. The psychological motives that led to the negotiations would continue to motivate major policy choices, cloaked in the rhetoric and perception of morality. However much the two nations would recognize mutual need, perpetuation of the special relationship would depend on the persistent appreciation of morality. German decisions have been underwritten for three decades by the sense of guilt expressed in 1951. In turn, Israeli demands for preferential treatment from the Federal Republic have been premised on a moral claim.

Gradually the Israeli public has come to share the policy-makers' view that Israel has not only a moral right to exact preference from Germany, but also a moral obligation to the past. The hostility of the generation of the Holocaust is perhaps diminished, but the decisions of January 1952 have guided policy, and apparently public opinion, ever since.

NOTES: CHAPTER 2

1 Before 1948, of course, there was no Israel, and before 1949, there was no Federal Republic of Germany. In the period 1945–8, then, the Jews inhabiting Palestine must serve as surrogates for 'Israel'; in the period 1945–9 Germans resident in the Western zones of occupation are surrogates for 'West Germany'.
2 Both Kurt Schumacher, the leader of the Social Democratic Party (SPD), and Theodor Heuss, the first President of the Federal Republic, made references to German blame for Nazi crimes. Yet neither of their statements constituted a real break in the silence, for they were made by individuals and not in the name of the German people; neither statement elicited a response from the German public or the German government. No policy initiative followed. For the text of the statement by Heuss on 'collective shame' made at a meeting of the Society for Christian-Jewish Co-operation in Wiesbaden in December 1949, see the *Stuttgarter Zeitung* (December 8, 1949). For Schumacher's attack on Adenauer over the latter's failure to mention German responsibility towards the Jews in his address to the first Bundestag session in September 1949, see Deutscher Bundestag und Bundesrat (September 21, 1949, p. 36). Adenauer made a brief allusion to the Jews in his September 20, 1949 statement to the Bundestag. For other references to Germans who did attempt during this period to concern their fellow citizens about Germany's recent past, see Bier (1980, pp. 10, 11, 14, 25); often these efforts were undertaken by victims of National Socialism. Adenauer himself hinted at the question of reparations as early as 1949 in an interview with the Jewish newspaper *Allgemeine Wochenzeitung der Juden in Deutschland* on November 11. His references to the Jews and to Israel do not represent an opening in the silence because of the omission of responsibility and because nothing ever came of Adenauer's concrete proposal that goods worth $10 million be put at the disposal of the State of Israel. Brecher notes that the offer was viewed as both premature and ridiculously inadequate (1973, p. 86). As with the statements by Heuss and Schumacher, Israel did not respond, nor did the German public. The question of silence and exceptions to it are dealt with in Lüth (1976), as is the whole history of the breaking of the psychological barrier in 1951.
3 Two special issues of the *New German Critique* (nos 19 and 20, 1980) have been devoted to 'Germans and Jews'; from different disciplinary perspectives, the authors see the silence breaking only after the showing of *Holocaust* on German television in 1979. The various essays elaborate on both the social-psychological and the politico-economic explanations for German reticence, borrowing particularly from the works of the Mitscherlichs, Adorno and Kühnl. See especially the articles by Herf and Huyssen. Other terms are used interchangeably with *Aufarbeitung der Vergangenheit*, including *Bewältigung der Vergangenheit*; alternative English renderings are 'confrontation with the past' or 'coming to grips with the past'.
4 Both the Mitscherlichs and Jacobsen recognize the inherent difficulties in attempting a psychological profile of a whole nation as opposed to individual citizens (Jacobsen, 1963, pp. 171–2; Mitscherlich and Mitscherlich, 1975, pp. xv–xvi). Jacobsen, it might also be noted, revised his findings in 1959 and again in 1962.
5 The questions involved in the Neumann and Noelle-Neumann polls, conducted in the Federal Republic, were: 'What is your attitude towards the Jews?' (August 1949 and December 1952); 'What would you say is the cause of anti-semitism: the characteristics of Jewish ethnic groups, the Jewish religion, anti-Jewish propaganda, or what else?'

(August 1949); 'Would you say it would be better for Germany not to have any Jews in the country?' (December 1952); 'If you had the choice of buying goods of the same quality in a Jewish or a non-Jewish shop and the Jewish shop was a little cheaper, where would you buy?' (August 1949); and 'Should people who today in Germany carry on anti-semitic activities be punished by court, or not?' (August 1949). All of the surveys involved a sample of 2,000 or more people aged 18 or over. The specific questions of the Merritt polls are not cited, but they related to the following topics: antisemitism (December 1946 and April 1948); expressions of National Socialist ideology (unspecified). For subsequent polls revealing similar evidence, see Merritt and Merritt (1980). For an analysis of antisemitism as reflected in public opinion polls in the period until 1952, and later, see Weil (1980).

6 Sixty-three per cent 'felt that the Germans were at least partly to blame for acts of the Hitler regime'; 83 per cent 'believed that both sides in World War II committed many crimes against humanity and peace'; 59 per cent 'agreed that Germany had tortured and murdered millions of helpless Europeans'; 28 per cent 'felt that the Germans were to blame for the outbreak of World War II'; 68 per cent 'stated that the harshness of the Versailles Treaty did not give the German people the right to start another war'; 52 per cent 'said the Versailles Treaty was a cause of the war'; and 56 per cent 'felt that Germany often found itself in a difficult situation because other people had no understanding of Germany'. The poll related to 'Attitudes towards collective guilt in the American zone of Germany' and was conducted in December 1946 with a sample of 3,005 persons (Merritt and Merritt, 1970, p. 149).

7 On denazification, see Fürstenau (1969).

8 It has been argued that the severity of the term 'collective guilt' was an obstacle to Germans confronting their past; it was too damning in its comprehensiveness. The seminal statement on this issue was made by Karl Jaspers immediately after the war (1946, p. 20) and more recently by Huyssen (1980, p. 120).

9 Israel's acceptance of Küstermeier as a 'good German' is demonstrated in the fact that Küstermeier was the first German press representative (and for some time the only one) in Israel. Küstermeier represented the Deutsche Presse Agentur, the Westdeutscher Rundfunk and the Norddeutscher Rundfunk from 1957 until 1968. In general matters Küstermeier served as Germany's 'unofficial ambassador' before diplomatic relations were established in 1965.

10 There were also, however, negative reactions to the Lüth–Küstermeier call, including antisemitic letters which Lüth cites (1952, p. 16, and 1976, pp. 89–94). See the *Allgemeine Wochenzeitung der Juden in Deutschland* of September 21, 1951 for references to the negative stand of the German Party.

11 Adenauer had been touched deeply by his personal relationship with Dannie Heinemann, who helped financially when Adenauer was removed by the Nazis from his position as mayor of Cologne (Adenauer, 1968, p. 155). Adenauer's indebtedness and desire to repay the kindness has been confirmed by Dr Josef Cohn, Chaim Weizmann's personal assistant for many years (interview, 1980).

12 An important public exception was the Israeli protest against the presence of German delegates at the Inter-Parliamentary Union's meeting in 1951 (Union Interparlementaire, 1952, p. 416).

13 Party opposition to direct negotiations with Germany over reparations reflected public sentiment. See, for example, *New York Times* (January 8 and 9, 1952); *Jerusalem Post* (January 8, 1952); *The Times* (January 9, 1952); the *Frankfurter Allgemeine Zeitung* (January 9, 1952); and *Die Neue Zeitung* (January 9, 1952). The reflection of public opinion in party opposition to negotiations is noted also by Brecher (1973, pp. 76, 92). The fact that party opposition, chiefly from Mapam and Herut, rooted its arguments in questions of morality was emphasized by Herut leader Menachem Begin (interview, 1975) and by Yona Golan, secretary for the International Relations Division of Mapam (interview, 1975).

14 Verified in interviews in 1975 with Avner, Eytan, Goldmann, Horowitz, Sharef, Shinnar and Scheck.

3
Mutual Needs

The Luxembourg Reparations Agreement of September 1952 was the product of one of the great ironies of the twentieth century. For four years the German government sought the physical annihilation of the Jewish people. The remnant of the Jewish people collected on territory some thousand miles away. After the four years of genocide, neither side could speak to the other. Yet within a decade after the Holocaust, Germans and Jews, the West German government and the government of the State of Israel, simultaneously concluded that they could not prosper without each other. Despite the horrors of the past relationship of their peoples, the two countries needed each other — and uniquely each other.

Motivations of morality on both sides allowed the silence to be broken and, in turn, led to direct negotiations over reparations. These moral motives were necessary for the special relationship to develop, but not sufficient. Mutual and simultaneous concrete need was even more important than morality. If the moral concerns of substantial segments of the population and certain members of government in both countries had stood alone, it is highly probable that Germany and Israel would have remained mutually hostile and silent. Morality, as a reflection of sentiment on both sides, was necessary for the initiation of the special relationship, but the weight of pragmatism was necessary to translate the wealth of emotions between the two countries into concrete acts.

Israel was in economic crisis when it broached the idea of reparations from Germany (the Israeli Notes of January and March 1951, and the Cabinet and Knesset decisions of December 1951 and January 1952). Similarly, only when Germany perceived overwhelming adverse external reactions to a failure to deal with Israel and the Jews, did Adenauer accept responsibility for past crimes against the Jews (Adenauer's statement of September 1951) and offer the possibility of direct negotiations over reparations. The silence was broken in these conditions of mutual and simultaneous need. The emotional outburst led swiftly to direct negotiations, which climaxed in the Luxembourg Reparations Agreement of September 1952.[1] The character of the special relationship between West Germany and Israel is a product of these further reasons for the relationship's creation.

EXTERNAL ENVIRONMENT: INTERNATIONAL AND REGIONAL SETTINGS

THE FEDERAL REPUBLIC AND WESTERN EUROPE

German political expediency with respect to Israel was influenced by the state of the world.[2] The division of Germany after 1945 resulted from tensions, disagreements and misunderstandings between the USSR and the Western Allies. Cold War antagonism did not abate with the formal division of Germany through the creation of the Federal Republic and the German Democratic Republic (GDR) in 1949. On the Western side efforts grew to integrate, through formal mechanisms, political, economic and military capabilities in order to provide a bulwark against the perceived growth of world communism.

Strategically located in the centre of Europe the Federal Republic of Germany gradually was viewed by the Western occupation authorities as a crucial, independent partner in collective Western arrangements. At the same time Konrad Adenauer believed that the future survival of West Germany was dependent on Germany's integration into the West.[3] In the period 1949–52 West Germany joined with other Western powers in a variety of international organizations; during the same period Germany regularized its relations with the three Western occupation authorities through the gradual abolition of the Occupation Statute.

Economic and political rehabilitation proceeded more easily than military acceptance. The debate began over Germany's inclusion in Western defence arrangements at the end of 1949. All the Western powers mistrusted German militarism, but the USA perceived a need for a German contribution to Western defence, especially after the outbreak of the Korean War in June 1950.

German rehabilitation proceeded rapidly, especially as the fear of communism tended to overshadow latent fears of German militarism. Nevertheless, Germany's recent past haunted the Western powers; item for item they were reluctant to integrate an independent Germany as a full and equal partner. Germany needed to overcome this reluctance by proving that the old Germany had disappeared. Its relationship with the Jewish survivors of National Socialism would be the acid-test for its candidacy as a full and equal partner in the Western 'family of nations'.

ISRAEL AND THE MIDDLE EAST

International conditions dictated Israel's needs as well. Despite armistice agreements with Egypt, Lebanon, Jordan and Syria in 1949, ending Israel's War for Independence, Israel saw the Arabs as a constant threat and believed the security of the state in permanent danger.[4] The Arab boycott of Israel had serious economic repercussions for the infant state: it was cut off from the markets of all its neighbours, deprived of cheap foodstuffs and outlets for Israeli manufactured goods. The severance by Iraq of the oil pipeline to Haifa meant that Israel was forced to pay foreign currency for oil. Moreover, and perhaps above all, the constant threat of war obliged Israel to maintain an army which was a severe drain on the economy of a small nation.

The constraints imposed by a hostile environment obliged Israel to make concerted efforts at home and abroad to improve its economy. Unlike West Germany, during its first years Israel pursued a policy of 'non-identification' with either Cold War bloc. Czechoslovakia had armed its first war with the Arabs; the USSR was one of the first to extend diplomatic recognition. Israel looked as much to the East as to the West for help in launching statehood. However, the Korean War had significance for Israel as well as for Germany.

The Korean War obliged most countries to take sides in the Cold War. In the fall of 1950 Israel aligned with the USA. The USSR and Eastern Europe ceased to be potential sources of economic and military aid. Although Germany and Israel were not direct partners, they were now on the same side of a bipolar international order. Moreover, they both had fundamental needs whose satisfaction would condition the role they could play as members of the Western camp. The international environment was now conducive to bilateral relations, but a supportive internal environment was also required for their concrete needs to be channelled into mutual satisfaction.

THE POLITICAL NEEDS OF THE FEDERAL REPUBLIC, 1949–52

> The world will carefully watch the new West German state, and one of the tests by which it will be judged will be its attitude towards the Jews and how it treats them. (John McCloy, US Military Governor, July 1949)

There is a broad consensus among leading observers and participants that German foreign policy after 1949 was premissed on a need to become accepted again, to be trusted, for with such acceptance and trust Germany could regain a degree of independence. Nevertheless, none of the analysts of this period identifies the significance of relations with Israel for German foreign policy and political rehabilitation; they ignore reparations to Israel in their analyses of West German foreign policy.[5] Yet even by Adenauer's own admission, relations with Israel were crucial for the objective of international rehabilitation.

There is an important dispute over whether morality or expediency counted more for Adenauer in opening relations with Israel. Both were present, but the domination of morality would imply a German choice; pragmatism implies a German necessity. If the Federal Republic needed Israel, it would fashion a bilateral relationship according to practical incentives and objectives.

52 Foundations

In his memoirs Konrad Adenauer sets out the framework of his early foreign policy:

> In the absence of its freedom and equality of rights, the German people cannot be the full partner of like-minded peoples. This was the *leitmotif* of my policies toward the Allies in all the years that I was Chancellor ... The most important precondition for partnership is trust ... We Germans should not forget what happened in the years from 1933 until 1945 ... the devastation the Nazis caused throughout the world ... In our dealings with the Allies we had to operate from the premise that to obtain progressively more power as a state, the psychological moment would play a major role ... We had to realize that trust could be regained only gradually and we had to avoid arousing mistrust towards us. (Adenauer, 1967, p. 236)

Here is the blueprint for Adenauer's relationship with Israel and the Jews: the need to generate trust from the Allies in the attempt to attain partnership, independence and equality. Adenauer's *post hoc* explanation here, moreover, is consistent with his earliest foreign policy pronouncements.[6]

WEST GERMANY'S NEED FOR ISRAEL

West Germany's need for Israel has been identified by the German Foreign Office as a responsibility of the Third Reich's successor state: 'the Federal Republic assumed the responsibility for the prewar debts of the German Reich and for the crimes committed in the German name before and during the war.' With respect to Nazi crimes, one step was taken in the form of personal restitution and 'the second step was taken towards Israel' (Auswärtiges Amt, 1972, pp. 34–5).

Adenauer openly stated the connection between Germany's needs and its consequent political actions when he returned from Israel in 1966: 'One of my chief aims as Chancellor was to put in order our relationship to Israel and the Jews, both for moral and political reasons. Germany could not become a respected and equal member of the family of nations until it had recognized and proven the will to make amends' (1966, p. 15). For as Adenauer stresses in his memoirs, 'Nothing had tarnished the German name and caused such contempt in the world for us as the annihilation of the Jews' (1968, p. 130).

Both Herbert Blankenhorn, one of Adenauer's closest advisers, and Franz Böhm, the leader of the German negotiation team to the reparations talks, appear to have influenced Adenauer's perception of the political necessity of positive relations with Israel. Blankenhorn recounts how

> In the very first weeks of the existence of the Federal Government ... there were talks between the Chancellor and me as to the way in which it would be possible to put the relationship of the German people to

the Jewish people and to the State of Israel on a new foundation. In these talks it was constantly maintained by me — and the Chancellor fully accepted this reasoning — that the new German state could regain confidence, reputation, and credibility in the world only if the Federal Government ... disavowed the past and contributed through impressive reparation payments to the relief of the incredible extent of distress suffered. (Quoted in Vogel, 1969, p. 21)

Adenauer has indicated that the views of Franz Böhm, as reported in a letter of April 23, 1952, to Adenauer describing the current state of German-Israeli contacts, coincided with his own. Böhm wrote: 'Presumably the most important and urgent task of German policy is to overcome the inconceivable bitterness evoked by the National Socialist crime in the Jews throughout the world and in all right-thinking people, and also to overcome the dreadful blow dealt by this crime to the German reputation' (text in Vogel, 1969, pp. 45–7). Both Böhm and Blankenhorn saw the importance of negotiations with Israel for the moral and political re-education of the German people, which was necessary if the Allies were to find Germany an acceptable partner.

Other participants in the political life of the early years of the Federal Republic also note the motivation of political expediency in Adenauer's overtures towards the Jews and Israel. Hermann Abs, for example, the German representative at the London Debt Conference in the spring of 1952 (involved also in strategy for the Hague (Wassenaar reparations talks), saw the political necessity of making the new German state credible in both the London and the Hague negotiations (interview, 1975). Despite Werner Kliesing's emphasis on Adenauer's moral motives for reparations, he, too, viewed Adenauer's decision to make his September 1951 statement as 'politically very opportune; Adenauer never would have missed such a politically opportune moment' (interview, 1975). Carlo Schmid, like Kliesing, perceived the moral motive as perhaps the strongest, but noted the importance of political expediency. He suggested that, as a statesman, Adenauer was reluctant to bring disgrace on the German name (interview, 1975). In the view of Rudolf Küstermeier the motive of political expediency was primary: 'He [Adenauer] wanted the Bundesrepublik to become a state with full and equal international rights and recognition ... To reach this aim he had to do something about the Jewish problem' (interview, 1975).

Contemporary observers of Adenauer's policy towards Israel and the Jews also evaluate the role of political expediency in Adenauer's relationship with Israel. On the basis of careful examinations of Adenauer's decisions on reparations Nicholas Balabkins (1967, p. 901) and Jekutiel Deligdisch (1974, pp. 14–15) recognize motives of both morality and political expediency.[7]

There are two basic ways to interpret the connections between morality and pragmatism in the motivation of foreign policy behaviour: either they genuinely coexist, or pronouncements of morality provide a cloak for pragmatic intentions that would be unpalatable if they stood alone. In Adenauer's case morality and pragmatism coexisted, but politically expedient reasons were ultimately decisive in his offer of direct negotiations. Professions of morality were not caused by political necessity, but morality could not be expressed in action without a perception of political necessity. John McCloy, US High Commissioner, had warned: 'I assure you that while I shall do everything in my power to help you get a fresh start and win a dignified and responsible place in the family of nations, I shall not forget Dachau and Belsen' (*New York Times*, August 10, 1949).

Expressions of Allied uncertainty about Germany's democratic tendencies, and particularly the mistrust expressed by the USA, led Adenauer to seek out Israel over the question of reparations. Adenauer never admitted that McCloy's warning was in mind, but his own words resemble McCloy's suggestion that German democracy would be tested by a willingness to sacrifice with reparations: 'We wanted a different Germany from the Germany of Hitler. We had to pass the test, and not just with fine words, but also with material sacrifices' (Adenauer, 1968, p. 153).

GERMANY REACHES OUT IN NEED: PRESSURES
FROM THE ALLIES

Despite the public silence, there were unofficial contacts between West Germany and Israel over reparations before September 27, 1951. These contacts were preceded by important events affecting on the one hand the question of Germany's acceptance internationally, and on the other hand Israel's economic situation. The contacts suggest mutual uncertainty that desire might be satisfied: Germany had to be sure that Israel would respond positively to the offer of direct negotiations, for if Israel continued to denounce Germany, the German government would be embarrassed at home and disgraced abroad. Israel on the other hand wanted to be certain that there were concrete economic possibilities behind the professions of moral obligation, for if Germany failed to deliver money or goods, the Israeli government would not likely survive the domestic recrimination attendant on dealings with Germany. Both sides needed to be sure, and both needed to perceive no other choices. Before September 1951 and January 1952, neither the need on both sides nor the perception that the need could be fulfilled by the partner was sufficiently strong to bring about direct and open contacts.

Germany perceived twin pressures, one concerning relations between Germany and the three Western occupation powers, and the other referring to Israel's public challenge to Germany's right to reoccupy a position in the 'family of nations'. In Adenauer's view Germany could not afford contempt from either the Allies or 'world opinion'.

Adenauer was never happy with the Occupation Statute that ordered relations between the German government and the occupation authorities. Soon after the establishment of the Federal Republic, he negotiated with the three Allied High Commissioners for its revision. Although Adenauer said the Petersberg revision was a political success, it also served to remind him of the distance between the Federal Republic's situation and the attainment of sovereignty. And when the three High Commissioners vetoed three tax laws passed by the Bundestag in April 1950, Adenauer was sufficiently enraged to resort to public protest (Baring, 1969, p. 67).

Behind this public rage Adenauer was working to improve Germany's image among the Allies, and such efforts meant, among other concerns, relations with Israel. The negotiations for revision of the Occupation Statute and the conclusion of the Petersberg Agreement (November 22, 1949) appeared to coincide with inquiries over the relationship between the Germans and Jews, Germany and Israel.[8] Adenauer dates the first unofficial contacts with representatives of the State of Israel in the spring of 1950.[9] He used both Jakob Altmaier, a Jewish SPD deputy, and Christian Democrat Herbert Blankenhorn as contacts with Jewish leaders and Social Democratic, Christian Democratic and Jewish domestic opinion. The 'good' character of both men with respect to Germany's past also meant the best possible basis for sounding out Israeli and world opinion. The timing of their first missions, however, is as notable as the choice of the men themselves.

There were contacts between Germans and Israelis throughout 1950, against a background of German efforts to regularize relations with the Western Allies. By the end of 1950 negotiations between Germany and the Allies began to focus on German responsibility for prewar debts,[10] a development previewing the emergence of German-Jewish relations as an issue affecting German rehabilitation. Adenauer pressed for further revision of the Occupation Statute, but the Allied concessions of March 6, 1951 indicated continued mistrust of the Federal Republic.[11]

Within a week of the Statute revision Israel formally requested from the four powers reparations from Germany. At the beginning of April 1951 David Horowitz visited the USA, France and England to seek support for the Israeli request. According to Horowitz, the USA was particularly supportive and arranged a meeting with Adenauer. Adenauer and Horowitz met on April 19, 1951 in Paris, the first high-level meeting over reparations.[12] Adenauer stated at this meeting that 'he would do all in his power to compensate for the material loss caused by the criminal Nazi regime' (Shinnar, 1967, p. 25).

The accumulation of events suggests more than coincidence in both the time and place of the Adenauer–Horowitz meeting. The meeting was on 'neutral' ground (outside Germany), while Adenauer was in Paris for final negotiations of the Schuman Plan: Germany's effort to achieve equal partnership with the West was simultaneous with efforts to make amends to Israel.

56 Foundations

At the end of June 1951 McCloy reported to Adenauer that, with reference to the military and political rehabilitation of the Federal Republic, there was still serious doubt in the USA about a real change of heart in Germany; 'What progress has Germany made on the path to real democracy?' was the American question (Adenauer, 1967, p. 440).

Similar doubts were expressed by all three commissioners soon thereafter. After months of preliminary exchanges, negotiations with the Allies over the complete removal of the Occupation Statute began on September 24, 1951. Adenauer expected a peace treaty in exchange for a German defence contribution, but the Allies suggested a transition state between the abolition of the Statute and the conclusion of a peace treaty. Adenauer was aware of the Allied scepticism: 'I asked the High Commissioners not to think that I had forgotten what misery Germany had caused throughout the world ... we Germans could not demand that the world forget' (1967, p. 459). Adenauer's statement on reparations followed by three days this disappointing start of negotiations with the Allies (Baring, 1969, p. 139).

A few days before the Adenauer statement, Fritz von Twardowsky, Adenauer's provisional press spokesman, asked Erich Lüth, 'How did you know that the Americans suggested that the Chancellor speak to the Jewish question before he makes his first trip to the States?' (Lüth, 1966, p. 274).[13] On September 6, at an informal meeting, Adenauer himself referred to the influence of American Jews in the American government's disinclination towards Germany (Baring, 1969, p. 402). The need to neutralize such hostility through positive moves towards the Jews and Israel was emphasized by Adenauer in an interview long after the events. When asked about the reasons for and significance of reconciliation with the Jews, Adenauer replied, 'One should not underestimate the power of the Jews, particularly in America' (quoted in *Deutschland-Berichte*, January 1966). And one should not underestimate, therefore, the power of the US government on this question, particularly in negotiations with Adenauer.

PRESSURES ON GERMANY: PERCEIVED WORLD OPINION
In addition to American prompting on Germany's relationship to the Jews, Adenauer faced the pressure of world opinion and the Israelis persisted in reminding the world of Germany's crimes. For example, during the September 1950 United Nations discussions of the principle of universal membership Moshe Sharett, the Israeli Foreign Minister, called for a single exception:

> The people of Israel and Jews throughout the world view with consternation and distress the progressive readmission of Germany by the family of nations, with her revolting record intact, her guilt unexpiated, and her heart unchanged. Judging by all accounts, the evil spirit of Nazism still dominates German mentality. The appeasement

now practised in both parts of Germany outrages the sacred memory of countless martyrs, betrays the sacrifices sustained in the overthrow of Nazism and sows the seeds of new aggression, savagery and horror. (Sharett, 1950, p. 394)

Israel gave no indication that it would hesitate to make such a statement again. Although there is no explicit evidence of German response to this attack, the tempo of Israeli-German contacts quickened; Israel's appeals to an international audience were an explicit obstacle to Adenauer's foreign policy objectives.

Israel continued to remind its international audience. The Note of March 1951 requesting reparations stated; 'The restoration of equal rights to Germany in the concert of nations is unthinkable until this basic measure of reparation is taken' (text in Vogel, 1969, p. 31). Then, in July 1951, when the state of war officially was ended with Germany by forty-seven states, Israel also reacted:

Six years after the end of hostilities the German people has not made any expiation or reparation for the crimes committed by the Nazis. To this day the German people has not found it within themselves to shake off the blood-stained heritage of their erstwhile masters, and have not abjured or solemnly dissociated themselves from the appalling record of those twelve years of Nazi rule. (*Keesing's*, 1950–2, p. 11589)

A month later Ben-Gurion reiterated this theme in a public criticism that did not go unnoticed in Germany.

By the end of August Germans themselves, in the Peace with Israel Movement, reminded the world that Germany so far had done nothing positive for the Jews or Israel. Israeli representatives emphasized the same issue. At the first session of the fortieth conference of the Inter-Parliamentary Union in Istanbul (August 31–September 6, 1951), the Israeli spokesman, Yitzhak Ben-Zvi, protested the presence of Germans in the organization. He said: 'The Germans have as yet offered no guarantee that the terrible crimes committed by them on their own territory and on the territories of other countries will not be repeated. Few of those who suffered personally have been compensated' (Union Interparlementaire, 1952, p. 416). Carlo Schmid, a member of the German delegation, defended Germany while expressing German shame for past crimes. After a fiery exchange, German and Israeli representatives met privately to discuss reparations. Schmid was accompanied by Heinrich von Brentano, the future Foreign Minister of the Federal Republic and a Christian Democrat. Before meeting the Germans, the Israeli delegation obtained the sanction of its political parties in the Knesset (Vogel, 1969, p. 19).

According to Schmid, the conversation resulted in an agreement 'that our interlocutors would inquire of the Knesset whether an offer from the German government to enter into negotiations about reparation payments to Israel would be entertained' (quoted in Vogel, 1969, p. 20). Israeli and German intermediaries, Schmid says, subsequently were in constant contact. According to a leading participant in the debate over ratification of the Luxembourg Reparations Agreement, there was a link between the IPU incident and Adenauer's September 1951 statement (Deutscher Bundestag und Bundesrat, March 18, 1953, p. 12274).

PRESSURES ON GERMANY: DOMESTIC

Adenauer wanted the world, and especially the Allies, to forget the German past. McCloy let the Germans know that the Allies would not forget, and diplomatic disappointments proved to Adenauer the Allies' concerns. Israel would not let anyone forget, especially with reference to crimes against the Jews. Germans inside Germany also brought pressure to bear on Adenauer's reticence to make his moral concerns public and political.

Some observers suggest that Adenauer's statement of September 27, 1951 was a direct consequence of the Lüth–Küstermeier appeal. According to *Die Neue Zeitung*, for example, 'The "Peace with Israel" movement...culminated in the corresponding decisions of the Bundestag and the Federal government' (January 18, 1952). *Die Welt*, three weeks before the Chancellor's appeal, offered information that the government was preparing to make a move towards Israel over reparations: 'The efforts of...Erich Lüth...and...Rudolf Küstermeier...will not go unheard this time' (*Die Welt*, September 7, 1951).

Other observers see an indirect link, suggesting that Adenauer used the Lüth–Küstermeier call to convince certain domestic forces that a statement about crimes of the past and reparations in the future was inescapable. Lüth himself traces Adenauer's delay in making such a statement to his fear that a confession of guilt and responsibility could provoke antisemitic reactions in Germany. Adenauer could not risk renewed German antisemitism visible to a world public, and according to Lüth, Adenauer was concerned particularly about the reaction of the nationalist German Party (DP). Now after the popular response to the 'Peace with Israel' appeal, Adenauer could go with evidence (such as newspaper clippings) to the DP and convince its members that the public demanded a government statement (Lüth, interview, 1975).

Lüth's reasoning is supported by the discrepancy between the reaction of the DP to Lüth's article of August 31 and the DP's statement of endorsement following Adenauer's speech of September 27. In response to Lüth the DP had commented:

> The aim of reconciliation might be a good one, but such a quest can lead to the betrayal of self-respect; one becomes servile and makes a pitiful impression. With this Mr Lüth, one has the impression that he's

a bag of wind, that he talks about things that don't exist anymore ...He should look at antisemitism in the United States...and convince himself of what real antisemitism looks like and compare it with the alleged antisemitism in Germany. (*Die Neue Zeitung*, September 18, 1951)

The reaction of the DP to Adenauer's statement was entirely different: 'We not only approve the statement of the government, we support it with all our hearts, because it is a matter of making good a profanation of divine and human law' (quoted in Vogel, 1969, p. 34).

Unlike the DP, the SPD as early as the first Bundestag session in September 1949, called for the government's acknowledgement of German responsibility towards the Jews. At this time the SPD also caused Adenauer difficulties on matters of defence. Ever since the idea of German rearmament first was raised in late 1949 and early 1950 the SPD had opposed vehemently any suggestion of German armed forces. Before the press on September 26, 1951 Kurt Schumacher, the leader of the SPD, once again reaffirmed his party's opposition to rearmament and to the notion of the political union of Western Europe. Two of the basic tenets of Adenauer's *Westpolitik* were under attack again by the opposition. The simultaneity of these SPD attacks and Adenauer's statement to Israel and the Jews cannot be ignored here, for it at least had the dividend of offering something favourable to the SPD, whose support for reparations and restitution was clear. At the very least, Adenauer knew that he was undercutting the agenda of the opposition.

There was, then, an accumulation of events, public statements and pressures inside and outside Germany during 1950 and 1951 (Table 3.1). By September 1951 Adenauer must have felt that the time had arrived to make a statement to the Jews and to Israel. Adenauer now knew, from the secret contacts, that the Israeli reaction would be positive. In the April 1951 meeting in Paris Israel had stipulated its two conditions for negotiations with Germany (and thus, presumably, for a positive reaction towards Germany): a 'guilt declaration' condemning the Nazi crimes, and negotiations on the basis of the Israeli claim (Brecher, 1973, p. 88). Adenauer took no chances with Jewish reaction. A draft of his planned statement, meeting the first condition, was approved by both Israeli representatives and representatives of world Jewry before Adenauer went before the public.[14] Reassured that Israel would not embarrass him, Adenauer also was clearly mindful of world opinion. Indeed, the statement opened:

Recently world opinion has concerned itself repeatedly with the attitude of the Federal Republic towards the Jews. Doubts have been expressed here and there as to whether the new state has been guided in this momentous question by principles that do justice to the frightful crimes of a past epoch. (Text in Vogel, 1969, p. 32)[15]

60 Foundations

Table 3.1 *Pressures on Germany and Overtures to Israel, October 1949 to May 1952*

Date	Pressure	Overtures
October–November 1949	Negotiations over Occupation Statute; Petersberg Agreement	Blankenhorn–Adenauer talks
April 1950	Veto by High Commissioners of tax laws	Altmaier–Livneh and Blankenhorn–Barou talks
March–May 1951	Incomplete revision of Occupation Statute; Israeli Note to four powers; Schumann Plan talks	Adenauer–Fischer–Horowitz meeting in Paris
July–September 1951	Israeli criticism of Germany; negotiations over complete removal of Occupation Statute; 'Peace with Israel'; SPD attacks	Adenauer statement in Bundestag
May 1952	Böhm–Küster resignations and negative reactions; imminent signing of Contractual Agreements with Allies	Böhm–Goldmann meeting in Paris together with Israeli representatives

Adenauer then proceeded to emphasize German good faith in this matter; the official silence finally was broken with the acknowledgement of responsibility for the past and future relationship to the Jews. The reparations negotiations began in Wassenaar, Holland, in March 1952.

CONFIRMING PRAGMATISM: NO PRESSURE, NO PAY
Confirmation that political need motivated Adenauer more than moral concern may be found in the conduct of the reparations negotiations. Adenauer's objective was to gain the trust of the Western Allies and reparations to Israel were means to this end. When the Allies indicated a general acceptance of the Federal Republic, Adenauer began retreating from his commitment to reparations; when the Allies indicated disapproval of this retreat, Adenauer reaffirmed his commitment. This zigzag in the conduct of negotiations would not have occurred if morality alone governed Adenauer's commitment to make amends.

By April 1952 Adenauer was confident about the treaties to be concluded with the Allies (the European Defence Community Treaty and the Contractual Agreements to end the Occupation Statute) (Adenauer,

1967, pp. 506–9, 514; Baring, 1969, pp. 143–4; *New York Times*, April 10, 1952). Negotiations, however, were deadlocked at Wassenaar. The Israeli representatives were demanding a firm offer from Germany. Both Böhm and Küster, the German negotiating team, were agreeable, but the matter had to be decided by Adenauer and the Cabinet, which met on April 5 in Bonn (Küster interview, 1975; Böhm interview, 1975). Adenauer's personal economic adviser, Hermann Abs, and Fritz Schäffer, the Finance Minister, argued that because of Germany's limited ability to pay, it would be better to offer some token, like the building of a hospital, until Germany knew better its own economic situation. According to Küster, Adenauer seemed convinced by this argument and noted that there need be no discussion of the figures Israel used in its claim because the Jews were just deceiving the Germans. Yet in a December 1951 letter to Nahum Goldmann, chairman of the Conference on Jewish Material Claims against Germany, Adenauer had agreed to base discussions on Israel's $1 billion (4·2 billion marks) claim.[16] Böhm and Küster argued vigorously against the proposal of Abs and Schäffer as inadequate and contrary to the prior understandings, but they found it exceedingly difficult to alter Adenauer's new opinion.[17]

It is notable that Adenauer might have been persuaded by Abs and Schäffer, and the arguments Küster used to deter Adenauer from tokenism are even more striking. He did not appeal to Adenauer's morality. Rather, he argued that Germany owed 'blood-money', and he contended that Adenauer would lose face if he accepted the Abs–Schäffer proposal. The thought of adverse public opinion seemed to disturb Adenauer more than any other consideration. Even then, the final outcome of the meeting was not totally to the liking of Böhm and Küster, and did not bode well for Israel.

Adenauer seemed much less positive towards Israel than six months earlier. Although the Abs–Schäffer proposal for a hospital was scrapped, the statement Böhm and Küster were authorized to make to the Israelis on April 7 was noncommittal: Germany would accept a figure of 3 billion marks (two-thirds of the 4·5 billion marks Germany considered necessary for immigration; Israel had assessed the total figure in its claim at 6·3 billion marks) as the basis for negotiations but would not commit itself to a concrete offer in terms of amount, timing, or form of payment, until the completion of the London Debt Conference, which had begun at the end of February and would reconvene in late May.[18]

The Israelis were dissatisfied and suspended negotiations. On April 9 the Germans told the Israelis that in all probability no firm offer could be made until June 20. The negotiations then were adjourned formally until late May.[19] Adenauer may have been persuaded by the practical considerations of Abs and Schäffer, thus suggesting again the secondary character of his moral concern.

Böhm and Küster were convinced Adenauer was not committed to reparations. They resigned. Three incidents in particular appear to have precipitated their resignations, and they all suggest the practical political linkages that dominated the policy of the Federal Republic. On May 7, 1952 Böhm and Küster met with Schäffer to discuss the Wassenaar negotiations. Schäffer had instructed the negotiators in March that there was no money, neither in the budget nor in domestic loans, for Israel; the most Germany could offer was to arrange a foreign loan.[20] Schäffer admonished Böhm and Küster for making statements on what they thought the German offer would be and accused them of violating instructions.[21] Schäffer suggested they return to the negotiations with his statement of March 7, declaring that Germany could afford to meet no part of the recognized claim at the moment. Böhm and Küster denied Schäffer's authority, suggesting that they took their instructions from Adenauer. Moreover, they told Schäffer that if the Chancellor had ever suggested to them that the only offer to Israel was to be a foreign loan, they would have refused his commission to be negotiators in the first place. Schäffer replied that it was for Böhm to make known to Adenauer Schäffer's instructions about the inability to pay. When Küster objected, they were ordered out of Schäffer's office. This incident provoked Küster's letter of resignation that same day (Küster, May 23, 1952, and interview, 1975), but there was further provocation before Böhm stepped down.

Adenauer at first refused Küster's resignation, but not because of a commitment to satisfying Israel's claims. At a meeting of the Cabinet and advisers on May 14 Küster tried to advance his views on the claims of representatives of world Jewry, with whom Germany was also negotiating at Wassenaar, but the Chancellor would not let him finish his presentation. Schäffer made personal attacks on Böhm and Küster. At this same meeting Böhm and Küster outlined their proposal for an offer to Israel, but Adenauer 'apparently sided with Herr Schäffer' in opposing such an offer (*New York Times*, May 20, 1952).[22]

Less than a week later Böhm and Küster learned that Abs had made an offer to Israeli representatives Shinnar and Keren in London. The Israelis considered the offer of an annual shipment of 100 million marks of goods, with no commitment to time or total amount, 'entirely inadequate' (Shinnar, 1967, p. 40; Goldmann, 1969, p. 265). And although Adenauer claims he knew nothing of this offer in advance (1968, p. 145), Shinnar has noted that Abs was authorized to clarify with the Israelis how much Israel would be willing to adjust its claim to Germany's capacity to pay (1967, pp. 39–41). Abs negotiated on the question of the Israeli claim only on the direction of Adenauer, and it is therefore unlikely that some range for an offer was not discussed with Adenauer before the meeting.

By this time Adenauer had accepted Küster's resignation; now both Böhm and Küster went to the public with their resignations (Baring, 1969, pp. 158–9, 409).[23] Their official reasons for resigning help explain Adenauer's commitment to the reparations, and also suggest why

Adenauer could be persuaded to change his position yet again. According to Böhm,

> The Federal Finance Minister and the responsible persons in Bonn are of the opinion that we cannot afford economically to make the sacrifices which are necessary if we are to make restitution as outlined in Chancellor Adenauer's statement of September of last year; they believe that such an offer of restitution will cause a total breakdown of the London Debt Conference. I hold this attitude [to be] completely wrong ... I think it is obvious that all the world would understand if the Federal Republic felt itself obliged to do all it possibly could to make amends for the Nazi crimes. The issue here ... is our debt of honour to the Jews ... [The final straw] was the authorization to the German representative at the London Debt Conference, Hermann Abs, to make known to the Israeli representatives at the London Conference the current German attitude, which is completely contrary to the statements we have been making in the Hague. (*Die Neue Zeitung*, May 21, 1952; *Frankfurter Rundschau*, May 21, 1952)[24]

Whereas Böhm blamed Abs, Küster held Schäffer to be the main culprit. In an interview with United Press Küster expressed the view he and Böhm had both already implied, that Adenauer had never been serious about reparations and had used them to improve Germany's world image (*Die Neue Zeitung*, May 21, 1952).

The meeting with Schäffer, the subsequent meeting with Adenauer and the Abs initiative in London were the three events that brought about the resignation of the German negotiating team, an event that shook the new foundations of German-Israeli relations and shook Adenauer as well. If morality had been Adenauer's prime concern all along, as so many critics and men close to him have claimed, then he would have succumbed to the moral arguments of Böhm and Küster rather than to the financial persuasions of Abs and Schäffer during meetings in early May; now that his relationship with the Allies seemed sound, Adenauer appeared to think he could afford to listen less to moral considerations. It is clear that Adenauer had been influenced in his overtures towards Israel largely by a desire to impress the Allies, for once he no longer perceived a need to impress, the negotiations with Israel began to founder.

CONFIRMING PRAGMATISM: YOU PRESSURE, WE PAY

Adverse reactions to the Abs offer and the Böhm and Küster resignations came swiftly from all quarters. On May 19 Nahum Goldmann, now one of the representatives of world Jewry to the Wassenaar negotiations, sent a letter to Adenauer with a copy to McCloy. He emphasized what he thought was important to Adenauer, pragmatism and world opinion:

> From all our discussions I had gained the impression that you and the

German Federal Government were seriously concerned to bring a true, if partial, reparation ... for ... the crimes committed against Jewry. The statements Mr. Abs made ... today contravened in spirit the statement of the Federal Government of September 27, 1951; still more do they contravene the substance of your letter of December 6, 1951 to me in which you accepted the claim of the State of Israel to the amount of $1 billion as a basis of negotiations ... If the order of magnitude in which Mr. Abs apparently sees the solution were to represent the official position of the Federal Republic, the Israeli government could not under any circumstances continue the negotiations, and naturally the same would apply to world Jewry. *The effects of breaking off negotiations ... a very real possibility ... would be hard to imagine in their extent. The confidence in the honest will of the new German state to make reparations will be profoundly shaken in all those persons who hope to see in you ... the spokesman and exponent of this new Germany. The violent reaction of the world ... would be inevitable and fully justified.* (Text in Vogel, 1969, pp. 47–8; emphasis added)

The same stern reminder of the effect on world public opinion if negotiations were to be abandoned was made in letters from the Israeli delegation at Wassenaar to Adenauer and to two supporters of the Böhm–Küster position, Economics Minister Erhard, and Walter Hallstein, another of Adenauer's close advisers (Shinnar, 1967, p. 42). The Israeli Foreign Minister, Moshe Sharett, arriving in New York on a fund-raising mission, spoke to world opinion two days after the Böhm–Küster resignations when he welcomed 'any moral pressure so that they, the Germans, will discharge their obligation' (*New York Times*, May 22, 1952).

As on prior occasions, domestic forces also contributed to Adenauer's change of heart. Much of the leading German press in the days immediately after May 19 regretted the developments in the reparations question (*Die Neue Zeitung*, May 23, 1952), and the SPD leadership expressed strongly its support for the exercise of Germany's moral obligation to the Jews (*Die Neue Zeitung*, May 21 and May 23, 1952). On May 20, to a certain extent on the prompting of Social Democrat Carlo Schmid, the Foreign Affairs Committee of the Bundestag issued a resolution emphasizing that moral obligations took precedence over all legal obligations and legal considerations, namely, the London Debt Conference (Adenauer, 1968, p. 145).

The treaties with the Allies were due for signature at the end of May. Adenauer realized now that the reactions to German negotiations with Israel could jeopardize signature. According to Adenauer's official biographer, Paul Weymar, the Chancellor had made elaborate plans for the ceremonial signing, for 'he perceived the signing of the Treaties as the crowning of his political work, he looked forward to the day and thought the occasion of the signing of the Treaties should be imprinted in the minds of all peoples as an occasion of pomp and circumstance' (1955, p. 671).[25] And according to Otto Lenz, a state secretary in the German Foreign Office at the time, the adverse world opinion, especially as expressed in foreign newspapers, deeply disturbed Adenauer (Baring, 1969, p. 409). Once again, Adenauer needed to convince the world of Germany's sincerity on the question of reparations.

Adenauer moved quickly: he promised Böhm that he would suggest a concrete offer before June 19, and as a result Böhm withheld his resignation. In addition, he arranged a meeting between Böhm and Goldmann to be held in Paris on May 23. McCloy was kept informed of these moves and was involved himself (Goldmann, 1969, p. 267). The Israeli delegation from Wassenaar participated in the talks.

At the meeting in Paris Böhm proposed 3 billion marks for Israel in the form of goods within eight to twelve years. The Israelis and Goldmann responded positively; meanwhile US Secretary of State Dean Acheson and British Foreign Secretary Anthony Eden, in Bonn to sign the Contractual Agreements, warned Adenauer of 'unfortunate consequences' if reparations talks failed (Goldmann, 1969, pp. 268, 279). On June 10, 1952 Israel and the Federal Republic settled the main outstanding problems in meetings with German representatives in Bonn and on June 17 the German Cabinet approved the formal offer. The deadlock had been broken and negotiations at Wassenaar to work out the final details began a few days later. The treaty was signed on September 10, 1952 in Luxembourg.

SUMMARY

One of the main ways in which Germany achieved political rehabilitation after the Third Reich involved reordering relations with Israel and the Jews. Although moral concerns contributed to Adenauer's offer of direct negotiations in September 1951, perceptions of political necessity were decisive.

Adenauer tried to find other ways for the Allies to recognize Germany as acceptable internationally, emphasizing Western dependence on Germany strategically, underlining the importance of Germany between East and West. It is true that Allied policy towards West Germany mellowed as the Cold War with the USSR developed, but the Allies were still not convinced that Germany's strategic indispensability could compensate for Germany's need for moral recovery. To a conference of German and international Jewish leaders in Heidelberg McCloy had said one of the tests for Germany was its relationship with the Jews (*New York Times*, August 1, 1949). Ultimately, and particularly in September 1951 and May 1952, only Israel could fulfil Germany's need for political rehabilitation. As we shall see, ultimately only Germany could be persuaded to fulfil Israel's economic need. The Federal Republic and Israel needed each other simultaneously and uniquely.

ISRAEL'S ECONOMIC NEED, 1948–52

As in Germany, in Israel morality did not govern policy. Perceptions of political necessity ultimately motivated German decisions on reparations, and perceptions of economic necessity pushed Israel into negotiations with Germany for material compensation for Nazi crimes. Moral concerns were genuine in Israel, as they were in Germany, but also as in Germany they were insufficient. As Fanny Ginor, assistant to David Horowitz, director-general of the Finance Ministry in the early years of Israel's development, has said: 'If Israel had not been in such severe economic straits, then it probably would not have entered into negotiations with Germany, nor concluded the Luxembourg Reparations Agreement' (interview, 1975).

ISRAEL IN ECONOMIC CRISIS

Participants, analysts, observers and journalists all agree that Israel was in economic need of help. This perception, which was based on the weight of considerable evidence, was crucial in the decisions of Israel's makers of foreign policy. Political disagreement and conflict was not over whether Israel was in need, but over whether Germany could, would, or should be the source of help.

A number of journals of the period 1950–4 refer to the severe economic conditions of Israel in the first few years after the creation of the state. Reasons vary: large-scale immigration, hostile environment, huge balance of payments deficits, unemployment, housing and lack of foreign currency. Different journals tend to stress different aspects of the problem, although all see immigration as the chief problem which resulted in other economic difficulties.[26] Even by 1954, Israel's economic situation had improved little, and the problems consonant with large-scale immigration were still discernible. Later analyses, in retrospect, tend to confirm the contemporary perceptions of the economic difficulties of the early years (for instance, Patinkin, 1960; Halevi and Klinov-Malul, 1968).

Michael Brecher's important analysis (1973) of Israel's decision on reparations elucidates the influence of the economy in the early 1950s. As Brecher points out, across a number of indicators of economic health, such as immigration, unemployment, gross national product per capita and foreign currency reserves, Israel fared poorly. Brecher limits his evidence to 1950 and 1951, emphasizing that the last months of 1950 were especially harsh for the economic situation (1973, p. 77).

Five points additional to the consensus of economic crisis should be made. First, during the first four years of the existence of the state, the economy's failure was constant and sustained. Secondly, there was a committed Israeli effort to solve the economic crisis domestically, while at the same time looking abroad to reduce the balance of payments deficits. Only failure in these efforts made acceptance of German reparations possible. Thirdly, the perception of economic necessity pervaded the Israeli government. Fourthly, there was an apparent relationship between the deterioration of economic conditions in Israel and the intensity of Israeli commitment to secure reparations (Table 3.2). Finally, if there were improvements in some indicators from year to year, they were either marginal or they were offset by a dramatic worsening in another

Table 3.2 *Israel's Foreign Currency Reserves and Negotiations with Germany, June 1950 to May 1952*

Date	Currency reserves (I£m.)	Contacts
June 1950	23·1*	First spring contacts underway
July	20·1	
August	17·1	
September	15·4	Horowitz's suggestion of Germany as source of help
October	13·8	
November	12·4	
December	10·9	
January 1951	9·6	First Israeli Note
February	8·3	
March	5·9	Second Israeli Note
April	5·0	Fischer–Horowitz–Adenauer meeting in Paris
May	3·6	
June	2·8	
July	2·8	
August	2·8	
September	2·8	
October	2·8	
November	2·8	
December	2·8	Cabinet decision on direct negotiations
January 1952	1·8	Knesset debate
February	0·8	
March	0	Opening of Wassenaar negotiations
April	0	
May	0	Agreement on basic settlement

*No monthly breakdown is available before June 1950.
Source: IMF, *International Financial Statistics*, October 1951, and July 1952.

Table 3.3 *Economic Indicators for Israel, 1949–52*

	Population (thousands)	Net immigration as % of population increase	Percentage of labour force unemployed, A*	Percentage of labour force unemployed, B†	Balance of payments deficit (million Israeli pounds)‡	Balance of trade deficit (million Israeli pounds)	Public debt (million Israeli pounds)	Real per capita income (index 1950 = 100)§	Foreign currency reserves (million Israeli pounds)¶
1949	1,173·9	91·1%	9·5%	13·9%	−54·6	−79·79	−8·48	—	28·7
1950	1,370·1	85·0%	6·9%	11·2%	−58·1	−93·54	−49·76	100	10·9
1951	1,577·8	81·9%	6·1%	8·1%	−69·4	−118·93	−71·42	112	2·8
1952	1,629·5	24·9%	7·2%	8·1%	−68·0	−98·78	−86·63	98	0

*Excludes labourforce potential in immigration camps.
†Includes labourforce potential in immigration camps.
‡Balance of payments deficit defined as difference between current account and capital account, using net figures (exchange rate: 1 Israeli pound = $2·8).
§No figures are available before 1950.
¶Year-end figures.
Sources: Halevi and Klinov-Malul, 1968, pp. 52, 54, 66, 141, 296–7; UN, *Statistical Year Book*, 1953, 1954; IMF, *International Financial Statistics*, July 1952, April 1959.

indicator, such that the overall state of solvency was drastically low (Table 3.3).

As early as 1949 Israel introduced measures at home aimed at solving these economic problems. The 'austerity period' of 1949–51, however, resolved neither the trade deficits nor the drain on foreign reserves, despite optimism that Israel would solve its own problems.

Like Israel itself, the immediate immigration problem, so broadly perceived as the key to economic distress, was an explicit product of the Third Reich. Inability to work, because of age or ill-health, reached as many as one of every five Israelis. These central problems, too, Israel sought to overcome independently. Faced with failure, it looked for help from abroad. Israel searched for ways of financing balance of payments deficits during the early days of the austerity programme, and on March 17, 1949 the Knesset authorized the Minister of Finance to accept a $100 million loan from the American Export-Import Bank that had been negotiated by the provisional government. By the spring of 1949 Israel already had signed trade agreements with Holland and Hungary and was seeking agreements with Czechoslovakia and Poland.

The third obvious potential source of capital, apart from the USA and other friendly but less powerful and affluent countries, all of whose contributions combined did not meet needs, was world Jewry. World Jewry did make large contributions: $118 million in 1949, and in 1950 $90 million came in the form of unilateral transfers, but the problem was far from solution. As Ben-Gurion explained: 'In the third year of the State of Israel [1950] it became clear that the tasks it faced could not be carried out by the State alone, not even with the help of the Zionist funds' (1971, p. 395). It was at this stage that Ben-Gurion suggested raising a popular loan of $1 billion for twelve to thirteen years, but his idea only began to be realized in September 1950 when foreign financial experts met in Jerusalem to work out the details of the Independence Loan (the State of Israel Bonds). The actual bond drive did not begin until May 1951.

Shinnar relates that 'knowing help would probably come later was not good enough in Israel's economic situation of near disaster' (interviews, 1975). Sharef recounts how attempts were made,

> but there was no hope. Truman was our friend, but certainly could not supply us with arms because of the Middle East embargo. We already had a $100 million loan from the United States and certain food supplies, but there was no immediate possibility of anything else. France was willing to supply arms, but no loan. (Interview, 1975)

Despite a policy of 'non-identification', attempts to obtain economic assistance from the Soviet bloc failed. Israel's economic need, moreover, could be expected to last as long as there was to be immigration, which could well mean throughout the life of the state. Several observers have suggested that, in looking to Germany, which he was now forced to do, Ben-Gurion recognized not only Germany's economic capability in the early 1950s, but foresaw Germany's economic success of later years (Pearlman, 1965, pp. 165–6; Brecher, 1972, p. 111; Ginor interview, 1975; Sharef interview, 1975).

Ben-Gurion saw the pursuit of a strong economy, an aim which required outside aid, not as an end in itself, but as a means of survival and security for the Jewish state (Brecher, 1973, pp. 79–80), a view shared by Foreign Minister Sharett. Sharett told the Knesset:

> Between renunciation and acceptance [of reparations] stands the decision of how strong we want to be in the future. It is a question of responsibility for the state. A state cannot renounce something which it is owed and must not pass up any opportunity to be strong and stable. Anyone who says no to reparations ... behaves as though we had no state. (Sharett, 1952a, pp. 38–9)

For both Sharett and Ben-Gurion, immediate concerns were economic; for both, the ultimate concern was survival and security.

Several government ministers of the early 1950s, notably Eliezer Kaplan, Golda Meir, Dov Joseph and Haim Shapira, professed the importance of the economic motive for the reparations negotiations, although in differing degrees (Brecher, 1973, pp. 82–3). Participants outside the Cabinet generally have confirmed the emphasis on economic considerations. Shinnar, for example, has said: 'There can be no doubt as to the importance of our awkward economic situation in the decision to seek reparations' (interviews, 1975). In his memoirs he states categorically that Israel's desperate economy overrode his own emotional disinclination and accounted for his agreement to be involved directly in questions of reparations from Germany (Shinnar, 1967, pp. 18–19).

Similarly, Nahum Goldmann said, 'the state was bankrupt and needed money' (interview, 1975). This perception provoked his involvement, despite expressions of emotion which might have kept him from contacts with Germany: 'large shipments of goods from the new Germany would be of crucial importance for Israel's future, whether we liked it or not, and ... it was the harsh duty of the Jewish representatives to enter into negotiations with Germany' (Goldmann, 1969, p. 257). David Horowitz made a similar economic assessment and drew the same conclusion (interview, 1975).

Giora Josephtal, co-chairman with Shinnar of the Israeli delegation to Wassenaar, was also treasurer of the Jewish Agency and head of its absorption department. In an interview in the *Allgemeine Wochenzeitung der Juden in Deutschland* Josephtal spent most of the discussion describing Israel's poor economic position and explaining how important the Reparations Agreement would be for the Israeli economy (January 16, 1953); letters to his wife during the Wassenaar negotiations confirm his preoccupation with the problems of immigration (Halpern and Wurm, 1966, pp. 147–73). Fanny Ginor, a Ministry of Finance official during the period, has reaffirmed that many of those involved in the decision to request reparations from Germany were influenced heavily by Israel's economic need (interview, 1975).

ISRAEL REACHES OUT IN NEED

In the spring of 1950 Ben-Gurion, realizing that Israel must have additional financial support from outside the country, opened contacts with the Federal Republic of Germany. Representatives of Israel and of world Jewry met separately with different representatives of the West German government. We have no complete record of the contents of those meetings, but there are some indications that material restitution, that is, Israel's economic concern, was the subject of discussion. For example, Noah Barou, one of the representatives of world Jewry, stipulated in his meetings with German representatives that 'Germany would make amends for the material losses suffered by Jewry and that representatives of Israel and world Jewry should be officially invited to discuss the matter' (Deutschkron, 1970a, p. 31). Already in February 1950 the Israeli Finance and Foreign Ministries were authorized to deal directly with officials of the Federal Republic over individual restitution claims under the existing Allied restitution laws (Brecher, 1975, p. 74). The Deputy Finance Minister travelled to Germany in the spring, and according to one newspaper account at the time, he suggested global settlement of Israel's individual claims to restitution, through delivery of goods to Israel (*Rheinischer Merkur*, January 27, 1951).

Thus, by the fall of 1950 it was abundantly clear to Israel that Germany was a possible new source of money. The initial contacts had taken place in the spring, and in July the Israeli government received an expert opinion, commissioned by the Ministry of Finance, that Israel should approach Germany directly over reparations and individual compensation. The study has been credited for an important role in Israeli decision-making (Deutschkron, 1970a, pp. 44–5; Balabkins, 1971, p. 87; Brecher, 1973, p. 84).

Hendrik van Dam, the secretary-general of the Central Council of Jews in Germany and author of the commissioned memorandum realized that the natural Israeli reaction was to abhor reparations from Germany, yet he stressed the economic necessity. He also advised speedy action. In the final section of his detailed memorandum van Dam concluded, 'For a number of reasons, direct government action now seems desirable, and the intervention of other institutions inappropriate'. He ended with a proposal: 'that the government dispatch a "Reparation and Indemnification Mission" with authority to negotiate with German government agencies ... on the indemnification of [individual] Jews resident in Israel ... and ... make preparations for the general reparation claim' (text in Vogel, 1969, pp. 21–6).

The final recognition that Germany was now the only possibility for financial assistance came when David Horowitz, director-general of the Ministry of Finance, visited London in September in search of foreign currency. Horowitz recalls how he found great difficulty and felt 'on the verge of crisis'. He telephoned Sharett – in New York for the United Nations General Assembly – and said, 'I am at my wits end, but I have a crazy idea to do with Germany which might just be realized' (interview, 1975).

At a subsequent meeting in Paris with Sharett, Horowitz outlined his proposal. The Foreign Minister was persuaded by the idea, both in terms of moral right and economic need: Israel should request through the four occupying powers a definite sum of money from the successor governments to Nazi Germany to help absorb Israel's immigrants. Horowitz realized that whatever help Israel got from elsewhere abroad would be insufficient. No other country could give the same amount that Israel expected of Germany, because no other country had a similar moral duty.

On his return to Israel Horowitz met with Ben-Gurion, who was quickly convinced of the validity of the proposal. The idea of an indirect claim to German reparations, later to be expressed in the Notes of January and March 1951, was born; its origin lay in Israel's desperate economic and financial situation, as perceived by the man who took care of Israel's day-to-day finances.[27]

The Cabinet decision to seek reparations from Germany through indirect means came on January 3, 1951. Shortly before, Israel had demonstrated again that Germany was a potential financial source. According to the *New York Times* of December 29, 1950, the Israeli government, 'which is desperately seeking foreign exchange to finance its import program for 1951', invited Robert Kempner, one of the American prosecutors at the Nuremberg trials, to advise on how to collect sums due Israeli citizens as restitution, indemnification and reparation for acts of the Nazi government. (The claims had been made by German Jews now residents of Israel, on the basis of laws the occupying powers had instituted in their zones of occupation. The problem was that no mechanism existed for transferring either goods or cash from Germany to Israel.)

Discussion between the Israeli government and Kempner appeared to lead to Israel's first Note of January 16. Once more reflecting Israel's economic concerns, Horowitz drafted the Note, together with Leo Kohn, political adviser to the Foreign Minister. In addition to demands for speedy restitution and indemnification, the Note introduced the idea of a general claim of the State of Israel to compensation because of Nazi crimes (State of Israel Ministry for Foreign Affairs, 1953, pp. 13–16). This idea was elaborated in the Note of March 12. Again addressed to the four powers, and again drafted by Horowitz and Kohn, the second Note referred to Israel's moral and economic right to reparations. The economic argument was made in the following terms:

6. ...between 1939 and 1950 almost 380,000 Jews from the territories conquered by the Nazis were brought in to the country. If we add to this number those Jews who had immigrated from central Europe during the pre-war years of Nazi persecution, we have a total of 450,000.
7. Most of these immigrants brought only their feeble strength with them. They had long since been plundered of their entire property. Many of them were difficult welfare cases, men and women whose health had been irremediably ruined and whom no state but Israel was prepared to admit... Israel had to make considerable exertions and spend substantial public funds to take care of the newcomers and, through investments, to create possibilities of employment for them. The entire economy of the new state was directed to this essential purpose from the very first ...Heavy tax burdens and a severe system

of economic restrictions had to be decided on in order to procure homes and the means of existence for these immigrants ... It is certainly not too much to demand that the German people, which is responsible for this predicament, and is still enjoying the use of the property taken from the Jews dead or alive, be called upon to help integrate the survivors.

9. The amount of these reparations must take into account on the one hand losses suffered by the Jewish people through the Germans and on the other hand the financial burdens involved in integrating in Israel the fugitives or survivors of the Nazi regime ... The number of these immigrants is estimated at some 500,000, which means a total expenditure of $1·5 billion. (Text in Vogel, 1969, pp. 30–1)

The demand, then, was only for the cost of absorption of immigrants, which Horowitz had assessed at $3,000 per immigrant (interview, 1975).

Only when all other means of foreign support appeared exhausted did Israel formally consider Germany as a source of finance, and then only through indirect approaches. Israel's economic situation needed to worsen still before Israel considered direct negotiations, and Israel needed to be certain of a positive German attitude and concrete subjects of negotiation. The deterioration of the Israeli economy and the confirmation of German attitudes came in the course of 1951, especially in the final months.

WHY DID ISRAEL FINALLY NEGOTIATE?

Israel was not eager to negotiate with Germany, and unofficial direct contacts were accompanied only by indirect official discussion. The idea of direct negotiations had been suggested in Israeli Cabinet meetings on October 30, 1950, and again on December 27; on both occasions the opposition of Dov Joseph, according to Brecher the most vociferous opponent of dealing with Germany, prevented direct talks (Brecher, 1975, p. 69).

The reluctance of the Israeli government to engage in direct negotiations with Germany no longer derived from insufficient need. The two most important factors – the perception of a moral claim and the perception of economic necessity – were clear by the end of 1950. But the Cabinet was still uncertain about three other matters: (1) whether the Israeli public could be persuaded that it was morally wrong to refuse German money; (2) whether Germany was disposed to pay; and (3) whether Germany was capable of paying.[28] To resolve the doubts the Cabinet undertook a number of initiatives, including informal talks with German officials and an assessment of the German financial situation.

High-level unofficial talks began in Paris in April 1951 but already at the end of 1950 Robert Kempner had warned the Israelis, 'If you want to collect money, you must talk. You cannot do it by telepathy' (*New York Times*, December 29, 1950). The Israelis knew that, should the

Germans be both willing and able to pay, negotiations would have to become direct.

While David Horowitz was leading the initial contact with Adenauer in Paris in April 1951, his assistant Fanny Ginor assessed Germany's ability to pay. On May 8, 1951, just after the first Paris meeting, she reported that Germany's 'economic miracle', as it would be called in retrospect, had begun already. According to Ginor, this assurance of German financial capability was a prerequisite to direct negotiations.[29]

In their April meeting Horowitz told Adenauer that talks with Israel could proceed only if Germany met moral and economic conditions. During the summer the Israeli government created a new Foreign Ministry section, the Claims Office of the Jewish People against Germany, indicating Israeli readiness and preparation for negotiation. One of Israel's leading economists, Felix Shinnar, was named head of the section.

Adenauer satisfied Horowitz's moral conditions in his September 1951 speech to the Bundestag. But Israel remained unsure of Germany's financial willingness. On December 6, 1951 Adenauer met with Nahum Goldmann in London. Goldmann informed Adenauer that Ben-Gurion could not respond to Germany's September 1951 offer of direct negotiations until Adenauer had recognized Israel's claim of $1 billion against the Federal Republic as the basis for negotiations. Adenauer, as we have noted already, agreed to this figure in a letter to Goldmann he wrote the same day.

Germany had now met all the conditions stipulated by Israel for direct negotiations, but Israel, apparently fearing domestic political difficulties, still baulked. Economic failure was decisive. By the end of 1951 the decline of the Israeli economy could not be arrested. There were virtually no reserves; the austerity programme had not worked; although there were reductions initially in the cost of living index (from March 1949 until June 1950 the index was reduced), by September 1951 it reached a new high (IMF, *International Financial Statistics*, July 1952; Balabkins, 1971, p. 102; Ginor interview, 1975). Unemployment continued also to be very high, and at least one-fifth of the population 'lived in ... temporary housing ... the black market [was now the] rule [rather] than the exception it had been in 1949' (Halevi and Klinov-Malul, 1968, pp. 6–7).

Yet again, Israel preferred measures at home to alleviate its severe economic problems: the government introduced the New Economic Policy at the end of the year, which called for cutbacks in government and private spending, and devaluation. In November 1951 the Jewish Agency, the chief agent of immigration into Israel, amended its liberal policy and instituted selectivity. These last-ditch efforts, including compromise in basic principles, were not enough. The potential economic benefits associated with direct negotiations could not be forgone for long.

Israeli leaders recognized the economic need for restitution from Germany; German leaders perceived its political benefits. These needs coincided. Both sides perceived the other as uniquely capable of fulfilling simultaneous needs, for only Israel could absolve Germany of past deeds, and only Germany could (and would) rescue Israel's economy. Here were the conditions necessary for the development of a special relationship.

Finally, the Cabinet decided to accept direct negotiations on December 30, 1951, more than a year after the Cabinet had first considered the idea. The government's proposal was supported by a small Knesset majority on January 9; the matter was finalized by the affirmative vote of the Knesset Committee on Foreign Affairs and Security six days later. For Israel, Germany was the last resort; it probably would have preferred help from elsewhere, but to some Israeli leaders it was right that matters developed this way, for Germany was, after all, the principal cause of the problems it was now being called upon to help solve.

MUTUAL NEEDS FULFILLED

Israel's need for economic help and Germany's need for political rehabilitation have been emphasized because need – mutual and simultaneous – is essential for the establishment of a special relationship. Germany and Israel saw each other as uniquely capable of fulfilling these needs and to a large extent their needs were satisfied.

Satisfaction came through the Luxembourg Reparations Agreement, which gave Germany international recognition as penitent and gave Israel economic and financial support. In an interview two months after Luxembourg, and later in his memoirs, Adenauer referred to the importance of the Agreement in terms of rehabilitation for Germany (*Die Neue Zeitung*, November 19, 1952). He called the Luxembourg Agreement 'a political event of equal importance with the Contractual Agreements and the European Defence Community Treaty', and noted that 'world opinion greeted' the accord (Adenauer, 1968, pp. 155–6). Felix von Eckardt, Adenauer's press secretary, said, 'International recognition and acceptance followed this struggle over Germany's future' (1967, p. 203), and several German newspapers at the time of the signing commented on the significance of the Agreement for Germany's political rehabilitation into the 'family of nations' (*Presse- und Informationsamt*, September 10, 1952).

Israelis also underlined the influence of the Luxembourg Agreement on Germany's international recognition. David Horowitz termed the Agreement 'Germany's visiting card to the civilized world'; Fanny Ginor has noted that 'Germany probably would have been rehabilitated sooner or later because of its economic strength, but the Agreement meant

Germany was accepted sooner internationally in political terms' (interview, 1975).

In a letter to the Conference on Jewish Material Claims against Germany Ben-Gurion, the Israeli Prime Minister, observed that 'the agreement will serve as an impressive contribution toward consolidating the economic independence of Israel and as substantial compensation to the victims of Nazi persecution who are still alive' (quoted in the *New York Times*, September 25, 1952). Even some of those in Israel who had opposed Ben-Gurion in the Knesset debate of January 1952 realized the economic importance of the Agreement. For example, a spokesman of the General Zionists stated: 'It must be conceded that the negotiations have succeeded beyond our expectations. Undoubtedly, Israel's economic difficulties will be eased, at least for the moment' (*New York Times*, September 12, 1952).

Moshe Sharett recognized the simultaneous significance for both Germany and Israel in the Agreement. In an interview ten years after the signing he said: 'It [the Agreement] was a political fact of enormous international significance, something quite unprecedented, which has taken a most momentous place in the history of Israel and Germany ... [It] brought honor to Germany, and ... constructive aid [to Israel]' (text in Vogel, 1969, p. 55). The Luxembourg Reparations Agreement was the first concrete step, the first act, in the special relationship between the states of West Germany and Israel.

DOMESTIC REPERCUSSIONS IN WEST GERMANY AND ISRAEL

West Germany and Israel concluded the Luxembourg Reparations Agreement in September 1952 after months of initial informal contact and of tough official bargaining. Despite this positive conclusion, in both countries there were strong elements of opposition that lasted from the time the idea of negotiations first was announced (September 1951 in Germany; January 1952 in Israel) until the ratification of the Agreement (March 1953 in both countries). A special relationship requires a supportive internal environment. Notwithstanding the opposition in both countries, on a number of decisive occasions the majority of German and Israeli elites looked favourably on the notion of reparations, such that negotiations could begin, proceed and lead to a positive agreement and, ultimately, to the ratification of the Agreement.

SUPPORT AND OPPOSITION IN WEST GERMANY
Opposition to the idea of a reparations agreement with Israel surfaced in Germany during the Wassenaar negotiations and was sustained during the ratification debate. At both times the opposition made its case on the basis of the economy.

During the Wassenaar negotiations opposition to a substantial reparations settlement (that is, on the order of the Israeli claim) came, as we have seen, from Finance Minister Schäffer and from Hermann Abs, the chief of the German delegation to the London Debt Conference and the chairman of the Administrative Council of the Credit Bank for Reconstruction. According to Böhm, Küster and Goldmann, Schäffer was opposed to making material amends to Israel because he believed the Federal Republic could not afford to pay. According to Shinnar, Schäffer advocated the fulfilment of *individual* restitution claims through the mechanism of the Allies' military restitution laws, which would be assumed and extended by the Federal Republic (1967, p. 43). The *New York Times* of May 20, 1952 reported that Schäffer opposed any settlement, and in June the newspaper reported him against most of the restitution proposals.

According to Inge Deutschkron, Schäffer had concurred with Abs's offer to the Israelis of May 19, 1952, and he 'tried to induce his ministerial colleagues to vote against the Israel treaty by threatening to eliminate all their pet projects from the budget plans' (Deutschkron, 1970a, pp. 50, 58, 63, 69). In the Bundestag vote on ratification of the Luxembourg Agreement, Schäffer, as a Christian Socialist Union (CSU) deputy, demonstrated his opposition by abstaining.

Schäffer himself shed some light on his opposition to financial commitments to Israel in his radio address of May 22, 1952, replying to attacks made on him by Küster. He did not dispute Küster's claim that he opposed a settlement on financial grounds; rather, he objected to Küster's personal attacks. Schäffer emphasized that it was Küster's obligation to negotiate on the basis of the material needs of Germany: 'As Minister of Finance, in all questions and dealings with all nations, I must always consider first the concerns, the needs and the burdens of my people' (quoted in *Die Neue Zeitung*, May 23, 1952).[30] Schäffer considered the burdens on Germany sufficiently great to preclude a substantial settlement with Israel, and on his insistence a clause was inserted in the treaty referring to contingencies should Germany be unable to pay.[31]

Abs did not oppose a settlement *per se*, but he believed Israel's claim must be considered in light of the claims of other countries against Germany. He saw to it that the Hague and London conferences were coordinated (*New York Times*, May 20, 1952; *Jewish Chronicle*, May 30, 1952; Vogel, 1969, pp. 39–41), and at one point he even persuaded Adenauer to await settlements in London before making other commitments. Abs warned Adenauer on December 3, 1951 (three days before Adenauer's letter to Goldmann accepting the Israeli claim as the basis of negotiations), that Germany should not incur any new financial responsibilities without prior approval of its international creditors (Deutschkron, 1970a, pp. 50–1). When Abs learned of Adenauer's commitment to negotiations with Israel on the basis of the Israeli claim, he let it be known that 'he was strongly opposed to the Israeli claims, which were unrealistic and calculated to compromise the London conference'. He threatened to resign and urged Adenauer to call off the talks with Israel (*Jewish Chronicle*, March 7, 1952).

Abs denies that he was opposed to the fulfilment of the Israeli claim. According to Abs, he supported the view that Israel should receive 3 billion marks, but he felt that he had to be careful in his statements because the London Debt Conference was still proceeding (interview, 1975).[32] This view certainly would account for his opposition to the Israeli claim in public, but does not explain why he persisted in his opposition to a major settlement in private meetings, as related by Adenauer, Böhm and Küster. Nor does it explain why he actually made a minimal offer to Israel.[33]

Despite the opposition of Abs and Schäffer, and their influence on Adenauer, at critical times the majority of the political parties, the Cabinet and Adenauer's close advisers supported a settlement with Israel. From the beginning a majority of German leaders supported a generous settlement (Vogel, 1969, pp. 33–5). Hallstein, Blankenhorn and Erhard supported Böhm and Küster at the Cabinet meeting of April 5, 1952, when Adenauer seemed swayed by Abs and Schäffer. Adenauer leaned to the majority view, and in subsequent meetings the debate divided consistently between these groups. Goldmann emphasizes the influence of Hallstein, Blankenhorn and Erhard, as well as of Franz Blücher, the Vice-Chancellor (1969, p. 277). In the Cabinet meeting on May 19, when Böhm's proposal for preventing the rupture of negotiations was considered, Adenauer 'carried everybody with him' in his support of Böhm (Deutschkron, 1970a, p. 64). At the conclusion of the protracted debate between the 'moralists' and the 'economists' a majority of the Cabinet endorsed the terms of settlement on June 17, 1952, and the Cabinet approved ratification of the Luxembourg Agreement on February 13, 1953.

The support of the political parties shown in September 1951, following Adenauer's Bundestag statement, continued throughout the negotiations, and Adenauer was apparently influenced in May 1952 by the resolution of the Foreign Affairs Committee, calling on Germany to fulfil its moral obligation to Israel, irrespective of other creditors. None the less, opposition, heavily influenced by Arab economic threats, was prominent prior to ratification. As soon as the Luxembourg Agreement was signed Arab representatives lodged their protest to the Bundestag and to various economic organizations in Germany, threatening a boycott of firms which participated in the delivery of goods to Israel.[34] Later the Arab states, through the Arab League, protested directly to the Federal government. In a Note of November 12, 1952 they called the treaty an affront not only to neutrality, but also to traditional German–Arab friendship. If the treaty were ratified, then the Arab World would break all economic ties with Germany.

Adenauer responded in a radio address the same day: 'I have signed the German–Israeli Agreement ... I stick to my word' (quoted in *New York Times*, November 1952; Adenauer, 1968, pp. 151–3). Adenauer said that his government was willing to negotiate with the Arab states, but was not willing to make ratification dependent on a favourable outcome of negotiations with the Arab League. Two days after Adenauer's response to the Arab Note, the Federal government did announce plans to send delegations to Arab capitals to clarify the content of the Agreement with Israel (*Neue Zürcher Zeitung*, November 17, 1952).

The Arab efforts to influence Bundestag deputies against the treaty had immediate results; thirty deputies representing four parties, including the DP and the Free Democratic Party (FDP), sent a letter to the government warning that the Luxembourg Treaty should not be ratified, in light of Arab concern (Kreysler and Jungfer, 1965, p. 46). At the same time a major financial newspaper, *Deutsche Zeitung und Wirtschafts-Zeitung*, began a series of articles, which lasted through the autumn, upholding the Arab cause (September 10, November 1, November 12 and December 17, 1952). The parliamentary opposition to ratification expressed by certain deputies in September 1951 was re-emphasized at the beginning of 1953. Franz-Josef Strauss of the CSU, in *Chemie* on January 5, opposed ratification because of the economic loss of Arab markets. In the same period the Bundestag Committee for Foreign Trade formally expressed to State Secretary Hallstein its concern over economic developments with Arab nations since the signing of the Luxembourg Agreement with Israel; the committee opposed ratification of the treaty (*Frankfurter Allgemeine Zeitung*, January 3 and February 23, 1953).

Opposition also was voiced in the Bundesrat, where various Länder doubted the money necessary to execute the Luxembourg Agreement was available; they saw no possibility for such appropriations in the budget. None the less, they recommended ratification unanimously, and the Foreign Affairs Committee of the Bundestag also stood by the treaty. When the Bundestag vote finally came in March, the FDP and the DP officially objected to the treaty because of its adverse effect on economic relations with the Arabs, and they allowed their deputies to vote freely. 239 deputies voted for the Agreement; there were 35 votes against ratification and 86 abstentions.[35] Opponents tended to represent special economic interests and were persuaded in their opposition by the Federal Association of German Industry whose president, Fritz Berg, convinced Adenauer of the need to reduce the damage in the Arab World (Grossmann, 1954, p. 34; Braunthal, 1965, pp. 193, 305). Despite limited Arab-lobby success, the government doubted the Arab threat and a majority of the German political elite remained committed to the Luxembourg Agreement. Ludger Westrick, state secretary and Adenauer's emissary to Egypt, advised proceeding with ratification; he doubted the boycott threat, and no boycott materialized (interview, 1975).

SUPPORT AND OPPOSITION IN ISRAEL

The very idea of direct negotiation with Germany had generated violent opposition in Israel which was sustained throughout the negotiation, signing and ratification stages of the Luxembourg Agreement. Herut staged demonstrations, and pursued other means of opposition (*New York Times*, March 26, 1952, March 23, 1953; *Die Neue Zeitung*, March 26 and November 3, 1952; *The Times*, March 24, 1952). In mid-January 1952 the party tabled a motion in the Knesset calling for a national plebiscite. At the beginning of the negotiations in Wassenaar Herut moved for the recall of the Israeli delegation and repeated its call in May when the talks between the Germans and Israelis appeared deadlocked.

Herut was not alone in opposition. In fact, at various times opposition was apparent within the coalition parties and within the opposition parties. When the Mapai leadership began discussion of direct negotiations in November 1951 Sprinzak, the first Speaker of the Knesset, Dvorjhetsky, a partisan leader in Europe during the Second World War, and to a lesser extent, Golda Meir, referred to the decline of Israel's moral standing if negotiations were to begin (Brecher, 1973, p. 91). The religious parties, especially Mizrachi, made their opposition known as soon as coalition members were invited to join discussions.

Outside the coalition Herut, Mapam, the General Zionists and Maki all resisted the idea of direct negotiations. The General Zionists, through their spokesman Elimeleh Rimalt, echoed the moral arguments of Herut, although in a more subdued tone, while Maki, the Israel Communist Party, shared one of Mapam's arguments that 'the direct negotiations project was a United States plot to whitewash the Germans and make it easier to line up West Germany in the western defense set-up' (*New York Times*, January 13, 1952). And by the time the ratification debate was started in the Israeli Cabinet the General Zionists were members of the government, now additional opponents within the coalition.

Opposition to direct negotiations with Germany came from all parties in Israel at different stages. However, as in Germany, when crucial votes were taken, the majority supported the Mapai leadership. Mapai was firm and carried a majority in Cabinet meetings in November and December 1951. In the meeting of the coalition members of the Knesset at the beginning of January the Cabinet position was sanctioned. Even the violence of the Knesset debate could not prevent a positive outcome; the vote was 60 in favour, 51 against, with 5 abstentions and 4 absentees. A week later the Knesset Committee on Foreign Affairs and Security upheld that decision by a vote of 8 to 6.

Majorities often were thin, and votes often were conditional, but majority support for reparations none the less was sustained. For example, although the Knesset voted 49 to 32 to continue the Wassenaar negotiations in May 1952, it was stipulated by a vote of 50 to 34 that the resumption of negotiations was contingent on a firm offer from Germany (*Jewish Chronicle*, May 9, 1952). And when Ben-Gurion submitted the

Agreement to the Knesset Committee on Foreign Affairs and Security ten months later, approval was only 7 to 5 with 1 abstention. The treaty was ratified by the Cabinet on March 22, 1953. Even at the very end, the majority was slight, but from beginning to end there was a majority.

In both Germany and Israel forces of opposition made negotiations difficult. Nevertheless, a majority of the political elite in both countries wanted the Agreement and perceived public support for its position, both for reasons of morality and for economic and political necessity. The special relationship began with strong traditions and deep commitments, but also with thin majorities and severe internal divisions. These divisions were overcome by an emphasis on need. Gemany gave greater priority to being accepted internationally than to guaranteeing Arab trade, and Israel gave greater priority to reparations than to self-righteousness. Both found moral arguments to support their perceptions of expediency, and both found certain needs satisfied almost immediately upon conclusion of the first agreements. But these divisive strains, present at the creation of the special relationship, would continue to test the relationship throughout its life.

CONTINUITY MORE THAN CHANGE

CHANGING NEEDS

The needs of Israel and of Germany were not met instantly by the signing of the Reparations Agreement. Israel's economic plight continued. One avenue for its resolution lay in technological and scientific advances, but they depended on outside financial assistance, and Israel's military situation also required aid from abroad. These economic, financial and military needs have been constant since the 1950s and have climaxed in times of crisis, such as the 1956 Suez campaign and the 1967 Six-Day War. After the Six-Day War, Israel encountered a new requirement for survival, to be found only beyond its own borders. Increasingly, and particularly after the Yom Kippur War and the oil crisis of 1973, Israel found itself in diplomatic isolation. Challenges to its position on the administered territories and on the Palestinian question were registered in many countries. Politically and psychologically, in addition to its economic and military requirements, Israel needed international friends. The Federal Republic, together with the USA, was the consistent focus in Israel's search for help after 1950. Until 1967 Germany was a more reliable and more generous donor and supporter than even the USA, and after 1967 when the USA diversified and increased its aid to Israel (especially in the military sphere), Germany remained a best friend (see Chapters 4 and 5).

For Germany, the political and psychological search for international acceptance persisted throughout the 1950s and 1960s. By the early 1970s,

82 Foundations

with its new membership in the United Nations and its established position in the EEC, Germany's return to the family of nations was obvious, an acceptance related closely to partnership with Israel as well as with the USA. Germany's continuing need to overcome the past is satisfied increasingly through leadership in the EEC, where its economic destiny has been anchored for almost twenty-five years. Israel's role as the purveyor of international approval for Germany has diminished since the late 1960s. However, it has not disappeared, and in science and technology, for example, Germany has increased its own need for relations with Israel.

In the early 1950s Germany and Israel shared the same sense of need and urgency; they viewed each other as the primary locus of satisfaction. Thirty years later the situation is less well-balanced. Israel has more needs and fewer opportunities for fulfilment than Germany, and Germany has felt the European dependence on the Arab World. As a result, the partnership has undergone major challenges. As we shall see, it remains none the less a special relationship.

THE CONSTANCY OF POSITIVE DOMESTIC POLITICAL CONDITIONS

Domestic politics continued to play an important role in the special relationship long after a supportive environment made its beginning possible. In the mid-1960s German politics were riveted on the questions of German scientists in Egypt and the creation of diplomatic relations with Israel; in the early 1970s re-establishment of relations with the Arabs figured prominently in German politics, and at the end of the decade the debate over the Statute of Limitations on Nazi crimes commanded German attention.

Israeli politics related to Germany no less, whether regarding the scientists in Egypt or the Munich Olympic Games assassins and their release, or the EEC's attitude towards the Palestine Liberation Organization (PLO) in the late 1970s. Germans and Israelis have remained preoccupied with each other for three decades, and despite periodic signs of German and Israeli opposition, their special relationship has been surrounded by fundamentally and continuously positive political forces in both countries (to be discussed later). As in the beginning, political leaders in both countries have interpreted international and regional conditions over time as perpetuating needs that Germany and Israel satisfy for each other.

NOTES: CHAPTER 3

1 Wherever possible, the retelling of events is based on descriptions and analyses written at the time, to try to minimize the difficulties which can result from a dependence on memoirs whose nature can be self-serving. Newspaper accounts, diaries and letters of

that period are, then, probably the most reliable sources. Where they do not exist, I have resorted to memoirs, checking assertions of fact against other memoirs and information given by the same people in interviews. Most useful have been the public statements made at the time by Schäffer, Abs, Böhm and Küster, and parts of Küster's diary. The letters of Josephtal to his wife from the Wassenaar negotiations are also revealing. In general, prominence is given to events which have not been recounted before or which previously have been told inaccurately. For a detailed discussion of the background to reparations negotiations and of the actual negotiations (including US involvement), see Sagi (1980).

Since the basic completion of this manuscript the Israeli archives on the period 1950–2 have been opened. For the most part, the flow of letters between Israeli officials in the Ministry for Foreign Affairs and Israeli representatives in Germany and France confirms the analysis presented here and in the previous chapter. However, in two central points the documents add to or alter slightly the arguments advanced in this chapter. (a) Most analysts suggest the first high-level meeting between Israelis and Germans occurred on May 6, 1951 in Paris and this author initially accepted that date. Israeli documents (State of Israel Ministry for Foreign Affairs Archives) reveal that the meeting took place on April 19 and Maurice Fischer, the Israeli representative in Paris, was intended as the primary interlocuteur with Adenauer. It was on the insistence of Foreign Minister Sharett that David Horowitz was included. The German government was motivated to set up the meeting (via Israeli, Jewish and German representatives) by the appearance of Israel's two Notes concerning reparations. From the encounter, Fischer considered Adenauer cold, reserved and calculating. Israel's moral arguments for making certain demands on Germany regarding the nature, content and timing of direct negotiations emerge clearly from these letters. (b) The April 1951 meeting was the first step in the chain that led to Adenauer's statement of September 27, 1951. Israeli documents indicate the statement went through three major drafts and that some of Israel's key suggestions for alteration were ignored. In particular, Israel stressed the notion of collective German responsibility for Nazi crimes (it had given up on the idea of collective guilt) but this was omitted from the final statement. In addition, Israel would have preferred far greater emphasis on Israel as the collective representative of the Jewish people.

The above points have been brought to my attention by Dr Yehudith Auerbach of the International Relations Department at the Hebrew University. The revision for publication of her doctoral dissertation has involved extensive examination of the Israeli archives. I am grateful for her materials, advice and insights on this question.

2 For treatment of the international setting in which the Federal Republic has found itself since the Second World War and its reaction to the international environment, see Hanrieder (1967, chs 2 and 3, and 1980); Seelbach (1970), ch. 1); Morgan (1974a).
3 For Adenauer's views during the immediate postwar period on West Germany's future, see the first volume of his memoirs (1967).
4 The question of Israel's external environment since 1948 is dealt with in Brecher (1972, chs 2 and 3, and 1975); Dippmann (1970, pp. 19–99); Sachar (1979, chs 13 and 16).
5 See Grewe (1960); Majonica (1965, 1969); Schwarz (1966); Baring (1969); Besson (1970); Hanrieder (1967, 1970, 1980); Löwenthal and Schwarz (1974): Hanrieder and Auton (1980). Baring does make a link between reparations and the general aim of German foreign policy, but there is no substantial treatment (1969, pp. 139, 158–9, 409).
6 See, for example, his inaugural address to the first Bundestag session on September 20, 1949 (Auswärtiges Amt, 1972, p. 153).
7 For a 1950s observer's view of the two motivations of morality and pragmatism, see Grossmann (1954). The importance of the political motive was underlined also by newspapers of the time. See, for example, the article by Jack Raymond in the *New York Times*, September 27, 1951; and *Tagesspiegel*, September 28, 1951.
8 Blankenhorn says he discussed with Adenauer the question of relations with the Jews and Israel 'around October and November of 1949' (text in Vogel, 1969, p. 21).

84 Foundations

9 See Adenauer (1968, p. 131). Adenauer's reference appears to be to the contacts between the Jewish SPD deputy, Jakob Altmaier, and Dr Eliyahu Livneh, Israel's consul in Munich from 1949 to 1953. There were also contacts between Blankenhorn and Dr Noah Barou, a prominent representative of world Jewry. For a note on the Altmaier-Livneh talks, see Brecher (1975, p. 74). For the Blankenhorn–Barou talks, see Fraenkel (1962, pp. 7–8); Goldmann (1962, pp. 10–11); Balabkins (1971, pp. 86–7). Nahum Goldmann was involved in both sets of contacts. For his role at this stage and in the subsequent developments, see Goldmann (1978, ch. 5). For Barou's account of the Luxembourg Agreement, see his 1952 article in *Congress Weekly*.

10 Negotiations between Adenauer and the Western Allies seemed to speed up in the second half of 1950. In mid-August McCloy suggested that Germany's chance to rearm would be improved by more emphasis on Germany's belief in democracy, particularly in statements by German politicians (Adenauer, 1967, p. 339). Adenauer then requested further revision of the Occupation Statute, which was discussed at the Foreign Ministers' Conference of the three Western powers in September; it was decided that there might be the possibility of revision, if 'in accordance with its new responsibilities, certain obligations [were] met and certain measures were taken by Germany' (Baring, 1969, p. 124; Adenauer, 1967, p. 447). These obligations, specified in late October by the British High Commissioner, included the assumption of Germany's prewar debts.

11 At the time of the revision Adenauer acknowledged German responsibility for prewar debts and postwar loans. The revision permitted Germany to conclude international agreements and allowed for the creation of a Foreign Ministry (until that time there had been the Dienststelle für Auswärtige Angelegenheiten, Department for International Affairs). Important powers remained with the occupation authorities.

12 In fact, according to Horowitz, all three Western powers were more sympathetic to Israel than their formal negative replies to Israel's Notes of January and March 1951 might have suggested (interview, 1975). See Brecher (1975) for the Allies' responses to the Notes, for the Paris meeting and the US involvement in arranging the meeting. American involvement also was indicated by the fact that Adenauer and Horowitz agreed to keep the meeting secret, except for informing the US State Department and the US High Commissioner in Germany. Of the three High Commissioners, McCloy in particular supported Israel's case. Horowitz attributes support also to some officials in the State Department. Adenauer makes no mention whatsoever of the meeting with Horowitz. It is clear that the Germans considered McCloy the most important and influential High Commissioner and that he was involved in subsequent dealings between Israel and Germany over reparations (Baring, 1969, p. 64; Abs interview, 1975; Küster interview, 1975; Böhm interview, 1975).

13 Adenauer visited the USA in April 1953. According to Nahum Goldmann, on this first trip Adenauer said to the Foreign Policy Association: 'Without this treaty I would not have dared to come to America' (*Das Parlament*, November 1972).

14 Inge Deutschkron quotes Blankenhorn: 'We met at least a dozen times until we reached a compromise' (1970a, p. 31). Brecher says, 'the draft was scrutinized by Jewish and Israeli representatives, including Barou, Goldmann and Shinnar. The first draft was prepared by the West Germans in July 1951. It took almost three months of negotiations to agree upon a text which met justified Jewish demands' (1973, p. 89). Adenauer confirms that he sounded out Jewish and Israeli opinion (1968, p. 134) and Goldmann writes of the prior approval of Adenauer's statement (1969, p. 256). Noah Barou refers to his evaluation of the statement, emphasizing that it took over two months to achieve agreement (1952, p. 7). According to Fraenkel, writing in memory of Barou, 'In the first draft of the Adenauer Declaration Israel was not even mentioned' (1962, p. 7).

15 Adenauer has justified the lateness of his positive statement by stressing that the obstacle in the unofficial contacts in 1950 was the Allied law concerning currency

Mutual Needs 85

which prohibited payments to Israelis who were entitled to restitution according to other Allied laws (1968, pp. 131–2). This law did not prohibit Adenauer, however, from making a statement on Germany's responsibility for the crimes against Jews.

16 The claim against the Federal Republic was two-thirds of the total claim against Germany of $1·5 billion (6·3 billion marks); the other third, or $0·5 billion, was claimed against the German Democratic Republic. The text of the letter is in Vogel (1969, p. 36).

17 Küster's diary account of the meeting is very important as are his radio address of May 20, 1952 and the text of his May 7 letter of resignation (Küster, May 23, 1952). See also his article of 1967 for a further account of his participation in the reparations negotiations. For detailed coverage of the breakdown in the reparations negotiations, see the *New York Times*, April 1 to April 10, 1952.

18 For details of the London Debt Conference, see *Bulletin* (June 4, 1952).

19 For the texts of the exchange of statements, see State of Israel Ministry for Foreign Affairs (1953, pp. 82–5). The German delegation's statement was formulated on April 5, but was delivered formally in negotiations with the Israeli team on April 7 (Halpern and Wurm, 1966, p. 150; Shinnar, 1967, p. 38).

20 On the nature of the loan proposal, see Adenauer (1968, p. 140) and Küster's May 20, 1952 radio address.

21 Böhm and Küster thought the 3 billion marks that the German government considered the basis of discussion should be the figure offered, but the delegation was precluded from taking this step because the amount and timing of payment had to await a clarification of Germany's economic position.

22 Adenauer makes no reference to Küster in his memoirs, nor does he mention the resignations of Böhm and Küster.

23 According to Küster, he and Böhm knew that Adenauer would be concerned about the reaction of public opinion to their resignations (interview, 1975). For a review of press reactions to the resignations, see *Allgemeine Wochenzeitung der Juden in Deutschland* (May 30, 1952).

24 Böhm already had made known his views to Adenauer on April 23 in a lengthy letter in which he suggested that priority be given to Israel's claim for moral reasons and because of the need to demonstrate to domestic and world opinion Germany's good faith (text in Vogel, 1969, pp. 44–7).

25 Adenauer emphasizes that the final talks over the treaties in April and May preoccupied him such that he could not involve himself intensively with the German-Jewish negotiations (1968, p. 143). On Adenauer's fear that the resignations might hamper the imminent return of sovereignty, see *New York Times* (May 21, 1952).

26 See, for example, *World Today* (1950); Stephens (1950); Lehrman (1951); Nasmyth (1954). On the general problem of immigration into Israel in the formative period of the state, see Sicron (1957).

27 The importance of Horowitz in the events leading to the Luxembourg Reparations Agreement was indicated by a telegram he received from the signatories: 'Today we are signing the Reparations Agreement. We remember with appreciation the tremendous role that you played in initiating the claim and in the first surge of effort' (Horowitz's private files).

28 According to Ginor, the USA also had to be convinced of Germany's ability to pay before it became actively involved (interview, 1975).

29 Ginor's basic measurement of Germany's potential economic growth was the size of its foreign trade, particularly exports. She detailed her positive assessment of Germany's future trade patterns in a memorandum of May 8, 1951 to the Israeli Ministry of Finance, entitled 'Foreign trade of Western Germany' (Ginor's private files). By 1951 German exports already were exceeding imports (Wallich, 1955, pp. 102–3, 238–9). Horowitz suggested that he had the content of the memo from Ginor before his meeting with Adenauer in Paris on April 19, 1951 (interview, 1975). It is probable that the essence of the study was transmitted before submission of the final report on May 8, 1951.

30 See also Adenauer for an explanation of the position of the Ministry of Finance (1968, p. 140).
31 Schäffer obviously was pessimistic about the future development of the German economy. There were optimists, like Erhard, who believed in the German capacity for hard work and ingenuity and supported a major commitment to Israel (Erhard interview, 1975). Böhm was an optimist too, suggesting, for example, in his letter of April 23, 1952, that reparations would have a positive effect on the capacity to pay (text in Vogel, 1969, pp. 44–7). As he saw it, the capacity to pay was more a political than an economic question.
32 Abs specifically challenged Deutschkron, and in 1970 he wrote to her, detailing the mistakes he believed she had made (Abs's private files). He claims that Deutschkron never interviewed him (interview, 1975).
33 For Abs's justification, see the interview with Vogel (1969, p. 40). Several participants in the reparations negotiations have said that Abs was much less opposed to a settlement than Schäffer.
34 For details of the Arab reaction, see Abediseid (1976, pp. 68–76).
35 Support came from all SPD members and most Christian Democrats; some CSU and FDP members also voted for the treaty. Opposition was largely on the extreme left and the extreme right. The majority of abstentions were among CDU, CSU and Free Democratic members (Deutscher Bundestag und Bundesrat, March 18, 1953, pp. 12290–92). For a discussion of the ratification in the Bundesrat, see *Bulletin* (March 20, 1953); Grossmann (1954, p. 32); Deutschkron (1970a, p. 73); Balabkins (1971, ch. 7).

Part Two

OPERATION

Conditions pertained by the autumn of 1952 for the development of a special relationship between West Germany and Israel. Knowing that there could be such a relationship, however, tells us little about what such a relationship is or might be. The existence of a special relationship depends more on the basis of what nations do than on the basis of what they say. Words are important, yet they represent but one of many expressions of policy. As it is not enough that conditions be right, so it is not enough that leaders may use the term 'special relationship' or say that they have a special relationship with another country. What do they mean when they say a relationship is 'special', and how do we know if their claim is warranted or justified?

The measure of a special relationship is a measure of deviation from a norm of bilateral activities. Although national leaders may use different terms to pronounce on relations with different countries, pronouncements tell us little about deviation from the norm. Philosophically it is always possible to equate words with actions, but the gap between them in international affairs warns us that the acid-test of bilateral relations must be what countries do, not only what they say. Moreover, frequently we must take note of the way they do things.

The existence of a special relationship, then, is subject to proof and measurement, which depends almost wholly on what the partners do to and with each other in comparison to what they do with other countries. If we relied merely on pronouncements in the German-Israeli case, we would be very confused. For a long time references to the special past were code-words for a special relationship in the present, but more recent commitment to pronouncements of 'balance' and 'neutrality', the effort to appear 'even-handed' and noncommittal, masks government activities that show little alteration in a continuously special bilateral relationship. Indeed, one of the special features of the relationship seems to require this gap between words and action. But the action is the proof, and it is the action we can measure.

Unfortunately, the instruments for measurement often are crude. Because the relationship is special – and contains inherent provocation for jealousy among other nations – there is great secrecy. Statistical evidence of quantitative relations is scarce and often ambiguous.

Qualitative assessment depends heavily on confidential interviews where much remains unsaid. Policy measurement, as the systematic assessment of government behaviour in bilateral relations, is largely an untested area; there are no reliable precedents for this mode of analysis, and therefore it is difficult to identify a norm from which to measure deviation.

Despite these difficulties, it will be evident in the next four chapters that it is possible to identify specific actions that distinguish the bilateral relationship between West Germany and Israel from bilateral relationships between most other nations in the world. These actions can be assessed both quantitatively and qualitatively. In some instances relations will be unique as well as special, preventing comparison with relations of West Germany and Israel with other countries. When possible, however, there will be an effort to demonstrate that when West Germany or Israel could have undertaken a given activity with some other country, they either choose each other uniquely, or they choose each other more or more often, or they strike special arrangements with each other. Comparison is crucial here, for we must understand the relationship as special more than unique. Hence, the measure from the norm involves a display of preference – not merely difference. If, for example, West Germany pursues a given activity with several countries, we will discover Israel near or at the top among those countries with respect to the level and kind of activity; there will be a concrete display of preference. We must remember as well, however, that whereas both sides must benefit, the flow of activity can be unidirectional. In the case of West Germany and Israel activity is usually identified through West Germany as a donor and Israel as a recipient. The key is that West Germany generally will give more to Israel than to others, and Israel will receive generally more from West Germany than from anyone else.

The special relationship between West Germany and Israel began with a single major action, reparations. The special relationship has been sustained and perpetuated through other major actions, which have multiplied and permeated into a full range of bilateral activities. As the reparations were peculiar and special, so subsequent actions would be. Indeed, the special relationship became so pervasive that almost every ministry of the West German government, no matter what its normal activity, has come to have someone concerned in some way with relations with Israel.

This special relationship is subjected to constant international pressures. Arab countries in particular want very much to break the German-Israeli bond. Hence, West German policy towards other countries in the Middle East is by implication policy towards Israel. The German commitment to the special relationship finds ultimate proof in the determination to withstand Arab pressure.

4
Economic Relations

> The relationship between Germany and Israel, including financial relations, is of a special kind. (Carl-Christian Kaiser, *Die Zeit*, November 16, 1973)

The special relationship between West Germany and Israel began as an economic agreement on reparations, and economic arrangements have dominated relations ever since. Agreements in other policy areas, such as the sale of Israeli weapons to Germany and joint research on desalination, have important economic implications, but will be considered separately in later chapters. Here, we shall concentrate on economic relations in three spheres: (1) fulfilment of the Luxembourg Agreement, both in terms of the goods and services West Germany delivered to the State of Israel, and in terms of restitution and compensation payments to individual Israelis in accordance with German laws: (2) West German development aid to Israel; (3) trade and investment relations, including Germany's initiatives on behalf of economic agreements between Israel and the EEC.

A liberal-democratic state can pursue essentially three types of economic activity with other countries. It can (*a*) give away money through outright government grants; (*b*) provide government loans; or (*c*) encourage private sector activity, whether through reciprocal exchanges, private investment, promotion of trade through preferences and tariff reductions, or through government guarantees of investments abroad. Germany's relations with Israel have embraced all these possibilities.

FULFILMENT OF THE LUXEMBOURG AGREEMENT

According to the Luxembourg Agreement, West Germany agreed to pay Israel the sum of 3·45 billion marks in twelve instalments (State of Israel Ministry for Foreign Affairs, 1953, pp. 125–57). Israel then was to transfer 450 million marks to the Conference on Jewish Material Claims against Germany (Claims Conference), the umbrella organization of world Jewry for victims outside Israel, with whom the Federal Republic had also negotiated at Wassenaar. The 3 billion marks received by the

State of Israel to help absorb 500,000 refugees came in the form of goods and services, whose exact nature was decided by a Mixed Commission of German and Israeli representatives. A Purchasing Mission (the Israel Mission) was set up in Cologne by the Israeli government to administer the Agreement; the mission's German counterpart was the Federal Office for Industry and Allied Trades in Frankfurt.[1] The Agreement also stipulated that Germany would provide a portion of the 3 billion marks in pounds sterling to enable Israel to import oil from Britain.

Payments to individual Israelis, as opposed to the transfer of goods to the State of Israel, were made in accordance with the Federal Indemnification Law and the Federal Restitution Law. The Federal Indemnification Law of June 1956 developed out of promises made by the German government within the framework of the Contractual Agreements with the Allies in May 1952 and the protocols of the Luxembourg Agreement dealing with the Claims Conference in September 1952. The first indemnification legislation passed in the Federal Republic (voted October 1953), the Federal Supplementing Law for the Indemnification of Victims of National Socialist Persecution, broadened the compensation legislation that had been in operation in the US zone of occupation.[2] The Federal Indemnification Law improved the conditions of the 1953 indemnification legislation; in September 1965 the Final Amendment of the Indemnification Law again increased the number of persons eligible for compensation and augmented the amount of payments. The Federal Restitution Law of July 1957 was to compensate for the seizure of property by the National Socialists. It went through four amendments, the final one in September 1969.

In the period of the fulfilment of the Luxembourg Agreement (1953–65) the total payments to Israel did not represent a significant financial burden to the Federal Republic. In most years less than 2 per cent of the Federal budget went to Israel; only in 1960 did total payments to Israel reach 2·36 per cent of Federal outlays. Länder expenditure for compensation to individuals exceeded 0·5 per cent of overall Länder expenditure only twice during 1954–65 (0·78 per cent in 1960, 0·55 per cent in 1961).[3] However, even if Israel and Jews did not receive any apparent preference over West Germans in terms of budget priorities, they do appear to have been extended preference over other countries in the form and in the content of both reparations and compensation.

Germany had no legal obligation to pay reparations to Israel. Under international law Israel had no claim, for it did not exist as a state when war crimes for which it claimed compensation were committed. Thus, any payment would have to be regarded as unusual, and many have called these payments unique (for example, Böhm, *Allgemeine Wochenzeitung der Juden in Deutschland*, May 9, 1952; Sharett, *New York Times*, September 11, 1952; Bentwich, 1965, p. 224; Adenauer, 1968, p. 153: Goldmann, 1969, pp. 249, 251). The Israeli claim, moreover, was made against a state that did not exist when the crimes were committed. Treatment of the claim, and the priority it received over other national claims (from states that had existed), displayed a preference logically consistent with the general uniqueness of the reparations and the enormity of the crimes.

SPECIAL TREATMENT THROUGH PREFERENCE

> The obligation to make compensation to Israel, which the Federal government and Federal parliament have recognized, can be fulfilled only when we also have acknowledged the Israeli right to preferential treatment. (Adenauer, 1968, p. 145)

A demonstration of preference requires comparison. Treatment of Israel's claim can be compared to the treatment accorded claims from other creditors. The Federal Republic had many other creditors and at the London Debt Conference had sought to settle prewar debts to a variety of them and to settle postwar debts to Britain, France and the USA.

Germany, on the insistence of Abs and Schäffer, had stated at Wassenaar that commitments to Israel could be made only after Germany could ascertain the commitments to other creditors at the London Debt Conference (see Chapter 3). In the end, however, for reasons of both morality and political expediency, Germany preferred Israel in two ways with reference to the London Debt Conference creditors. First, the two conferences were separated and the Israeli case was decided on its merits. Israeli and German representatives reached basic agreement on the amount of reparations and the form and timing of payment two months before conferees in London produced recommendations for the settlement of claims. The Agreement with Israel was signed a full six months before agreement was reached with the creditors in London. Abs and Schäffer were completely overruled. Secondly, eighteen creditors in London were promised a total of 14·3 billion marks; Israel alone was to receive 3 billion marks. Germany agreed to pay almost three-quarters of Israel's original claim. By contrast, the claim of the prewar creditors had amounted to 13·5 billion marks, of which Germany agreed to little more than half; postwar creditors claimed 16 billion marks, of which Germany agreed to pay less than half (Auswärtiges Amt, 1972, pp. 234–8; Rumpf, 1973). Thus, Germany agreed to pay Israel irrespective of London, agreed to a far greater proportion of the claim and for a proportionately much greater sum.

A number of states wanted to claim reparations from Germany and perhaps were justified under international law, but art. 5 of the Debt Agreement stipulated that such claims would be postponed until a peace treaty with the whole of Germany (both the German Democratic and Federal republics) would allow a 'final settlement of the reparations question'. Reparations to Israel were allowed, in annex VIII to the London

Debt Agreement, as an exception to art. 5 because the Luxembourg Agreement was prior. Once extended preference in terms of timing, Israel was now privileged as the only country among the creditors at the London Debt Conference that also could claim reparations (Auswärtiges Amt, 1972, pp. 228–9; Rumpf, 1973, pp. 357–8, 363).

Various Arab states opposed ratification of the Luxembourg Agreement. Adenauer, however, preferred the commitment to Israel: 'It would be shameful, if we had wavered in our resolve just because of the threat of economic disadvantages. There is something loftier than good business' (1968, p. 153). In his speech during the ratification debate in the Bundestag Adenauer stressed that Israel should be treated in a special way: 'The Jews ... had to undergo the cruelest of persecutions. The extent of this persecution, the sacrifice of human and material values that it brought, not only justifies but demands a special treatment of the reparation to the Jewish [victims]' (quoted in Vogel, 1969, pp. 69–74). In the end Adenauer, and those who supported the Luxembourg Agreement, believed Israel should take precedence over all other creditors, over Arab threats and over export considerations.

The preference shown Israel over other creditors through negotiations and over the Arabs through ratification was sustained during the development of bilateral relations. By 1964, Israel was one of thirteen countries with whom global agreements on reparations and compensation had been concluded, and although the bases for these agreements were obviously different, countries that received compensation under similar provisions (exceptions to art. 5) can be compared to one another.* Such comparison highlights the preference shown Israel.

Israel received 3 billion marks to provide for 500,000 immigrants. Eleven other countries received a total of 876 million marks, and Austria, in a separate arrangement, received 102 million marks to augment its own restitution payments. It has been estimated that the payments to other countries were calculated on a per capita of approximately 4,000–5,000 marks, compared to 6,000 marks to Israel (Bundesministerium der Finanzen, 1979a, p. 9). Moreover, only between 175,000 and 219,000 recipients were allowed for all other countries, fewer than half the number allowed Israel.

Once the Federal Republic had concluded and ratified the Luxembourg Agreement, its obligations were defined formally. Nevertheless, Germany allowed modification and further interpretation of the Luxembourg Agreement favourable to Israel. For example, by 1955 Israel was able to

---

* The agreements with eleven European countries were to compensate victims of Nazi persecution in those countries excluded by the provisions of Federal compensation legislation. The payments were made to the states to be passed on to individuals. In the case of Austria, the twelfth country, the payment was to supplement the financial compensation it was making to Nazi victims. Agreements were exceptions to art. 5 because they repeated German domestic legislation on compensation for persecution for religion, race, or political views.

revise the commodity breakdown of the Agreement and was allowed to order greater amounts of capital goods than originally intended (Balabkins, 1971, p. 171). Annual instalments of goods were increased. Israel was allowed in 1955 to place advance orders worth 280 million marks, to be delivered in the period 1956–9, but with payment to be made only by 1962.

Another type of 'speed-up arrangement' was a 1958 loan of 450 million marks which the Deutsche Bank, on the encouragement of its president, Hermann Abs, made to Israel. As collateral the Deutsche Bank was promised payment from future instalments of the Agreement. Shinnar allegedly claimed that 'no other banker in the world would have given him this loan', considering Israel's insecure political and military situation at the time. Through a variety of 'speed-up' provisions, the State of Israel had received 95 per cent of the total sum due by 1962. Article 4 of the Agreement had noted that West Germany would try to pay the full amount in a shorter time, but there was no guarantee. The Federal Republic chose, in accordance with Israeli wishes, to make art. 4 a reality (Balabkins, 1971, pp. 178–81).

Two other countries, Poland and Russia, might have claimed, like Israel, a moral right to compensation to incorporate into society those who had suffered physically and mentally from the Third Reich and the Second World War. The non-Jewish civilian populations of Poland and Russia experienced great loss of life, forced labour and internment. Poland repeatedly had demanded such compensation,[4] and in August 1975 the Federal Republic agreed to compensate Poland $500 million to satisfy its claims and $400 million in trade credits at low interest in exchange for allowing some 120,000 ethnic Germans to migrate to the Federal Republic (*International Herald Tribune*, August 4, 1975). In real money terms (1975 vs 1952) the Polish compensation was much smaller than the compensation to Israel. Moreover, Germany refused to call these payments to Poland 'reparations', although the Agreement has been seen by German financial and foreign policy officials as an example of Germany's 'special relationship' with Poland, in which Germany had felt a moral commitment to make payments because of the past (confidential interviews, 1975).

Germany never acknowledged owing compensation to the USSR, believing the latter had taken on its own initiative sufficient compensation. One could argue that it was inconceivable that Germany could have concluded an agreement with Poland in the 1950s because of the nature of the East–West split. One, then, would argue that Israel cannot be compared to Poland, that the Agreement with Israel in 1952 was an isolated phenomenon. Such an argument is deceptive, for it forgets that in 1951 very few people imagined negotiations with Israel. Both Israel and Poland were unlikely negotiation partners, yet only with Israel did Germany reach early agreement.

The Federal Republic might also be compared with the German

Democratic Republic. The USSR extracted its own reparations from its zone of occupation, but otherwise the other part of the former German Reich has never made compensation in any way comparable to the responsibilities assumed by the Federal Republic. The Federal Republic, compared to the German Democratic Republic, has shown preference to all its creditors, and especially to Israel. The question of the responsibility of the German Democratic Republic for a third of Israel's claim in its Note of March 1951 was raised at the time of the discussions between Western countries, particularly the USA, and East Germany over diplomatic relations. To date the efforts of Nahum Goldmann, as president of the Claims Conference, to negotiate the matter of compensation with East German authorities have shown few results.

INDIRECT AID TO ISRAEL: PAYMENTS TO ISRAELIS
By the end of 1978 Israelis had received some 40 per cent of the total payments made in accordance with both the Federal Indemnification and Federal Restitution Laws and other compensation arrangements, approximately 22 billion marks (Bundesministerium der Finanzen, 1979b, pp. 1–2).[5] The consular section of the German Embassy in Tel Aviv has been staffed specially by some fifteen people – a large number for any single task in a consulate – to accept and expedite Israeli applications more readily than applications from other countries.

The Federal Indemnification Law applied basically to four categories of victims of Nazi persecution: (1) persons who were residing in the Federal Republic or West Berlin on December 31, 1952; (2) persons who, prior to that date, had emigrated or had been deported from the territory of the German Reich (1937 borders); (3) persons who, on October 1, 1953, were stateless or refugees according to the Geneva Convention definition (para. 160); and (4) persons from German-speaking areas and areas of German culture outside the Federal Republic who left these places before October 1, 1953 (para. 150). The territorial and time constraints contained in paras 150 and 160 of the law meant that those Jews who had not left or been forced out of Eastern Europe by 1953 were not eligible for compensation. By the time emigration did occur for some of these people from Eastern Europe (in the mid-1950s from Poland, Hungary and Rumania) the deadline for leaving (October 1953) already had passed. West Germany remedied this exclusion. The Final Amendment to the Indemnification Law of September 14, 1965 applied specifically to those people who left Eastern Europe after 1953: the Federal government set up a 'special fund' of 1·2 billion marks to compensate victims who had no rights under paras 150 and 160, and who had left the areas designated by December 31, 1965. These 'post-1953' cases represent a significant example of German willingness to reach beyond legal obligation in order to show preference for Israel (for many would emigrate there), even indirectly. Of the subsequent 170,000 claims, 120,000 were accepted and 81 per cent of the recipients are residents of Israel (Federal Ministry of Finance correspondence, 1980; State of Israel

Ministry of Finance correspondence, 1980). The creation of the 'special fund', therefore, had clear foreign currency benefits for Israel.

The 'special fund' in remedying an exclusion, of course, created another, for as there were immigrants after 1953 so there would be after 1965. For several years German officials and Nahum Goldmann (as president of the Claims Conference) had discussed the possibility of a final payment of 600 million marks by the Federal Republic to compensate the 'post-1965' cases (*Deutschland-Berichte*, October 1973, December 1974, February 1975, January 1976, January 1978, February and June 1980). Many of the prospective recipients live now in Israel.[6] Israeli representatives were included in discussions, underlining the potential significance for Israel of a new settlement.

After protracted and intermittent negotiations, all parliamentary parties (CDU/CSU, FDP and SPD) approved a resolution on December 14, 1979, calling for a total sum of 440 million marks to be paid over three years, beginning in 1980, through the Central Council of Jews in Germany for German residents and through the Claims Conference for residents abroad (Deutscher Bundestag und Bundesrat, *Drucksache* 8/3511, 1979). In October 1980 the matter was decided finally and favourably, for 400 million marks, by the Federal government. Jews who have encountered serious health problems as a result of Nazi acts of violence and who have not met the requirements of the Federal Indemnification Law or its final amendment (for reasons of non-compliance with time and location prerequisites) are eligible for lump-sum payments of up to 5,000 marks (Bundesministerium der Justiz, 1980).

Foreign opposition to the idea of a final payment included specific objection to demonstrations of preference for Israel. Poland, before settlement of its claim, and Arab countries, felt that such a payment would harm them, in Poland's case because of its own claim against Germany, and in the Arab case because of the economic advantage they believed Israel would derive.[7]

Domestic opponents of payment to Jews in Israel cited an overburdened federal purse. They also feared public objection. Despite opposition, the German government and the German people continue to view compensation (which benefits Israelis more than any other national group) as a moral obligation. However, both the government of Israel and the Claims Conference, as part of the agreement, were required to give written assurances that this 'special fund' would be their final demand (Weismann interview, 1980). Payments to individuals under existing legislation, of course, will continue.

GETTING SPECIAL TREATMENT: THE ISRAELI PERSPECTIVE

> There can be no doubt that the past nine years [1953–62] have seen a revolution in the Israel economy, brought about in large part by reparation goods. (Bank Leumi Le-Israel, May 1962, p. 9)

The main sources of aid for the economic survival of Israel have been the government of the Federal Republic, the government of the USA and

Table 4.1 Unilateral Transfers to Israel from the Federal Republic Compared to Payments from Other Major Contributors, 1953–65

	(1) Reparations from Germany	(2) Individual compensation from Germany*	(3) Reparations plus individual compensation (1 + 2)	(4) US grants-in-aid	(5) World Jewry	(6) Total payments (3 + 4 + 5)	(7) Payments from Germany as percentage of total (3:6)	(8) Payments from USA as percentage of total (4:6)	(9) Payments from world Jewry as percentage of total (5:6)
	(Million $)	(Million $)	(Million $)	(Million $)	(Million $)	(Million $)			
1953	40·7	—	40·7	47·3	84·6	172·6	23·6	27·4	49·0
1954	79·4	8·0	87·4	39·0	133·2	259·6	33·7	15·0	51·3
1955	84·5	18·8	103·3	20·5	83·2	207·0	49·9	9·9	40·2
1956	79·2	25·7	104·9	6·8	128·4	240·1	43·7	2·8	53·5
1957	77·0	45·9	122·9	24·1	98·0	245·0	50·2	9·8	40·0
1958	68·8	66·3	135·1	16·4	111·8	263·3	51·3	6·2	42·5
1959	66·3	70·8	137·1	9·5	104·1	250·7	54·7	3·8	41·5
1960	72·9	100·5	173·4	13·9	123·5	310·8	55·8	4·5	39·7
1961	87·3	111·3	198·6	10·4	137·0	346·0	57·4	3·0	39·6
1962	43·0	137·5	180·5	8·0	141·8	330·3	54·6	2·4	42·9
1963	24·6	141·6	166·2	5·9	173·2	345·3	48·1	1·7	50·2
1964	16·9	132·6	149·5	8·2	191·8	349·5	42·8	2·3	55·0
1965	16·7	111·4	128·1	4·7	206·3	339·1	37·8	1·4	60·8
Total 1953–65	757·3	970·4	1,727·7	214·7	1,716·9	3,659·3	47·2	5·9	46·9

*Amounts received by Israeli citizens but not transferred are excluded.
Sources: State of Israel Central Bureau of Statistics, 1971; Halevi and Klinov-Malul, 1968, p. 298.

world Jewry.* Total payments in the form of unilateral transfers in the period 1953–65 (the duration of the Luxembourg Agreement) were greatest from West Germany, $1·72 billion or 47·2 per cent of the total of $3·6 billion (Table 4.1). World Jewry was close behind with $1·71 billion, while the US government supplied $214·7 million, only 5·9 per cent of the total. Only in 1953 did the USA – Israel's second source of government financial aid – provide Israel more money than did Germany. The Federal Republic in the period 1953–65 contributed approximately eight times more money in total payments than did the government of the USA. Since 1965 the USA has been the only government to provide unilateral transfers to the State of Israel, including $6·4 billion during 1972–9 (Israeli Embassy, Washington, correspondence, 1980). Personal transfers to individuals from the German government have continued and in the period 1970–8, 41–58 per cent of all personal unilateral transfers to Israel have come from West Germany (Bank of Israel, 1973, p. 106, 1975, p. 104, 1978, p. 114). During 1972–8 unilateral transfers from Germany amounted to 17·1 per cent of all unilateral transfers to Israel, while transfers from the USA stood at 41·2 per cent of the total for the same period (ibid.).

Several prominent analysts of German-Israeli economic relations, including Shinnar (1967, pp. 85–90), Ebeling (1966), Schürholz (1968) and Balabkins (1971, chs 11 and 12), have underlined the importance of the Luxembourg Agreement and individual compensation for the Israeli economy. The most thorough analysis was made in a report for the Bank of Israel in 1965 by Fanny Ginor and J. Tishler (1965).[8] In an article in 1972 reviewing the 1965 Hebrew report Ginor claims the following specific benefits for the Israeli economy:

(1) The capital imports from Germany, both reparations and compensation payments, amounted to more than one-quarter of Israel's capital imports during a nineteen-year period and accounted for 16 per cent of the additional capital invested in the economy.
(2) Of all the goods and services, 38 per cent was in the form of investment goods, 24 per cent raw materials, industrial and agricultural products, 8 per cent transportation goods and bank charges, and 30 per cent oil from Britain. However, approximately 80 per cent of the total amount eventually went into investments.

---

* Compensation payments from Germany, unlike donations from world Jewry, Luxembourg Agreement goods and US grants-in-aid, have been made to individual Israelis and not the State of Israel. However, these payments are included here in the comparison because of their significance for the state's foreign currency reserves and because they lighten the state's welfare burden. World Jewry, although not a government, is included because of its scope and because contributions have been made to the State of Israel. One should note, too, that from the Israeli perspective restitution payments are unlike other contributions; Germany was transferring merely what it had expropriated, not what it owned

98 *Operation*

(3) Germany virtually built Israel's commercial fleet, which was important because of the lack of land access to other countries.
(4) Industrial equipment which came from the Agreement amounted to 14 per cent of the total Israeli investment in industrial equipment.
(5) In the period 1954–64 Germany supplied around one-quarter of the total investment in power installations, a prerequisite for industrialization.
(6) In the agricultural sphere reparations paid for one-fifth of the imported equipment for the Mekorot Water Co. in the period 1954–61, which helped Israel's irrigation programme.
(7) During the period 1954–9 Germany supplied one-half of all railway investment.
(8) During 1954–9 one-quarter of the capital investment in the port of Haifa derived from reparations.
(9) Twelve per cent of the total assets of the telephone network in 1962 came from reparations.

Ginor claims that if reparations had not been pumped into Israel, general economic growth would have been markedly slower. She calculates that 'the share of the reparations in Israel's economic growth [was] 6% of the additional product during the thirteen-year period, representing about 4% of the total gross national product in 1966'. Calculating what the GNP would have been without reparations Ginor contends that 'In the absence of the reparations, all other things remaining equal, the total GNP in 1966 would have been some 12% less than it was'. For the whole period, 'the impact of the reparations receipts may be estimated at about 17% of the additional GNP' (1972–3, p. 40). Although other sources of foreign capital may have been available, they would have involved large debt and interest payments later on.

Payments to individuals in Israel had amounted to 22 billion marks by the end of 1978; the Federal Ministry of Finance estimates that Israel will receive another 10·47 billion marks by the year 2000, or approximately 40 per cent of the total estimated future compensation payments of 26·15 billion marks (Bundesministerium der Finanzen, 1979b, pp. 1–2, 1979c, p. 1). These payments, too, have had a number of distinct advantages for the Israeli economy, especially in the contribution to foreign currency reserves. In the past when compensation recipients were advantaged by Israel's foreign currency rules (Schürholz, 1968, p. 20), 90 per cent of all foreign currency accounts were estimated to be based on restitution payments (Ginor, 1972–3, p. 44); at the end of 1979 following the removal in October 1977 of certain foreign currency restrictions for all Israelis, restitution deposits amounted to approximately 50 per cent of all foreign currency deposits (State of Israel Ministry of Finance correspondence, 1980; Bank of Israel correspondence, 1980).

Compensation payments to individuals have relieved the state of embracing financial responsibility for immigrants, especially those unable to work because of Nazi persecution. Some recipients in Israel have even enjoyed a measure of affluence by investing successfully in real estate. About half of the lump-sum payments have gone into real estate, accounting for about 20 per cent of all real estate investments in Israel. This investment of foreign capital has increased demand and inflation, but it has contributed also to the alleviation of Israel's housing shortage. Restitution payments may have exacerbated social differentiation, both among recipients and between recipients and non-recipients, but most observers consider the net effect of such individual payments as positive for the whole Israeli economy.

Both reparations and compensation were, then, decisive for the Israeli economy, particularly in the early years of extreme foreign currency shortage and an economy overburdened with massive immigration. Ginor appears to echo the view of both German and Israeli observers in her positive conclusion:

> Reparations and restitution payments had a considerable impact on the size and composition of investments and savings, and therefore on the country's economic growth and employment ... Together both sources paid for 12% of total imports during 1953–71, and for 27% of the excess of imports over exports. Their greatest importance lay in the fact that over a prolonged period they constituted a sizeable part of the foreign currency receipts without creating foreign exchange debts or the obligation to pay interest. (Ginor, 1972–3, p. 45)

MOTIVES AND CRITICS

The faithful execution of the Luxembourg Agreement was a perennial way for Germany to show its new face to both Israel and the world, and it helped win international approval (Shinnar, 1967, p. 90; Schürholz, 1968, p. 3; Balabkins, 1971, pp. 205–11; Scheck interview, 1975). The New Left in Germany and Arab critics of German-Israeli relations, however, suggest a darker motive: that in the execution of the Luxembourg Agreement West Germany acted on the direction of the USA, which saw Israel as an important Middle East outpost in its global imperialist strategy (Coburger, 1964; Asad, 1966; Abdel Hadi, et al., 1973; Lewan, 1975). A necessary corollary of this argument is that the Federal Republic merely passed on to Israel in the form of payments in kind (goods) the payments it had received from the USA. The USA did donate sums to the Federal Republic through the Marshall Plan, but there is no evidence of an American stipulation that such money should be transferred into payments in kind to Israel. Marshall Plan money surely fostered a healthy German economy which could sustain payments to Israel, but there are indications that the USA hesitated to encourage Germany to negotiate with Israel until it was convinced that the German economy, on its own, could support such a burden. Horowitz commissioned Ginor's report following concerns expressed to him during his visit to the USA in April 1951 about Germany's ability to pay (interview, 1975), and Ginor says the report was written in English primarily to convince Americans before negotiations with Germany could proceed (interview, 1975). Josephtal says the USA was constantly concerned about the burden on Germany for fear that if Germany could not pay, then the USA as a power of occupation would end up footing the bill, something the US government was apparently not prepared to do (Halpern and Wurm, 1966, p. 154).

The New Left also suggests an economic advantage for the Federal Republic in the execution of the Agreement. Nicholas Balabkins agrees that reparations to Israel stimulated the West German economy, and he suggests that the Federal Republic deliberately wrote art. 6, relating to specific commodities and amounts Israel was obliged to order annually, on behalf of the domestic economy. But Balabkins does not see economic stimulation at home leading to what the left called neo-colonialism (1971, ch. 9.).

Germany's economy may have benefited, then, from fulfilment of the Agreement, but non-economic moral behaviour continued to be prominent. The 'speed-up' procedures Germany adopted are one example, and Adenauer's decision, at the time of the Suez crisis in 1956, to continue delivering goods despite international pressure for a cessation of supplies is another. These motives, along with the more apparently pragmatic, helped the Luxembourg Agreement grow into other special economic relations. In light of the unique moral basis of the Agreement, and the preference shown in its conclusion, ratification and execution, Germans and Israelis, from politicians to bureaucrats to ambassadors, have considered the Luxembourg Agreement a chief example of the special relationship and a central cause for the relationship's development.

DEVELOPMENT AID

In the 1950s the Federal Republic took unco-ordinated 'tentative measures', such as technical training, export credits and multilateral finance, in a small programme of development aid to several countries. There were also private initiatives. Not until 1960, however, did the government decide to initiate a comprehensive aid programme. In 1961 the Federal Ministry for Economic Co-operation was created, and a special entry for development aid appeared in the Federal Budget (Bundesministerium für wirtschaftliche Zusammenarbeit, 1975a, 1977, 1978a, 1979a, 1979b, 1979c; White, 1965; Holbik and Myers, 1968; Knusel, 1968; Hesse, 1969; Sohn, 1972; Schwarz, 1975).

Stripped of empire Germany appeared free of obligation, 'without the burden of outstanding commitments', as one analyst described the situation in 1960 when aid policy was formulated (White, 1965, p. 10). Israel was one of the first recipients of German development aid with the conclusion of an agreement in March 1960 and from the start aid to Israel would prove outside the norm of general aid policy.

Development aid to Israel falls into two discrete yet related time periods; 1960–5 on the basis of a controversial 'agreement' between Adenauer and Ben-Gurion, and after 1965 on the basis of a formal economic agreement. Since the beginning Germans and Israelis have regarded the aid programme as a preferential policy expression of the special relationship between the two countries.

THE 'AGREEMENT'

Despite Jekutiel Deligdisch's assertion that the agreement made with Israel in 1960 was viewed by Germany not as development credit, but rather as a commercial loan (1974, p. 65), the terms and purpose of the loan and the involvement of the Federal Ministry for Economic Cooperation require an appreciation of the agreement in the context of an emerging German policy for development aid.[9] In March 1960 Adenauer and Ben-Gurion met at the Waldorf Astoria Hotel in New York to discuss, among other things, economic aid for the further development of Israel, particularly of the Negev desert which comprised over 60 per cent of the country's territory. Ben-Gurion proposed a Federal Republic loan of $500 million (2 billion marks) over a ten-year period, and left the meeting believing that Adenauer had agreed to the proposal (Ben-Gurion, 1971, p. 538; *New York Times*, February 13, 1965). Adenauer later claimed, 'I could not reply to this question with a firm answer' (1970, p. 38), although he said he would do all in his power to help Israel. This meeting and interpretive disagreement were the genesis of development aid to Israel.[10]

There was no written agreement and the two sides disagreed over what had transpired. One Israeli official involved in arranging the meeting itself and later in negotiating the loan, explained the absence of a written agreement as the 'colour-blindness' of the two statesmen with respect to figures, neither being economists, as Ben-Gurion has noted (1971, p. 539). Ben-Gurion claims he did not insist on a written agreement because he trusted Adenauer. Whatever the reason, the absence of a written agreement led to difficulty, for although Adenauer and Erhard were committed to helping Israel (Shinnar, 1967, p. 103), others in German officialdom – as in 1952 and 1953 – did not necessarily share their desires. Only after a long exchange of letters of clarification among Abs, Adenauer, Shinnar and Ben-Gurion did the first payment emerge in December 1961. After the fourth biannual instalment, the loan was extended two years and the annual sums were reduced (Shinnar, 1967, pp. 101–3). By June 1965 Israel had received 560 million marks.

As far as is known, the Federal Republic extended such aid to no other country with whom it had no diplomatic relations. Nor did leaders from

Table 4.2 *German Development Aid to Israel as a Percentage of Total, Bilateral and Capital Aid, 1961–5 (Gross Figures)*

Million DM	1961	1962	1963	1964	1965	Total 1961–5
Multilateral aid	1,143	409	101	96	156	1,905
Bilateral aid*	1,282	1,316	1,553	1,796	2,094	8,041
Total aid†	2,425	1,725	1,654	1,892	2,250	9,946
Capital aid	1,173	1,159	1,265	1,448	1,691	6,736
Aid to Israel‡	75	150 (75 + 75)	140 (75 + 65)	130 (65 + 65)	130 (65 + 65)	625 (560 until June 1965)
Aid to Israel as percentage of total	3·1	8·7	8·5	6·9	5·8	6·3
Aid to Israel as percentage of bilateral	5·9	11·4	9·0	7·2	6·2	7·8
Aid to Israel as percentage of capital	6·4	12·9	11·1	9·0	7·7	9·3

*Technical and capital aid.
†Excludes reparations to Israel and Greece.
‡The total aid figure to Israel until June 1965 is from Shinnar, 1967, p. 106.
 The annual breakdown of aid to Israel, which does not appear in any official publication, has been estimated: according to Deutschkron, 1970b, p. 137, and Vogel, 1969, p. 121, the German Minister for Economics (Erhard) and the Israeli Minister of Finance (Eshkol) agreed that the annual sum should not exceed 150 million marks. Payments were negotiated every six months, Ben-Natan, 1974, p. 32. After four instalments, the time period and amount were changed, Shinnar, 1967, pp. 101–3. It is assumed here that until December 1963 Israel received the maximum amount of 75 million marks for each of the four instalments (December 1961; June and December 1962; June 1963).
 After June 1963, the biannual payment is calculated at 65 million marks (for December 1963; June and December 1964: June 1965) on the following basis: in 1979 the Federal Ministry for Economic Co-operation, 1979c, p. 60, cited a figure of 1,935 million marks for aid to Israel up until the end of 1978. From published figures we know that Israel received 160 million marks in each of the years 1966 and 1967 and in 1968–78 received 140 million marks per annum, giving a grand total of 1,860 million marks for the period 1966–78, and leaving unaccounted 65 million marks (1,935 minus 1,860 million marks). It is clear that the Federal government considered as part of the regular and public development aid package to Israel any payments made after the establishment of diplomatic relations in August 1965, Shinnar, 1967, p. 104; German Embassy, Israel, interview, 1975. One such payment was made before the conclusion of the 1966 economic aid agreement, namely, the second instalment of aid for 1965 delivered in December. The 'additional' 65 million marks was the December 1965 payment.
 According to Shinnar, Adenauer agreed to 160–200 million marks per annum for ten years, a total of 1·6–2 billion marks. By December 1963 when the terms changed, Israel had received 300 million marks (four payments at 75 million marks). Using the lower figure (1·6 billion marks) 1·3 billion marks remained to be paid. The total number of years changed from ten to twelve, leaving ten years in which payments would be made. In each biannual instalment beginning in December 1963, therefore, Israel would receive 65 million marks.
Source: Statistisches Bundesamt, 1965, 1968.

other countries receive large sums with no more than a confusing verbal understanding. Such was the special character of aid to Israel.

Nothing legal bound the parties to the agreement. The details of the meeting in New York were wrapped in secrecy, as was the agreement itself, in order to escape Arab knowledge.[11] Consequently the agreement could not be put before the Bundestag for a legal *imprimatur*. Secrecy also hid the sums involved from the annual reports of the Credit Bank for Reconstruction, which was involved in executing the loan, and from the budget of the Ministry for Economic Co-operation. The 'special act', as the agreement has been called in the Ministry for Economic Co-operation, was so remarkable that analysts of German development aid tend to ignore completely aid to Israel in this period despite, as one analyst describes, German pride in the new general policy departure of the early 1960s (White, 1965, p. 25).

Despite the special way in which Israel came to receive development aid, it is possible to compare the size of arrangements with agreements for aid that the Federal Republic concluded with other countries in the period 1961–5. Israel, as only one of some sixty-five recipients, took in 6·3 per cent of Germany's total aid bill. Israel received more than 6 per cent of Germany's bilateral aid each year (except for 1961 when its portion stood at 5·9 per cent), and for the five-year period Germany gave 7·8 per cent of all bilateral aid to Israel (Table 4.2).

Israel received only capital, not technical, aid. In the period 1961–5

Table 4.3 *Development Aid to Israel Compared to Government Development Aid to Principal Recipients, 1960–3*

Recipient	Amount 1960–3 (Million DM)	Rank
India	1426·6	1
Turkey	472·0	2
Israel*	365·0	3
Liberia	307·7	4
Pakistan	266·2	5
Brazil	153·1	6
Chile	148·2	7
Argentina	84·1	8
Spain	60·1	9
Iran	15·4	10
Peru	2·0	11

*White does not include Israel in principal recipients; author's calculation is from Table 4.2.

Note: If private aid figures are added, the ranking changes. There are no published figures for private aid to Israel.

Source: White, 1965, p. 78.

Israel received 9·3 per cent of the total German capital aid to all countries (Table 4.2). In 1960–3 there were eleven principal recipients of German development aid and Israel ranked third after India and Turkey (Table 4.3).

Terms were favourable to Israel. For industrial projects it was charged 5 per cent, less than the usual interest rate of 5·5 per cent, and for infrastructure projects only 3 per cent was charged. The repayment time for industrial projects, twelve years, was normal, but for infrastructure projects Israel was granted twenty years, the best repayment time Germany offered anyone. Israel's average interest rate for all aid was 3·6 per cent and repayment time averaged 17·6 years; the general average for other countries showed an interest rate of 4·3 per cent in 1963 and a repayment schedule of nineteen years (White, 1965, p. 117; Shinnar, 1967, p. 102; Deutschkron, 1970a, pp. 128–9).

THE 1966 ECONOMIC AGREEMENT
The May 1966 formal, written agreement between the Federal Republic and Israel replaced the 1960 'agreement' for both development and military aid (Ben-Natan, 1974, pp. 50–2; *Le Monde,* April 28 and May 2, 1966; *Neue Zürcher Zeitung,* May 1, 1966). Informal and secret agreements precipitated a crisis in German-Israeli relations in the spring of 1965, and formality followed the establishment of diplomatic relations.

Differing explanations for the informal accord in 1960 led to disagreement in 1966. The Germans emphasized the absence of a firm agreement; the Israelis said Adenauer had made promises manifested in German aid since 1961 and, moreover, the promises were not yet fully realized. Some German officials insisted that Germany had paid its debts already in the form of reparations. Negotiations were difficult and threatened to rupture, but finally an agreement was signed in Bonn to 'promote... economic relations by means of continuous cooperation' (text in Vogel, 1969, pp. 176–8).[12] Germany committed 160 million marks in development aid for specific projects for the year 1966.

For the first time in German-Israeli relations, emphasis now turned to 'normality'. The press communiqué declared: 'The agreement concluded today can be regarded as an essential element of German policy in the sphere of economic cooperation, through which the Federal Republic of Germany supports other countries in the build-up of their economies' (quoted in Vogel, 1969, p. 178). *Le Monde* (May 14, 1966) interpreted this statement as a final indication that Israel received neither favour nor preference in the negotiations over the agreement, and that Israel was now being treated as any other country to whom Germany gave development aid.

Now that diplomatic relations were established and the economic agreement was formal and public, was Israel no longer a special German partner? Certainly, the form of relations was now normal. Before diplomatic relations, agreements with Israel were often secret; the public could not know of preference. After the establishment of diplomatic relations, secrecy gave way to a relationship officially and publicly non-committal or non-preferential. Yet just as secrecy masked favour, public non-commitment cloaked preference. The gap between public pronouncement and government behaviour reveals continuity in the special relationship.

Despite the public pronouncements and press reactions of May 1966, this second period of development aid from 1966 until the present has become a frequently cited example of a special relationship. Germany's criteria for 'developing' countries are consistent with criteria of the Organization for Economic Co-operation and Development (OECD), largely based on the GNP per capita of the country (Bundesministerium für wirtschaftliche Zusammenarbeit, 1978a, pp. 21–2). Although Israel qualifies under these criteria, it is at a higher development level requiring corresponding help; the disproportionate aid Germany extends is not normal in the context of other German development aid.

Normally recipients of development aid submit applications that they review together with the Ministry for Economic Co-operation to determine what projects will be supported and how. For Israel, there has existed a 'simplified and abbreviated procedure' (Federal Ministry for Economic Co-operation interview, 1975), generally free of negotiation. Until 1976 only 20 million of the annual 140 million marks were tied to specific projects (*Die Zeit*, November 16, 1973; Israeli Embassy, Bonn, interview, 1975). Since 1976, 40 million marks have been earmarked for specific projects in advance with Israel enjoying flexibility over 100 million marks (120 million marks until 1976) (Federal Ministry for Economic Co-operation interview, 1979). Israel has submitted applications for basically the same projects every year (mainly for construction) and annual signature seems guaranteed. In other words, Israel alone, unlike other countries, essentially has decided which projects should be funded.

Israel's share of total German government aid, and especially of bilateral aid, can be seen in Table 4.4. During 1966–79 Israel received 1·7–6·7 per cent of total aid, 2·8 per cent over the fourteen-year period. Israel received 2·3–7·2 per cent of all German bilateral aid during this period, all in capital aid, 3·7–9·0 per cent of the total after the 1966 agreement. Of some 100 countries with whom the Federal Republic had agreements for development aid from 1950 until 1977, Israel still ranked in the top four in total amount and was first by per capita contributions (Table 4.5).

The conditions of the loans granted to Israel have continued to be better than the norm. For the first two years Israel received 160 million marks per annum at a maximum interest rate of 3 per cent, to be paid over twenty-five years with a seven-year period of grace (Vogel, 1969, p. 179). In 1965 the average interest rate for all German aid to all

Table 4.4 German Development Aid to Israel as a Percentage of Total, Bilateral and Capital Aid, 1966–79 (Gross Figures)

Million DM	1966	1967	1968	1969	1970	1971	1972	1973	1974	1975	1976	1977	1978	1979
Multilateral aid	145	266	440	236	688	783	772	843	1,091	1,359	1,450	1,594	1,589	2,183
Bilateral aid*	2,234	2,447	2,578	2,559	2,814	3,368	3,274	4,188	4,107	4,529	4,535	4,156	5,143	6,155
Total aid†	2,379	2,713	3,018	2,795	3,502	4,151	4,046	5,031	5,198	5,888	5,985	5,750	6,732	8,338
Capital aid	1,783	1,907	1,944	1,746	1,911	2,395	2,294	3,108	2,896	3,160	3,247	2,778	3,567	3,765
Aid to Israel	160	160	140	140	140	140	140	140	140	140	140	140	140	140
Aid to Israel as percentage of total	6·7	5·9	4·6	5·1	4·0	3·4	3·5	2·8	2·7	2·4	2·3	2·4	2·1	1·7
Aid to Israel as percentage of bilateral	7·2	6·5	5·4	5·5	5·0	4·2	4·3	3·3	3·4	3·1	3·1	3·4	2·7	2·3
Aid to Israel as percentage of capital	9·0	8·4	7·2	8·0	7·3	5·8	6·1	4·5	4·8	4·4	4·3	5·0	3·9	3·7

*Technical and capital aid.
†Includes payments from Credit Bank for Reconstruction.
Sources: Statistisches Bundesamt, 1968, 1974a, 1980; German Embassy, Israel, interview, 1975.

Table 4.5 Development Aid to Israel Compared to Government Aid to Principal Recipients, 1950–78

	Amount, 1950–77 (million DM)*	Rank	Population in 1977 (millions)	Amount per capita (DM)	Rank†	Category of development‡	Amount (million DM)§		Rank		Population (million)		Amount per capita (DM)		Rank†	
							1976	1978	1976	1978	1976	1978	1976	1978	1976	1978
India	4,033·4	1	631·7	6·4	7	LDC/MSAC	424·2	372·0	1	1	613·3	638·4	0·7	0·6	7	7
Pakistan	1,926·2	2	74·9	25·7	5	LDC/MSAC	209·2	181·6	3	3	72·4	76·8	2·9	2·4	5	5
Israel	1,674·3	3	3·6	465·1	1	TO	149·5	161·0	4	4	3·5	3·7	42·7	43·5	1	1
Turkey	1,465·3	4	41·9	35·0	3	TO		315·2		2		43·2		7·3		3
Indonesia	1,331·7	5	133·5	10·0	6	OPEC	114·2		6		138·5		0·8		6	
Yugoslavia	1,298·1	6	21·7	59·8	2	TO	145·0		5		21·6		6·7		3	
Egypt	1,168·9	7	37·8	30·9	4	LDC/MSAC	309·9	153·3	2	5	37·8	39·6	8·2	3·9	2	4
Algeria¶						OPEC	96·7		7		17·3		5·6		4	
Bangladesh¶						LLDC/MSAC		116·4		6		84·7		1·4		6
Tunisia¶						TO		114·2		7		6·1		18·7		2

*Net figures.
†Ranking relates to other countries who are main recipients of total aid amounts. Real per capita ranking regardless of total amount may be different in some cases; Israel still would be in first place.
‡Since 1976 Germany's five categories for development are: take-off (TO), Organization of Petroleum Exporting Countries (OPEC), less developed (LDC), least developed (LLDC) and most seriously affected (by the increases in oil prices after 1973) (MSAC).
§1976 and 1978 figures are gross and include special extra payments.
¶These countries appeared among the top seven in 1976 or 1978 but not in 1950–77.
Sources: Bundesministerium für wirtschaftliche Zusammenarbeit, 1977, pp. 133–6, 1978a, pp. 21–4, 1978b, p. 9, 1979a, pp. 94–6, 125–7, 1979c, p. 45; UN, 1979.

countries was 3·7 per cent, repayment was expected within 20·3 years and grace periods averaged 5·3 years (Schwarz, 1975, p. 736). Terms improved during the next half-decade for all countries, but in the period 1968–77 Israel received 140 million marks per year on better terms than before and on terms still better than the norm for recipients of German aid: 2 per cent interest rate, a thirty-year repayment period and a grace period of ten years (German Embassy, Israel, interview, 1975). (In 1970 the average interest rate for German aid was 2·9 per cent, the repayment period was 28·2 years and the grace period was 8·5 years.) Only in the 1970s did Israel's terms become more 'normal', and normalization meant that other countries began receiving the favourable arrangements Israel had enjoyed already since 1968.

Germany began to distinguish by degrees of development in January 1976. Thereafter, the more developed or 'take-off' countries received aid on less favourable conditions than the least developed.[13] The more developed countries paid 4·5 per cent interest with a twenty-year repayment and a five-year grace period. In sharp contrast the least developed countries had the option of receiving planned credits as grants (since 1978), and the most seriously affected paid only a 0·75 per cent interest rate with fifty years to repay and ten years' grace. The standard

Table 4.6 *Repayment Terms of Different Loans to Israel, March 31, 1977*

IBRD	8.5% interest, 2 years' grace, 13 years to repay
EXIMBANK	8.5% interest, 3–5 years repayment periods (for special projects, 5 years' grace followed by 30 equal and consecutive, semi-annual payments)
Food surpluses	2 years' grace at 2% interest, 19 years for repayment of principal at 3% interest
AID housing	8.8% interest, 7 years' grace, 45 equal and consecutive, semi-annual payments
Loan from West Germany	4.5% interest, 5 years' grace, 21 equal and consecutive, semi-annual payments
Commercial loans	8% interest, 1 year's grace, followed by 12 equal and consecutive, semi-annual payments
Supportive aid	10 years' grace at 2% interest followed by 61 equal and consecutive semi-annual payments at 3% interest
IMF	Special drawing rights at 4% interest for the first year plus an annual increment of 0.5% for every additional to a maximum of 6%; the credit is payable as from the end of the third year and it must be fully repaid no later than by the end of 5 years
Defence loans	10 years' grace at 2% interest, followed by 20 years to repay principal at 3% a year, 30 years altogether

Source: Liviatan, 1980, p. 41.

conditions for developing countries have been 2 per cent interest with a thirty-year repayment period and ten years' grace. OPEC countries sometimes have received aid (for example, Indonesia) but also have been required to pay for technical assistance (as Saudi Arabia) (Bundesministerium für wirtshaftliche Zusammenarbeit, 1979b, pp. 12, 18). Since 1977 Israel has counted as a 'take-off' country, thereby operating on less favourable terms.

The German government has lightened Israel's burden while changing its loan status. Germany agreed in December 1977 to a two-year moratorium on repayment. There was opposition from some Cabinet members, who feared a precedent, but Chancellor Schmidt 'brushed this problem aside' (*Deutschland-Berichte*, January 1978). Israel stands out for its sophisticated industrial development among the 'take-off' countries, yet the German government still applied 'special conditions' (Lewan, 1975, p. 63; Federal Ministry for Economic Co-operation interviews, 1975, 1979).

Loan terms from Germany consistently have been better than terms available from other lenders. When other loans averaged 4·9 per cent interest, a nineteen-year repayment period and 5·5 years of grace

Table 4.7 *Loans to Israel from Major Donors, 1961–78 (Gross Figures)*

Million $	West Germany*	USA	World Jewry
1961	19	26	63
1962	38	34	67
1963	35	62	79
1964	33	61	98
1965	33	64	100
1966	40	48	124
1967	40	37	232
1968	35	48	182
1969	38	86	184
1970	39	367	231
1971	43	283	285
1972	44	300	300
1973	52	342	302
1974	58	290	326
1975	54	1,319	290
1976	61	836	292
1977	67	633	355
1978	77	982	400
Total, 1961–78	806	5,818	3,910

*The $–DM exchange in this period fluctuated from $1 = 3.99 DM in 1961 to $1 = 1.82 DM in 1978.

Sources: State of Israel Central Bureau of Statistics, 1971, 1977b; Bank of Israel, 1979; Federal Ministry for Economic Co-operation interviews, 1975, 1979; and Tables 4.2 and 4.4.

(1967–70), German terms were 2·0 per cent interest, thirty years for repayment and ten years of grace. Germany maintained soft terms into the 1970s, even when other lenders adjusted terms for more demanding rates of interest (Liviatan, 1980, pp. 26–7).

West Germany and the USA are the only two countries today whose governments provide capital aid to Israel, and they always have been the principal donors (ibid., pp. 16–20). Both the International Monetary Fund and the World Bank have furnished Israel loans, but nowhere near the magnitude of the German or US governments (ibid., pp. 21–3). Only world Jewry (Independence and Development Bonds) has been comparable (Table 4.7). Liviatan has explained the motives of soft loans: 'These easy terms are received owing to the government's special standing with its foreign creditors, whose motives for lending are not necessarily economic but may be political (governments and international organizations) or other (Israel Bonds)' (ibid., p. 3). The West German government plainly combines political and sentimental reasons for providing loans on soft terms to Israel.

MOTIVES AND ADVANTAGES FOR WEST GERMANY AND
FOR ISRAEL

Why, with its Luxembourg Agreement obligations fulfilled and world opinion satisfied, did Germany enter into further special economic arrangements with Israel? And why did Israel, with a public still suspicious of Germany, press the Germans for new agreements? Did the motives of 1952 still persist, or did new concerns inspire the partners?

Both Shinnar and Ben-Gurion recognized in 1960 that reparations would run out soon and Israel would need substantial economic help. Ben-Gurion, looking to the Bible, urged development of minerals from the Dead Sea and the Negev in order to export to Asia and East Africa through the Red Sea. He presented this economic argument to Adenauer, while pressing again Israel's moral claim:

> The moral [reason for my request] was that the generation born after the defeat of the Nazi regime hearing of the Nazi atrocities that had no parallel in human history, would be ashamed of their nation and its deeds during World War Two; they would find some moral satisfaction in knowing that their nation had helped Israel to gain independence and develop the desolate Negev. (Ben-Gurion, 1971, p. 538)

Ben-Gurion also now wanted diplomatic relations, and expansion of relations in many fields could enhance political recognition.

Israel's motives, focusing above all on perceived economic need, remained the same, and so did Israeli tactics for obtaining German commitments. Negotiations were on the verge of collapse when Adenauer visited Israel at the beginning of May 1966. In his speech at a dinner for Adenauer Levi Eshkol told the Federal Chancellor that reparations agreements could not atone for the terrible past, and he reminded Adenauer of 'the obligation of the Christian peoples to render their aid in the consolidation of Israel's independence' (quoted in Vogel, 1969, p. 184). The threat of public moral pronouncements was used again.

In its annual dealings with the Federal Republic over development aid Israel does not make public pronouncements about Germany's past. But it is clear that Israelis involved believe Germany owes this kind of ongoing support to Israel. Ben-Gurion's immediate political necessity, diplomatic relations, had been achieved by the time the 1966 Agreement was negotiated, yet there remained the need both for economic help and for general political recognition. Development aid from Germany has been one way of showing the world that Israel's diplomatic relations are not confined to the USA and that isolation is not complete.

A few months before Adenauer and Ben-Gurion met in March 1960 there had been a wave of antisemitic activity, such as the swastika-daubing of synagogues, in Cologne. Adenauer thought American opinion would be, consequently, less than friendly during his visit. According to the *New York Times* of March 15, 1960, Adenauer told a luncheon audience in New York that 'he had been warned before flying to New York that he would find American opinion had become more "difficult". He said this [prediction resulted from] a reaction to the "minute minority of neo-Nazis" in West Germany, the recent series of anti-semitic incidents'. Yet again, Germany was concerned about American and world opinion,[14] and Ben-Gurion obliged with moral absolution after the Waldorf Astoria meeting: 'The Germany of today', Ben-Gurion intoned, 'is not the Germany of yesterday' (quoted in Vogel, 1969, p. 121). Germany felt that it could not conclude the diplomatic relations Israel wanted in 1960. Compensation was given, therefore, through development aid (Seelbach, 1970, p. 103; Ben-Natan, 1974, p. 31). And Adenauer has cited yet another political reason for aiding Israel, to keep it in the Western camp: 'I was prepared to do everything possible to help Israel...also for reasons of political wisdom. Israel belonged to the West as a country with a Western orientation, and it was in the general interest of the free world that Israel should develop' (1970, p. 38). American and world opinion, and political expediency, continued to motivate Germany, and so did morality. Adenauer told Ben-Gurion that Germany would give Israel aid because of an 'inner obligation', and Ludwig Erhard, who was involved in the granting of development aid to Israel both as Minister for Economics under Adenauer and subsequently as Chancellor, said 'I myself have repeatedly stated that a country like the Federal German Republic, which received aid in its darkest hour, must in turn respond to the moral obligation to help less fortunate peoples' (quoted in Knusel, 1968, p. 10). Israel was considered a particularly needy case, and according to officials involved in development aid to Israel, a sense of morality as a basis for granting aid persists today.

TRADE AND INVESTMENT

In liberal-democratic states like the Federal Republic foreign commercial exchanges are based largely on the classical liberal principle of free trade and domestic commercial exchanges are based on a market economy. The role of liberal-democratic government is to promote private sector trade and investment, whether through export and investment guarantees to its own citizens, through trade and investment treaties with other nations, or through the reduction of tariffs and the granting of preferences.

Trade relations between Germany and Israel developed to a certain extent from the Luxembourg Reparations Agreement (Ebeling, 1966, pp. 65–6; Shinnar, 1967, p. 83; Deutschkron, 1970a, pp. 169–70; Hess interview, 1975; Levinsky interview, 1975). German goods and machinery were introduced into Israel, and much of Israel's infrastructure was built with German equipment. By the time the Reparations Agreement expired in 1965 Israel had built many commercial connections with Germans, who often spoke the same language, whether German or English. It was much simpler for Israelis to continue with the German connection than to look for a new trading partner, especially given the generally good quality of German machinery. German development aid furthered the purchase of German goods for industrial purposes.

Since 1960 the Federal Republic consistently has been one of Israel's three most important trading partners, both as an importer of Israeli goods and as an exporter to Israel (Table 4.8). The Israel–German Chamber of Commerce and Industry in Tel Aviv has been one of the largest such bilateral groups in Israel, emphasizing the importance of German trade (Moosberg, 1973). In the period 1964–70 the Federal Republic was second only to the United Kingdom as a foreign purchaser of Israeli citrus fruits, and in 1973–5 and 1978 Germany continued this role, close behind the UK. In 1971–2 and 1976 Germany was the leading purchaser (State of Israel Central Bureau of Statistics, 1966, 1968, 1972, 1973, 1974, 1975, 1979). One of the few agricultural attachés in the Israeli diplomatic service works in Bonn, and since 1977 there has existed the government-sponsored Israel Trade Centre in Düsseldorf, again testifying to the centrality of trade relations with West Germany (*Deutschland-Berichte*, February 1977).

Germany is a much more important economic force than Israel. Although its purchases of Israeli goods are substantial by Israeli standards, they are small, ranging over $0\cdot2-0\cdot4$ per cent in imports, for Germany (Statistisches Bundesamt, 1964, 1966, 1968, 1972, 1973, 1974a, 1976, 1980). Similarly, Germany is a major supplier for Israel, but no more than $0\cdot5$ per cent of Germany's exports in fact go to Israel. Nevertheless, per capita, Germany's trade with Israel is substantial. For the Germans, too, there is a perception of common language and culture

Table 4.8 Israeli Imports and Exports According to Most Important Countries, 1963–78

Million $	All countries	Exports FRG	FRG as %	USA	USA as %	UK	UK as %	All countries	Imports FRG	FRG as %	USA	USA as %	UK	UK as %
1963	351·5	39·5	11·2	46·4	13·2	47·8	13·6	673·6	61·4	9·1	185·2	27·5	134·0	19·9
1964	372·4	33·3	8·9	54·7	14·7	46·0	12·4	839·3	65·7	7·8	208·6	24·9	159·0	18·9
1965	429·1	40·1	9·3	62·2	14·5	50·7	11·8	835·4	74·9	9·0	212·2	25·4	164·2	19·7
1966	503·3	47·3	9·4	77·5	15·4	62·2	12·4	832·6	68·7	8·3	220·0	26·4	157·8	18·9
1967	555·0	59·3	10·7	89·9	16·2	70·5	12·7	758·8	62·3	8·2	197·1	26·0	146·2	19·3
1968	639·6	58·1	9·1	119·4	18·7	70·7	11·0	1,089·3	115·1	10·6	245·9	22·6	218·4	20·0
1969	729·3	64·7	8·9	135·7	18·6	74·9	10·2	1,330·6	157·5	11·8	313·8	23·6	248·5	18·7
1970	778·7	66·9	8·6	149·1	19·1	81·4	10·5	1,454·9	174·9	12·0	324·2	22·3	227·7	15·6
1971	957·2	90·5	9·5	185·5	19·4	97·5	10·2	1,807·6	235·0	13·0	426·5	23·6	276·4	15·3
1972	1,149·0	103·6	9·0	223·4	19·4	111·2	9·7	1,983·1	229·3	11·6	373·2	18·8	365·3	18·4
1973	1,148·6	137·6	12·0	267·0	23·2	140·7	12·2	2,987·3	511·8	17·1	549·4	18·4	478·8	16·0
1974	1,825·6	135·6	7·4	302·1	16·5	157·6	8·6	4,215·3	535·7	12·7	783·8	18·6	552·1	13·1
1975	1,940·7	160·5	8·3	307·5	15·8	169·3	8·7	4,172·6	457·5	11·0	1,001·5	24·0	560·7	13·4
1976	2,415·2	201·7	8·4	440·1	18·2	183·9	7·6	4,132·4	416·6	10·1	888·3	21·5	633·6	15·3
1977	3,081·7	275·6	8·9	564·6	18·3	223·8	7·3	4,844·4	447·5	9·2	980·8	20·2	484·9	10·0
1978	3,921·3	340·3	8·7	686·4	17·5	282·6	7·2	5,870·6	594·4	10·1	1,125·5	19·2	542·5	9·2

Source: State of Israel Central Bureau of Statistics, 1964, 1966, 1968, 1972, 1973, 1974, 1975, 1977a, 1979.

enhancing trade, and the German Society for Economic Relations with Israel is Germany's counterpart to the Israel–German Chamber of Commerce and Industry. Perception of a common past and the impact of the flow of goods and services from the Luxembourg Agreement provided conditions for trade that began to flourish in the mid-1960s.

Despite special conditions, spokesmen of German and Israeli industry insist that trade is strictly commercial (Hess interview, 1975; Levinsky interview, 1975). Israeli importers buy goods from Germany because of quality and the efficiency of German exporters, and Germans sell to Israel because it has a reputation for paying its bills. Germans import from Israel because Israel offers high-quality, well-priced goods in certain areas, and Israelis sell to Germany because it is a willing buyer (*Deutschland-Berichte*, 1977, November 1977, July–August 1978).

For these commercial reasons, both private sectors have termed the relationship 'normal' in the sense that rational economic criteria of quality, profitability and efficiency are applied. However, whereas businessmen on both sides of the relationship may be motivated by market criteria, governments are involved in trade also because of politics and sentiment. According to one economic counsellor at the Israeli Embassy in Bonn, wherever there is a government role Israel expects special treatment on the basis of sentiment. The Federal Republic is often, although not always, responsive to this expectation.

SPONSORING ISRAEL FOR THE EEC

Israel has been concerned especially about trade relations with the European Economic Community, and Germany has helped in a supportive and preferential way. Culturally, philosophically and even geographically (as part of the Mediterranean area) Israel has regarded itself since the 1950s as part of Europe and has placed great emphasis on economic and political relations with Western Europe accordingly.[15] Israel was one of the first countries to have representation with the EEC and already in 1958 it submitted an *aide mémoire* to the Commission, announcing its desire for a formal, associate relationship. From the beginning West Germany has been crucial for Israel's attempts to forge formal links with the Community.[16]

The first agreement between the EEC and Israel in 1964 was largely the result of efforts made by Holland, Israel's other main advocate in the Community. Israel, however, was dissatisfied with the commercial agreement, which covered only about 10 per cent of its total exports to the Community. In 1966 it submitted an application for the replacement of the 1964 agreement by association status. It was at this point that the Federal Republic became an active proponent of the Israeli cause.

French opposition to the Israeli application, following the 1967 war, poisoned Israel's chances and caused great delay, but Germany championed Israel's case in the protracted negotiations inside the EEC. Association status became impossible, and France also opposed preferential agreements while proposing preferential status for Morocco, Tunisia and Spain. Holland's vigorous support of Israel could not have beaten back the French, but the 'emergence of Germany as a major protagonist certainly changed the political balance' (Henig, 1971, p. 115).

The Dutch and German proposal for Israel was based on a two-stage agreement for the establishment of full free trade, beginning with a preference rate of 60 per cent. As this formula was debated (France countered with a proposal for a 40 per cent rate), only Germany stood by the original 60 per cent. When France yielded to Holland's compromise of 45 per cent put forward with Italy, Belgium and Luxembourg, Germany finally agreed. But on a related issue Germany would not compromise at all. France said the Community should show also its willingness to negotiate with the Arabs during negotiations with Israel. Germany formally objected to the linkage (Henig, 1971, p. 118).

The Preferential Trade Agreement finally concluded with Israel in June 1970 was a definite improvement over the first agreement of 1964: an immediate 30 per cent tariff preference in the industrial sector to be increased gradually to 50 per cent; in the agricultural sector there was to be a 40 per cent tariff reduction. When France objected to the agreement's preamble, which promised a progressive elimination of trade barriers, the Dutch and Germans, this time with Italian support, overrode the French (Henig, 1971, pp. 121–23).

The Federal Republic gradually replaced Holland as Israel's chief EEC backer and is credited for the dominant role in concluding the 1975 Free Trade Agreement with Israel.[17] The negotiations again were protracted, running parallel to negotiations with Morocco, Algeria, Spain and Malta all of whom were unhappy with the Community's offer.[18] Israel made it clear that it wanted the agreement signed as soon as possible. Federal Foreign Minister Genscher successfully pushed the Israeli case and Israeli Foreign Minister Yigal Allon publicly praised Genscher for facilitating a conclusion to negotiations. Allon hailed the accord, which provides for complete free trade in industrial goods at the earliest in 1985 and at the latest by 1989, and significant tariff reductions for Israel's agricultural exports, as a 'foreign policy success of tremendous significance' (*Frankfurter Allgemeine Zeitung*, May 9, 1975). Again, Germany contributed to the removal of barriers to Israeli exports and to the delay in the removal of Israeli duties in action frequently cited by policy-makers, politicians and businessmen in Germany and Israel as an example of a special economic relationship.

Additional protocols were signed with the Community in February 1977 providing for development loans to Israel from the European Investment Bank and for technical and industrial co-operation. Although Israel clearly preferred the 1975/1977 agreements to none, 'the Israel–EEC Free Trade Agreement is far from satisfactory', in the view of Yaacov Cohen of Israel's Ministry of Industry, Trade and Tourism

(1979, p. 7). There are both industrial and agricultural problems, in part because the Community's Common Agricultural Policy, which by 1979 embraced 91 per cent of Community agricultural production compared to 50 per cent when the Agreement was signed (Cohen, 1979, p. 8), discriminates against Israeli agricultural goods. One of Israel's primary objectives in the Agreement, to reduce the trade imbalance with the Community, clearly has not been reached. In fact, the balance of trade deficit grew by 25 per cent from 1977 to 1978 (Cohen, 1979, p. 7), and Cohen remained pessimistic about the overall consequence of the 1975 Agreement: 'The erosion of preferences caused by agreements concluded by the EEC with other countries, the widening of the gap in the balance of trade, the protectionist tendencies in the Community combined with the lack of progress in the removal of non-tariff barriers – all this leads Israel to make a sober reevaluation of the balance achieved until now in the implementation of the Agreement' (Cohen, 1980, p. 36). Cohen's pessimism is not shared universally. In a joint German-Israeli research project on the 'Economic integration of Israel in the EEC' two of his colleagues argue through detailed statistical analyses that free trade will have dynamic consequences such as the growth of economies of scale, productivity and foreign direct investment. They conclude that the Free Trade Agreement 'will yield considerable economic benefit to Israel' (Pomfret and Toren, 1980, p. 187). In 1980 and 1981 the Community recognized some of Israel's concerns in deferring the schedule for tariff reductions on certain Israeli imports (Commission of the European Communities, 1981, 1982a).

Whether the 1975 Agreement will benefit Israel or not, the industrial and agricultural sector will face increasing difficulties because of the Community's second enlargement.[19] Israel and the Community expect Greek membership to harm Israel's food, textile and fur industries, and especially its fresh agricultural exports (Cohen, 1979, p. 9; *Deutschland-Berichte*, March 1980), and Spanish membership in general will be damaging to Israel. To meet those new challenges Israel has been pursuing two strategies: a change in the present Agreement, and an industrial revitalization to make Israeli products more competitive. In 1981 the Community did adjust the Co-operation Agreement with Israel to account for Greek accession (Commission of the European Communities, 1982a), but by the beginning of 1982 an arrangement to mitigate the probable effects of Spanish and Portuguese membership still had not been struck between the Community and its non-member Mediterranean partners. German government help is crucial in Israeli endeavours to adjust to an enlarged Community, providing political support in the EEC and encouraging private investment in Israel. Although past German behaviour is promising for Israel, some Israeli officials fear that automatic German verbal support may not be translated readily into formal activity on Israel's behalf.

PROMOTING GERMAN-ISRAELI TRADE

At the end of his visit to Israel in December 1975 Genscher and the Israeli Minister of Trade and Industry, Haim Bar-Lev, issued a statement announcing agreement on the creation of a Mixed Economic Commission:

> the two ministers have decided to exhaust the possibilities of intensifying economic relations in the interest of both countries and...to appoint a mixed commission which will be led by the Foreign Ministers [and] which will...bring in representatives of industry; [it] will be concerned with the mutual promotion of trade, industrial cooperation and investment, as well as other economic matters. The commission will coordinate and develop relations in these spheres, which embrace a large proportion of the substantive cooperation between the two countries. (*Deutschland-Berichte*, December 1975)

The Federal Republic, of course, does have economic commissions with other countries, but for Israel's size and its share of the German market the constitution of a mixed commission at ministerial level was significant.

Most of the economic discussions between West Germany and Israel have been informal. The Mixed Economic Commission has met only once, in June 1976, because both sides think economic problems can be resolved best through quiet diplomacy; yet both sides appreciate that the creation of the Mixed Economic Commission as a formal institution and its continued existence have been a demonstration of goodwill, of a public signal of the importance Germany attaches to the development of the Israeli economy (*Deutschland-Berichte*, 1977; Israeli Embassy, Bonn, interview, 1979; Federal Ministry for Economics interview, 1979). Nevertheless, Israel remains concerned about the absence of German law effective against the Arab boycott. The German government simply considers the boycott 'an obstacle to trade and a practice incompatible with its policy of free economy' (*Deutschland-Berichte*, 1977).

INVESTMENT

Investment, like trade, is essentially private in liberal democracies. German investment in Israel is substantial compared to investments from other countries. For the period 1967–78 German investments (at 12·6 per cent of the total) were second only to those from the USA (49 per cent of the total) (Bank of Israel correspondence, 1980). The government of the Federal Republic has been active in investment promotion. At 585 million marks in 1978 (since 1952), Israel topped countries such as Japan, Australia and Singapore for German investments, and German firms have invested more in Israel than anywhere else in the Asian region (which includes most of the Middle Eastern countries) (Bundesministerium für Wirtschaft, 1979b).

Israeli investment in Germany has been small, amounting to only 0·02 per cent of all foreign investment in the Federal Republic by the end of 1978. Germany and Israel signed a Treaty on the Encouragement and Reciprocal Protection of Investments in June 1976. There were some difficulties in the ratification procedures, but the treaty has been implemented.

German investments in Israel are encouraged further by the provisions of the German Tax Law for the Promotion of Investments in Developing Countries and by German export guarantees. The Federal government normally grants insurance to exporters and investors against non-payment and expropriation by a recipient country, but guarantees investments only when it has cause to expect compensation in the case of nationalization (White, 1965, pp. 131–2; Knusel, 1968, pp. 85–7; Bundesministerium für Wirtschaft, 1973, 1976, 1977a; Gröner, 1975, p. 421; Schwarz, 1975, p. 731; MEED, 1979, pp. 17–18). Should a country default, either in paying for its imports or in compensating for nationalization, the Federal government will not renew insurance. German investors and exporters to Israel, however, readily receive government insurance; 12·5 per cent of all guarantees for capital investments since 1960 have been in Israel, making it second only to Brazil in total amount guaranteed by the German government (Bundesministerium für Wirtschaft, 1979a). According to one German official, an Israeli default would not prevent the renewal of insurance. Such financial risk would not be contemplated for investments in other countries. The Agreement for the Avoidance of Double Taxation between the Federal Republic of Germany and Israel is a final factor providing a favourable atmosphere for investment. German investment in Israel is all the more remarkable when one considers how far the Middle East deviates from the German preference for regional stability as a criterion in investment decisions.

MOTIVES AND ADVANTAGES FOR ISRAEL AND FOR GERMANY

Clearly, the most immediate reason for Israel's desire for improved trade relations with Germany has been economic necessity, the need to open up German and European markets to more Israeli goods in an effort to improve Israel's balance of trade (34·3 per cent of export trade and 41·8 per cent of import trade was with the EEC in 1978). There has existed also a political motive, perceived by Ben-Gurion, Shimon Peres and Eshkol, among others, to have economic relations highlight diplomatic acceptance.

To a certain extent economic agreements have awarded Israel political recognition, but its long-term aim of inclusion in Western Europe through association status in the EEC has not been achieved. Nevertheless, Germany has been supportive of Israel on economic questions in the Community, despite generally following France's political lead which from 1967 through the presidency of Giscard d'Estaing was firmly negative towards Israel. German support of Israel seems to be, then, an act of compensation for political hesitation, consistent with other compensatory behaviour notable throughout German policy towards Israel.

Germany makes no particular economic sacrifice in supporting Israel, whereas countries like Italy, with its own citrus products, do perceive an economic threat. Indeed, economic arrangements between Israel and the EEC and between Israel and the Federal Republic appear mutually advantageous for Israel and for the Federal Republic. Finally, as part of the thread that runs through all of Germany's actions with respect to Israel, there is the sense of moral obligation to aid the survival of the State of Israel; this commitment finds expression most clearly in efforts within the EEC and with respect to investment promotion and guarantees.

The nuances and emphases of motive have altered over time, but the main lines of economic advantages for Israel and moral and political absolution for Germany, continue to dominate the special relationship, in economics as in other spheres. For its size Israel is disproportionately important in German trade and investment and in German policy in the EEC; Israel's economic progress is dependent to a significant degree on its various economic relationships with the Federal Republic. It is second only to the USA in trade, investment and development aid;[20] as an avenue to the European Economic Community, it is of greater help to Israel than the USA can be. Both in form and content Germany has treated Israel as a special friend in economic questions. In turn, Germany has developed a sturdy and reliable partner in the Middle East.

NOTES: CHAPTER 4

1 Everyday workings of the Israel Mission were reported by the information department of the mission in *Israel-Informations-Dienst*, a bulletin begun in the spring of 1953 to keep Germans informed of events concerning Israel; there were no German journalists in Israel until 1957 when Rudolf Küstermeier began his work (Naor interview, 1975).

2 For details of the origins and development of Federal legislation to compensate the victims of National Socialism, see: van Dam (1963a); Robinson (1964); Bentwich (1955, 1965, 1969); Schwerin (1972); Bundesministerium der Finanzen (1975, 1979a). For an important work on Jewish efforts to receive compensation for forced labour (not covered by Federal indemnification legislation), see Ferencz (1979).

3 Percentages are based on the author's calculations. Figures for Federal and Länder budgets are taken from the annual editions of the Statistical Yearbook of the Federal Republic, starting in 1957. Figures for the annual Luxembourg Agreement and individual compensation payments are from State of Israel Central Bureau of Statistics (1971). For a full analysis of the effect of the Luxembourg Agreement on the German economy, see Balabkins (1971, ch. 9). He has assumed that the Federal government carried the whole burden for compensation; according to German financial officials,

however, approximately 37·5 per cent of all compensation to individuals has been borne by the Länder.
4   In 1970 Parliamentary State Secretary Moersch of the German Foreign Office indicated the government's awareness of Polish demands (Deutscher Bundestag und Bundesrat, October 8, 1970, pp. 3855–6). The claims, which amounted to 10–13 billion marks, received much attention in the German press in 1970 and 1972 (*Deutschland-Berichte*, May 1975). As a completely separate issue. Poland had received by 1972 100 million marks from the Federal Republic for victims of medical experiments (Bundesministerium der Finanzen, 1979a, p. 7).
5   According to German financial officials, these figures represent rough estimates for two reasons: (1) political considerations deter the Federal government from offering an exact statistic; (2) contrary to the desires of the Israeli government, some of the compensation to individuals has not occurred via official mechanisms of payment. In the estimation of the Israeli Ministry of Finance the amounts reaching Israel have been less than 40 per cent of restitution payments because once-wealthy Jews who would be compensated at high levels often chose to emigrate to the USA rather than to Israel (correspondence, 1980). Israelis have received about 40 per cent of a third category of compensation that included payments to former German civil servants (Bundesministerium der Finanzen, 1979b, p. 2).
6   In 1979 the Federal Ministry of Finance estimated that 60–70 per cent of the prospective recipients would be residents of Israel (interview, 1979).
7   According to a Foreign Office official, both the Arabs and the East European countries did not like the 'assertion of a special relationship, a policy of privilege', which they believed would be involved in the granting of a special fund (confidential interview, 1975). Poland, Syria and Kuwait apparently threatened retaliation if the payment went ahead. For details of the opposition of Arab and East European countries, see: *Die Welt* (March 18 and March 26, 1975); *Jerusalem Post* (March 28, 1975); *Israel-Nachrichten* (June 18, 1975); Deutsche Presse Agentur (March 30, 1975).
8   In 1966 the Ginor–Tishler report aroused debate in Israel when a number of newspapers, particularly the *Jerusalem Post*, doubted the report's claim of the Agreement's positive effects; the *Jerusalem Post* of mid-April 1965 cited Israel's increased dependence on foreign aid to finance balance of trade deficits and blamed German help. Shinnar defended the Agreement against the newspaper attack. The various analyses mentioned do note the negative effects of the Luxembourg Agreement, especially Balabkins (1971), but all on balance perceive a positive effect on the Israeli economy. Ginor is perhaps the most comprehensive because she attempts to measure the influence of German goods and services and payments to individuals on different sectors of the economy.
9   Abs did write Adenauer that 'financial assistance...will be given on a commercial basis' (quoted in Ben-Gurion, 1973, pp. 504–5). However, his further reference to 'capital aid for the continuation of the economic development [of Israel]' (ibid.), and the fact that the terms were too soft to qualify as a normal commercial loan, lead one to the conclusion that Abs was implying a distinction between Luxembourg Agreement goods, which were an outright gift, and the aid for development which would be a loan requiring interest and repayments. Shinnar alludes to the German characterization as a commercial loan, but he himself uses the term development loan (*Entwicklungsdarlehen*) (1967, pp. 101–2).
10 Seelbach notes that, despite denials to the contrary, there was confirmation of an agreement between the two countries; the information was disclosed by SPD deputy Frenzel who was chairman of the parliamentary committee on compensation (1970, p. 103). A discussion of whether there was an agreement and the nature of the accord can be found in Shinnar (1967, pp. 99–107); von Eckardt (1967, pp. 609–10); Deutschkron (1970a, ch. 6). Deutschkron's account is based on the notes of the interpreter at the meeting (interview, 1975).
11 According to Shinnar, the Arabs learnt of the agreement but did not disclose it in exchange for German development aid (1967, pp. 102–3).

12 According to one high–level Israeli official, this sentence in the preamble to the agreement signifies that economic aid should continue indefinitely (confidential interview, 1975). *Le Monde* of May 14, 1966 on the other hand said the agreement was not a long-term arrangement as Israel had wanted. But as the *Neue Zürcher Zeitung* of May 1, 1966 pointed out, there is no provision for a Federal ministry to make a long-term commitment. In these circumstances 'continuous co-operation' must be understood as the limit of the commitment German negotiators were empowered to make with any country.

13 The differentiation was part of the new development aid concept of the then Minister for Economic Co-operation, Egon Bahr (*Frankfurter Allgemeine Zeitung*, May 7 and May 20, 1975). For details of the criteria for identifying 'take-off' countries, see Bundesministerium für wirtschaftliche Zusammenarbeit (1978b).

14 Werner Kliesing has emphasized Adenauer's constant awareness of US opinion (interview, 1975).

15 For two of the first articulations of the Israeli position towards the EEC, see Bartur (1961) and Eshkol's statement of November 26, 1962. An overview of the relationship during 1958–78 is in Cohen (1980). On the various aspects of Israel's economic ties to the EEC, see the companion pieces to Cohen's article in Giersch (1980).

16 On German support in the mid-1950s, see Yisrael (1971). For the German offer of help during meetings between German Minister for Economics Erhard and Israeli Finance Minister Eshkol in the early 1960s and for the talks between German Minister for Economics Schmücker and Israeli Finance Minister Sapir in February 1965, see Shinnar (1967, pp. 91–2, 151–2). Details of Germany's offer of support during the negotiations over arms termination in 1965 are offered by Birrenbach (1972, p. 378). For statements by German officials on various occasions in the late 1960s and 1970s, see, for example, the remarks by then Foreign Minister Willy Brandt (*Deutschland-Berichte*, December 1967); German political parties (*Deutschland-Berichte*, April 1967); Chancellor Kiesinger (*Deutschland-Berichte*, May 1968); Minister of Economics Schiller (*Deutschland-Berichte*, February 1968); Minister of Agriculture and Forests Höcherl (ibid.); Foreign Minister Scheel (*Deutschland-Berichte*, August 1971); Foreign Minister Genscher (*Deutschland-Berichte*, June 1975); Ambassador Schütz (*Deutschland-Berichte*, November 1977); Foreign Office State Secretaries Jahn and Moersch (Deutscher Bundestag und Bundesrat, February 14, 1969, pp. 11718–20 and January 22, 1971, pp. 5008–9).

17 Information on the background, details and implications of the 1975 agreement is contained in the *Frankfurter Allgemeine Zeitung* (May 2, 3, 8, 9 and 12, 1975); *Süddeutsche Zeitung* (May 10–11, 1975); *International Herald Tribune* (May 12, 1975); Golan (1976); *Jerusalem Post* (July 1, 1977); Commission of the European Communities (1977); Cohen (1979, 1980); Mushkat (1980); Pomfret and Toren (1980).

18 Since 1972 the EEC economic policy towards Israel has been conducted in the framework of its 'global Mediterranean policy'. For the history of the EEC Mediterranean policy and Israel's role in it, see Shlaim and Yannopoulos (1976); Tsoukalis (1978); Pomfret and Tovias (1980). The 1975 agreement was the first manifestation of the global Mediterranean approach.

19 For Israel's position on the second enlargement and EEC-Israeli negotiations on the issue, see *Jerusalem Post* (June 29 and June 30, 1978, October 7, 1980); *Europe* (1979, 1980b, 1980c, 1981a, 1981b); Commission of the European Communities (1979a, 1979b, 1980); Aeikens and Guth (1980); Taylor (1980).

20 The UK also has been important for Israel in trade (see Table 4.8) and in banking.

5
The 'Special' Special Relationship: Military Affairs

> We left with the definite feeling that the foundations had been laid for a special relationship between the two countries and between the two Ministries of Defence. We were not mistaken. (Peres, 1970, pp. 71–2)

There are many features of the special relationship between West Germany and Israel, but the military relationship in the period 1957–65 was so extraordinary that it, alone, often has been called the special relationship itself (for example, in Yisrael, 1971). The military relationship led to a major crisis in foreign military aid policy for West Germany and contributed to the rupture of diplomatic relations with ten Arab countries (see Chapter 7). For Israel, the military arrangements were of great importance for security, and the termination of military agreements with West Germany in 1965 gave way to diplomatic relations and to a much-desired military aid relationship with the USA (Peres, 1970, p. 85).

The military relationship unfolded with a cloak-and-dagger style worthy of the finest fiction.[1] Because of its obvious importance and style, it has been the object of a number of detailed studies both descriptive and analytical. The story will not be retold here, nor will there be an account of commercial arrangements that were not the activities of the two governments;[2] rather, the aim is to measure the military relationship in comparison to arrangements West Germany and Israel have had with other countries.

THE MILITARY RELATIONSHP, 1957–65

There are at least twenty-four different accounts of military relations between West Germany and Israel, including those of officials on both sides, scholars, newspapers and journals from West Germany, Israel, the Arab World and the USA. Unfortunately, there are discrepancies in the accounts of events,[3] inconsistencies in estimated values of arms[4] and in the weaponry involved.[5] Despite these discrepancies, overall preference can be seen because, whichever account or analysis one chooses, West Germany deviated sharply from its norm in its policies of military aid, showing preference to Israel. This practice of preference is the key to a special military relationship.

MILITARY AID: THE GERMAN PERSPECTIVE

During the period 1957–65 Germany showed Israel preference in military aid in at least five ways. First, the Federal Republic's military aid policy always has been restrictive, to a large extent for 'fear of damaging the West German reputation through reappearing in a militaristic guise' (SIPRI, 1971, p. 295). As Ludwig Erhard explained: 'The granting of military aid to Israel was an exceptional situation' (Deutscher Bundestag und Bundesrat, February 17, 1965, pp. 8103–5). Therefore, the fact that Israel received military aid at all was unusual, and it was one of only a handful of countries singled out for advantage in this way.

Secondly, within the exception to the rule Israel also proved an exception. In the period under consideration it was the only country in the Middle East to receive large amounts of military aid from Germany. As one observer has explained:

> With the exception of the rather large programme to Israel between 1962 and 1965, the emphasis has been placed on Africa. Africa provided the most promising market, since several states were anxious to avoid dependence on the former colonial powers and on the United States. Further, West Germany was encouraged by its allies to provide such aid when requested, in order to prevent the recipients from turning to socialist countries. (SIPRI, 1971, p. 309)[6]

Israel was, then, the only non-African major recipient of German military aid.

Thirdly, diplomatic relations between West Germany and Israel did not yet exist. Germany maintained diplomatic relations with all the African states with whom it had military relations (Guinea, Madagascar, Nigeria, Somalia, Sudan and Tanzania). As with development aid, the amount of German support, in view of the absence of formal relations, was remarkably high. The military agreements of 1962 and 1964 were top secret, for Germany feared Arab reaction and Israel feared opposition at home. Although the agreements with the African states were also secret, the enforcement of secrecy was not nearly as extreme, and it has been with Israel that the constitutionality and legality of the secrecy have been questioned.[7] The agreement with Israel, once it was disclosed, was referred to as the 'Secret Agreement', even though it was not disclosed by the government for some twenty months after the revelation of other military aid agreements.[8] Even when the agreement with Israel was disclosed by the Federal government in February 1965, details remained secret and still remain secret.

There was no written agreement with Israel, as Shimon Peres explained:

> We worked out nothing that can be described as a formal agreement. However, we reached a considerable degree of understanding. We did not bother ourselves too much with putting things in writing ... Most of our agreements were verbal and were carried out in a way that was true to the letter and spirit of our talks. (Quoted in Vogel, 1967, p. 142)

The agreements with the African countries were, according to Werner Knieper (who was involved in both sets of arrangements), written and precise and thus more normal (interview, 1975).

Table 5.1 *Comparison of German Military Aid to All Recipients, 1962–72*

	Recipient	Amount (million DM)	Period
1	Turkey (NATO)	300	1964–70
2	Israel	149*	1962–5
3	Sudan	106	1961–5
4	Greece (NATO)	101	1964–8
5	Guinea	47	1962–71
6	Ethiopia	46	1965–71
7	Iran	40	1966–72
8	Somalia	18	1962–71
9	Morocco	16	1968–72
10	Kenya	16	1966–70
11	Nigeria	15	1963–7
12	Tunisia	8	1968–72
13	Niger	8	1966–71
14	Tanzania	6.2	1963–5
15	Ghana	6	1969–71
16	Chad	6	1969–71
17	Madagascar	6	1962–4
18	Togo	4	1969–71
19	India	3.5	1962
20	Mali	2	1969–70
21	Jordan	1.7	1964–5

*Haftendorn adds to this 140 million marks paid to Israel in compensation for the curtailment of military aid. Because actual weapons were no longer given, the sum is not included here.

Source: Haftendorn, 1971, p. 130.

Fourthly, the military arrangements with Israel were quantitatively different. Above all, Israel received at least 30 per cent of all German military aid to all non-NATO countries (Table 5.1), and perhaps more than 70 per cent of all aid to major non-NATO recipients (Table 5.2). Most countries received only software, whereas Israel was one of the few to receive hardware (Knieper interview, 1975). Only Israel, Nigeria, Tanzania and Sudan received aircraft; Israel was the only country to receive fighter planes. It is true that Nigeria received more planes (188 in all), but most of them were trainers; more importantly, Nigeria paid for most of the equipment received. Israel and the Sudan both received armoured fighting vehicles, but Israel received some 150–200 M-48 Patton main battle tanks and Sudan acquired only 97 small tanks or reconnaissance cars of the Ferret and Saladin variety. Israel was the only country to receive submarines, helicopters, anti-tank and anti-aircraft equipment (*Frankfurter Allgemeine Zeitung*, February 20, 1965; *Der Spiegel*, February 3, 24, 1965: Haftendorn, 1971, pp. 109–17; SIPRI, 1971, pp. 310–12, 844–5).

Finally, the agreements with Israel by far exceeded the cost of any other West German military agreement in the period 1958–65. Even if one accepts the lowest cost estimate for Israel and the highest estimate for any other non-NATO country, West Germany spent at least 20 per cent more on Israel (based on Israel at $37·5 million and Somalia at $30 million; see Table 5.2). On the basis of the highest estimate for Israel ($266 million), compared to the highest estimate for any other country (Somalia at $30 million), the agreement with Israel cost West Germany

Table 5.2 *Comparative Highest and Lowest Estimates of Military Aid for the Federal Republic to Major Recipients, 1960–5*

Recipient	Israel	Sudan	Nigeria	Guinea	Tanzania	Madagascar	Somalia
Highest estimate	266[a]	26·5[b]	26·0[c]	9·25[d]	1·55[e]	6·3[f]	30·0[g]
Lowest estimate	37·5[h]	10·2[i]	3·75[j]	7·5[k]	1·55[l]	1·5[m]	4·5[n]
Period	1958–65†	1961–5	1963–7	1962–5	1963–5	1962–5	1962–71‡

Million US $*

*$1 = 4 DM; amounts received.

†1958 is the starting-date for Israel because there is no exact figure for 1958–60.

‡Somalia end-date is 1971 because the highest figure is not broken down for 1962–5 and 1965–71.

Sources: (a) Rathmann, 1966, pp. 110–11; (b) Haftendorn, 1971, pp. 114, 130; (c) SIPRI, 1971, pp. 310–11; (d) Haftendorn, 1971, pp. 109–10; (e) ibid., pp. 114, 130; (f) SIPRI, 1971, pp. 310–11; (g) ibid.; (h) Haftendorn, 1971, pp. 26–7, 110, 130; (i) SIPRI, 1971, pp. 310–11; (j) Haftendorn, 1971, pp. 112, 130; (k) *Der Spiegel*, March 3, 1965; (l) Haftendorn, 1971, pp. 114, 130; (m) ibid., pp. 111, 130; (n) ibid., pp. 113, 130; for the period until 1965, *Der Spiegel* of March 3, 1965 gives an estimate of $1·6 million; Haftendorn's estimate for same period is $2·75 million, 1971, pp. 113.

some 800 per cent more. Even in comparison with military agreements made with other countries after the period under review (Table 5.1), most money (with the single exception of Turkey) had been spent on Israel.

Even when West Germany was buying (instead of selling or giving away), Israel was shown preference. The Federal Ministry of Defence looked to Israel for purchases of ammunition, grenade-throwers, uniforms, tyres and particularly Uzi submachine guns (Vogel, 1969, p. 125; Deutschkron, 1970a, pp. 112–14). It was not unusual for West Germany to buy weapons from other countries, but it was exceptional to buy weapons from a country to whom it was giving military aid. Moreover, the way in which Germany approached the matter was, according to Knieper, not normal: 'Our attempt to give Israel preference in the purchase of weapons for the Bundeswehr was an exception' (interview, 1975). Several countries might have offered the same goods to Germany with comparable conditions, but the Federal Republic attempted to stimulate Israel's infant armaments industry.

Israel clearly received special, in the sense of preferential, treatment compared to all other recipients of German military aid. From Israel's perspective, Germany was one of the few countries supplying Israel with arms, such that the aid was, as we shall see, automatically preferential.

MILITARY AID: THE ISRAELI PERSPECTIVE

In his book *David's Sling: The Arming of Israel*, Shimon Peres, former Minister of Defence, lists four possible suppliers of arms in the mid-1950s (1970), pp. 37–8, 41–3). For different reasons, Sweden, the USA and Britain had to be excluded from the list and, as Peres put it, 'there remained France'. France became a very important supplier in the period 1956–67, until its Middle East policy reversed in favour of the Arabs after the Six-Day War (Peres, 1970, ch. 3; Crosbie, 1974). Israel's 'success in France stimulated [it] to seek ties with other European countries, without of course halting [its] efforts to try and secure a change in the policy of Washington'. Arrangements with France served as Israel's model when it sought a military relationship with a potential second European military partner, the Federal Republic (Peres, 1970, pp. 65–8; Crosbie, 1974, pp. 100–2).

A comparison of military aid from France and from the Federal Republic emphasizes the importance of the Federal Republic for Israel. France and Germany were Israel's two main suppliers and were also important recipients of goods from Israeli military suppliers (SIPRI, 1971, p. 769; Crosbie, 1974, pp. 155–6). However, there were differences. One advantage of the military relationship with France not shared in the military relationship with Germany was the fairly open collaboration on weapons technology (SIPRI, 1971, pp. 530–1; Crosbie, 1974, ch. 7). There was speculation in 1964 that Germany and Israel were engaged in joint military research and weapons technology, based on the presence of several German atomic scientists at the Weizmann Institute. They denied vigorously, as did Israel, that they were involved in anything but peace-related research, and there is no concrete evidence of joint German-Israeli military research or production (*Der Spiegel*, November 4, 1964; *Neue Zürcher Zeitung*, October 29, 1964; *Die Welt*, October 31, 1964; *Jerusalem Post*, January 6, 1965). Both countries, however, did train Israeli officers and soldiers (*Die Welt*, June 17–18, 1963; *Le Monde*, June 18, 1963; *Der Spiegel*, February 24, 1965; Vogel, 1969, p. 128; Deutschkron, 1970a, pp. 270–1; Haftendorn, 1971, p. 117; Crosbie, 1974, pp. 103–5).

There can be no comparison of actual military supplies because the terms were different and they were complementary to Israel's needs. With respect to dollar values, France supplied Israel with military equipment worth $600–$1122 million in the period 1955–67 (SIPRI, 1971, p. 531; Crosbie, 1974, p. 217); from Germany, Israel received somewhere between $37·5 million and £266 million during 1958–65. Whereas the quantities purchased from France were much greater, from Germany the weapons were an outright gift. Peres has described Germany's unique role: 'the United States was helping us with funds, but not with arms; France was helping us with arms but not with money; Germany would be taking a far-sighted step in building bridges to the past if she would help us with arms without requiring either money or anything else in exchange' (1970, p. 71). In November 1964 a German journalist was able to observe: 'The military aid to Israel from the Federal Republic has been given at a level never before realized in terms of either recipient or donor' (quoted in *Der Spiegel*, February 10, 1965). Ben-Gurion was to say at the same time, 'The contribution of the German government for our military security *exceeds* what any other government does for us' (*Maariv*, November 22, 1964). In February 1965 German Foreign Minister Schröder confirmed that Israel had received arms free of charge (*Die Welt*, February 26, 1965).

The military relationship with France has been referred to as a 'special relationship' by Israeli officials. Peres's description of the bases of the friendship with France (both a psychological relationship from the past and mutual interest) certainly conforms to the foundation and need aspects of German-Israeli relations (1970, pp. 44–5, 63–4). The policy expression of the relationship was preferential to Israel. However, other aspects of a special relationship were missing, such as preferential treatment in non-military policy areas and adequate support mechanisms; the brief and incipient special relationship could not weather the brewing crisis which erupted in 1967. When the military supplies stopped, so did other aspects of relations. In contrast, when German supplies stopped, other special arrangements were made. Thus, in our terms military relations with France were special, but an enduring and embracing relationship did not exist.

PERCEPTIONS OF A MILITARY 'SPECIAL RELATIONSHIP'

In *David's Sling* Peres makes several explicit references to the special military relationship with West Germany. For example, in his comments on the 1960 Waldorf Astoria meeting where the first agreement is alleged to have been discussed, Peres writes: 'Dr Adenauer confirmed to Ben-Gurion that he had already given his support to the policy presented by his Defence Minister for a special arms relationship with Israel' (1970, p. 75). When Franz-Josef Strauss, the main German initiator of the special military relationship, resigned, Peres feared the policy might end, for 'the very advantage of the special relationship we had established carried a built-in disadvantage – it rested to a large extent on the mutual trust and friendship between individuals' (ibid., p. 78). Basically, however, the policy did not change. Even when the relationship was about to be terminated, Peres still referred to it as special: 'After the Arab diplomatic break with Germany, the Germans informed us that the time had come to discontinue our special relationship in the field of defence' (ibid., p. 79).

From his explicit references to the special relationship and his other comments in the discussion of German military aid, one can find the following features on which Peres's perception of the special relationship seems to depend: the giving of any aid at all; the preference shown to Israel once aid was given in terms of amount, quality and absence of cost; the 'under-the-table' contacts necessary to maintain secrecy; the personal relationship that resulted from clandestine arrangements and, in turn, reinforced such arrangements.

Peres was the arms negotiator; Shinnar was the administrator who arranged initial contacts in the military relationship. Like Peres, Shinnar saw German arms supplies as a prime policy expression of the special relationship, 'an impressive manifestation on the part of the post-Hitler Germany of a moral consciousness and a desire to contribute to the maintenance of peace in a part of the world where peace seems threatened' (1967, p. 171). Elsewhere, Shinnar has stressed that German military aid was special because of its unusual motive of morality, because of its preferential content, and because of the secrecy of its execution (interview, 1975).

Both the negotiator and the executor of the military aid on the German side also characterized the military relationship as special. Strauss, the Minister of Defence who concluded the military agreements with Peres, has said:

> We [Strauss and Adenauer] agreed, notwithstanding our mutual desire to continue normal and friendly relations with the Arab states, that the German–Israel relationship was of a special type with special meaning – a matter of *sui generis* ...I saw in this [military co-operation] not only financial and moral but also historical reparation. (Quoted in Vogel, 1969, p. 123)

According to Werner Knieper, who was responsible for carrying out the agreements on behalf of the German Ministry of Defence, the military relationship with Israel was always understood as an expression of the overall special relationship. Its justification, form, content and execution were all considered exceptional and Knieper believed that the special military relationship should be continued even after the Arabs protested (interview, 1975).[9]

THE MUTUAL AND SIMULTANEOUS NEED FOR MILITARY RELATIONS, 1957–65

Israel and the Federal Republic shared four motives for entering a special military relationship: morality, politics, security and economics. In addition, the Federal Republic was subject to the pressure of world opinion in general, and American opinion in particular. Finally, both countries were motivated by perceptions of need, which were consistent with the needs generating the Reparations Agreement.

ISRAEL

The most comprehensive and clear statement of Israel's perceived need for a military relationship with the Federal Republic was offered by David Ben-Gurion, Prime Minister and Defence Minister for most of the period 1957–65. In an address to the Knesset on July 1, 1959, just prior to his second resignation (due to the opposition of coalition members to a military relationship with the Federal Republic) (Brecher, 1972, pp. 415–18), Ben-Gurion compared divisions in Israel to the debates of January 1952: 'In the last few days', he said, 'there has been a repeat performance of the interesting and educational spectacle we witnessed seven years ago during the debate over the reparations agreement' (Ben-Gurion, 1959, p. 1). Ben-Gurion held the same ground in 1959 as he did in 1952, and so did his opponents, especially Herut, Mapam and Achdut Haavoda (Brecher, 1972, pp. 418–26). Again, the debate was between pragmatism and sentimentality (or morality, depending on the point of view), and again, the forces of pragmatism won, endorsing Ben-Gurion's policy towards the Federal Republic.

After 1955, the USSR became heavily involved in the Middle East, supplying arms and money to Israel's enemies. The Suez crisis had highlighted both the USSR's influence and the fragile quality of American support for Israel. From Ben-Gurion's perspective, the basic positions of the two superpowers had not changed by 1959: the USSR was interventionist on the other side and, despite the Lebanon landing the year before, the USA was neutral in the Middle East (Ben-Gurion, 1959, p. 12).

Israel had few political and military friends, which imposed additional burdens on an already strained economy. As in 1952, Israelis perceived economic growth and stability to be necessary for military security. Israel needed arms and, as Ben-Gurion saw it, should take them from wherever possible:

> The small State of Israel does not belong to an alliance or a bloc ... Membership in a bloc strengthens security, facilitates the acquisition of arms and lessens the expenditures for security purposes. However, we are isolated; we must bear the heavy and constantly growing burden of defence alone – and more than any other people we are dependent on friends. (Ben-Gurion, 1959, p. 13)

France already had indicated its friendship at Suez, and Ben-Gurion now looked to Germany. The Federal Republic could fulfil Israel's immediate need for arms, and could satisfy other short- and long-term needs. The Federal Republic, Ben-Gurion reasoned, would be a political friend, an economic partner, and an influential advocate of Israel's political, economic and military interests with other countries:

> Germany has developed as a factor of great significance in its region and this region also includes France. Germany needs France as much as France needs Germany ... Their cooperation in economic, political and defence matters is increasing constantly, which means in matters which could be decisive for our fate. Just as we are obliged to nurture relations with France, so we must with Italy and even more so with Germany, for its position and significance are even greater...all my Jewish feelings and instincts, my whole being as a Jew and man tell me: do what is right for Israel and its safety! When I say that Germany of today...is not the Germany of Hitler, I am referring not only to the new regime...but also to the geo-political transformation...in Western Europe and in the world ...Germany as a force hostile to Israel...also endangers the friendship of the other countries of Western Europe and might even have an undesirable influence on the United States and the other countries of America. [It] is a rising force ... Its attitude to us will have no small influence on the attitude of other countries that are allied with it.
>   In my profound conviction, the injunction bequeathed on us by the martyrs of the Holocaust is the rebuilding, the strengthening, the progress and the security of Israel. For that purpose we need friends...especially friends who are able and willing to equip the Israel Defence Forces in order to ensure our survival ...But if we regard Germany, or any other country, as Satan, we shall not receive arms. (Ben-Gurion, 1959, pp. 17–21)

Thus, Ben-Gurion emphasized, first, the need for friends, and secondly, the need for friends capable of ensuring Israel's survival. As in 1952, he contended that the State of Israel owed a moral obligation to the victims of the Holocaust, and it was Israel's moral duty to make Germany fulfil a moral obligation to the Jews' only homeland.[10]

Ben-Gurion's successor as Prime Minister and Minister of Defence, Levi Eshkol, shared his view when the military relationship was threatened in 1965: 'It is Germany's primary moral duty to make every possible contribution to the strengthening of Israel' (quoted in *Jerusalem Post*, February 16, 1965). The attitude of Ben-Gurion and Eshkol was not determined by their affection for Germany. Their bitterness about the events of the Holocaust was in no way diminished. But they argued pragmatically. Describing Franco-German relations, Ben-Gurion obviously had German-Israeli relations in mind: 'I cannot assume that France has forgotten what the Germany of the Kaiser and the Nazis did to her ... But the two countries are moving closer and closer... not because they love one another, but because they need each other. This is the basis for international friendship' (1959, p. 16). There can be no doubt that, by 1959, Israel needed Germany as much as in 1952.

Ben-Gurion's assessment of Germany's importance for a range of Israel's needs has been shared by both observers and participants of the relationship. Both Shimon Peres and Felix Shinnar, for example, have referred not only to Israel's motive for accepting German aid, but also for selling arms to Germany. Israel saw the sale of the Uzi machinegun to Germany as an opening to the whole NATO market, which had distinct economic advantages for Israel's armament industry and meant foreign currency (Shinnar, 1967, p. 139; Shinnar interviews, 1975; Deutschkron, 1970a, p. 112; Peres, 1970, p. 73). Ben-Gurion, Peres and Shinnar probably saw other advantages in selling arms to Germany, including creation of contacts between the military establishments that would in turn facilitate the sale or donation of German arms to Israel. Shinnar certainly saw the connection (interviews, 1975). Peres noted that the arms relationship had the potential of leading to diplomatic relations (Vogel, 1969, p. 127; Federal Ministry of Defence interview, 1975). Germany was to be Israel's window to the West, its provider as well as its harbinger. Germany, as a rapidly growing European power, was capable of providing such help, and in any case Israel had no such moral influence, on which it was so dependent, with anyone else.

THE FEDERAL REPUBLIC
The motives or needs of the Federal Republic in pursuing a military relationship with Israel have not been expressed as succinctly as Ben-Gurion described Israel's. Nevertheless Germany's rationale and motives are clear. Franz-Josef Strauss, in 1967, perhaps came closest to offering a comprehensive statement:

> In principle, Adenauer and I were agreed that where lives were concerned aid to Israel was more than a matter of obligatory reparation; it was of especial moral and political consequence to us all...millions

of Jews were murdered as a result of criminal German policy and with German weapons...the Jews of the world have found a new home and accomplished a marvellous task of reconstruction. Many threats have been uttered against this country and its people; threats from a hostile world that it will be conquered and its people wiped out. If therefore the Federal Republic of Germany can make a modest contribution to keeping the peace in the Middle East – a critical factor for us too – then this goes some way towards reparation in the very sphere in which Germany committed some of her worst crimes. (Quoted in Vogel, 1969, p. 124)

Strauss had in mind Germany's moral obligation for the survival of Israel but clearly he was persuaded, too, by political and security considerations relating to the interests of the Federal Republic.

In his initial contacts with the Israelis Strauss showed an interest in captured Soviet weapons from the Sinai campaign. Furnishing Israel with arms helped offset the Soviet threat in the Middle East, and a Middle Eastern military balance was in Germany's interest:

in the case of an Arab-Israeli conflict...there would be the danger of a confrontation between Russia and America...it seemed advisable to make some contribution towards preventing military action, apart from the inevitable border clashes. My aim was to ensure that military action could not be taken either by the Israelis...or by the Arabs. (ibid., p. 124)

As a result of Germany's military aid to Israel, Strauss says, the Federal Republic expected Israel to distinguish the new Germany from the old at the time of the Eichmann trial in 1961. Unlike others, Strauss does not say that a deliberate motive in the granting of aid was to gag Israel from reminding world opinion of Germany's past. His emphasis lay on German security and moral obligation.

There were also economic motives for Germany's military relationship with Israel. The Federal Republic bought Uzis, ammunition and mortars from Israel because the quality and the price were right (Vogel, 1969, p. 125).

The moral motive, the perceived obligation to ensure the survival of Israel because of the Holocaust, has been cited by other Germans involved in the administration and execution of the arms agreements. A typical official explanation, from a well-placed deputy, runs, 'We Germans could hardly stand by and let the Jews be murdered a second time' (Jaeger interview, 1975).[11] Even when officials saw morality as an unusual motive, they still contended that it dominated military relations between West Germany and Israel (Knieper interview, 1975; Federal Ministry of Defence interview, 1975).

Germans saw a moral motive, and Israelis accepted German sincerity.

Shimon Peres, for example, has indicated that morality was a driving force for Strauss: 'Although we talked about military affairs, the background was always political and moral' (*Der Spiegel*, February 24, 1965). Peres also attributed moral motives to Fritz Erler, an SPD deputy involved, and to Adenauer, who, Peres thought, was motivated by religious belief (1970, pp. 74–5). According to Arthur Olsen of the *New York Times*, the moral motive continued with Erhard: 'Chancellor Ludwig Erhard authorized the arms aid ...on the ground that West Germany has a moral obligation to contribute to the security of the Jewish state (*New York Times*, January 21, 1965). And Erhard in his statements to the Bundestag in February 1965 on the issue of the arms agreements, emphasized that on this, and other, questions Germany had been motivated by a sense of guilt: 'Nobody can dispute that we have made extraordinary contributions to Israel because of a deep moral commitment ...We owe nobody an explanation for our support for Israel's struggle with its existence ...We have always seen our contributions to Israel as a duty' (Deutscher Bundestag und Bundesrat, February 17, 1965, pp. 8103–5).

Peres saw the moral motive of Germans like Strauss and Adenauer complemented by a concern for politics and security. He describes how, in one of their first meetings, Strauss 'spoke with concern about Soviet penetration of the Middle East' (Peres, 1970, pp. 70-1). When Peres met with Adenauer in June 1962, the Chancellor also referred to Soviet influence in the world. Israel seemed to be conjured by German leaders as a Middle Eastern Berlin standing against communist expansion. In these terms Germany needed to aid Israel's military defence as a counterpart to Germany's own defence.

Others, including Ludger Westrick, who served as an aide to both Adenauer and Erhard, have echoed this perception of a German concern for its own security in fostering the special military relationship. Westrick put the case simply: 'We felt Israel was NATO's most reliable partner in the Middle East' (interview, 1975).[12]

Still another feature of Germany's political motivation has been observed by Israeli participants: because of its inability to accord Israel diplomatic relations, the Federal Republic compensated with military aid. Peres, Shinnar and Ben-Natan all have stressed that in place of diplomatic relations Israel received military aid (Peres, 1970, p. 68; Ben-Natan, 1974, p. 32; Shinnar interview, 1975).

None of the participants, neither Germans nor Israelis, has stressed the economic motive that Helga Haftendorn has underlined in her study of German military aid: granting military aid would encourage later military purchases from Germany. She does not indicate the source of her observations, but claims economic motives were important (1971, p. 22).

Finally, there was the question of Germany's image abroad.[13] In 1951 and 1952 Adenauer perceived the need for Germany to project an image of responsibility and democracy, if sovereignty was to be regained. Although Germany had acquired a large degree of independence by the mid-1950s, if a position of some importance in European and world affairs was to be assumed, then a favourable image would have to be maintained. Wherever possible, Germany would have to quell Israeli references to Germany's Nazi past. There is no evidence that the Federal Republic and Israel ever had any explicit *quid pro quo* on this question (for instance, Israeli silence for German arms), but there are indications that an implicit understanding of the requirements of each side did exist. For example, in March 1960 in his meeting with Ben-Gurion, Adenauer had been concerned about disquiet resulting from antisemitic activities in Germany at the end of 1959. According to Seelbach, sensitivity to the damage Israel could have inflicted on Germany's world image accounted for Adenauer's readiness to agree to military and economic aid (1970, p. 99).

Seelbach and others perceive a similar German need in 1961 at the time of the Eichmann trial (1970, p. 106; *Der Spiegel*, February 24, 1965; Deutschkron, 1970a, p. 139; Haftendorn, 1971, p. 22). The trial itself could not be avoided, but there was great potential for embarrassment. In February 1965 the editor of the German magazine *Der Stern* claimed that Strauss and Israeli representatives reached an agreement whereby Germany would supply arms to Israel in return for an Israeli guarantee that during the trial Hans Globke, one of Adenauer's closest aides, would not be summoned as a witness (*New York Times*, February 23, 1965; *Der Spiegel*, February 24, 1965). Globke was implicated during the trial (*Neue Zürcher Zeitung*, May 15, 1961). The Israeli mission in Cologne vigorously denied the allegation, but Strauss, as we have seen, suggested an indirect relationship, as has Peres:

> We met frequently and had discussion lasting...hours...we made no settlements concerning this matter; however...I endeavoured to explain to the Israelis, and to the Jews in the United States, the importance of the new relations between ourselves and Germany. Of course I also mentioned the action that Herr Strauss was taking to help Israel. (Peres, 1970, p. 127)

Peres's statement is hardly an admission of collusion or corruption of the trial. However, just before the Eichmann trial began Ben-Gurion distinguished between the new Germany and the one with which Eichmann identified (*Neue Zürcher Zeitung*, April 5, 1965). Of course, Ben-Gurion had been issuing such statements since 1957, for political reasons, but the timing in 1961 should not pass unnoticed. Globke was never called to testify.

There is no concrete evidence of an agreement between Israel and Germany. Israel already was receiving arms from Germany and did not need to be reminded that Germany could ill-afford a negative public image. Ben-Gurion, as a logical development of the policy adopted in 1951 towards Germany, probably would have distinguished between Nazi Germany and Adenauer's Germany on his own initiative.

Israeli silence was considered during discussions in Israel over Germany's desire to terminate the arms agreement in 1965. A Mapam deputy accused Peres of having made a deal to protect Germany's image in return for arms: 'The only way I can even begin to explain our German policy is by assuming that there must have been some deal: German arms shipments in return for our keeping quiet on the scientists.' Peres replied: 'I categorically deny that there ever was any such deal!' (*Jerusalem Post*, February 16, 1965). The scientists were German ex-Nazis participating in Egypt's development of bacteriological weapons to be used against Israel (see Chapter 7). It is sufficient for our purposes here to observe that Ben-Gurion had made little issue of the scientists' presence in Egypt in 1963, which caused a furor in Israel. His management of the problem was consistent again with the philosophy and policy he had adopted by 1952. Whether any explicit arrangement with the Federal Republic could account for this silence in 1963 is, therefore, moot.

Together with the allegations that Germany was endeavouring to impress world opinion in general are the assertions that Germany sought to satisfy the USA in particular. Such assertions come from both leftist observers of West German Middle East policy (who claim West Germany is extending US imperialism) and from more conservative and traditional analysts and participants. Neither side provides concrete evidence of US instigation of West German military aid to Israel. It does seem clear, however, that the initial contacts and the first agreement were with the explicit approval of the USA, and the second agreement was probably related to an American initiative.[14] Such US involvement is not surprising. The Federal Republic was a formal ally of the USA within NATO. The arms in question were often American, now obsolete, and there were strict rules about transfer of such obsolete weapons.[15] The USA still had rights and responsibilities for the Federal Republic resulting from the wartime agreements of the Allies.

For Germany, then, there were motivations for granting military aid to Israel that were notable politically and economically, and for German as well as Israeli security. These motives were also typical for the granting of aid to African countries. But the motive of moral obligation and the influence of perceived world opinion seemed to be unique for the relationship with Israel. For Israel, the political, security and economic needs were not unusual either. But again, the motive of morality was unique. And when non-aligned African countries went to market, they could shop at Soviet as well as German counters. Israel could not. Indeed, for a large segment of Israeli opinion, military arrangements with Germany were undesirable but necessary.

Germany, as one of the few countries to deal with Israel in military matters, gave Israel preferential treatment. On the receiving end, in the critical question of cost, Israel received better treatment from no one. From the German point of view, Israel was clearly a special case in military affairs. In military exchange Germany mostly gave and Israel mostly received, but the moral and political value of being permitted to give, along with the perception of Middle East partnership against the USSR were, as the Germans saw it, invaluable.

AN ONGOING MILITARY RELATIONSHIP?

Yitzhak Yisrael reports that, with the establishment of diplomatic relations in 1965, Israel no longer received arms supplies as it had under Adenauer (Yisrael, 1971, p. 332). Many observers share Yisrael's view that the military relationship indeed ended in 1965. Since that time, however, there have been indications of an ongoing military relationship.

As Yisrael notes, there was suspicion in 1965, with the exchange of ambassadors, that military relations were continuing. The first Israeli ambassador to Bonn, Asher Ben-Natan, had been director-general of the Israeli Ministry of Defence and had been involved in the first arms negotiations in the 1950s.[16] Angelika Bator, from Germany's New Left, is more specific in her assertion of a German-Israeli military relationship after 1965, characterizing it as part of a general relationship between two imperialist powers, Israel and the Federal Republic. In 1969, she says, Israel received from the Federal Republic a large number of Noratlas planes for which Israeli pilots were being trained in the Federal Republic. Bator reports that Israel obtained further military equipment from the Federal Republic in 1970, this time shipped through Belgium. In its 1968–9 and 1975 yearbooks the Stockholm International Peace Research Institute (SIPRI) also alludes to arms deliveries to Israel involving the Federal Republic: in 1968 France supplied twenty-five Fouga Magister trainers which were ex-Bundeswehr stock (1968–9, p. 230); in 1974 Germany supplied fifteen Dornier light transport planes (1975, p. 225). Arab sources also have commented on relations, suggesting that the Federal Republic increased its arms supplies to Israel after March 1966 (*Süddeutsche Zeitung*, June 16–18, 1967).

Citing Arab sources Bator maintains that a number of officers of the Israeli armed forces received training at Bundeswehr schools; others, she says, were trained in helicopter techniques (1970, p. 20). Helga Haftendorn also has doubted that military training ended in 1965 with the termination of arms supplies (1971, pp. 30–1).

Official German and Israeli views on the current military relationship are not entirely clear. From the early 1950s Germany and Israel exchanged technological, strategic and defence information; weapons deliveries were one feature of a 'going concern' (confidential interview, 1980). Until 1965 the training of armed forces and German purchases of military equipment from Israel were additional expressions of preference. Weapons deliveries do seem to have ceased, but relations in the other three defence areas may continue into the 1980s.

Guidelines set in 1965, with the end of arms shipments to Israel, were essentially reconfirmed in a 1971 Cabinet decision that forbade Germany from sending arms to 'areas of tension' (*Spannungsgebiete*), including the Middle East (Haftendorn, 1971, pp. 64–7, 75–88; Albrecht and Sommer, 1972, p. 66; *Die Zeit*, February 6, 1981; *New York Times*, March 26, 1981; *Der Spiegel*, April 27, 1981).[17] The conclusion of the Egyptian-Israeli Peace Treaty in March 1979 did not change this classification for the Middle East (Federal Ministry of Defence correspondence, 1980; State of Israel Ministry of Defence correspondence, 1980). Nevertheless, at least since 1975 the Israeli embassy staff in Bonn has included a military attaché who was entered in the embassy's diplomatic list as a political attaché until the spring of 1976. The Israelis called him a 'purchasing officer'. Due to Germany's restrictions, purchases appear limited to software or borderline military goods that are permitted under other guidelines.[18]

Enforcement of legislation restricting the export of defence-related goods, and of companion legislation limiting the export of weapons of war depends on governmental control and co-ordination mechanisms whose 'extent of effectiveness', according to a high-ranking official involved in German-Israeli relations, 'are overestimated' (confidential interview, 1980). Nevertheless, the furor precipitated by revelation of German arms supplies to Israel until 1965, make it likely that any relations now derive from the Foreign Trade Act rather than the Act for the Control of Weapons of War or the guidelines on 'areas of tension' (confidential interview, 1980; *Der Spiegel*, May 11, 1981).

Evidence on the training of armed forces is incomplete. Israel's Ministry of Defence states categorically that joint training has been discontinued since 1965 (correspondence, 1980), but the ministry is disinclined generally to discuss any military matters. The Germans are less emphatic: 'With Israel there is contact in the areas of weapons technology and support for military training.' However, the relationship is not deemed unusual, for it occurs 'with every state that considers itself part of and committed to the Western world' (Federal Ministry of Defence correspondence, 1980). 'Support for military training' can be construed several ways, including the normal activities of military attachés, which Germany and Israel exchanged in the first half of 1976. Both sides now say the exchange of military attachés testifies to the 'normalization' of relations. 'Normal' activities of a military attaché include participation in manoeuvres, tours and visits with the host's armed forces, and reporting on the military situation in the area to one's own Ministry of Defence and Foreign Office (Federal Ministry of Defence correspondence, 1976, 1980; State of Israel Ministry of Defence correspondence, 1976, 1980). A written reply from the German Foreign Office to a question by an SPD deputy during the controversial consideration of arms sales to Saudi Arabia in the spring of 1981 suggest that German-Israeli relations go beyond the normal activity of military attachés. According to *Der Spiegel* of May 11, 1981, the German government confirmed German military training for Israeli officers and mechanics.

'Normal' military relations, according to both Ministries of Defence, refer also to mutual commerce in military equipment when permitted by law. Germany probably no longer supplies Israel, but it does still purchase equipment (*Deutschland-Berichte*, October 1978; *International Defense Review*, 1979) and 'on the basis of ministerial directives, where possible the agencies of the Bundeswehr place orders in Israel' (confidential interview, 1980). Moreover, 'The exchange of information on technological, "strategic" and defence questions never has been broken' (confidential interview, 1980).[19]

The extent of today's special military relationship is uncertain. Training seems to extend beyond the regular activities of military attachés, and the special relationship clearly exists in German purchases and in information exchanges. Officials on both sides have hinted at the continued preference of ties since 1965. Officials in the Israeli Ministry of Defence have noted that

> the special relationship of Israel and Germany is conducted at many levels. Whether with reference to the military or any other special relationship, these matters are confidential and very delicate. We do not want to embarrass ourselves or West Germany. It is a matter of integrity. (State of Israel Ministry of Defence confidential interview, 1975)

As recently as 1981 spokesmen for the Israeli defence industry called Germany their 'best partner after the United States' (*Der Spiegel*, May 11, 1981).[20] German officials also suggest a special relationship: 'As the occasion offers, technical qualifications and moral impetus oppose tenaciously political changes of course and frequently remove [military] projects from control because of their long-term nature, the appearance of normalcy, or secrecy' (confidential interview, 1980). The intensity and diversity of the special military relationship of the late 1950s and early 1960s have waned, but a special relationship involving preference and based on both morality and pragmatism appears still to exist.

NOTES: CHAPTER 5

1 See, for example, the semi-fictional treatment of the arms deals and the attendant political issues by Forsyth (1972). Erhard compared the arms deals to a detective novel (interview, 1975).

2 Until the 1970s Germany traded little in arms and virtually not at all with Israel (Haftendorn, 1971, ch. 5, pp. 122–5; SIPRI, 1971, p. 296). In the 1970s German arms trade increased as the needs of the Bundeswehr were easily met and surplus potential, therefore, existed. On German arms trade and the efforts of the arms lobby to change Germany's restrictive export policy, see Haftendorn (1971, pp. 64–88); Albrecht (1972); SIPRI yearbooks (1972, 1973, 1974, 1975, 1976, 1977, 1978, 1979, 1980); *Christian Science Monitor* (June 22 and September 22, 1976); *Washington Post* (December 2, 1977); *International Defense Review* (1978); *The Economist* (January 13, 1979); *Die Zeit* (February 6 and February 20, 1981); *New York Times* (March 26, 1981). Most of the trade had been with Latin America and Africa. In 1978 Germany was the sixth arms exporter, accounting for 2 per cent of the world total (SIPRI, 1979, p. 175). For the period 1970–9, Germany ranked seventh among major arms-exporting countries (SIPRI, 1980, p. 79). The debate over arms export policy surfaced again in the spring of 1981 over the question of tanks to Saudi Arabia (see Chapter 8).

3 For newspaper reports of the chain of events comprising the military relationship, see *New York Times*, *Le Monde*, *Die Welt*, *Neue Zürcher Zeitung*, *Frankfurter Allgemeine Zeitung*, *Frankfurter Rundschau*, *Süddeutsche Zeitung* and *Jerusalem Post* for the months of December 1957, June 1963, October 1964, February and March 1965 and February 1967. *Der Spiegel* is also useful, particularly the editions of June 24, 1959, and February 3 and February 24, 1965. For different interpretations of key events, see Rathmann (1966); Shinnar (1967); Vogel (1969); Peres (1970); Deutschkron (1970a); Seelbach (1970): Ben-Gurion (1971); Haftendorn (1971); SIPRI (1971); Yisrael (1971); Albrecht and Sommer (1972); Brecher (1972, 1975); Deligdisch (1974); Abediseid (1976). The interview with Knieper (1975) was also helpful for details of the relationship.

The relationship in the period 1957–65 can be divided into nineteen separate events falling into four main areas: initial contacts and agreements on small deliveries; first major agreement; second major agreement; and disclosure.

4 Figures for projected military aid in 1958–65 vary widely from $62 million (*Die Welt*, October 27, 1964, February 20 and March 2, 1965; *Neue Zürcher Zeitung*, October 28 and November 1, 1964; *Frankfurter Allgemeine Zeitung*, February 20, 1965; *Die Zeit*, November 16, 1973) to $80 million (*Jerusalem Post*, February 12, 14, 17 and 20, 1965; *Der Spiegel*, February 3, 10 and 24, 1965) to $270–285 million (Rathmann, 1966, pp. 110–11). Estimates of actual aid differ, too: $37·5–50 million (Haftendorn, 1971, pp. 26–7, 110–11, 130), $45 million (West German government, quoted in Vogel, 1969, p. 299), $50–62 million (*Der Spiegel*, February 3 and February 24, 1965; German newspapers as in projected; Seelbach, 1970, p. 107), $60–64 million (SIPRI, 1971, pp. 310–11), $125 million (Knieper interview, 1975), $250 million (Brecher, 1975, p. 103) and $254–266 million (Rathmann, 1966, pp. 110–11). The dollar–mark conversion used is 1:4.

5 Sources differ with respect to both the nature of military weapons and the amounts. The following items were mentioned by at least one source: ammunition, spare parts, grenades, machineguns, parachutes, communications equipment, trucks and ambulances, boats, submarines, airplanes (fighters, monoplanes, transport planes and trainers), anti-aircraft equipment, helicopters, tanks, anti-tank rockets, howitzers and military training.

6 There were, in fact, two other countries besides Israel and African nations that received military aid from Germany at the time, and Jordan, a Middle Eastern country, was one. The amount it received, however, was minimal (1·7 million DM), and of a paramilitary nature as with the other recipient, India (Haftendorn, 1971, pp. 110–11).

7 Legality was questioned because of the general ignorance of the Bundestag on the question of arms to Israel. On the constitutionality of the agreements, see Müller (1965). He points out that the issue was whether the secrecy involved violated art. 59, para. 2 of the Basic Law which stipulated that 'political treaties' required parliamentary approval in the form of a law. Knieper denies absolute secrecy: 'We had an

140 *Operation*

  agreement not to speak about it' (interview, 1975). In fact, select members of the Bundestag gradually were apprised of the situation. In June 1962 a six-man committee (two deputies from each party) was formed; it was expanded in June 1964 to a nine-man committee. Details of this arrangement were revealed in February 1965 by Erhard in the Bundestag debate over arms to Israel (Deutscher Bundestag und Bundesrat, February 17, 1965, pp. 8103–5).
8 In June 1963 the Federal government disclosed its military aid relationship with the African countries (*Die Welt*, June 11, 1963; *Le Monde*, June 14, 1963). Deutschkron (1970a, p. 273) and Haftendorn (1971, p. 67) note that Israel was excluded from the list of countries disclosed, despite media pressure on the German government to confirm the existence of the relationship. Disclosure did not halt aid to African states, but declaration did involve risk that the Federal government was not prepared to take in the case of Israel.
9 The 'special' view was shared by German Defence Ministry officials and by Bundestag deputies Richard Jaeger (CSU) and Werner Kliesing (CDU), members of the parliamentary oversight committee that had followed the arms arrangement with Israel since the middle of 1962 (interviews, 1975).
10 On Germany's moral responsibility for supplying arms, see the interview with Ben-Gurion in *Der Spiegel* (March 31, 1965). In December 1959 he had suggested that Israel had no other possible supplier of arms than the Federal Republic (Deutschkron, 1970a, p. 110).
11 In addition to being a member of the parliamentary oversight committee, Jaeger was chairman of the parliamentary Defence Committee at the time. Jaeger's view was confirmed by Knieper (interview, 1975); Erich Mende, head of the parliamentary party of the FDP at the time of the arms deals with Israel (interview, 1975); Kliesing, CDU senior deputy and a member of the oversight committee (interview, 1975); Dr Hohmann, chief aide to Erhard during the latter's chancellorship (interview, 1975); and Kurt Birrenbach, CDU deputy and negotiator of the termination of arms shipments to Israel and the establishment of diplomatic relations (interview, 1975).
12 The political-security argument for Germany's military relationship with Israel has been outlined in several places: Shinnar (1967, p. 141); Haftendorn (1971, pp. 10, 22); and Deligdisch (1974, pp. 94–5).
13 Strauss said on this issue: 'I was of the opinion that effective cooperation between the Federal Republic of Germany and Israel would be a significant contribution towards the task of leaving the past behind us. I meant this in the sense, not only of the reacceptance of Germany in the world, but acceptance ... as a state with equal rights in the field of present-day world politics' (quoted in Vogel, 1969, p. 123).
14 For leftist analyses, see Coburger (1964, pp. 189–206); Asad (1966, pp. 3–5, 43–5); Rathmann (1966, pp. 110–13); Abdel Hadi, *et al.* (1973, pp. 10, 25, 27, 51, 55); Lewan (1975, pp. 56–60). For other analyses, see Deutschkron (1970a, pp. 272–3); Peres (1970, pp. 76, 85); Seelbach (1970, p. 102); Haftendorn (1971, pp. 63, 72); SIPRI (1971, p. 295); Deligdisch (1974, p. 94). Newspapers in 1965 also referred to US involvement in differing degrees: *New York Times* (February 1 and 20, 1965); *Die Welt* (February 1, 20 and 22, 1965); *Der Spiegel* (February 3, 1965).
  On February 17, 1965 a State Department spokesman 'acknowledged that the U.S. had been consulted in advance about the arms deal and had given its approval for the transfer of U.S.-made tanks from West Germany to Israel' (*New York Times*, February 18, 1965). Adenauer had said there were discussions over arms 'at the wish of a friendly power', presumably the USA (*Die Welt*, February 17, 1965; *Neue Zürcher Zeitung*, February 18, 1965). A German government spokesman later denied that Germany had shipped arms to Israel at American instigation (*Die Welt*, February 27, 1965), but did not contradict Erhard's statement of February 17 to the Bundestag, 'we found ourselves in agreement with our allies' (Deutscher Bundestag und Bundesrat, February 17, 1965, pp. 8103–5).
15 The USA sold to Germany in May 1962 its right to reclaim equipment that had been given under the grant aid programme of 1954–9; any transfers from Germany

prior to 1962 would have required US approval; subsequently, US approval was still required for major items such as tanks (SIPRI, 1971, pp. 301–2).
16 For the exchange of ambassadors, see Deutschkron (1970a, pp. 333–43); Yisrael (1971, pp. 320–30).
17 According to Haftendorn, the principle of 'areas of tension' was formulated to prevent discrimination against Israel alone (1971, p. 75).
18 Article 5 of the Foreign Trade Ordinance of September 1961, requires approval from the government for the export of items relating to three lists (arms, ammunition and armaments material; nuclear energy; and other goods of strategic significance). If these items relate to weapons of war, then approval is declined in general. The production, ownership and export of weapons of war are regulated by the Control of Weapons of War Act of April 1961. These laws prevent the export of arms or military equipment that could impair Germany's friendly relations, disturb international peace, or contribute to a military attack. For details of the legislation, see Haftendorn (1971, pp. 42–3); SIPRI (1971, pp. 299–301).
19 Before meeting with the author, officials in the Federal Ministry of Defence in Bonn sought clearance from Israeli embassy personnel, indicating the extent of information exchange.
20 For details of US military aid to Israel, see the SIPRI yearbooks from 1968–9 on, and Congressional Quarterly (1979, pp. 45–53). On the closeness of ties between Israel and the USA in the military sphere, see the articles by Wolf Blitzer, 'Comrades and arms' (1979), and Hirsh Goodman, 'Friends in need' (1980).

6
Exchanges in Science, Technology and Youth

> If I may resort to the expression 'special relations', then they do in fact play a role in promoting international youth exchange ... particular stress must be laid on the people with whom we had 'very special relations' in the past. A symbiosis such as was very rare in the history of Jewry in Europe ... that is the background which plays a great role for the German-Israeli youth exchange ... From the standpoint of political instruction we must say that we attach very great importance to this youth exchange. (Fichtner, 1977)
>
> In the history of German-Israeli relations scientific contacts have occupied a special position. (Popp, 1972)

The aim of a foreign cultural policy, according to the German Foreign Office, 'should be to advance and to strengthen cultural, scientific and social contacts with other peoples, with their institutions, special groups and individuals' (Auswärtiges Amt, 1970, p. 6).[1] The prominent features of culture, especially language, literature and music, have been central to a great antagonism between the German and Israeli peoples. Despite these difficulties, however, the remaining aspects of culture, knowledge and wisdom of the two nations, have contributed to important government programmes in the special relationship; those arrangements in science, technology and youth exchange constitute the essential elements of bilateral cultural exchange between West Germany and Israel.

SCIENCE AND TECHNOLOGY

Both Israel and the Federal Republic of Germany consider programmes in science and technology among the strongest features of their bilateral relations.[2] Relations began essentially in 1959, first with a March 6 meeting between Dr Josef Cohn (former personal secretary to Chaim

Weizmann and since the 1950s the Weizmann Institute's 'ambassador') and Konrad Adenauer, and then with the December visit to the Weizmann Institute of the German scientists Otto Hahn, Wolfgang Gentner and Feodor Lynen.[3] These contacts were followed immediately by a German government grant of 3 million marks to the Weizmann Institute, formalized by Adenauer in his March 1960 meeting with David Ben-Gurion (Cohn interview, 1980); four years later a contract was signed between the Weizmann Institute and the Minerva Foundation (a subsidiary of the Max Planck Society) (Popp, 1972).

Minerva disbursed more than 37 million marks in the period 1963–72 for basic research at the Weizmann Institute and sponsored through 1977 70 million marks of co-operative German-Israeli scientific work (*Max-Planck-Gesellschaft*, 1979). These funds were donated by the Federal Ministry for Education and Science (after December 1972, the Federal Ministry for Research and Technology), making Minerva primarily a conduit for German government monies supporting German-Israeli relations in science and technology.

Although Minerva is a German organization, the research it funds is chosen by a joint committee of some thirty Germans and Israelis. And apart from Minerva, the Federal Ministry for Research and Technology has paid for the construction of new facilities, the purchase of equipment and for educational development. In December 1975, for example, the Federal government announced a 700,000 mark gift to the Weizmann Institute for the Duckwitz chair of cancer research.

Minerva's student exchanges were organized and financed until 1973 by the Volkswagen Foundation, one of several private German organizations funding scientific research in Israel (*Deutschland-Berichte*, May 1974). After 1973, the Ministry for Research and Technology assumed the financial responsibility for the stipend programme, extended it beyond the Weizmann Institute and increased the annual commitment from 500,000 marks to 1 million marks; the Volkswagen Foundation meanwhile continued its own scholarship and research programmes in Israel (*Deutschland-Berichte*, 1977). The net exchange during the first ten years favoured German scientists visiting Israel, but since then more Israelis have gone to research institutes in the Federal Republic (*Max-Planck-Gesellschaft*, 1979).

German-Israeli co-operation no longer is concentrated exclusively at the Weizmann Institute. A May 1970 agreement between Israel's National Council for Research and Development (NCRD) and the German Research Foundation provided for annual joint conferences in Germany or Israel and for research in Israel to be conducted by some fifteen senior German scientists, largely chosen by Israelis (NCRD, 1977). According to a second agreement with the NCRD, concluded in 1973, the Ministry for Research and Technology funds applied research in projects preselected by Israel. Unlike the basic research at the Weizmann Institute,[4] these projects include desalination and water purification, new forms of energy, medical technology, information and documentation systems, computer science and applied cancer research. Research areas of common interest are co-ordinated by a German-Israeli Commitee for Scientific and Technological Co-operation comprised of official representatives of the respective government agencies.

The Federal Republic's 'normal' relationships for science and technology, as with France and the USA, involve joint co-ordination, exchanges of information and joint funding (usually in equivalent sums). Governments control the purse. The Minerva programmes, by contrast, are not controlled exclusively by governmental personnel and even non-Germans join in their supervision. The joint NCRD–Ministry for Research and Technology programmes were planned as 'normal', but the Yom Kippur War made the Israeli financial contribution impossible. Germany therefore has carried the entire cash commitment, with Israel writing off 20 per cent of overall programme costs as institutional overhead.

These relations with Israel have been recognized by both German officials and scientists as special. Professor Heinz Stab, as the new German chairman of the Minerva Committee, noted in November 1978 closer co-operation between German and Israeli institutes of higher learning than Germany enjoys with most West European neighbours (*Max-Planck-Gesellschaft*, 1979). Bundestag President Karl Carstens in 1978 called the ties between German and Israeli scientists a model of understanding in Europe, adding that the Bundestag always held a special interest in relations between the Weizmann Institute and German research institutes (*Deutschland-Berichte*, January 1979). In March 1980 Minister for Research and Technology Volker Hauff renewed the partnership during a visit to Israel with substantial donations to the Weizmann Institute for equipment and an Einstein Centre for theoretical mathematics (*Deutschland-Berichte*, April 1980).

During 1960–75 Israel probably received 84–87 million marks for science and technology from the Federal Republic (Table 6.1). Since 1975 Germany has provided 13–14 million marks per year (6 million marks to the Weizmann Institute, 1 million marks for the fellowship programme and 6–7 million marks for the applied research programme) (Federal Ministry for Research and Technology interview, 1979). The statistical evidence is not available, but countries eligible for unilateral payments from the Federal Republic for science and technology certainly have not received comparable support.

The relations are also unusual for Israel. The Weizmann Institute's president has referred to the 'unique collaborative effort with the Minerva Foundation' (Weizmann Institute, 1979) and according to Josef Cohn, 'without money from Germany, the whole budget of the Weizmann Institute would have collapsed' (interview, 1980).

Israel's scientific relations with the USA provide a useful benchmark for measuring the German ties. The USA has been involved with the

Table 6.1 *Federal German Expenditure for Scientific and Technological Relations with Israel, 1960–80*

Year	Amount (Million DM)
1960	3·0
1961–3	8·9
1964	3·5
1965–6	10·2
1967	4·0
1968	4·0
1969–71	10·5
1972	5·0
1973	10·0–11·0
1974	12·0–13·0
1975	12·7–13·7
1976	13·0–14·0
1977	13·0–14·0
1978	13·0–14·0
1979	13·0–14·0
1980	13·0–14·0
1960–80	148·8–156·8*

*Does not include annual amounts devoted to Israel by organizations such as the German Academic Exchange, a private agency funded mainly from public sources on the federal and state level, including the Federal Foreign Office.

Sources: Vogel, 1969, p. 265; Popp, 1972; Federal Ministry for Research and Technology interviews, 1975, 1979.

Weizmann Institute since its founding. Scientists have been exchanged with the National Institutes of Health; the Agency for International Development has made grants to the Weizmann Institute's Feinberg Graduate School (chartered by the New York Board of Regents), yet in the last five years of the 1970s US government contributions to research at the Weizmann Institute averaged only $2 million per annum, approximately one-third of the German government's support (Hill correspondence, 1980).

A further indication of Germany's special role in Israel's science and technology may be found in a pair of 1977 NCRD publications. One treats relations with the Federal Republic, and the other relations with the rest of Europe. It is not surprising, therefore, that Israel assigns a science attaché to its embassy in Bonn.

MOTIVES AND ADVANTAGES FOR GERMANY AND FOR ISRAEL

One of the key elements in Israel's potential for self-reliance is an extraordinary capacity in science and technology. But the advancement of science and technology is expensive, and Israel needs money. Thus, again, economic necessity has driven Israel's scientific and technological relationship with the Federal Republic as it has driven other features of the special relationship. From the beginning Israel saw practical and mutual advantages (Cohn interview, 1980), a point stressed today by the NCRD. Germany, as one of the science giants in Europe, proffers not only its own benefits, but also acts as a conduit for Israel's relations in science and technology with other European countries and inter-European institutions (NCRD, 1977). Yet as with other fields of common endeavour, there are other motivations for Israel. Like Israel, Germany has a strong tradition of scientific talent and success, such that there are academic or professional reasons for close association with the Federal Republic. Moreover, until 1933 Jews and Germans were part of a common scientific tradition in Germany (Nachmansohn, 1979); for some, co-operation with the Federal Republic has been part of a natural tendency to return to positive roots (*Max-Planck-Gesellschaft*, 1980).

The same desire for a return to a natural co-operation also has been attributed to the Federal Republic. Some Israeli officials have suggested that this special co-operation is a form of restitution like the other forms of German restitution, the Federal Republic trying to make good something that the Nazis destroyed. German officials have agreed with this view; the apparent altruism of some of the arrangements, especially with the Weizmann Institute, they attribute to a sense of guilt and moral obligation. At the same time they, too, refer to the natural affinity of Germans and Jews in scientific co-operation and allude to the close personal friendships that abound now between German and Israeli scientists (Popp, 1972; Scheel and Carstens speeches, *Deutschland-Berichte*, January 1979).

Of course, there are scientific and academic advantages for the Federal Republic from the results of Israeli research, most keenly felt with the new expanded relations which, according to one German official, would have occurred irrespective of Germany's past because of the extraordinary capability Israel had to offer. Volker Hauff has emphasized Israel's intellectual advantages for Germany and its geographical and climatic characteristics that offer Germany research opportunities closed to it in Europe (*Deutschland-Berichte*, January 1979). There can be no doubt, however, that the past helped propel forward developments with Israel. The 'great momentum' of relations described by the NCRD in 1977 continues into the 1980s. According to former German President Walter Scheel, the ties in science and technology have formed a crucial element in the history of German-Israeli relations in general (*Deutschland-Berichte*, January 1979).

YOUTH EXCHANGE

Unlike science and technology, youth exchange is an area where the Federal Republic has had relations with other countries comparable to those with Israel. But as with science and technology, Israel has been accorded a special place even in these programmes. And like science and technology, officials of high rank in both countries have considered youth exchanges an expression of the special relationship between Germany and Israel (for example, Heinz Westphal, former state secretary in the Federal ministry for Youth, Family and Health; Felix Shinnar interviews, 1975).

As we shall see, youth exchanges mean more to the Germans than to Israel. Indeed, Israel has been reluctant about most cultural contact despite German interest. Youth exchange is, in fact, the only area in which positive cultural relations, outside science and technology, are well developed.

The development of relations between Israel and the Federal Republic in youth exchange falls into three periods.[5] Private contacts without German government funding had started at the end of the 1950s, but the first period really began in 1960 when the Federal government, through the Ministry for Youth, Family and Health, committed funds from the Youth Plan to exchanges with Israel. Thereafter, the Federal government has made serious and consistent efforts to promote youth exchange with Israel.

The attitude of the Israeli government in the 1960s was generally negative. The Knesset Resolution on Cultural Relations with the Federal Republic of December 1961 approved visits of young Germans to Israel, so that they might learn about the new state and its achievements, but nothing was said about young Israelis visiting Germany. Education of Israelis in the Federal Republic was frowned upon and it was clear there would be no government support for contact between the youth of the two countries (Ott, 1972). The number of programmes and the number of young Germans going to Israel increased, but very few young Israelis visited the Federal Republic. There were no formal bilateral consultations between Israeli and German representatives in this period, and Israelis who did visit the Federal Republic were sponsored locally, especially through the Israeli Municipalities Association.

Bilateral annual consultations through a Mixed Commission of Experts began in 1969. The main institutional parties to the talks were the Federal Ministry for Youth, Family and Health and, at first, the Israeli Municipalities Association; the delegates were individuals actively involved in the planning and execution of the youth exchanges, whether youth leaders or politicians. The consultations offered potential for a 'better platform for the planning and realization of common youth programmes in both of the countries' (Ott, 1972).

The Israeli government now became involved. At the end of 1971 the Education and Home Affairs Committee of the Knesset was assigned the task of reviewing German-Israeli youth exchange. The committee stressed the importance of the exchange and recommended the creation of an interministerial commission, which was established by the Minister for Education and Culture at the beginning of 1972 under the chairmanship of the Deputy Minister for Education and Culture; at his invitation

German-Israeli governmental talks on youth exchange, which 'documented the willingness of the Israeli government for co-participation and co-responsibility in the planning and execution of German-Israeli youth exchange' (Ott, 1972), took place in Israel in April 1972.

The Knesset committee also recommended the transfer of responsibility for implementation of youth exchange from the Municipalities Association to a special body. Subsequently, in 1973 the Public Council for Youth and Young Adult Exchange with Other Countries was established, entrusted by the government to deal with the whole question of youth exchange. The Secretariat of the Public Council was housed in the Israeli Ministry for Education and Culture, and it has become the chief partner to the Federal Ministry for Youth, Family and Health in the annual bilateral consultations of the Mixed Commission. Since the inception of the bilateral consultations and direct involvement of the Israeli government, the number of programmes and participants has grown steadily.

The German-Israeli Mixed Commission met in Berlin in November 1974 to work out joint regulations for the implementation and promotion of youth exchange. Otto Fichtner, ministerial director in the Federal Ministry for Youth, Family and Health, who headed the German delegation, saw the meeting as 'an important stage in the development of our common relations; [the joint regulations] underline the close and friendly co-operation which exists with our Israeli partner' (1977). The directives refer to the aims of youth exchange, the type of programme desired, the nature of participants, and the division of financial and administrative responsibility; they went into effect in January 1975.

From the beginning youth exchange between West Germany and Israel has been unusual and special. A formal cultural agreement between two countries is normal for most German youth exchanges, but there is still no such agreement with Israel. The German-Israeli Mixed Commission is the largest one Germany has with any exchange partner, and whereas the head of the German delegation to the mixed commissions is normally at the senior civil servant level, until 1979 the head of the Department of Youth in the Federal ministry personally led the German delegation with Israel (Federal Ministry for Youth, Family and Health correspondence, 1980). In addition to the normal funding procedures to sponsor youth exchanges,[6] Germany has provided a third and unique procedure available only for Israel, a special contribution of approximately 500,000 marks per annum from the Land Nordrhein-Westfalen established primarily by the Land's former Minister-President Heinz Kühn. Moreover, particular effort is made in Germany with the selection of participants and of the programme. In the view of former Minister for Youth, Family and Health, Bruno Heck, there has been a clear qualitative difference in the programmes with Israel compared to other countries (interview, 1975).

After the Franco-German exchanges, which are in a category by themselves with their own institutional base (the Franco-German Youth Office),[7] exchanges with Israel have been considered by past (Westphal and Bierhoff interviews, 1975) and present German officials in the Ministry for Youth, Family and Health (correspondence, 1980) to be the most important. Germany has youth exchange programmes with a variety of countries on most continents, but the emphasis (in terms of financing and the number of programmes) has been with France, Israel, Western Europe and Eastern Europe. Of the total expenditure on international youth questions during 1970–8, Israel received 15·3 per cent (Table 6.2). Although the number of youths involved remains small as a percentage of the total, the scale of financial commitment, compared to programmes with other countries, is considerable. If we look at comparable years (1970, 1971, 1972, 1974, 1975 and 1976) across Tables 6.2–6.4, we notice that in each the percentage of funds spent on programmes with Israel is much higher than the percentages of Israelis or Germans involved in youth exchange programmes. Moreover, Israel ranks among the top few in number of programmes and even number of participants after disaggregating Western and Eastern Europe. The two countries have not stinted financially to make visits successful, nor have they limited the number of programmes for small numbers of participants.

Although the Franco-German Youth Plan is atypical in its extent (see Tables 6.2–6.4), the way it is financed is normal for youth exchanges: Germany and France share the burden equally. Another method adopted in Germany's international youth exchanges is that the country sending young people assumes travel costs to and from the Federal Republic,

Table 6.2 *Federal Government Expenditure on Youth Exchange with Israel Compared to Total Expenditure on International Youth Activities and to Expenditure via the Franco-German Youth Office, 1970–8*

Thousand DM	1970	1971	1972	1973	1974	1975	1976	1977	1978
Total expenditure*	14,380	14,380	16,330	16,950	17,610	17,553	14,610	15,822	16,243
Expenditure for Israel†	2,050	2,350	3,100	3,200	2,500	2,000	2,160	2,267	2,447
Israel as percentage of total	14·3	16·3	19·0	18·9	14·2	11·4	14·8	14·3	15·1
Expenditure for France	17,400	17,552	16,875	14,874	13,688	13,221	13,890	13.036	13,911

*Excludes amounts for Franco-German Youth Office.
†Includes amounts via Mixed Commission and via Länder and youth organizations.
Sources: Federal Ministry for Youth, Family and Health interviews, 1975, and correspondence, 1980; *Deutschland-Berichte*, February 1972, May 1973; Franco-German Youth Office correspondence, 1980.

Table 6.3 *Israelis Participating in Youth Programmes in the Federal Republic Compared to Participants from Other Areas, 1970–6*

	1970	1971	1972	1974	1975	1976
Total foreign participation in programmes in Germany*	22,503	22,510	27,083	24,061	24,809	22,687
Israel	1,041	1,350	972	1,149	1,311	1,468
Israel as percentage of total	4·6	6·0	3·6	4·8	5·3	6·5
Western Europe	17,531	16,927	21,334	11,199	14,028	10,677
Western Europe as percentage of total	77·9	75·2	78·8	46·5	56·5	47·1
Eastern Europe	1,394	1,723	1,732	1,455	1,171	921
Eastern Europe as percentage of total	6·2	7·7	6·4	6·0	4·7	4·1
North America	1,112	809	883	722	—	—
North America as percentage of total	4·9	3·6	3·3	3·0	—	—
Latin America	210	213	308	29	59	52
Latin America as percentage of total	0·9	0·9	1·1	0·1	0·2	0·2
Africa	561	502	451	8	190	53
Africa as percentage of total	2·5	2·2	1·7	0·03	0·8	0·2
Asia (excluding Israel)	650	975	1,382	1,220	1,131	921
Asia as percentage of total	2·9	4·3	5·1	5·0	4·6	4·1
Arab World†	—	—	—	302	322	651
Arab World as percentage of total	—	—	—	1·3	1·3	2·9
Other areas	4	11	21	—	587	627
Other areas as percentage of total	0·02	0·05	0·08	—	2·4	2·8
France	83,785	79,607	77,937	49,737	48,612	46,825

*Excludes numbers for French youth participating via the Franco-German Youth Office.
†Includes North Africa; programmes began with consistency only in 1974.
Note: Figures not available for 1973 or 1977, 1978 and 1979.
Sources: Federal Statistical Office, correspondence, 1976; Federal Ministry for Youth, Family and Health correspondence, 1980; Franco-German Youth Office correspondence, 1980.

while the Federal Republic pays for the stay. Neither of these 'normal' procedures applies in the case of Israel. There are two categories of participants, one which comprises youth leaders, youth workers and experts in youth affairs, and one which comprises youths from the age of 16, whether young workers, pupils, or students. The 1979 funding provisions of the Federal government for both categories are offered in

Table 6.4 *Germans Participating in Youth Exchanges in Israel Compared to German Participants Elsewhere, 1970–6*

	1970	1971	1972	1974	1975	1976
Total German participation in programmes abroad*	45,749	46,047	47,136	42,936	39,170	33,180
Israel	2,952	3,879	4,224	3,139	3,473	2,598
Israel as percentage of total	6·4	8·4	9·0	7·3	8·9	7·8
Western Europe	30,130	29,213	29,302	28,931	26,610	22,608
Western Europe as percentage of total	65·9	63·4	62·2	67·4	67·9	68·1
Eastern Europe	10,944	11,343	11,135	7,567	6,389	5,124
Eastern Europe as percentage of total	23·9	24·6	23·6	17·6	16·3	15·4
North America	554	434	801	1,381	726	1,226
North America as percentage of total	1·2	0·9	1·7	3·2	1·9	3·7
Latin America	17	59	38	166	107	47
Latin America as percentage of total	0·04	0·1	0·08	0·4	0·3	0·1
Africa	835	486	1,031	442	416	390
Africa as percentage of total	1·8	1·1	2·2	1·0	1·1	1·2
Asia (excluding Israel)	317	633	605	597	583	494
Asia as percentage of total	0·7	1·4	1·3	1·4	1·5	1·5
Arab World†	—	—	—	582	783	643
Arab World as percentage of total	—	—	—	1·4	2·0	1·9
Other areas	—	—	—	131	56	50
Other areas as percentage of total	—	—	—	0·3	0·1	0·2
France	112,567	110,348	99,544	63,262	54,717	54,137

*Excludes numbers for German youth participating via the Franco-German Youth Office.
†Includes North Africa; programmes began with consistency only in 1974.
Note: Figures not available for 1973 or 1977, 1978 and 1979.
Sources: As Table 6.3.

Table 6.5; they indicate that the Federal government has been assuming the lion's share of financial responsibility whether the events occur in Israel or in the Federal Republic. Because of the amounts and numbers involved and the procedures employed, German officials think a special effort has been made with respect to Israel: 'In line with the special nature of the youth contacts with Israel the Federal Government has not only provided considerable funding, but also has accorded Israel decisive exceptions to the current guidelines for youth exchanges' (Ott, 1972). According to a German expert on German-Israeli youth exchange, 70 per cent of all Israeli youth exchanges with non-Jewish groups has been devoted to contacts with Germany (Bierhoff interview, 1975), and

152   *Operation*

Table 6.5   *Contributions of the Federal Government to German-Israeli Youth Programmes in the Federal Republic and Israel, 1979*

(1) *For events in the Federal Republic*

Category A:	Travel costs to the Federal Republic for Israeli participants	75%
	Per diem per participant (Germans and Israelis)	28 DM
Category B:	Travel costs to the Federal Republic for Israeli participants	up to 50%
	Per diem per participant (Germans and Israelis)	20 DM

(2) *For events in Israel*

Category A:	Costs involved in visit for German participants	75% (with 600 DM ceiling)
Category B:	Costs involved in visit for German participants	60% (with 600 DM ceiling)

Source: Federal Ministry for Youth, Family and Health correspondence, 1980.

exchanges with Germany have been larger than those with the USA (Federal Ministry for Youth, Family and Health interview, 1979; correspondence, 1980). Apparently the Israeli government has no fixed formula for making contributions to the cost of the programmes, and contributions have been made in an *ad hoc* way if at all (*Deutschland-Berichte*, July–August 1974; confidential interviews, 1975);[8] the remainder of the costs involved, that is, those not borne by the Federal government, have been covered by Länder in Germany, by municipalities in Germany and Israel or by private persons and institutions.

Some exceptions have been made to general Israeli youth exchange policies to the advantage of contacts with the Federal Republic. For example, in December 1971, Minister of Education Yigal Allon announced that he had requested of all bodies which dealt with youth exchange 'that in 1972 for economical reasons no exchange of youth groups with other countries should be implemented' (*Deutschland-Berichte*, 1972). However, it was noted at the time that the Israeli Ministry for Foreign Affairs wished to continue youth exchange with the Federal Republic, and in April 1972 during bilateral consultations in Israel, Deputy Minister of Education Yadlin emphasized 'that despite the economy measures brought into force for the travel programme of Israeli groups to Germany, his government advocated the unlimited implementation of German youth programmes in Israel' (*Deutschland-Berichte*, May 1972). An apparent exception to Israel's exit tax rule was adopted as well. The joint regulations, updated in May 1977, stated that 'the competent Israeli ministry or the agency appointed by it...shall grant Israeli participants in German-Israeli exchange programmes in the Federal Republic of Germany full or partial exemption from the Israeli exit tax'. The imposition of the tax, even in a reduced form, had been seen by German officials as a serious obstacle to the growth of German-Israeli youth exchanges. The possibility of a full removal of the tax was welcomed.

MOTIVES AND ADVANTAGES FOR GERMANY
AND FOR ISRAEL

In a 1973 interview Dr Fichtner outlined the general aim of German youth exchanges:

> We were always of the opinion, and have remained so up to the present, that above all international youth encounter also belongs to the political instruction of youth ... Young people must overcome frontiers, must get to know other young people in other countries. Through these contacts, they can get to know the countries themselves. This includes the structures of other states...their history, their national psychology, their particular features and their form of behaviour. (*Deutschland-Berichte*, May 1973)

The Federal government has desired such encounters especially with those peoples who suffered because of Nazi rule, that is, with the countries of Europe and with Israel. Of those who suffered, the Jews suffered the most and, according to Germans, the very darkness of the past relationship between Germans and Jews has determined the intensity of effort with respect to youth exchange with Israel, an expression of the special relationship.

The historical setting formed the focal point of the aims enunciated in the Joint Regulations for the Promotion and Execution of German-Israeli Youth Exchange in November 1974 and remained prominent in May 1977:

> In the necessary awareness of the terrible and irrevocable events of the National Socialist dictatorship the young generation of both countries have and use the opportunity of creating an atmosphere of mutual respect and friendship between the two peoples. The constant aims of German-Israeli youth exchanges must be then in a special way mutual knowledge, understanding and action. (IJAB, 1977, p.1)

With Israel, in particular, but also with other countries, through youth exchanges the Federal Republic is attempting to meet a moral obligation to educate its young in the events of the past, while at the same time trying to create peace and harmony for the present and future.

Youth exchange has been considered by the German government as an instrument for political education, but there has been criticism in the Federal Republic from those actively involved in youth exchange programmes that, with respect to Israel, the aims set by the government have not been achieved and that the instrument has been inadequate. According to a series of articles by Hartwig Bierhoff, the former assistant for youth questions at the German-Israeli Society, German-Israeli youth exchanges were viewed by some committed to youth exchange as state-subsidized tourism, and they questioned whether the special procedural and financial efforts made for German-Israeli youth exchange should continue when they saw greater possibility of their aims being realized, at reduced financial cost, in other countries (1973a, 1973b, 1974). More recently Bierhoff has argued that youth exchanges with Israel have done little to remove the roots of antisemitism and do not permit the development among German youth of critical faculties that would facilitate an understanding of Germany's past and Israel's present (1979). Visits of young Germans to Israel have produced a high level of information, but there has been no conclusive evidence, according to a controlled study of youth groups to Israel, that they have contributed to political education or understanding (von Gizycki, *et al.*, 1972).

Despite these criticisms, the Federal government emphasizes the importance of youth exchanges in its relationship with Israel, as the then Minister for Youth, Family and Health, Dr Katharina Focke, made clear in a statement during Prime Minister Rabin's visit to Germany in July 1975:

> The development of the German-Israeli youth exchange from its first personal contacts to the broad programme of today...shows that the historical ties between the German and Jewish people, which were dealt the most severe of blows through twelve years of the Hitler dictatorship, were not completely destroyed, and could be revived. The bilateral programme in the last few years has also shown that the critical confrontation of the young generation of both countries did not, as many perhaps feared, encumber the opening up of new relations, but rather gave impetus to them. (Bundesministerium für Jugend, Familie und Gesundheit, July 11, 1975)

Youth exchange with Israel, from the German perspective, has helped the general development of relations with Israel; this point has been repeated by various German officials, including Foreign Minister Genscher (for example, *Bulletin*, May 3, 1978) and Ambassador Schütz (*Jerusalem Post Magazine*, May 8, 1981). No doubt, it has served also as a constant reminder to the world that the Federal Republic has attempted to deal with its past. Finally, it seems German officials believe the youth exchange has taught young Germans about their more unfortunate history in a positive framework.

The more positive attitude of the Israeli government to youth exchange at the end of the 1970s also appeared to result from its position in the world. A long time ago the Israeli government decided that West Germany was important for its political, economic and military future. The pragmatism of Ben-Gurion, Sharett and Eshkol was reaffirmed by such former opponents of Germany as Allon. The Israeli government cannot forget the past, but in a time of relative diplomatic isolation it realized more than ever the importance of outside links for the present and future and acknowledged that the support it needs from the Federal Republic will result, to a certain extent, from the positive encounters between the youth of the two countries. Youth exchange with Germany also provides a means for contact with other European countries, for as part of their visits to the Federal Republic young Israelis often make side-trips elsewhere.

The development of youth exchanges, like pingpong diplomacy, signals an opening between the German and Israeli peoples, sponsored by their governments, which seemed as inconceivable even a decade ago as direct negotiations had seemed in 1950. The special relationship has been strongest where government policy has meant preference and where perceived need has accompanied perceived advantage. In the fields of science and technology these conditions have fostered a special relationship, but in other spheres of culture, more oriented to the peoples than to the states, development is more tentative (see Chapter 9). Nevertheless, the youth exchange experience suggests that wherever Israel and West Germany do meet, arrangements are special.

NOTES: CHAPTER 6

1 For details of Germany's foreign cultural policy and its future direction, see the 1978 report of the Division for Foreign Cultural Policy of the Auswärtiges Amt.
2 For information on German institutional research beyond its borders in general, see Hauff and Haunschild (1978, pp. 305–35); Bundesministerium für Forschung und Technologie (1979, pp. 359–79). On Germany's contribution to the solution of problems in the developing world through science and technology, see the Federal Ministry for Research and Technology (1979a, 1979b); Association of National Research Centres of the Federal Republic of Germany (1979); the speeches by Minister for Research and Technology Hauff (*Bulletin*, May 22 and August 24, 1979). For details of Israel's relations with other countries in science and technology, see National Council for Research and Development (1977); on research and technology in Israel compared to developments in other countries, see National Council for Research and Development (1978).
3 For the origins of relations, see the article by Manfred Popp, an official in the Ministry for Education and Science (1972); the interview with former Minister for Research and Technology, Horst Ehmke (*Deutschland-Berichte*, May 1974); articles in the *Max-Planck-Gesellschaft* publication for its members and friends (1979, 1980). In the latter articles personal accounts of relations are given by Josef Cohn and Gentner. Interviews with past and present officials of the Ministry of Research and Technology (1975, 1979), including Horst Ehmke, have been useful; Dr Josef Cohn (interview, 1980) has emphasized the importance of Adenauer's personal commitment to the development of

relations in science and technology, telling Cohn in March 1959, 'I am your man on these questions' (*Ich bin Ihr Mann*).

4   In its 1977 annual report the Weizmann Institute said it would pursue applied research (speech of German Minister for Research and Technology, Volker Hauff, *Deutschland-Berichte*, January 1979). It qualifies, therefore, also for the second major programme between Germans and Israelis.

5   For information on the development of youth exchanges, see interviews and articles in *Deutschland-Berichte* (February 1972, May 1972, May 1973, July–August 1975, 1977); Ott (1972); Bundesministerium für Jugend, Familie und Gesundheit (July 11, 1975); Schultheiss (1976); Klein (1978).

6   The costs for youth exchange are borne by the Federal government, Länder, municipalities and youth organizations. Normal funding is through two channels: (*a*) the Mixed Commissions of Experts which Germany has with its individual foreign partners; and (*b*) the Länder and municipalities, whether by the highest youth authority in the Land or by the Central Youth Association. In the first instance the Mixed Commission for a particular country will use all its funds for the bilateral programme it approves only with that country; in the second instance the Länder and Central Youth Association decide with which countries they wish to promote and fund exchanges; some of these programmes also receive financial support from the budget of the Ministry for Youth, Family and Health. In the case of Israel exchanges have been funded heavily by all methods. It is the Länder, municipalities and youth organizations, not the Federal government, which initiate, plan and execute youth exchanges.

7   For information on Franco-German youth exchange, see Deutsch-Französisches Jugendwerk (1980). The Franco-German Youth Office was created by the Franco-German Friendship Treaty of 1963.

8   Material on the Israeli viewpoint has been unavailable from the Public Council for Youth and Young Adult Exchange in the Israeli Ministry for Education and Culture. Information on the Israeli side of youth exchange has been culled, therefore, from German sources.

7
Political Support

'Political support' refers to diplomatic behaviour. Both West Germany and Israel have perceived public statements, the discourse of diplomacy, as a significant feature of their relations. At different times each has perceived a need for either public approval or silence from the other. West Germany generally has shown Israel preference in political support and Israel has returned this support as in no other policy area of the special relationship.

Political support has defined the limits of the special relationship, and like the relationship itself, it has undergone great change. The period 1952–65 was characterized by mutual need and occasional mutual satisfaction. During 1966–9 Germany's need for Israeli support declined, at the same time that Israel's need for German support grew. As West Germany's need declined, so did its public expressions of approval for Israel; and as Israel's need for support grew, its emphasis shifted from Germany's unfortunate past to prospects of a co-operative future. More than in any other area West Germany has been forced to choose between Israel and the Arab World in expressions of political support, and the German choice has become more and more a function of need for Arab oil and German membership in the EEC. In the most recent period of the special relationship after 1977 Israel has displayed a vital need for West German public approval, only to compete with a constantly growing German perception of need for the Arab World.

POLITICAL SUPPORT: THE GERMAN PERSPECTIVE

WEST GERMANY, 1952–65

Between 1952 and 1965 West German policy was two-sided. Adenauer and Erhard guaranteed approval in the rare public statements that concerned the two countries, but on two vital matters they failed to satisfy Israeli desires. Formal diplomatic recognition was withheld, and the German government did not act to remove German scientists working in Egypt on weapons intended for Israel's destruction. In both cases West Germany was unwilling to jeopardize relations with the Arab World.

German policy favoured Israel over the Arabs in almost every sphere of activity. Why in these two matters, then, was Israel to be disappointed? Adenauer had indicated a desire for diplomatic relations during the debate over ratification of the Luxembourg Reparations Agreement (text in Vogel, 1969, p. 73), and in September 1954 he reiterated a hope that the Reparations Agreement might be a first step towards 'full normalization of relations with Israel' (*Die Welt*, September 14, 1954). Article 12 of the Agreement accorded Israel's mission the rights and privileges of other diplomatic missions in Germany, but without formal recognition. The German Foreign Office in late 1955 proposed a German visa office in Israel, and Israel responded positively in January 1956. In March the German Foreign Minister, von Brentano, broadened the proposal to the creation of a mission in Israel equivalent to Felix Shinnar's mission in Cologne. Both sides agreed to pursue these discussions secretly.

Soon after von Brentano's note, Egyptian President Nasser warned that he would recognize East Germany if West Germany recognized Israel (Deutsche Presse Agentur, April 4 1956).[1] West Germany's claim to be the sole German nation, as embodied in the Basic Law, was enforced by preventing international recognition of the GDR. Nasser's threat addressed the most vital principle of German policy and, at the same time, meant that German relations in the Arab World could be severed because, according to the Hallstein Doctrine, West Germany recognized no nation that recognized the GDR.

German ambassadors to the Middle East, in a secret meeting chaired by Walter Hallstein in May 1956, vetoed the planned German mission in Israel. Hallstein, with government approval, personally conveyed the decision to Shinnar. He said that growing Soviet influence in the Middle East forced West Germany to maintain relations with the Arabs, and he added that the Federal Republic feared Arab recognition of East Germany (Shinnar, 1967, pp. 114–15). After the abortive Suez invasion in the autumn, the Western Allies endorsed the German decision because they feared Soviet influence in the area (Deutschkron, 1970a, p. 91; Seelbach, 1970, pp. 33–5).

Unexpectedly, from the German point of view, the Hallstein Doctrine 'proved to be a double-edged weapon' in the Middle East (von Imhoff, 1971, p. 19). To prevent Arab recognition of East Germany, West Germany complied with Arab demands and denied Israel diplomatic recognition. At the same time, however, West Germany perceived a need to compensate Israel. West Germany could now be pressured (if not simply blackmailed) from both sides.

Challenged to choose between recognition of East Germany and support for Israel, West Germany stood by the Hallstein Doctrine. Such a choice did not signify, however, preference for the Arab World. Short of diplomatic recognition, West Germany made clear both to Israel and to the Arabs the enduring commitment to the special relationship. Nevertheless, the affair of the scientists confirmed the political paralysis inflicted by the Hallstein Doctrine.

Some time after Suez, President Nasser committed Egypt to the development of a rocket for his struggle against Israel; he recruited German scientists to help. Israeli intelligence discovered the activities of the scientists in Egypt, and the Israeli government appealed to the German government to intercede because the scientists involved came from a Stuttgart institute supported by government funds.[2] The German Cabinet had the scientists dismissed from the institute, only to see some of them move to Cairo to work full-time. Israeli appeals had been respected, but the outcome was not to Israel's liking. To Israel's dismay the German government would go no further.

The Egyptians successfully launched several rockets in July 1962. Israeli intelligence was authorized by Ben-Gurion to solve the problem and launched a campaign of physical violence against the German scientists working for Egypt. Less than a year later Israel learned of German scientists working in Egypt on atomic, biological and chemical weapons for use against Israel. In March 1963 the Knesset denounced the German activity and Israel again appealed to the German government.

This second time the German government was less sympathetic. The Germans accused Israel of exaggeration, demurred that they could do nothing about the private activities of German citizens and denied outright the allegations of research in atomic, biological and chemical warfare. The Germans promised only to look into the complaint.

Adenauer's government was trying to protect the Hallstein Doctrine, but Adenauer's parliamentary party joined the SPD and the FDP in a call for legislation that would outlaw the weapons research of German scientists anywhere. The German public squarely supported this initiative in particular and Israel in general.

Despite the initiative and the weight of public opinion, and even after Erhard replaced Adenauer as Chancellor, the government was reluctant to act. Erhard complained that a law could not solve the problem (there was discussion of new passport legislation); he did not want a 'special law' reminiscent of the problem-solving formulae of the Third Reich (*New York Times*, June 5, 1964), and he was unwilling to appear to choose publicly between the Arabs and Israel. Arab diplomats warned the German government not to interfere with the scientists, and the controversy dragged on through the next year.

As with diplomatic relations, in the matter of the scientists Germany did not extend Israel the kind of support and preference to which it had become accustomed in other policy spheres. Non-recognition of East Germany was more important. But Adenauer and Erhard both attempted to compensate Israel for these two disappointments.

During the Sinai Campaign, as Israel advanced on the Suez Canal, the United Nations, the USA, and several Arab countries all asked Germany to halt the payments and flow of supplies to Israel that were contracted under the Luxembourg Agreements. The German government rejected the appeals in favour of supporting Israel.

Many Arab officials thought the imminent end of reparations would signal the warming of German-Arab relations (*Frankfurter Allgemeine Zeitung*, March 16, 1960). The Adenauer–Ben-Gurion meeting at the Waldorf-Astoria in 1960 disillusioned them, and Adenauer publicly promised Israel future co-operation (text in Vogel, 1969, pp. 119–21). During the Eichmann trial a year later West Germany absorbed considerable embarrassment in silence.

Erhard sustained the public nature of Germany's commitment to Israel despite Arab objection. In October 1964 he affirmed: 'The Federal Republic sincerely regrets that there have been certain events taking place that have upset the progressive improvement of German-Israeli relations and have given rise to feelings of anxiety in Israel ... we shall leave no stone unturned to eliminate the possibility of the Israeli people feeling threatened by Germans' (text in Vogel, 1969, p. 165). Still, Erhard took no action on the scientists, and in February 1965 he stated explicitly the German dilemma:

> There are three facts which German policy in the Middle East cannot ignore: our relationship to Israel and the whole Jewish world is overshadowed, as in the past, by the fact of a tragic and still unforgotten past. Then there is the division of our fatherland, which increasingly is being exploited by the Soviets to make the puppet regime acceptable in the non-aligned world. Then there is the increasing division of the world into a host of opposing, mistrusting forces. (Deutscher Bundestag und Bundesrat, February 17, 1965, p. 8103)

The issue of the scientists was resolved ultimately when most of them returned to Germany. The German government had engaged quietly in a campaign to lure the scientists out of Egypt with more lucrative posts in Germany; fears for their safety and the expiration of contracts were additional reasons for the scientists' departure. In his letter to Eshkol concluding the negotiations on diplomatic relations Erhard noted that in the future 'legal action will be taken against those who seek to encourage German nationals to take up scientific, technical or expert activities abroad in the military sphere' (Shinnar, 1967, p. 168). There was hope for the future, then, on the role of its scientists in Egypt or elsewhere, but up until May 1965 the German government had been committed to public inaction.

The Arabs had checked effectively German support for Israel in one area of policy, and German public declarations were contradicted by German inaction. But when the Arab nations moved for checkmate, preference for Israel and the special relationship again prevailed.

DIPLOMATIC RECOGNITION

The Arab World had used the Hallstein Doctrine for leverage. Egypt extracted development aid, although Israel's portion was greater. After threatening to expose publicly German arms shipments to Israel, the Arabs successfully halted the arms through threats to recognize the GDR.[3] In fear of antagonizing the Arabs neither Adenauer nor Erhard acted to oust German scientists from Egypt. But Germany never criticized Israel publicly, even during the Eichmann trial. When Germany spoke of Israel, it spoke only with praise. And when the Hallstein Doctrine no longer stood in the way, West Germany recognized Israel diplomatically.

The press in October 1964 exposed West German arms supplies to Israel (*Frankfurter Rundschau*, October 26, 1964; *New York Times*, October 31, 1964). Arab states soon threatened to recognize the GDR (*Die Welt*, November 20, 1964; *New York Times*, November 20, 1964), and the West German government immediately began to reassess arms policy (Shinnar, 1967, pp. 145–8). The President of the Bundestag, Eugen Gerstenmaier, was dispatched to Cairo where he offered to cease the shipment of arms in exchange for non-reprisal in the event of diplomatic recognition for Israel. Gerstenmaier invited Nasser to the Federal Republic, and apparently in recognition of agreement on the arms proposal Nasser accepted. Nasser stipulated, however, that the shipments should stop immediately.

The German Cabinet did not bow to Nasser's stipulation, largely because the USA was involved in the execution of the second arms agreement, and German hopes for compromise faded. Syria demanded 350 million marks for the construction of the Euphrates Dam and threatened to sever relations with West Germany if a commitment were not made within six weeks (Deutschkron, 1970b, pp. 297–8). It was now abundantly clear to West Germany that the Hallstein Doctrine invited blackmail, and not only in reference to Israel. Israel declared Germany morally bankrupt for ignoring the scientists and Egypt accused Germany of fuelling tension in the Middle East. The Syrian ultimatum was rejected in mid-January, but arms to Israel continued to flow.

Now Nasser acted. Motivated both by Germany's repudiation of his stipulations and by Soviet pressure to recognize East Germany (enhanced by significant economic incentives), Nasser invited East German Premier Walter Ulbricht to Cairo.[4] At the end of January Nasser repeated his threat of recognition for East Germany to West Germany's ambassador. West Germany was left to ponder whether the invitation to Ulbricht already constituted *de facto* recognition of the GDR.

The German Cabinet promptly halted arms shipments to Israel but postponed an invocation of the Hallstein Doctrine, hoping to dissuade Nasser from following through on the Ulbricht visit.[5] Erhard warned Egypt, at the same time, that it would lose economic aid if the invitation were not withdrawn.

Until Ulbricht's official ten-day visit to Cairo at the end of February 1965, no East German leader had been received in a country outside the Soviet bloc. Two days after Ulbricht returned home, Nasser announced plans to establish a consulate-general in East Berlin. The West German Cabinet was paralysed, evenly divided between CDU/CSU members demanding invocation of the Hallstein Doctrine and severance of relations with Egypt (except for Schröder, who sided with the FDP), and FDP members preferring at most the discontinuation of development aid. As a temporary compromise, an emissary, Kurt Birrenbach, departed for Israel, offering to establish consular relations in exchange for the cessation of arms shipments. There was little expectation of Israeli agreement.

Five days after the Cabinet compromise on March 7, Erhard applied his powers to set guidelines of policy (*Richtlinienkompetenz*) to end the stalemate. He directed his press secretary, von Hase, to announce a German offer of full diplomatic recognition for Israel, knowing that the move invited Arab retaliation. Later he explained:

> It was never an issue of whether there would be diplomatic relations, but rather a question of when. It was the fear of recognition of East Germany which had prevented relations. But then there was the Ulbricht visit to Cairo and I saw that as *de facto* recognition by Egypt. If they could recognize East Germany, then we could recognize Israel. Why should we be different from many other countries? (Interview, 1975)[6]

Nasser, as Erhard saw it, finally had fulfilled his threat. There was no further cause to be blackmailed or deterred from desired relations with Israel.

There were, too, other factors influencing Erhard's surprise decision. Rainer Barzel, returning from the USA, reported American dissatisfaction with the failure to grant diplomatic recognition.[7] There was considerable domestic pressure on Erhard, and his own party was firmly committed to diplomatic relations. There is little doubt, too, that Erhard's own moral conscience pushed him to act.

Negotiations concerning the full range of German-Israeli relations followed immediately (Eban, 1977, pp. 300–1), and within two months Erhard and Levi Eshkol exchanged letters of initial agreement. Germany promptly paid the expected price: ten of the thirteen members of the Arab League broke diplomatic relations with West Germany. Erhard had sought to avoid such a rupture, sending personal emissaries to several Arab states and personal notes to all the members of the Arab League. He stressed a German commitment to improve German-Arab friendship, just as Adenauer had with the Westrick mission in 1952. The Arab states did not, in fact, begin to recognize East Germany until 1969, but for public consumption at least, the German–Arab friendship was now over.

WEST GERMANY, 1966–8

Israel and West Germany exchanged ambassadors with contradictory expectations. West Germany thought 'normalization' would reduce the 'special' relationship and German vulnerability to evocation of the past. Israel thought, in contrast, that diplomatic recognition would lead to preference in political support. Mutual disillusionment was almost inevitable.

The special relationship gradually normalized over 1966–9 in the area of political support. Germany gradually became critical of Israel as its need for Israeli approval declined. Germany was, once recognized diplomatically by its former victims, a member of the family of nations, free to speak out as any other nation. Although Germany's criticisms would be reserved, these transition years presaged the outspoken governments of Willy Brandt and Helmut Schmidt.

There were three key indications of the shift in German policy and attitude. Germany's choice for a first ambassador was greeted by opposition in Israel. West Germany did not endorse Israel's role in the 1967 Middle East war, and West Germany sought constantly to curry favour with the ten Arab states that had severed relations in 1965.

The selection of Rolf Pauls as ambassador to Israel signalled West Germany's determination to treat Israel diplomatically as it would treat any other nation. According to Inge Deutschkron:

> Foreign Minister Schröder insisted on Pauls as ambassador because of the necessity, within the framework of a 'normalization of relations', of appointing a career diplomat as the first ambassador. If a political figure with an impeccable past had been chosen this would have been making an exception which could have set a precedent for the next two or three ambassadors. (*Maariv*, June 10, 1965)

During his first year in Israel Pauls resounded the themes of Adenauer and Erhard, emphasizing the tragic past and a hope-filled mutual future (*New York Times*, August 12, 1965; Vogel, 1969, p. 175; *Jedioth Chadashoth*, November 5, 1965; *Al Hamischmar*, February 23, 1966). But Pauls never called German-Israeli relations 'special', nor did he personally consider himself involved in a special relationship, one he thought connoted 'close relations of intensive co-operation' (correspondence, 1976).

After a year at his post, Pauls openly criticized Israel, a first for any German official. On the occasion of his first public speech in Israel, at the Israeli Industrial Fair on June 30, 1966, Pauls outlined the terms for future relations between the two countries. He argued that the past should cease to dominate relations, and he cautioned Israel that

Germany was sensitive to political support as much as any other nation. Thus, he objected to Israel's recognition of the Oder-Neisse Line, and he objected to Israeli criticism of German–Arab relations. He reminded Israel that Germany had extended itself more than any nation in diplomatic history in order to satisfy Israeli expectations for diplomatic relations. Both in tone and in content the speech was a watershed in the special relationship:

> We Germans are in a special position with regard to you...we are doing everything practically possible ...We understand that you cannot forget what has happened. We are convinced that we may not be allowed to forget...we have been making every effort to build up relations of the kind which exist between other governments and other states ...It is inevitable that in our relations the past overshadows the present ...We do not want however to deprive ourselves of confidence in the future ...It is only with great concern that we can note how the sufferings of the past are continually stirred up for political and other reasons and for egoistic motives, in order to disrupt the present, so that it cannot serve the future ...It is a vain attempt to want to portray the Germany of 1966 on Nazi lines ...Important people have said repeatedly during the last few weeks that the Jewish people expect deeds from Germany, so that she can take her place again in the family of peoples. I should like to say in that respect: Germany already has a respected place in the family of peoples again. She no longer needs permission for this ...Remarks, which have a discriminatory tendency and only serve to be insulting, have never held a happy place in the relations between states. It seems opportune for me in this connection to remind my listeners that Germany in recognising Israel consciously underwent the risk of losing her in part normal, in part good relations with ten states ...There is no like example in the history of diplomacy and foreign politics ...There is...little reason for disagreeable reactions in Israel, when we express the desire to revert our relations with the Arab states to normal. The treatment of German interests by Israel is of basic significance for the quality of German-Israeli relations ...We react to any undermining of our position with the same sensitive attention displayed by any other government in a similar position ...Cooperation should ensue in particular where emotions are least involved, for example in the economic sphere ...Relations with Germany will improve in the measure that policies are not only conceived in the past, but also with an eye to the future. (Text in Vogel, 1969, pp. 188–91)

Pauls put Israel on notice that the relationship would need to be more balanced in the future. He promised 'normal' relations in the future, by which he meant that Israel would have to be more generous to Germany in the international arena and would have to accept public criticism when views did not coincide. Diplomatic recognition would be the end, not the beginning, of special political support.

Pauls regarded relations with Israel as neither normal nor special. They were not normal because

> For generations one will not be able to refer to a normal relationship between Germany and Israel. Too many awful things have happened. Only much later will younger generations be able to approach one another unfettered and unconstrained by the past. (*Die Welt*, August 8, 1967)

Emotion and the past were obstacles to normal relations, but the objective remained. According to Pauls, normal relations 'are basically free of difficulties' (correspondence, 1976), and it was to this end, substituting pragmatism for emotion and the future for the past, that he tried to shape the course of relations between his country and Israel.

Pauls came to be admired and respected in Israel; Ben-Gurion became one of his chief defenders (*Die Welt*, August 10, 1967; July 17, 1968; *Kölnischer Stadtanzeiger*, August 2, 1968). His departure after only three years surprised many observers, some of whom suggested that Pauls gave Israel greater importance in Germany's Middle East policy than Foreign Minister Brandt. Several Arab countries, it was said, saw Pauls as representative of those circles in Bonn that preferred Israel to the Arab World at a time when Germany wanted to alter that impression of its Middle East policy (*Kölnischer Stadtanzeiger*, August 2, 1968). Pauls moved on to Washington and then Peking, suggesting no fall from Willy Brandt's favour.

Rolf Pauls's successor, Karl Hermann Knoke, was also a career diplomat and, like Pauls, felt a personal commitment to Israel (*Allgemeine Wochenzeitung der Juden in Deutschland*, July 26, 1968). When he presented his credentials in August 1968, he, too, evoked the past only to emphasize hope for the future. He, too, focused on pragmatic politics. And, like Pauls, he studiously avoided the term 'special' (*Deutschland-Berichte*, September 1968).

It was by this time apparently official policy not to use the term 'special relationship' publicly. Publicly, at least, Germany now sought a 'balanced' policy towards both Israel and the Arab World. Statements self-consciously stressed balance or neutrality.[8] Normal relations, to Knoke and other German officials, were 'relations which in no way stand out from the majority of relations with other states' or 'relations without special privileges or emphases or particularly negative points' or 'diplomatic relations between states as recognized in international law' (interviews, 1975). Normal – neither special nor unusual – relations had become, more than ever before, the German objective.

This objective was challenged often after the establishment of diplomatic relations, but no more so than during war, for it is then that sides most commonly are chosen. A year after Pauls enunciated the new policy, the German government put it into practice by maintaining strict official neutrality during the Six-Day War. Chancellor Kurt Kiesinger declared: 'Despite the conflict, [the Federal government] will do all that it can to maintain its contact with the countries in this area – and this also applies to matters of trade and economics; at the same time, the Government will remain true to its principle of non-intervention and will not supply weapons to the warring parties; it will make sure that this decision is strictly adhered to' (text in Vogel, 1969, p. 290). Germany was not to antagonize the Arabs on behalf of Israel even if, as Foreign Minister Brandt claimed, there was no 'neutrality of the heart'.[9]

The establishment of diplomatic relations with Israel also changed German policy in the Middle East generally. For the first time Germany began to examine closely its interests in the whole area, not only with Israel and world opinion. The relations between the two states encouraged Germany to distinguish between German-Israeli and German-Jewish relations. The interests of the German state would not always coincide with the interests of the State of Israel. Whatever special relationship existed between the states would be expressed economically, not in public statements, for it had to be kept from the watchful eyes and listening ears of the Arab World (confidential interviews, 1975). German politicians and diplomats asked themselves with increasing frequency what limits might exist in their obligations to the Jews, especially where the interests of the German state might seem jeopardized.

WEST GERMANY, 1969–73

It is clear that by 1969 West Germany's policy in the area of political support had shifted from approval or silence to an incipient policy of 'even-handedness', 'balance', or open criticism. This shift was simultaneous with Germany's growing appreciation of economic and political power in the Arab World. During the period 1969–73 Germany's formal neutrality in the Middle East was accompanied by constantly improved East–West relations, growing German political power (to complement its unquestioned economic importance) and the new influence of the FDP in the formulation of foreign policy.

Ostpolitik in the late 1960s, probably the most important symbol of Germany's international acceptance and foreign policy independence, was the setting for Middle East neutrality. Brandt was preoccupied with overtures to the East; his Foreign Minister, Walter Scheel, whose party was historically uncomfortable with aspects of the special relationship,[10] was preoccupied with the Middle East. The objectives of the FDP, above all to secure friendly relations with the Arab World, became the objectives of the Federal Republic.

There were two central indications confirming the change in policy. First, there were the public pronouncements of Scheel and Brandt. They redefined policy towards Israel, although Scheel leaned more towards the

Arab World than his colleague. Secondly, there was the policy of the EEC, for Germany cloaked its neutrality in its responsibilities to Europe, even though the basis of change lay in dependence on Arab oil.[11]

When asked, soon after taking office in 1969, whether Germany would continue the 'special attitude' of former governments towards Israel, the new Foreign Minister replied:

> At the time of the conclusion of diplomatic relations with Israel ... the Federal government declared that it saw in this move a step towards the normalization of relations. This attitude was reiterated in countless statements by the Grand Coalition. The new government will continue that line ...Our relationship to Israel is as our relationship with other countries. Normalization consists of our having discharged, through perfectly normal cooperation, former contractual agreements as a settlement for certain events in the past. There is nothing special in that. (*Bulletin*, December 18, 1969)

Asked to elaborate on Germany's Middle Eastern policy Foreign Minister Scheel noted that 'We will continue to make every effort to have a balanced policy'. 'Nothing special' would be the hallmark of Scheel's public policy.

When Israel's Foreign Minister, Abba Eban, visited Bonn a year later, Scheel emphasized the future and suggested that the debt from the past had been paid. The new generation of 'political responsibility' in Germany, he said, had not even been born by the time Germany's criminal regime had been overthrown. Toasting Eban at an official banquet Scheel declared, 'It is good for the relationship between the Israeli and German peoples that the relations are so completely normal, so open. That is necessary if one wants open relations. And we have such relations' (*Bulletin*, February 26, 1970).

Scheel returned the Eban visit in the spring of 1971. Although the trip was meant, in part, to mark the normal quality of relations, Scheel did remark, 'I cannot arrive here with the same feelings as on a visit to any other friendly country. No German can escape our past. No one in the Federal Republic can or will forget what Germans did to your people' (*Bulletin*, July 13, 1971). But Scheel now introduced a new explanation for the changes in German policy. Whatever a German might feel, he suggested, the Federal Republic's policy in the Middle East was part of the foreign policy of the European Economic Community. When asked to reconcile his special feelings with normal, 'balanced' relations, Scheel explained,

> An even-handed policy in the Middle East means, on the one hand, that we have and want to develop with Israel good, friendly relations which, because of the past have a special accent. On the other hand we are trying to reestablish diplomatic relations in the near future with

those countries with whom there have been no relations for some years. The Israeli government understands that the interests of the Federal Republic dictate an even-handed relationship with all countries of the region. (*Bulletin*, July 13, 1971)

The 'special accent' would not permit the past to govern the future.

In Egypt two years later Scheel said, 'We ourselves do not speak of a special relationship or of privileged relations' (*Frankfurter Allgemeine Zeitung*, May 24, 1973; *Le Monde*, May 23, 1973). The fact of the awful past, he conceded, did give the relationship a 'special character', but the views of Adenauer and Erhard notwithstanding, circumstances of the past, he asserted, would not dictate preference in the future.

Chancellor Willy Brandt placed some of the 'special accent' on concerns that Scheel downplayed. Like Scheel, Brandt emphasized normalization and even-handedness, but Brandt gave the past greater importance and he made a firm commitment to the survival of the State of Israel.

Publicly and officially Brandt supported Resolution 242 of the United Nations Security Council, desired 'good relations with all states' in the Middle East and promised to send no arms into the region (Deutscher Bundestag und Bundesrat, October 28, 1969, p. 32). In his first inaugural address Brandt made no mention of special positions or special relations, the first time a new German Chancellor had made such an omission (*Die Welt*, March 20, 1971; *Die Zeit*, June 11, 1971).[12] Four years later, in his second inaugural, he referred to 'traditional German–Arab friendship', but also referred to the inviolability of the State of Israel (Deutscher Bundestag und Bundesrat, January 18, 1973).

To some extent, at least, the changes in rhetoric were meant to signal deliberate changes in policy. Brandt told the inaugural session of Brotherhood Week in 1971:

> We have been accused of no longer entertaining special relations – as past governments – but rather normal relations with Israel. Some have said that this has something to do with our *Ostpolitik* ...Our relationship in fact still carries a special sign: the fact of the murder of millions of Jews in Europe...I admit that we have to use the term normalization carefully. (*Bulletin*, March 23, 1971)

Brandt also emphasized what Scheel often ignored, repeating a statement he had made some months earlier to the Yugoslav News Agency: 'We believe, especially after all that has happened in this country in the past, that we cannot be indifferent to the crisis and that we cannot allow Israel's right to exist to be questioned. But we also are attempting to do justice to the legitimate rights of all and to improve our relationship with the Arab world.' The commitment to Israel's right to exist Brandt repeated often during his administration, but he would never explain what he would do in case of a threat to Israel's survival. It was clear that he would not use troops or arms (for legal and political reasons). And unlike German Chancellors in the past, Brandt rarely referred to Israel without a friendly reference to the Arabs at the same time.

Scheel and Brandt, both committed to overcoming the notion of a special relationship, struggled for a comfortable description of relations with Israel. During the first state visit to Israel of a sitting German Chancellor in June 1973 Brandt seemed to settle upon a formula, 'normal relations with a special character'. Now references to the past were couched in the terms introduced by Pauls:

> The visit of a German head of state in Israel is not automatic. The fact that it has been possible indicates a wise pragmatism ...We need patience and signs of goodwill to ensure that we learn the right lessons from the past but do not become captives of the past. But I know this is easy to say. I also know how extremely difficult the seemingly simple can be ...The recognition of our responsibility for our crimes was the decisive act of inner freedom for us, without which external freedom would have been unreliable. The thirteen years of horror will not be forgotten. German-Israeli relations must be seen against the grim back-ground of the National Socialist terror regime. This is what we mean when we refer to our normal relations with a special character. (*Deutschland-Berichte*, July 1973)

An important past, the right to a secure existence, but acceptance of less preference over neighbours: this was Brandt's description of Germany's political support for Israel.

WEST GERMANY AND EEC POLICY, 1973-80

The Middle East has been a central focus in the EEC's efforts to formulate common external policies since the early 1970s.[13] Germany was not the chief initiator of this policy effort (that role falling largely to France), but Germany's acquiescence has been necessary for consensus. As the primary economic power within the Community, moreover, German participation has been crucial.

The first clear indication of an EEC Middle East policy came in a 'working paper' of the Community's Political Committee, accepted by EEC Foreign Ministers in May 1971. They adopted the French interpretation of Resolution 242 of the United Nations Security Council – withdrawal from '*des territoires*' (all territories) occupied in 1967 by Israel. Prior to the *Die Welt* leak of the paper (July 14, 1971), Israel had assumed that German support for Resolution 242 was premissed on a British interpretation of 'withdrawal from territories' (some territories). (Britain was not yet a member of the EEC.) Germany, when questioned by Israeli officials, claimed to support the British interpretation (*Jerusalem Post*, July 15, 1971), but as one Foreign Office spokesman explained, 'It is in the interests of all that the beginnings of a common European policy are not disturbed' (*Die Welt*, May 22, 1971); Walter Scheel said, 'The Foreign Ministers, in drawing up the paper, were merely fulfilling their European duty' (*Süddeutsche Zeitung*, May 23, 1971),[14] and he emphasized that the working paper enjoyed unanimous adoption by the Community (Deutscher Bundestag und Bundesrat, July 19, 1971, p. 7759). Hence, Germany was pretending to have matters both ways: Israel could be told that Germany was partial to the British interpretation, but at the same time German commitments to Europe obliged acceptance of the French interpretation.

Germany's public position was equally ambivalent during the Yom Kippur War, but public neutrality camouflaged material assistance. Observers everywhere considered military disaster for Israel a genuine possibility during the war's first stage in October 1973, so the war gave a measure of Israel's friends, both in the arena of public statement and political support, and in the arena of material assistance.

For Walter Scheel, the 1973 war was an opportunity to state relations with the Arab World more boldly than ever before:

> Our relations with Israel are relations, as I have said before, which have a special character and that must be considered in this difficult situation in which we find ourselves. But not only relations with Israel are of a special kind; also relations with the Arabs must be seen in this way. (Presse- und Informationsamt, October 28, 1973)

Balance now referred to equally special relations, and other officials plainly reflected Arab and European pressure (especially French) during the war. By contrast, Chancellor Willy Brandt avowed, 'For us there can be no neutrality of the heart and the conscience' (*Washington Post*, November 10–11, 1973). Despite the division, official German policy conformed to the view of the Foreign Minister, not of the Chancellor.

While Germany pleaded neutrality, the Organization of Arab Petroleum Exporting Countries (OAPEC) warned that Israel's friends were soon to face an oil embargo. A week later the press disclosed American use of Bremerhaven to resupply Israel. With its alleged neutrality either contradicted or violated, the German Foreign Office promptly announced:

> The American Ambassador in Bonn has been told that Germany's strict neutrality in this conflict forbids any deliveries of weapons using West German territory or installations from American depots in West Germany …The Federal Republic is absolutely determined not to be dragged into the Middle East conflict. It stands by its neutrality and by the policy of balance despite the strain on the new Middle East War. (Presse- und Informationsamt, October 25, 1973).

Germany may have been complicitous in supplying Israel (*Süddeutsche Zeitung*, October 27–8, 1973; Eban, 1977, p. 514), but public exposure touched the most vulnerable area of the special relationship.

Germany imported 85 per cent of its oil from the Middle East in 1973. The Libyan demand of 'positive neutrality' during the war threatened Germany's energy supplies, for 23·1 per cent of all German oil came from Libya alone, more than from any other Middle Eastern country. Both Scheel and the Minister for Economics, despite Brandt's denials, attributed Germany's behaviour during the war to dependence on Middle East oil (Scheel, 1973; *Süddeutsche Zeitung*, October 29, 1973; *Washington Post*, November 10–11, 1973). Whether the Arab threat caused German behaviour is not absolutely certain; Germany, however, did escape the embargo in part because it subscribed to the EEC's November 6 Declaration on the conflict;

Commitment to a European position unacceptable to Israel was reiterated in the EEC Declaration. The EEC had proposed that Israel submit to the internationalization of Jerusalem in 1971, and in November 1973 Europe emphasized the inadmissibility of annexation of territory through force and the necessity for Israel to evacuate all territory occupied since 1967; the EEC called for the recognition of the 'legitimate rights of the Palestinians' in the formulation of a just and lasting peace.

Germany apparently did not oppose the formulation even though observers, including Israel, have regarded the Community Resolution of November 1973 as contrary to Israel's position (Lieber, 1976, p. 13). Willy Brandt claimed German adherence to the Resolution resulted chiefly from Europe's need to unite on issues affecting all members of the Community, but no German officials were then able to explain the divergence between Germany and Holland in the face of Arab oil.

By 1973 German public policy was prepared to take a course neutral, even possibly favourable, to the Arabs in case of crisis. If oil was critical for German 'neutrality', membership in the European Economic Community was an additional incentive, and adherence to Community statements constituted an important example of change in German political support for Israel.

The 'European' position, more pro-Arab than neutral, with the notable exception of Holland, was the culmination of a developing Community policy in the Middle East. Walter Scheel, as Foreign Minister, was the architect of German policy on political co-operation within the European Community, and the stance that emerged in 1973 was consistent with his views.

The EEC has pronounced often on the Middle East conflict since November 1973,[15] but in the period 1977–80 the European position evolved from vague references to a 'homeland for the Palestinian people' (declaration, June 29, 1977), to severe criticism of Israel's settlement policy (statement of June 18, 1979), to culminate in *de facto* recognition of the PLO (Venice 'initiative' of June 13, 1980). Germany has been careful in this process only to avoid *de jure* recognition of the PLO. A similar process, with similar results, evolved in the Euro-Arab Dialogue established after the Yom Kippur War.[16]

Israel has reacted to the development of EEC policy on the Middle East conflict and on the Palestinians with outrage and frustration. Whereas the Israeli government castigated the whole Community, characterizing its behaviour as, for example, 'A Munich-like surrender to tyrannical extortion' (*Jerusalem Post*, June 16, 1980),[17] it was most disappointed, privately and sometimes publicly, with Germany. In response to the June 1979 declaration, in which for once Germany played a leading role (Sicherman, 1980, pp. 852–3), Israeli Minister of Transport Haim Landau 'warned Germany against joining hands with the PLO "within living memory of the Holocaust" ' (*Jerusalem Post*, June 24, 1979). To Israel's disappointment neither the EEC nor Germany actively supported the 1979 peace treaty with Egypt, and Germany had moved, as Israel saw it, 'from a stance of outspoken support for the Camp David accord ... towards the French position which has consistently opposed the American-orchestrated peace efforts in the region' (*Jerusalem Post*, June 21, 1979).

Although the Israeli government has been vitriolic over EEC positions on the Middle East conflict, it generally has been less critical of Germany. There is an important difference in Germany's posture on the Middle East conflict. In the framework of European Political Co-operation Germany has angered Israel, but in the bilateral relationship private discussion usually has inspired continuing confidence.

WEST GERMANY, 1974–80

Despite West Germany's firm commitment to the European Economic Community, bilateralism also has shaped its stand on the Middle East conflict. Consequently, in every year since 1974, Germany has appeared both friendly to Israel and sympathetic to a solution of the Palestinian problem that Israel considers unacceptable.[18]

Germany's ambassador to the UN, von Wechmar, first tried to explain the confusing policy to the General Assembly in November 1974:

> We consider it inadmissible to acquire territory through force and deem it necessary for Israel to end the territorial occupation which it has maintained since the conflict of 1967. As a consequence of the right of self-determination, we recognize the right of the Palestinian people to decide itself whether to create its own authority on the land vacated by Israel, as was decided at the Arab summit in Rabat, or whether to choose another solution. (Presse- und Informationsamt, November 19, 1974)[19]

Yet von Wechmar emphasized Israel's right to a secure existence, and

Germany abstained from both the UN vote on Palestinian self-determination and the vote to grant the PLO observer status.

This position was clarified in early 1975, first, by Chancellor Schmidt. He sustained sympathy for the Palestinians but said Germany could not take seriously the question of the PLO participation in the Euro-Arab Dialogue until the PLO recognized the right of Israel to exist in secure borders and renounced acts of terrorism (*Le Figaro*, February 4, 1975). Germany's new ambassador to Israel, Per Fischer, elaborated two weeks after Schmidt's statement:

> In every case and unflinchingly we will support Israel's right to exist in secure and recognized borders. In the context of our capabilities and in all international fora, particularly in Europe, this is the clear position of the German government; the Israeli government knows that we will not leave it in the lurch. (*Zweites Deutsches Fernsehen*, February 16, 1975)

And Foreign Minister Genscher told his counterpart, Yigal Allon, in Bonn: 'You can rely on us. We will not leave you in the lurch' (*Die Welt*, February 28, 1975).

The German government now refrained deliberately from the language of a 'special relationship' (*Die Welt*, February 28, 1975), but normalization always was tempered by reference to the past. Schmidt spoke in these terms on American television (Bill Moyers' Journal, January 23, 1975), and Genscher employed them in Israel at the end of 1975, particularly concerning his government's negative UN vote on an Arab resolution that condemned Zionism as racism:

> We note with gratitude that it has proved possible to open up a way out of a past full of horror and suffering into the future. None of us can or wants to act as if the events of the past had been forgotten... we rejected with all determination the effort to identify racism with Zionism. For us this is not only a political decision. This is a challenge to our conscience and wherever we will again be confronted with this challenge we shall stand by you. (*Deutschland-Berichte*, December 1975)

Yet on the same occasion Genscher noted the need for an expression of Palestinian national identity as part of a peace settlement. The special relationship no longer defined German political support in the Middle East, but its remnants delimited change.

During various meetings with Arab leaders in 1976 Foreign Minister Genscher and Chancellor Schmidt reconfirmed Germany's position on the Palestinian question, but also pledged Germany to Israel's survival.[20] When Genscher visited Syria, Jordan and Egypt in February 1977, German adherence to EEC policy dominated. Yet before leaving for the

Middle East, Genscher conferred with Allon in Brussels; while in Damascus he reminded the Syrians of Germany's friendship with Israel (*Die Welt*, February 9, 1977; *Die Zeit*, February 18, 1977). In August 1977 Schmidt named one of Israel's closest friends, former Berlin mayor Klaus Schütz, Germany's sixth ambassador to Israel, and in late November the German Minister for Economics hailed Foreign Minister Dayan's visit to Bonn:

> The destiny and future of the State of Israel mean a great deal to the Federal Government and the German public. As in the past, we continue to accept our responsibility towards Israel. This applies both to our bilateral relations and the development of the situation in the Middle East. (*Deutschland-Berichte*, January 1978)

An apparently serious conflict in German-Israeli relations erupted in 1978 because of remarks during the Bonn visit of Saudi Crown Prince Fahd. Chancellor Schmidt said at a concluding press conference:

> We very much admired the extremely courageous step taken by President Sadat at the end of last year. We feel that Israel's response to that step has so far been inadequate ...The Federal Government's attitude is ...laid down by Resolution 242 and the several constant statements by the European Community ...We emphasize Israel's right to exist within secured boundaries. We also emphasize the legitimate right of self-determination of the Palestinian people, the right of the Palestinians to *organise themselves as a state*. (*Deutschland-Berichte*, July–August 1978; emphasis added)[21]

Genscher, in Israel soon thereafter, was asked to explain Schmidt's statement. He did not deny Schmidt's remarks, but he did deny that either the EEC or Germany had a ready solution to the Palestinian problem. Indeed, he said, 'That is a matter for the parties to the conflict' (*Deutschland-Berichte*, July–August 1978; *Jerusalem Post*, June 28, 1978; *Frankfurter Allgemeine Zeitung*, June 30, 1978; *Neue Zürcher Zeitung*, July 2–3, 1978). In an article six months later Genscher gave relations with Israel priority (*Rheinischer Merkur*, December 15, 1978), so that a year passed without an official explanation of Schmidt's formula for a Palestinian state.

A year after his innovative characterization of a solution to the Palestinian problem Schmidt hardened his view of German-Israeli relations. The *Jerusalem Post* quoted him admonishing Begin for his settlement policy and warning that 'Israel is on a very dangerous path' (*Jerusalem Post*, June 22, 1979). 'If Israel goes on with its present political course', according to Schmidt, 'it will be difficult to remain a friend'. He also downgraded the foundation of German-Israeli relations: 'I agree with Mr. Begin that the Germans should have a bad conscience about Hitler and the Nazi past. Contrary to Mr. Begin, though, I think that bad conscience should not be the reason for West Germany's support for Israel.' Schmidt's prompt denial of these remarks (*Jerusalem Post*, June 24, 1979; *Washington Post*, June 26, 1979) was not entirely credible in Israel, especially when former Chancellor Brandt and Austrian Chancellor Bruno Kreisky met with PLO leader Yassir Arafat in July.

Another German politician, FDP deputy Jürgen Möllemann, met with Arafat in August, but Genscher quickly distanced himself from Möllemann's advocacy of closer links with the PLO (*Jerusalem Post*, August 12, 1979). Nevertheless, Genscher's two Middle Eastern trips during this period continued to raise Israeli doubts about German sympathy. His visits to the 'Rejection Front' (Libya and Iraq in June 1979, and Syria in September), his own rejection of a separate peace between Israel and Egypt, and advocacy of the 'Abukir Principles' (the rights of the Palestinians to self-determination, a homeland and choice of representation; and the need for a comprehensive peace) hardly inspired Israeli confidence (*Süddeutsche Zeitung*, September 3, 1979; *Frankfurter Allgemeine Zeitung*, September 3, 1979; *Die Welt*, September 3, 1979). Nor did Genscher's answers in an interview upon his return to Germany. He even subsumed the special history of German-Israeli relations under the need to be critical of Israel:

Question: German-Israeli relations have a special character because of the past. How can that specialness be manifested in relations today?
Answer: I believe that in our search for peace we ought to be conscious of our special responsibility. For peace in the Middle East also means peace and security for Israel.
Question: That means that our guilt requires us to be particularly honest towards Israel?
Answer: I am of the opinion that both historical responsibility and the friendship that has now developed between us necessitates our being candid and honest with one another. (*Deutschland-Berichte*, October 1979)

Establishment of the notion that friendship demands criticism appears to be a turning-point in the area of political support in German-Israeli relations.[22] Germany's critical and frequently negative attitude towards Israel was crowned by Chancellor Schmidt's open disinclination to reciprocate Prime Minister Rabin's state visit of 1975. German government officials claimed scheduling constraints (German Foreign Office interview, 1979), but the real reason was Schmidt's disapproval of Begin's peace policy, particularly the active development of settlements on the West Bank (*Der Spiegel*, August 6, 1979).

Despite the German drift into conformity with EEC (largely French) Middle Eastern policy, contradictions and ambiguities continued into the

1980s. Iraqi Foreign Minister Sadoun Hammadi told a luncheon audience in Bonn in February 1980 that Israel was attempting 'the annihilation of the Arab people'. He accused Israel of 'racist and colonial aggression'. Although the German Foreign Minister had spoken at the luncheon already, he rose again to emphasize the German view that all parties desired peace and deserved respect. Germany had come to this view 'after the bitter experiences of European history'. Genscher concluded by stressing his government's comprehensive approach: 'We know no greater wish than for an order in the Middle East in which all peoples of the region, Israel and the Arab peoples, find peace' (*Deutschland-Berichte*, March 1980).

During two 1980 visits of Saudi officials (Prince Saud al Faisal in March and King Khaled in June), German support for their impatience with the American-led peace efforts of Egypt and Israel was clear (*Deutschland-Berichte*, April 1980; *Süddeutsche Zeitung*, June 20, 1980). Yet, German officials also endorsed the Egyptian position in meetings in Bonn and Cairo during March and May (*Deutschland-Berichte*, April and June 1980). Later Germany and Israel agreed 'to maintain closer and more frequent high-level contacts – especially before taking new steps in its Middle East policy' (*Jerusalem Post*, September 1, 1980).

Both countries were determined by 1980 to improve relations, and Ambassador Schütz served continually during his term (1977–81) as a vital force of encouragement. As Genscher and Schmidt emphasized the shift to a European position, Schütz throughout his ambassadorial term spoke for Germany's more traditional policy. He reiterated his long-standing position early in 1980:

First, Germany's relationship to Israel was never as normal as its ties to any other country. Relations were always special. Second, one should know that relations were not as disrupted as it often appeared. Third, and this is the most important point, one must be aware that in such relations there are always new developments. (*Welt am Sonntag*, January 6, 1980)[23]

German policy clearly had more than one voice, and more than one direction. Despite the linear development of EEC policy from an emphasis on Palestinian rights in the early 1970s to an advocacy of the PLO in the early 1980s, West Germany withheld formal endorsement of the PLO. Nevertheless, there has been a departure from an absolutely firm public commitment to Israel, largely the product of German oil dependence and membership in the EEC. Hence, even as Germany refuses to call its political relationship with Israel 'special', a political commitment endures.

POLITICAL SUPPORT: ISRAEL'S PERSPECTIVE

ISRAEL AND POLITICAL SUPPORT: AN OVERVIEW

Israel was slow to appreciate the shift in German policy and throughout the 1960s failed to heed German warnings that public reciprocity was important. But as the new German policy took hold around 1970, Israel increasingly pleaded in public for German support by bearing public witness to Germany's friendship. Conforming to German wishes Israel also reduced its commitment to the public characterization of relations as 'special'.

The Third Reich certainly had given Israel cause to denounce Germany, and before the Luxembourg Reparations Agreement Israeli officials freely made very damaging statements. But Israel did not bite a feeding hand; after 1952, condemnation became little more than chiding, playing on the past more for advantage than for vengeance. Germany knew Israel was willing to exploit the past, but rarely was it necessary to be inflammatory. Levi Eshkol's rhetorical denunciations of Germany's decision to end arms shipments and failure to remove German scientists in Egypt were exceptional.

Germany effectively bought Israeli silence during the period 1952-66, not through praise of Israel but through material assistance. Israeli silence was all Germany seemed to want, and it made the special relationship reciprocal across policy areas. But after 1966, facing diplomatic isolation, Israel began to praise Germany in an effort to regain public praise. What Israel won was a role reversal: in response to Israel's praise Germany granted Israel muted criticism (compared to the French, for example) or silence, precisely what Israel had granted Germany during difficult diplomatic years.

ISRAEL, 1952-65

For Israel, as for Germany, the period between the Luxembourg Agreement and the establishment of formal diplomatic relations was dominated by consideration of those relations and by concern over the German scientists in Egypt. When Israel finally achieved diplomatic relations, it came as something of a concession. But in the early 1950s Germany had indicated a desire for formal diplomatic exchange and Israel had been reluctant to formalize relations.

According to Terence Prittie, relying on information from Hans Globke, 'Adenauer tentatively offered Israel diplomatic relations...at the time of the Luxembourg Agreement' (quoted in Brecher, 1975, p. 105). Brecher and others say Germany offered diplomatic relations in 1953 (ibid.). Shinnar denies any formal offer was received before March 1965, but he does indicate that talks on a German visa office did begin as early as the middle of 1955 (1967, pp. 108-14). Not before January 1956, however, did Shinnar inform the German Foreign Office of Israel's willingness to talk about formal relations.

Hallstein's meeting with Shinnar in June 1956, halting discussion of formal relations, disappointed Israel. Some saw it as a political victory for the Arabs. According to Inge Deutschkron, in response three factions emerged within Israeli government circles: (1) a group, including Foreign Minister Sharett and Golda Meir, that saw the German move as a breach of confidence. When Meir replaced Sharett in June 1956, she pretended that Germany did not exist; (2) a smaller group, including Moshe Dayan, that thought the incident should be publicized in an effort to overcome the Arab victory by achieving diplomatic relations; and (3) the largest group, including Eshkol and Shimon Peres, that accepted the situation but worked towards concrete co-operation with Germany in other areas (1970, pp. 105–6; Shinnar, 1967, pp. 115–16). Prime Minister, David Ben-Gurion, actively wanted diplomatic relations but was also pleased with Germany's compensation for the failure.

Ben-Gurion diplomatically said nothing when the discussions failed, but in June 1957 he hoped publicly that 'normal diplomatic relations will be established with the Federal Republic of Germany in the near future' (*Jewish Chronicle*, July 5, 1957; *Die Welt*, June 29, 1957), He repeated this desire twice in July, the second time in a comprehensive statement in the Knesset responding to a motion from the opposition for clarification of policy towards Germany: 'Increasingly Germany is assuming an important place in Europe ...Israel's economic and financial relations with Germany are of special importance for our future ...Relations with Germany, in my humble opinion, are also necessary for political reasons ...[to do with peace and our future]' (quoted in Deutschkron, 1970b, p. 115).[24] Ben-Gurion also said that 'The Germany of today is not the Germany of yesterday' (*Frankfurter Allgemeine Zeitung*, July 16, 1957). The development of a new Germany and the recognition of Germany's importance for Israel were to dominate his public statements concerning Germany from then on.[25]

Increasingly, Israel saw the absence of diplomatic relations as a political advantage for the Arabs. Shinnar has written,

> In the area of foreign policy the absence of diplomatic relations was becoming increasingly a politically damaging policy for Israel. Nasser tried...to pull the African states...away from Israel. His argument was that a power of the economic and political importance of Germany was not willing to recognize Israel in order not to jeopardize its relations with the Arabs; he expected the African countries to follow suit. (Shinnar, 1967, pp. 121–2)

Israel understood Nasser's thinking on this subject and feared that Germany's example would lose Israel friends.

Ben-Gurion argued that diplomatic relations were normal and, hence, desirable. He called for 'relations which ought to be like our relations with any people' for Israel 'to win Germany's friendship, as we would win the friendship of any people, for that is necessary for us' (*Haaretz*, October 2, 1959). But Ben-Gurion never suggested that relations in general between Germany and Israel could be 'normal'. Thus, Germany's past was to be remembered but the sons of the Nazi years were not forever to be held accountable for their fathers' sins:

> First, one must not forget or excuse the crimes of the Nazis. The whole German people is responsible...for the people went along. Second, the sins of the Nazis cannot necessarily be taken out on present day Germany. That would indeed be subscribing to a race theory ...If a German father was inhuman but his sons are decent, then I have nothing against the sons. (*Haaretz*, October 2, 1959)

Ben-Gurion said he would visit Germany if it were politically expedient, for in political questions pragmatism had to prevail. According to Ben-Gurion, Israel needed Germany and needed diplomatic recognition. Nevertheless, when asked in 1968 why Israel had not pursued formal relations more vigorously, he replied, 'Money was more important to us then than diplomatic relations' (Deutschkron, 1970a, p. 119).

Shimon Peres offered similar explanations in 1968. In reference to arms supplies Peres said, 'I found security more important than diplomatic relations. Frontiers cannot be defended with ambassadors' (Deutschkron, 1970a, p. 282). Ben-Gurion and Peres understood that material assistance was in some part a compensation for the absence of diplomatic relations, and they perhaps feared loss of these advantages when diplomatic relations might be established. They also understood that there were limits to the public pressure they could apply to Germany and continue to be rewarded materially.

Once it was clear to Israel that Germany considered diplomatic relations impossible but was willing to compensate, Israel ceased public appeal on the subject. Indeed, Israel began to go further in public statements supporting Germany. During the preparations for the Eichmann trial in 1961 Ben-Gurion remarked,

> Concerning the crimes that the Nazis perpetrated against us, I feel as every other Jew. But for those Germans who condemn those acts, then I feel towards them as I do towards any other people. One must never forget the past, but one must see reality as it is. For me a decent German is no different than a decent Englishman. (*Bulletin*, March 1, 1961)

The official German government information publication, *Bulletin*, noted Germany's appreciation for the content and timing of Ben-Gurion's statement, and on the eve of the trial Ben-Gurion reiterated his regard for the new Germany and distributed blame for the tragedy that had befallen European Jews to Britain, France and the USA for their failure to act positively in the 1930s (*Frankfurter Allgemeine Zeitung*, April 4, 1961; *Neue Zürcher Zeitung*, April 5, 1961).

Ben-Gurion was out of step with popular Israeli feeling. His apparent indifference to the German scientists in Egypt led to charges that he was buying arms with Israeli silence over a major threat to security (Harel interview, 1975; *Jerusalem Post*, February 16, 1965). He was reluctant to complain to Adenauer lest Germany's troubles in the Arab World be exacerbated, and it was this reluctance that led to the programme of physical violence and harassment conducted privately by Israeli intelligence (*Der Spiegel*, March 27, 1963).

Ben-Gurion's failure to achieve diplomatic relations was not a major issue in Israel, probably because there was significant domestic opposition anyway. But the threat posed by the German scientists and Ben-Gurion's failure to extract German government action plunged his government into crisis. Foreign Minister Golda Meir, addressing Germany, declared, 'We demand that the German government put a stop to the activities of these scientists, and if legislative or other measures are required for the purpose, we demand that such measures be taken at once' (*Jerusalem Post*, March 21, 1963). The Knesset presented a resolution to the German government:

> The German people cannot absolve itself ...It is the duty of the German Government to put an immediate end to this dangerous activity of its citizens and to take all steps required to prevent this cooperation with the Egyptian Government. The Knesset calls upon enlightened world opinion to exercise its influence without delay in order to put a stop to this activity of German experts, whose aim is [the destruction of] the State of Israel, the home of the remnants of our people who have survived the Nazi holocaust. (*Jerusalem Post*, March 21, 1963)

The Israeli government and the Israeli people were particularly disturbed that Germans, especially Germans known for their pro-Nazi activities, were involved in the development of deadly weapons aimed at Israel; they held the German government responsible and evoked the ghosts of the Third Reich. The press ran an anti-German campaign.

Ben-Gurion considered the public attack on Germany too vigorous, and he objected to the violent methods the Intelligence Service had chosen for solving the problem. He downplayed the danger of the Egyptian weapons.

At the end of March 1963 the Chief of Intelligence, Isser Harel, resigned in protest at Ben-Gurion's conservative policy on the scientists.[26] The resignation fuelled criticism of Germany and of Ben-Gurion, and in mid-June Ben-Gurion himself resigned as Prime

Minister, although the role of the German scientists in his resignation is unclear.[27]

Ben-Gurion's resignation did not halt his public support of Germany.[28] He returned to appeals for an Israeli commitment to the establishment of diplomatic relations and even suggested that diplomatic recognition had displaced German arms in importance (*Neue Zürcher Zeitung*, March 23, 1965). But Levi Eshkol, his successor, did not share Ben-Gurion's view.

Eshkol refused to minimize the importance of the scientists and concluded that the German government was not submitting to friendly persuasion. He levelled at Germany one of the severest public attacks since the Luxembourg Agreement. In October 1964 he told the Knesset:

> [We are filled with] bitterness and disillusionment...as a result of the activities of the German scientists ...The destruction of European Jewry by Germany in those unhappy days...will forever remain a component part of our collective and personal consciousness...our understandable disgust at the work that is being done...should not be conveniently dismissed as illogical prejudice. Surely a people that has suffered as much as our people...has the right to expect special consideration in these matters? ...We need only point to the similarity between the exponents of the blind Arab hatred and the murderous executives of terror from the Hitler days in order to obtain a true view of the situation. And this applies...to scientists and technicians of this kind from any country – and of course with still greater force to those coming from Germany. (Text in Vogel, 1969, pp. 162–3)

Eshkol and the Israeli government no longer divorced Nazi Germany from the Federal Republic; they linked the past to the present. They expected and demanded special treatment from Germany, not indifference.

Eshkol was not prepared, however, to go as far as Sharett at the UN in 1950. He recognized that Europe was important to Israel and that Germany was important in Europe. He was not prepared to destroy Israeli ambitions through hatred for Germany:

> In connection with the special system of relations existing between us and Germany...we do not wish the idea to become public that this chapter of history is closed on a note of bitterness, arising...because of the activities of...unprincipled and unscrupulous scientists ...The economic and political importance of the Federal Republic is growing steadily... [Our relations with Europe] are of very great importance to our progress in all fields; consequently the mission that Federal Germany has in the Western World and in Europe makes it incumbent upon us to make a comprehensive assessment of the situation and

maintain a strictly objective and effective watch over all the problems arising. (Text in Vogel, 1969, pp. 164–5)

Eshkol wanted to be just critical enough to make the German government act on the scientists without forsaking the crucial material assistance Israel enjoyed.

Indeed, Eshkol wanted more from Germany. As the end of the reparations agreement approached, he suggested that Germany had repaid only a fraction of what had been plundered from the Jews, in addition to psychological loss. Eshkol suggested German credit could be a substitute for the end of reparations, and he made a public pitch for development aid (*Jerusalem Post*, January 6, 1965). Eshkol appeared to feel free, in light of the pending termination of arms supplies and German inaction on the scientists not only to criticize Germany, but also to suggest how Germany should compensate in the future.

Once Germany had announced the decision to cease arms shipments to Israel in February 1965, Eshkol appeared totally unconstrained in his criticism. In the Knesset he said:

Germany must face a special responsibility of unexampled gravity [with a] fundamental duty to advance world peace...reinforced by a unique fabric of memories which call for the eternal mourning, anger and grief in the hearts of the Jewish people and cast a heavy shadow on the conscience of this generation ...The whole of civilized humanity rightly tends to judge and evaluate the extent to which Germany has liberated herself from the burden of the past by her actions in the sphere of relations with Israel and the Jewish people. It is also natural to regard Germany's policy towards Israel as the touchstone for her aspiration to find her place in the family of nations ...For several years the Government of West Germany displayed a favourable approach to the vital needs of Israel ...Nevertheless the account still pending between the Jewish people and the German people – an account written in blood – goes far beyond the limits of the political and the material spheres ...The decision of the West German government [to end arms supplies] is based on the principle of not supplying arms to areas of tension ...Gemany is not entitled to regard Israel as one of the world's areas of tension. Israel is not an area of tension. Israel is the remnant that has remained to the Jewish people after the most dreadful of all the tribulations that have ever been visited upon any member of the family of nations. Germany's obligations to Israel belong to a unique and unexampled fabric of history and cannot be subsumed under any general definition of 'areas of tension'. (*Jerusalem Post*, February 16, 1965)

Eshkol sought to embarrass Germany in the court of world opinion as Israel had done before 1952. He advised the world that Germany should yet be judged on fitness for the family of nations. He rejected compensation for the lost arms, and his statement probably affected Erhard's decision three weeks later to recognize Israel.

After Erhard's announcement, Eshkol softened his public tone. He still chastized Germany for surrendering for several years to Arab pressure on the question of the scientists and diplomatic relations, but he also returned to the importance of Germany and Europe. He made clear in his March 16 speech to the Knesset that Israel would agree to the German proposal because it was in Israel's interest to do so (text in Vogel, 1969, pp. 169–72).

Up through 1965, then, Israel was restrained in public criticism of Germany (and, with Ben-Gurion, perhaps even in private criticism). In exchange Israel received significant material assistance as well as public German support or silence. But when sorely disappointed, Levi Eshkol and Golda Meir, at least, were prepared to recall the consequences of Nazism as justification for their expectations of German behaviour.

ISRAEL, 1966–9

After diplomatic recognition, Germany emphasized 'normalization'; Israel insisted on characterizing the changes as a 'formalization of relations'. The different terms reflected the different perspectives on the meaning of what had happened. Israel refused to let go of the special relationship; publicly, at least, Germany thought it was over.

Asher Ben-Natan, Israel's first ambassador to Germany, held to the language Israel always had used respecting Germany. Presenting his credentials in August 1965 he looked towards German help in the future and he reminded the President of the Bundesrat of the past, stressing that the moral future of the world depended on the lessons of the Holocaust (State of Israel Ministry for Foreign Affairs, August 24, 1965). During his four-year term in Bonn Ben-Natan never wavered from these themes of close relations, an important and tragic past and a brighter future.[29]

On several occasions Ben-Natan commented on the term 'normal relations', and his interpretation was different from Germany's: 'Through the establishment of diplomatic relations normal channels were created ...This is how I understand the concept "normalization" in German-Israel relations' (*Allgemeine Wochenzeitung der Juden in Deutschland*, November 19, 1965). However normal the form, the content of relations would never be normal:

> By normalization between two countries one generally means a mutual *de jure* recognition which expresses itself in the exchange of ambassadors. The past state of affairs was, according to this definition, an anomaly ...But this does not mean that the substance of our relations can be fit into a normal scheme. It cannot be expected that feelings, thoughts and historical associations will just end. The significant

content of a normalization is a deepened mutual respect between peoples as a prerequisite for understanding. (Ben-Natan, 1966, p. 3)

Ben-Natan denied that diplomatic relations were suggested by Germany to 'force Israel out of its special position in Germany's array of foreign relations' (*Haaretz*, March 1966), and he noted that there was no consensus in German officialdom on the meaning of 'normalization'. In this respect Ben-Natan's choice of language on the subject of normalization typified the Israeli refusal to succumb to the implications of change in German diplomatic behaviour. He introduced 'normalization between peoples' to distinguish from 'normalization between states', and he insisted that history could not be overcome by formal arrangements. And he plainly did not want to accept what Germany seemed to be saying.

Willy Brandt eventually endorsed Ben-Natan's distinction between states and peoples,[30] but whereas German officials chose to emphasize the concept of normalization, Israelis discussed the concept only reluctantly and in response to questions. What was 'normal' to the Germans remained 'formal' to the Israelis.

ISRAEL, 1969-75

The visit of Israeli Foreign Minister Abba Eban to Germany at the end of February 1970 was seen by some observers as a 'new stage in German-Israeli normalization' (*Handelsblatt*, February 24, 1970; *Neue Zürcher Zeitung*, February 28, 1970). It was certainly the beginning of the public recognition of German-Israeli relations as always friendly.

Eban shifted the emphases of Israeli rhetoric in recognition, finally, of change in the political support features of German-Israeli relations. His first remarks on arrival in Germany were concentrated in the present, not the past, and he discussed the past only as a bridge to the future: 'Let us use these thoughts and experiences of the past to aid our work for a peaceful future for Europe, the Middle East, and the world. It is in the service of the future that I have come here' (*Bulletin*, February 25, 1970). Israel's recent political isolation had changed its perceptions of Germany and of Europe, and Eban was prepared publicly to accept Germany as part of Europe. 'My visit here', he said, 'is part of an Israeli effort to emphasize as much as possible our relationship with Europe' (ibid.). Like Ben-Natan, Eban did stress that relations between the German and Israeli peoples were unique, and he still claimed a 'special character' for the relationship. He referred to 'the central philosophy – that our relationship has a special context of history'. But he allowed, too, for German–Arab relations. Despite different emphases, Israel and Germany were beginning again, for the first time since diplomatic recognition, to speak of their relationship in like terms.

Abba Eban repeated his friendly, future-oriented remarks about Germany and Europe in Israel when Walter Scheel visited in July 1971.

He emphasized the special past but, for the first time, he suggested that Israel should not be a captive of the past. He referred to 'normal political relations' (*Bulletin*, July 13, 1971). But Israel also expressed displeasure over German attitudes towards the Middle East conflict. Israel was particularly chagrined by Germany's stand on the 1971 European Economic Community Middle East paper (*Frankfurter Rundschau*, May 19, 1971; *Die Welt*, May 22, 1971; *Publik*, July 2, 1971). If Germany and Israel were now to speak of each other in similar terms, they both perceived renewals of their licences to criticize each other as well.

A year after the Scheel visit, Israeli athletes were assassinated at the Munich Olympics. The Palestinians responsible had hoped, among other things, to drive a wedge between Israel and Germany, for nothing could have been more painfully symbolic than the death of Jews under German care on German soil. Israel, however, did not blame Germany for the terrorist attack nor for the loss of life. To a significant degree there was mutual understanding.

Israel did find unconscionable, however, the German response to the hijacking of a German airliner in October 1972. The Federal government released those responsible for the Munich murders. The Israeli ambassador was recalled; Israel, exponent of a hard line with terrorists everywhere, denounced Germany publicly, and the disagreement between the two countries over the release marked one of the lowest points in the history of their relations. Israel's ambassador declared: 'The release of the three terrorists is unbelievable. It is not just a question of capitulation to Arab threats. Three murderers...are now free...to murder more Israelis ...One should not be surprised by the disappointment and shock evoked in Israel by the German decision' (*Das Parlament*, November 4, 1972). The ambassador said Israel deserved better treatment: 'One should be aware...that the real issue is the struggle of the remainder of the Jewish people for a meaningful life in peace and security ...Israel has a right that this reality take precedence over diplomatic or other considerations of the Federal Republic' (ibid.). Prime Minister Golda Meir put the Israeli view succinctly: 'The decision to release the Arabs was a shocking and retrograde step that put humanity at the mercy of brutal force' (*New York Times*, October 31, 1972).

Some nine months later, in June 1973, Meir's old doubts about Germany surfaced during Willy Brandt's visit to Israel. Although she paid lip-service to the themes of the future and of Europe, she stressed Germany's past and a consequent special obligation to Israel (*Deutschland-Berichte*, July 1973). Meir asked Brandt to remember two Hebrew words, *ain breira*, which mean 'we have no choice'. Israel's diplomatic options were limited. Meir was both asking and demanding German understanding, not unlike German appeals to Israel in 1952.

Germany continued to disappoint Israel publicly in the Middle East, especially through the EEC during the 1973 war. Germany's abstention in the vote on the Palestinian debate at the United Nations in 1974 only confirmed Israel's worst doubts about Germany as a potential champion of Israeli causes in the international arena. Moreover, Israel no longer understood how to coax Germany. Officials began to complain that they appreciated the German need for neutrality in public statements, but they could not accept an apparent preference for the Arab side (confidential interviews, 1975). Israel had become aware, however, that matters could be much worse; Germany could have gone the pro-Arab way of France. Thus, for relatively mild treatment, Israel remained grateful.

Israel publicly repudiated German policy on the Middle East conflict and publicly approved German-Israeli relations. Such distinctions signified the growing sophistication of their mutual contact. Foreign Minister Yigal Allon and Prime Minister Yitzhak Rabin praised Germany during state visits there in 1975. Allon, who had opposed reparations and arms and had rejected Ben-Gurion's mild attitude on the scientists, now stressed German-Israeli friendship in Bonn. On arriving in Germany Allon said, 'I feel I am among friends' (*International Herald Tribune*, February 27, 1975). He described his pleasure in accepting Foreign Minister Genscher's invitation because it 'came from a friend who represents a friendly government' (*Deutschland-Berichte*, March 1975; also *Bulletin*, February 28, 1975; *Die Welt*, February 26, 1975). He insisted that the relationship was special, unlike a usual relationship between countries, but he added that relations were becoming more normal (Westdeutscher Rundfunk, February 27, 1975). In private conversations Allon was alleged to have shown understanding for Germany's Middle East policy. In light of Allon's own political background the change was remarkable.

Rabin's was the first visit of a sitting Israeli Prime Minister, echoing the pragmatic and perhaps prophetic promise of David Ben-Gurion a decade earlier. Rabin articulated what had become clear Israeli policy since Eban's formulation linking past and future five years earlier:

> I believe there is something which no Jew, no Israeli can ever forget. At the same time, however, I am certain that we must build good relations for the future between the Federal Republic and Israel. My visit is of a special kind, for I come on the one hand with the burden of the past, but on the other I am attempting to create bridges to the future. (Deutsches Fernsehen, July 7, 1975)

Before leaving Israel Rabin told German journalists, 'Because of the past, Germany has moral obligations to Israel' (Deutsche Presse Agentur, July 3, 1975). During the visit in Germany he did not refer to the relationship itself as special, but he did emphasize its unusual aspects and, while extolling Germany's leadership in Europe, reiterated responsibility to Israel.

ISRAEL, 1977-80

The Labour Party fell from power in Israel for the first time in 1977. The new Prime Minister, Menachem Begin, had led the opposition to the Luxembourg Reparations Agreement. He had been throughout Israel's life an implacable foe of friendship with Germany. It was reasonable, therefore, to expect a radical change in Israeli policy.

The Begin government continued through 1980 a tradition of pragmatism established by its predecessors. Criticism of Germany focused on Middle Eastern policy, whereas the bilateral relationship remained, outside the sphere of diplomatic support, the object of praise.[31]

Prime Minister Begin's diplomatic relations with Germany did not start well. He was too preoccupied forging a close relationship with the USA to receive Per Fischer, the German ambassador, before his final departure for Bonn in July 1977 (*Süddeutsche Zeitung*, July 23, 1977). And when Begin's Foreign Minister Dayan visited Bonn at the end of 1977, he chastized the Federal Republic for pursuing 'an erroneous policy merely for the sake of maintaining solidarity with the European Community' (*Deutschland-Berichte*, January 1978). The criticism escalated in early 1978, however, with news of a sale of anti-tank rockets to Syria by the joint Franco-German armaments production company Euromissile. The German government stressed that it had neither initiated the sale nor had any legal power to prevent it, but Israel's anger was directed, nevertheless, against Germany (*Die Zeit*, February 10, 1978).

Germany was criticized again for the Syrian arms (*Le Monde*, June 29, 1978; *Jerusalem Post*, June 30, 1978; *Der Spiegel*, July 3, 1978), and for Schmidt's endorsement of Palestinian rights (*Frankfurter Allgemeine Zeitung*, June 26 and 28, 1978; *Jerusalem Post*, June 28 and 30, 1978) during Genscher's visit to Israel in June 1978. Following Schmidt's attack on Israeli policy a year later Begin advised Germany to 'keep faith with us, the remnant of the Holocaust' (*Jerusalem Post*, July 6, 1979; *Frankfurter Allgemeine Zeitung*, June 29, 1979). And when Dayan visited Bonn in September 1979, he felt relations had changed 'for the worse' (*Jerusalem Post*, September 12, 1979). Germany, he observed, was 'an outsider to the conflict' and he implied that it had no right, therefore, to pronounce on peace negotiations.

Dayan's successor, Yitzhak Shamir, told *Der Spiegel* after the Venice Declaration that the Germans 'have a special responsibility to the Jewish and Israeli people, a responsibility which should not be forgotten'. 'If Germany had not wanted the Venice resolution', he argued, 'it would not have come to pass', for Germany 'is one of the most important and influential members of the Nine' (July 28, 1980). Nevertheless, Israeli officials recognized that the German attitude could be worse. Ambassador Yochanan Meroz observed that 'Even today there is no complete identity of views between the Federal Republic of Germany and France [in the EEC]' (correspondence, June 1980). He continued to focus on Germany's special responsibility for Israel (*Die Welt*, May 10, 1980).

Because Israel values relations with Germany, criticism usually has concentrated on other actors. When Brandt and Kreisky met Arafat in 1979, for example, Kreisky and the Austrian government were the chief targets of Israeli scorn. The Israeli ambassador to Austria was recalled for consultations, and public statements were vituperative. Brandt, of course, no longer held an official government position; none the less, Israel spared him a personal attack.

Prime Minister Begin was less temperate than his Foreign Minister and his ambassador in Bonn after the Venice Declaration. He recalled the collaboration of Vichy France and Fascist Italy; he said Europe's behaviour during the Second World War disqualified it from offering Israel advice about the 'Nazi-like' PLO (*Jerusalem Post*, June 15, 1980). But the criticism of Germany remained strictly within the European context.

Developments in the spring of 1981 sharpened Begin's rhetoric and escalated verbal antagonism with Germany to a level unknown for nearly three decades. During a state visit to Saudi Arabia in April Chancellor Schmidt said,

> In the Palestinian conflict, one cannot attribute all morality to the one side and shrug one's shoulders in reference to the other side ... Particularly this cannot be if one is a German, living in a divided nation and raising the moral claim of self-determination for the German people. Then one must recognize also the moral claim of the Palestinian people to self-determination. (Deutsches Fernsehen, April 30, 1981)

Foreign Minister Shamir objected to the apparent equation of Palestinian and Israeli moral claims on Germany (*Jerusalem Post*, May 3, 1981), but it was Begin who attacked Schmidt personally:

> From a moral point of view, Schmidt's statements certainly rank as the most callous ever heard. It seems that the Holocaust had conveniently managed to slip his mind, and he did not make mention of a million and a half small children murdered, or of entire families wiped out ... He doesn't care if Israel goes under. He saw this almost happen to our people in Europe not so long ago. He served in the armies that encircled the cities, until the work was finished by the *Einsatzgruppen*. (*Jerusalem Post*, May 4, 1981)

Begin continued these criticisms on Israel Radio (*Jerusalem Post*, May 8, 1981) and before a rally of Likud supporters (*Jerusalem Post*, May 11, 1981). In all of Begin's statements on Schmidt the Holocaust and history dominated as they had in the 1950s, when he opposed any relations with Germany.

The German government characterized Begin's remarks as campaign rhetoric (*Jerusalem Post*, May 5, 1981), and Schmidt appealed for restraint. In a Bundestag speech of May 7, 1981 he tried to end the verbal exchange by reviving earlier language: 'I am aware of the special moral and historical quality of German-Israeli relations, as I have always been in the past and shall continue to be in the future.'

Begin's attack on Schmidt may have been campaign rhetoric (parliamentary elections were in June).[32] It is notable, nevertheless, that criticism of foreign leaders was not reserved for Germany. Harsher words had never been directed towards Germany by any Israeli leader, but a similar vocabulary was deployed for France and President Giscard d'Estaing. Even Menachem Begin, once Prime Minister, found *raison d'état* compelling, and even Helmut Schmidt was still prepared, under duress, to call German-Israeli relations 'special'.

CONCLUSION

What national spokesmen say is not necessarily what their nations do, but symbolic politics can be important. To the casual observer political support is the essence of bilateral relations, and to the casual observer of German-Israeli relations the dramatic changes in public statements have signalled the end of the special relationship. We know, however, that special arrangements continue between Germany and Israel in a variety of policy areas.

Changes in political support are important above all because nations attach much importance to them. Germany believed it had overcome international repudiation by securing public acceptance from the survivors of its chief victims, and it was prepared to sacrifice materially and even, to a lesser extent, diplomatically, in order to gain that acceptance. On the other side no sooner did Israel grant public approval than it found itself needing such approval returned by Germany. Reciprocity, however, could not be simultaneous, for once Germany had secured approval, Israel had lost its leverage over German foreign policy.

For at least three years after the establishment of diplomatic relations German statements alerted Israel to a change in policy. Israel was slow to recognize or accept the change. Only when Israel acutely needed Germany after 1969 did Israel respond to the German warning. For in political as in other areas of the special relationship, behaviour is predicated as much on need and pragmatism as on emotion and perceptions of morality.

Menachem Begin appeared during his first government to pursue the policy of his predecessors, highly sensitive to the past but always pragmatic. Germany's most vociferous critic in Israel seemed to learn David Ben-Gurion's lesson that Germany's friendship, crucial to Israel, was best attained through quiet diplomacy. But Begin also learned, like Ben-Gurion, Levi Eshkol and Golda Meir before him, that the act or threat of public castigation can help obtain objectives: arms and development aid in 1960, diplomatic recognition and development aid in 1965 and 1966, quiet German political support after the Munich massacre of 1972 and Brandt's visit to Israel in 1973.

How useful is the tool of language for Israel's relations with Germany today? Can Israeli public denunciation of Germany's past change German policy towards the Palestinians? The international community accepts Germany as an economic and political power far more in the early 1980s than it had in 1960 or 1965 or even 1972. Germany's commitment to the EEC remains as firm as ever. Its dependence on Arab oil has increased since 1965. Under these circumstances a German retreat on policy towards the Palestinians is unlikely.

Israel does not like the direction of German political support in the past decade, but leaders recognize privately that the situation could be far worse. History has constrained Germany, but it is not obvious that memory will continue to shape German policy in the Middle East through the 1980s. It may not be strategically as useful as in the past, therefore, for Israel to seek its goals this way. However, until the point of diminishing returns is clearly reached, the rhetorical heat in German-Israeli relations may provide a misleading impression that the bilateral bonds are being consumed in verbal fire.

Even if Germany's political support for Israel has undergone a change in kind because of oil dependence and the EEC, other aspects of the bilateral relationship continue to thrive. Downturns in diplomatic support are nothing new in German-Israeli relations, and as in the past, Israel may well be compensated for oral criticism with other more material fruits of the special relationship.

NOTES: CHAPTER 7

1 The literature on the problem of diplomatic relations between West Germany and Israel is extensive. The most useful accounts are provided by Knauss (1960); Bretholz (1963); Wewer (1963); Baade (1965); Böhm (1965); Hottinger (1965); von Imhoff (1965a, 1965b); Ben-Vered (1965); Wagner (1965a, 1965b); Wasser (1966); Shinnar (1967); Deutschkron (1970a); Seelbach (1970); Birrenbach (1972); Deligdisch (1974). More recent analysis, emphasizing the Arab perspective, has been offered by Abediseid (1976). See also the accounts in *Der Spiegel* and *Jerusalem Post* of 1964 and 1965 and the press files of the Deutsche Gesellschaft für Auswärtige Politik for 1957, 1959, 1963, 1964, and 1965.
2 On the question of the scientists, see Lönnendonker (1964); Shinnar (1967); Deutschkron (1970a); Seelbach (1970); *Der Spiegel* (March 27 and May 8, 1963); *Jerusalem Post* (1963, 1964); the press files of the Deutsche Gesellschaft für Auswärtige Politik on the United Arab Republic (1962, 1963, 1964). Abediseid's 1976 account is also useful. According to Abediseid, German technicians and researchers had been working on Egypt's armaments industry since 1950 (1976, p. 132).
3 The Arabs also threatened to expose the arms deal if Germany interfered with the German scientists in Egypt (Seelbach, 1970, pp. 109, 112).
4 In an interview Nasser denied the existence of Soviet pressure to invite Ulbricht (*Der*

Spiegel, February 24, 1965). According to Abediseid, Ulbricht took the initiative and asked to be invited (1976, p. 171).
5   Strauss and Adenauer, consulted by Erhard together with other CDU/CSU politicians, were for the continuation of arms (Deutschkron, 1970a, p. 289). The Israelis saw Foreign Minister Schröder behind the move to halt arms shipments (*Jerusalem Post*, February 15, 1965).
6   Birrenbach called the offer of diplomatic relations one of Erhard's most important political decisions (interview, 1975). Yet the decision has received scant attention from German foreign policy analysts; an exception is Besson (1970).
7   Birrenbach agrees that Barzel influenced Erhard's decision, but suggests the USA thought it was important for the Western world that Germany, as a voice of moderation, should not be excluded from the Middle East (1972, pp. 370–1).
8   See, for example, Willy Brandt (*Bulletin*, September 8, 1967; *Deutschland-Berichte*, February 1967); Karl Hermann Knoke (*Jedioth Chadashoth*, September 6, 1968).
9   Brandt referred to 'neutrality of the heart' during the 1973 Middle East war. At the time of the 1967 war Brandt noted that 'our non-intervention...cannot by any means be interpreted as any moral diffidence or as emotional sluggishness' (text in Vogel, 1969, p. 295).
10 Mende said the FDP and CDU had their differences in the coalition until 1966 with respect to Israel. It was not that the FDP was anti-Israel, but rather that traditionally the party valued a balanced relationship with both Israel and the Arabs. The FDP voiced objection to arms supplies to Israel and diplomatic recognition for fear of losing the Arabs (interview, 1975). Shinnar notes that Scheel, as Minister for Economic Co-operation, suggested a reduction in the annual development aid to Israel (1967, p. 101). Mende saw Scheel's reference in October 1973 to special relations with both Israel and the Arabs as a logical development of traditional FDP attitudes to the Middle East. Of course, some FDP politicians, like Thomas Dehler, were well known for their pro-Israeli positions.
11 For the dependence of individual European countries and the EEC on Arab oil, see Maull (1980a, ch. 3).
12 On this issue, see the exchange between Walter Scheel and Rolf Vogel in *Deutschland-Berichte* (January 1970).
13 On the development of political co-operation and foreign policy in the EEC, see Dahrendorf (1971, 1973); Morgan (1974b); Hoffmann (1974); Palmer (1976); Wallace and Allen (1977); Allen (1978). For European policy towards the Middle East within the framework of European Political Co-operation, see Steinbach (1979b); Sicherman (1980); Artner (1980); Liber (1979–80). On efforts to fashion a common energy policy, see Lieber (1979). For a review of the various aspects of European-Arab relations, see Steinbach (1979a).
14 For a discussion of the 1971 paper and whether Germany accepted the French or the British interpretation of Resolution 242, see *Neue Zürcher Zeitung* (May 15, 1971); *Frankfurter Rundschau* (May 19, 1971); *Die Welt* (May 22, 1971); *Süddeutsche Zeitung* (July 5, 9, 11 and 23, 1971); *Die Zeit* (July 9, 1971); *Handelsblatt* (July 13, 1971); *Jerusalem Post* (July 15, 1971); *Aufbau* (July 16, 1971); *Le Monde* (July 16, 1971); *Deutsche Zeitung Christ und Welt* (July 19, 1971); *Bulletin* (July 21, 1971).
15 The following EEC statements on the Middle East are deemed important by Israel's Ministry for Foreign Affairs (correspondence, 1980): declaration of the EEC Foreign Ministers, Brussels, November 6, 1973; declaration of the European leaders, Copenhagen, December 15, 1973; speech of the Italian ambassador in the name of the Nine, UN, November 5, 1975; speech of the Italian ambassador in the name of the Nine, UN, December 2, 1975; speech of the Dutch Foreign Minister in the name of the Nine, UN, September 28, 1976; speech of the Dutch Foreign Minister in the name of the Nine, UN, December 7, 1976; declaration of the European Council, London, June 29, 1977; speech of the Belgian Foreign Minister in the name of the Nine, UN, September 26, 1977; declaration of the Nine Foreign Ministers after Sadat's visit to Jerusalem, November 22, 1977; declaration of the European Council, Copenhagen,

April 7–8, 1978; declaration of the Nine Foreign Ministers after the Camp David Agreements, September 19, 1978; speech of the German Foreign Minister in the name of the Nine, UN, September 26, 1978; declaration of the Nine on the treaty between Israel and Egypt, March 26, 1979; declaration of the Nine, June 18, 1979; speech of the Irish Foreign Minister in the name of the Nine, September 25, 1979; statement by the Foreign Ministers of the EEC on Lebanon, April 22, 1980; declaration of the European Council, Venice, June 13, 1980.

16 On the Euro-Arab Dialogue, see Braun (1977); Allen (1978b); Taylor (1978); Steinbach (1979a); Maull (1980a); *European Report* (1980).

17 For Israel's other reactions to EEC statements, see *Jerusalem Post* after the dates noted in n. 15, above. For the Israeli response to the fact-finding mission of Gaston Thorn, Luxembourg's Foreign Minister and the EEC's plenipotentiary on the Middle East after the Venice summit, see *Europe* (1980a); *Guardian* (August 30, 1980); *Jerusalem Post* (September 30 and October 1, 1980). For further developments in the EEC after the June initiative, see *Jerusalem Post* (October 13 and 14, November 26, December 3 and 28, 1980); *Guardian* (November 29, 1980); European Community Information Service (1980).

18 For comprehensive documentation of the German position, see the files of the Pressedokumentation section of the German Press and Information Office and the clippings in the press library of the Royal Institute of International Affairs. On the development of Bonn's policy of 'balance', see Oppermann (1980) and Steinbach (1981). Steinbach calls for a greater recognition by policy-makers of Germany's economic and strategic interests in the Gulf, while Oppermann believes that Germany's responsibility for the Holocaust and the creation of the State of Israel must remain the chief determinant of policy towards the Middle East.

19 For excerpts from other major German statements on the Palestinians since 1974, see *Deutschland-Berichte* (April 1980). See also von Wechmar (1972) for a fuller statement of his own views on Israel and the Middle East.

20 For examples of German statements made during the visits of the Saudi Foreign Minister, the Egyptian Foreign Minister and President Sadat in 1976, see *Deutschland-Berichte* (April 1980).

21 For press reports of the visit and Schmidt's remarks, see: *Frankfurter Allgemeine Zeitung* (June 26, 1978); *Süddeutsche Zeitung* (June 28, 1978); *Le Monde* (June 29, 1978); *Neue Zürcher Zeitung* (July 2–3, 1978); *Der Spiegel* (July 3, 1978).

22 See the article by Theo Sommer (*Die Zeit*, July 13, 1979) for an elaboration of this point.

23 Schütz sets the relationship between Israel and Germany in a positive light also in interviews with *Haaretz* (March 14, 1980) and *Jerusalem Post Magazine* (May 8, 1981).

24 Ben-Gurion was to say later that Germany was perhaps the greatest power in Europe (*Le Monde*, December 26, 1957).

25 See, for example, Ben-Gurion's statement to the Knesset on July 1, 1959, and his statement after meeting with Adenauer in March 1960 (quoted in Vogel, 1969, pp. 119–21).

26 On the differences between Ben-Gurion and Harel, see *Jerusalem Post* (April 1, 1963). Harel appreciated Germany's importance in Europe and the need for pragmatism, but he could not accept Ben-Gurion's directive to cease moves against ex-Nazis bent on the destruction of the State of Israel.

27 According to Harel, it was important, but others such as Ben-Natan disagree (correspondence, 1980). For additional interpretations, see *Jerusalem Post* (June 17, 1963).

28 See statements in *Die Welt* (February 4, 13, and 22, 1965); *Jerusalem Post* (February 14, 1965); *Neue Zürcher Zeitung* (March 19 and 23, 1965); *Der Spiegel* (March 31, 1965).

29 See *Jedioth Chadashoth* (August 25, 1965); Deutsches Fernsehen interview (Presse- und Informationsamt, September 6, 1965); *Allgemeine Wochenzeitung der Juden in Deutschland* (November 19, 1965); Bayerischer Rundfunk interview (Presse- und Informationsamt, November 19, 1965); *Vorwärts* (December 8, 1965); *Diskussion*

(February 1966); *Haaretz* (March 3, 1966); Deutsches Fernsehen (July 3, 1966); *General-Anzeiger* (August 25, 1966); *Emuna* (September 1967); *Rhein-Neckar Zeitung* (January 20, 1968); Westdeutscher Rundfunk interview (Press- und Informationsamt, May 5, 1968); *Allgemeine Zeitung Mainz* (June 14, 1969); *Deutschland-Berichte* (October 1969); *Kölner Stadt Anzeiger* (December 3, 1969); *Publik* (December 12, 1969).

30 Ben-Natan made the distinction in an interview on Deutsches Fernsehen (July 3, 1966); Brandt made the distinction in his formulation 'normal relations with a special character', referring to relations between the peoples of Germany and Israel (*Deutschland-Berichte*, July 1973).

31 See, for example, the speech by Foreign Minister Dayan during a visit to Bonn in November 1977 (*Deutschland-Berichte*, January 1978), the interview with Ambassador Meroz on May 10, 1980 (*Die Welt*), and statements by Genscher (*Deutschland-Berichte*, July–August 1978) and Ambassador Schütz (*Deutschland-Berichte*, February 1980; *Jerusalem Post Magazine*, May 8, 1981).

32 For an analysis of the series of exchanges between Prime Minister Begin and Chancellor Schmidt, see *Der Spiegel* (May 11, 1981).

8
An Overview of German-Arab Relations

Resolution of conflict in the Middle East often seemed to require in the past a choice between the Arabs and Israel. German neutrality has tried to avoid such a choice. But declarations of a 'balanced' policy since 1973 have exposed Germany to an inevitable Arab challenge: if Israel has enjoyed preference, then balance must imply preference for the Arabs also. Squeezing with this one simple point the Arab states have forced Germany into concessions in policy spheres that sometimes parallel, but do not yet rival, relations with Israel.

Germany always has been aware of the Arab states and, even in the warmest moment of relations with Israel, it has sought to maintain friendships throughout the Middle East. Arab states, beginning with German-Israeli negotiations in 1952, have attempted to isolate Israel by threatening reprisals against Germany, and Germany always has responded. German responses satisfactory to the Arabs, however, began only when Germany began to appreciate the economic might of the anti-Israel world.

THE EARLY STAGES, 1952–65

When the Arab League threatened to break economic ties with the Federal Republic if Germany ratified the Luxembourg Agreement, the Federal government promptly dispatched delegations to Arab capitals to clarify the content of the agreement with Israel and to seek to avert reprisals. On the same day that the Arab League threatened to break economic ties Adenauer said: 'We did not forget the Arab world when we began to negotiate with Israel' (*Bulletin*, November 13, 1952).[1] Businessmen in Germany did not want to lose Arab markets, even though the volume of trade between Germany and the Arabs was, in 1952, still very small (Tables 8.1 and 8.2). The Arab World was regarded generally as a potential market, and Germany's growth economy had faith in the future value of the Middle East (*Neue Zürcher Zeitung*, November 23, 1952).

Table 8.1 *German Imports from the Middle East and North Africa, Selected Years and Countries, 1950–79*

Million DM	1950	1951	1952	1956	1960	1963	1965	1966	1967	1969	1971	1973	1975	1977	1978	1979
Egypt	98·9	103·0	127·8	108·5	127·5	139·7	146·2	122·7	115·0	157·9	165·8	148·1	127·6	193·3	273·3	344·5
Syria	4·5	5·4	15·1	51·0	22·4	24·6	32·3	35·8	34·1	18·2	61·9	62·5	159·5	290·0	295·1	257·3
Lebanon	—	4·4	2·5	12·1	4·6	19·6	24·1	32·4	19·0	30·6	32·2	46·1	50·1	21·4	18·9	14·1
Iraq	76·4	138·4	169·6	258·6	382·7	388·3	327·0	251·5	105·0	151·2	323·1	144·8	294·5	294·6	411·5	610·6
Saudi Arabia	67·7	154·0	145·9	310·1	528·1	310·8	529·1	576·7	817·6	786·2	1,270·9	1,923·3	3,897·5	4,463·3	3,033·4	4,308·6
Jordan	—	—	0·22	0·59	0·50	0·16	0·78	0·66	0·81	0·51	0·98	0·94	4·0	7·9	8·7	11·0
Kuwait	13·6	48·6	58·0	138·8	111·3	168·5	145·2	113·3	236·7	182·1	324·1	321·2	548·7	369·5	529·6	996·7
Libya	0·01	0·16	1·0	4·8	3·3	442·4	1,484·4	1,611·4	1,402·0	2,550·1	2,331·0	2,222·2	3,446·7	5,026·9	3,416·5	5,540·7
Algeria	64·5	38·3	45·5	70·3	107·5	242·5	238·8	357·2	515·3	624·0	966·0	1,409·0	2,527·2	2,728·6	2,341·2	3,096·4
Tunisia	22·3	8·5	13·5	12·6	15·6	12·1	27·2	46·9	78·7	86·8	132·9	45·9	282·4	384·6	443·8	400·4
Morocco	187·3	116·1	170·5	194·6	223·7	193·6	225·3	192·2	172·4	193·0	203·9	292·4	324·0	410·3	408·2	492·7
United Arab Emirates*	—	—	—	—	—	—	—	—	—	—	—	651·7	1,824·8	2,111·5	1,395·7	2,108·7
Iran†	39·1	106·7	68·9	118·0	598·1	885·4	618·9	686·1	659·7	717·7	1,150·1	1,686·4	3,634·9	4,335·2	4,214·8	4,225·3
Total Middle East and North Africa	574·31	723·56	818·52	1,279·99	2,125·3	2,827·66	3,799·28	4,026·86	4,156·31	5,498·31	6,962·88	8,954·54	17,121·9	20,637·1	16,790·7	22,407·0
Total all countries	11,373·9	14,725·5	16,202·9	27,063·8	42,722·6	52,277·3	70,447·6	72,669·8	70,183·2	97,972·4	120,118·5	145,417·4	184,312·5	235,177·8	243,706·6	292,160·9
Middle East and North Africa as % of total	5·0	4·9	5·1	4·7	5·0	5·4	5·4	5·5	5·9	5·6	5·8	6·2	9·3	8·8	6·9	7·7

*Figures were recorded first in 1972.
†Not included in figures for the Middle East of the Federal Ministry for Economics.
Note: Certain African countries (Sudan, Mauritania and Somalia) included by the Federal Ministry for Economics are excluded here. Some Middle Eastern countries (Bahrein, Qatar, Oman, North Yemen and South Yemen) also have been omitted because of the inconsistencies in recording figures; the amounts are not significant.
Sources: Statistisches Bundesamt, 1974b, 1976, 1980; Bundesministerium für Wirtschaft, 1977b, 1979a, 1980.

German trade in the Middle East was already growing. Exports to the Middle East and North Africa increased 81 per cent in the year preceding the Arab threat. Germany's principal partner and first diplomatic contact in the area was Egypt, which Adenauer recognized when he sent one of his closest economic advisers, Ludger Westrick, on a mission to Cairo to negotiate with several Arab leaders (*Bulletin*, February 20 and March 20, 1953; *Frankfurter Allgemeine Zeitung*, February 12, 1953). The government made clear Westrick's objective:

> In addition to traditional friendship between the Arab world and Germany, this area provides a market with many possibilities for exchange. Therefore, the Federal Republic has always stressed that it does not desire an impairment of relations with the Arabs. (*Bulletin*, February 20, 1953)

Adenauer empowered his emissary to offer 400 million marks in credit to Egypt in exchange for continuing normal trade relations. If there were to be payment to Israel, there would be payment to Egypt, although not in comparable sums or terms.

Westrick concluded that the Arabs would not carry out their boycott threat because it would hurt them more than it would hurt the Federal Republic, and it was at least partly on the basis of this economic and political assessment that Adenauer ratified the Luxembourg Agreement in March 1953 (interview, 1975). Adenauer had not succumbed to Arab pressure because he had judged, correctly, that Arab threats were idle.

During the next four years Federal Republic exports to the Middle East and North Africa increased by 125 per cent. In addition to continuing private economic interest in the Arab World, the West German government sustained the concern it had shown before the Luxembourg Agreement ratification. Germany and Egypt had decided during Westrick's Cairo negotiations in February 1953 to commit a German study group to analysis of technical possibilities for construction of the Aswan Dam (*Bulletin*, March 20, 1953). The group arrived in March, and the Federal government promptly promised to support companies interested in the construction of the dam (*Bulletin*, March 10, 1956; Adenauer, 1969, p. 216).

Egypt and Germany signed a major trade agreement in February 1956, and the Egyptian Minister of Production visited Bonn a month later. The German government observed:

> This is the first official visit of an Egyptian Minister to the Federal Republic. Its significance lies not only in the concrete economic talks but also in the fact that Egypt and the Federal Republic for the first time have acknowledged their close contact on a high level ...The Federal Republic and Egypt can be viewed as two states which, building on different foundations, strive for a new development ...it

Table 8.2 German Exports to the Middle East and North Africa, Selected Years and Countries, 1950–79

Million DM	1950	1951	1952	1956	1960	1963	1965	1966	1967	1969	1971	1973	1975	1977	1978	1979
Egypt	80·6	124·7	160·5	265·1	474·0	400·4	409·3	365·2	219·7	312·1	353·6	328·7	1,044·4	1,363·7	1,350·7	1,509·3
Syria	30·3	32·4	39·3	81·2	107·2	112·3	92·9	101·5	73·3	119·6	112·5	203·7	609·9	635·0	527·5	687·5
Lebanon	—	16·9	48·0	87·2	155·3	153·7	195·5	206·3	174·1	213·9	283·8	345·2	394·3	265·9	249·5	349·9
Iraq	1·4	9·5	19·5	110·1	136·3	110·3	158·7	233·7	153·5	70·1	102·5	112·8	2,565·5	1,811·3	1,606·5	2,086·2
Saudi Arabia	10·6	12·8	18·6	65·0	68·5	81·4	146·5	171·2	187·9	268·0	189·2	333·5	1,396·4	3,957·1	4,159·7	4,416·7
Jordan	0·2	3·2	6·4	19·8	54·5	42·4	52·1	63·2	77·2	63·2	42·2	74·8	212·4	397·5	323·5	385·4
Kuwait	2·2	1·9	8·4	27·7	78·1	103·0	121·1	127·1	189·6	222·6	146·2	186·0	499·7	858·3	693·5	691·7
Libya	0·13	0·45	1·5	22·0	86·2	125·0	126·3	168·4	156·4	238·3	208·3	559·9	1,321·0	1,507·8	1,631·2	2,157·1
Algeria	5·1	12·0	13·5	21·4	57·6	46·3	62·5	53·9	77·2	331·4	431·9	826·0	1,503·3	2,501·6	2,552·8	2,276·6
Tunisia	2·4	4·4	6·5	12·3	37·7	36·5	47·6	58·0	77·5	71·4	87·7	149·1	258·1	528·1	568·6	650·5
Morocco	15·1	36·6	57·4	118·1	82·6	104·8	118·9	113·5	175·2	218·7	209·1	229·4	454·2	486·2	416·5	418·1
United Arab Emirates*	—	—	—	—	—	—	—	—	—	—	—	74·3	357·7	851·2	857·8	863·9
Iran†	39·0	83·4	87·5	220·6	494·0	398·8	629·6	827·8	928·3	1,094·2	1,279·2	1,885·7	5,192·0	6,350·7	6,767·2	2,349·2
Total Middle East and North Africa	187·03	338·25	467·1	1,050·5	1,832·0	1,714·9	2,161·0	2,489·8	2,489·9	3,223·5	3,446·2	5,309·1	15,808·7	21,515·1	21,705·0	18,842·1
Total all countries	8,362·1	14,576·7	16,908·8	30,861·0	47,946·1	58,309·6	71,650·8	80,628·3	87,045·1	113,556·6	136,010·5	178,396·2	221,588·6	273,614·1	284,907·1	314,621·3
Middle East and North Africa as % of total	2·2	2·3	2·8	3·4	3·8	2·9	3·0	3·1	2·9	2·8	2·5	3·0	7·1	7·9	7·6	6·0

*Figures were recorded first in 1972.
†Not included in figures for the Middle East of the Federal Ministry for Economics.
Note: See Table 8.1.
Sources: As Table 8.1.

is obvious that political contact between our two countries has increased and our relationship has taken on greater political significance ...The possibilities for the exchange of goods between our two countries is very large. (*Bulletin*, March 10, 1956)

The German government noted that technological, trade, cultural and archaeological relations between Egypt and Germany already were flourishing.

Adenauer had strong political, as well as economic, interests in relations with the Arab World. The German Cabinet had decided in November 1955 to counteract efforts of the German Democratic Republic to gain international recognition through the Arab World (Abediseid, 1976, p. 99). Moreover, Adenauer hoped to obstruct the entry of Soviet arms into the Middle East by co-operating with Nasser; he sorely regretted American withdrawal from participation in the Aswan Dam (Adenauer, 1969, pp. 134, 215–19).

Despite the Suez invasion which followed the American withdrawal, damaging relations between the Arabs and the West, trade between Germany and the Arab states continued to flourish. Over the next decade Federal Republic exports rose 137 per cent (Table 8.2); imports, reflecting Germany's increased dependence on imported oil (88.2 per cent of all oil used for fuel in 1965 – see Table 8.3), rose 215 per cent (Table 8.1). The Federal government granted trade guarantees to Egypt in May 1958, April 1963 and September 1964 (*Bulletin*, February 20, 1965). Economics Minister Erhard visited Cairo to discuss trade in January 1960, and at year's end the Federal Republic and Egypt concluded a cultural agreement (Deutsche Welle, March 29, 1972).

In addition to successful Arab pressure against German recognition of Israel, the Arabs demanded and were promised development aid, 230 million marks according to an economic agreement signed by Germany and Egypt in April 1963. This capital aid was supplemented by 50 million marks in technical aid and Egyptians were to be trained in the Federal Republic at a cost of 18 million marks. From 1963 until aid was cut off in 1965 Egypt received 198 million marks (*Bulletin*, February 20, 1965); Israel received 400 million marks in capital aid during the same period.[2]

If relations with Israel were 'special', with the Arabs they were 'traditional'. To Germany, at least, there were no 'normal' partners in the Middle East. Principal pressure for maintaining traditional relations came, inside Germany, from the CDU's coalition partner, the FDP, and according to former party leader Erich Mende, the FDP commitment was almost entirely the product of industrial interests. They feared the loss of markets in a period when German economic growth depended on exports (interview, 1975). When Walter Ulbricht visited Cairo, FDP Minister Walter Scheel opposed stopping aid to Egypt (*Der Spiegel*, February 10, 1965).

The tension between the CDU and the FDP over Israel was equally

Table 8.3 *Imported Oil as a Percentage of Total Oil Use in the Federal Republic of Germany, 1955–78*

1955	69·3
1960	80·8
1965	88·2
1966	89·6
1967	90·1
1968	91·3
1969	91·9
1970	92·9
1971	93·1
1972	93·5
1973	94·3
1974	94·3
1975	94·0
1976	94·7
1977	94·8
1978	95·0

Source: Bundesministerium für Wirtschaft, 1979d.

present over relations with the Arabs, and in crucial decisions the CDU prevailed. Thus, Erhard defied FDP wishes in recognizing Israel and stopping aid to Egypt. Nevertheless, Erhard did try to mitigate the effects of the decision, sending personal emissaries – political experts and businessmen – to a number of Arab countries (Deutschkron, 1970a, pp. 323–5; Seelbach, 1970, pp. 139–40; von Imhoff, 1971). He sent personal letters to all thirteen Arab League nations stressing a German commitment to German–Arab friendship. Erhard was less successful in these tactics, however, than Adenauer had been in 1952. Ten of the thirteen (Egypt, Syria, Jordan, Iraq, Yemen, Sudan, Algeria, Saudi Arabia, Kuwait and Lebanon) broke off diplomatic relations with the Federal Republic.

The example of Israel had proved that the Federal Republic was capable of intense relations without formal diplomacy. After the break in diplomatic relations, Erhard repeated his desire for friendly relations with the Arab World, promising to remain neutral in the Arab dispute with Israel. His efforts to guarantee relations continued throughout his administration (*New York Times*, December 23, 1965; Deutsche Presse Agentur, September 15, 1966), and at least one major threat was overcome: the Arabs then did not recognize East Germany.

CHANGES IN PERCEPTION WITH THE SIX-DAY WAR

Chancellor Kurt Georg Kiesinger, in his 1966 inaugural address, underlined the need for relations with the ten Arab countries (Deutscher

Bundestag und Bundesrat, December 13, 1966, p. 3664), and Jordan responded positively by re-establishing relations in February 1967. Willy Brandt, the new Foreign Minister, launched a systematic effort to encourage other countries to emulate Jordan and, in April 1967, the secretary-general of the Arab League came to Bonn to discuss German–Arab relations with Brandt and Kiesinger.

Secretary-general Hassouna attached both economic and political conditions to the re-establishment of relations. He demanded economic aid and a change in German policy towards Israel. The Germans refused to negotiate economic aid until after the resumption of diplomatic relations, but in now characteristic fashion the Federal Republic compensated for this affront by increasing its aid to the United Nations Relief Agency for Palestinian refugees. Politically Brandt stressed that Germany would continue its policy of normal relations with Israel; it would continue to grant economic aid and would support Israel's application for association with the EEC. Hassouna requested a formal written statement of Germany's policy towards Israel; Brandt refused, but he did write Hassouna that 'Arab fears are unfounded that our relationship to Israel could or must be to the detriment of the Arabs' (*Deutschland-Berichte*, May 1967; *Bulletin*, September 8, 1967).

Despite the absence of diplomatic relations, trade between Germany and the Arab World continued to flourish (Tables 8.1 and 8.2).

Table 8.4 *Major Energy Sources as a Percentage of German Energy Use, 1955–78*

	Hard coal	Lignite	Oil	Natural gas	Nuclear energy	Hydroelectric power	Other
1955	71·7	14·8	8·5	0·3	0	3·3	1·3
1960	60·7	13·8	21·0	0·5	0	3·1	0·9
1965	43·3	11·3	40·8	1·4	0	2·6	0·6
1966	38·3	10·6	45·7	1·6	0	3·1	0·6
1967	36·2	10·2	47·7	2·1	0·1	3·0	0·6
1968	34·0	10·0	49·4	3·3	0·2	2·7	0·5
1969	32·3	9·5	50·9	4·2	0·5	2·1	0·5
1970	28·7	9·1	53·1	5·5	0·6	2·5	0·4
1971	26·6	8·6	54·7	7·1	0·6	1·9	0·5
1972	23·5	8·7	55·4	8·7	0·9	2·3	0·4
1973	22·2	8·7	55·2	10·2	1·0	2·2	0·4
1974	22·6	9·6	51·5	12·7	1·1	2·0	0·5
1975	19·1	9·9	52·1	14·1	2·0	2·2	0·5
1976	19·1	10·2	52·9	14·0	2·1	1·2	0·5
1977	18·0	9·4	52·1	14·9	3·2	2·0	0·4
1978	17·7	9·1	52·5	15·6	3·0	1·7	0·4

Source: Mineralölwirtschaftsverband, 1978.

Moreover, the German government began to appreciate the Arabs as major suppliers of oil. As German dependence on oil as an energy source grew, its oil imports from the Arab World steadily increased (Tables 8.3–8.5). In 1965 the Federal Republic depended on oil for 40·8 per cent of its energy, and in 1969 for 50·9 per cent (Table 8.4). During this same period dependence on foreign oil climbed to 91·9 per cent of all oil consumption (Table 8.3), and 88·9 per cent of that oil came from the Middle East and North Africa (Table 8.5). German awareness of dependence on the Arabs began during the three-month oil embargo of Germany, Britain and the USA after the 1967 Six-Day War (Lieser, 1975). During the Arab embargo, West Germany redoubled efforts to re-establish formal relations with the Arab World.

Willy Brandt was asked by a Lebanese interviewer in September 1967:

> In connection with the problem of Germany and Israel, responsible Arab politicians have always feared that, in the framework of its diplomatic relations with Israel, the Federal Republic has accorded Israel a 'special position'. People cite arms and considerable aid to Israel as results. Are these fears justified?

Anxious to accommodate Arab demands and pacify Arab fears Brandt answered by characterizing relations with Israel as normal. He denied any special arrangements for Israel:

> Now with the establishment of diplomatic relations a normal relationship to Israel has been created and it will remain as such. The Arab fears you mentioned are unjustified for you know our wish and determination for a balanced policy. Moreover since 1965 we have supplied no more weapons. The economic agreements with Israel do not differ from conditions we set for many other countries. (*Bulletin*, September 8, 1967)

Economic aid conditions for Israel did deviate from the norm, but Brandt was keen to deny it. Publicly, the Arab World was winning against the special relationship. The oil embargo and public pressure seemed to affect German public policy.

Before leaving for Morocco (one of three countries in the area with whom formal relations continued), in February 1968, Brandt argued that the Arabs as well as Germany needed formal relations for reasons of *Realpolitik*. He revealed that unofficial contacts had been taking place with different Arab governments on the renewal of diplomatic relations, and he declared that legally binding development aid projects were being completed despite the absence of relations (*Deutschland-Berichte*, March 1968).

Throughout the period of formal rupture German–Arab relations continued. The Federal government worked particularly hard to please

Table 8.5 German Oil Imports from the Middle East and North Africa as a Percentage of Total Oil Imports and According to Rank, 1965–79

	Percentage															Rank														
	1965	1966	1967	1968	1969	1970	1971	1972	1973	1974	1975	1976	1977	1978	1979	1965	1966	1967	1968	1969	1970	1971	1972	1973	1974	1975	1976	1977	1978	1979
Libya	39·2	38·6	30·8	43·0	44·4	41·4	29·8	27·8	23·1	16·3	16·8	21·6	20·0	15·5	16·2	1	1	1	1	1	1	1	1	1	2	2	1	1	2	2
Saudi Arabia	13·8	13·3	17·0	15·9	13·3	12·2	13·2	18·5	23·0	24·5	20·0	19·3	19·7	15·5	16·7	2	2	2	2	2	2	2	2	2	1	1	2	2	3	1
Algeria	4·3	6·7	9·1	8·3	9·4	8·1	11·3	11·1	12·3	9·5	11·5	10·8	10·3	10·5	9·1	8	4	4	3	3	4	3	3	4	5	4	4	4	5	6
United Arab Emirates	—	—	6·2	5·9	4·4	3·4	5·8	6·2	7·1	8·6	9·0	7·1	9·0	6·9	7·0	—	—	5	5	5	9	6	6	6	6	6	6	6	6	7
Iraq	8·8	5·9	2·3	3·2	2·6	3·5	4·2	1·8	1·4	3·5	1·5	1·5	1·4	2·0	2·1	4	5	10	8	9	7	8	9	9	8	9	7	10	10	11
Kuwait	4·4	3·2	5·1	3·2	3·3	4·0	5·1	4·2	3·9	4·2	2·8	1·3	1·1	1·8	2·5	7	9	7	9	8	6	7	7	7	7	7	9	11	11	10
Qatar	0·03	0·1	2·1	1·5	0·4	0·3	0·9	1·1	0·6	1·1	1·5	1·2	0·9	0·6	0·5	12	11	11	—	12	13	12	10	10	10	10	10	13	17	15
Syria	—	—	—	—	0·02	—	0·3	0·4	0·5	0·8	0·9	1·2	0·7	1·5	0·8	—	—	—	—	18	—	15	14	13	12	13	11	15	12	13
Oman	4·9	5·7	1·5	0·9	2·4	2·5	2·8	0·1	—	0·1	—	0·6	—	0·4	0·3	6	—	12	11	10	10	11	16	—	16	—	14	—	18	18
Tunisia	—	—	1·3	1·3	1·5	0·9	0·8	1·0	0·1	0·7	1·0	—	0·8	1·0	0·3	—	—	13	10	12	12	13	11	15	13	12	16	14	13	17
Egypt	—	—	0·07	0·03	0·6	1·3	0·7	0·1	0·2	0·1	0·2	—	0·3	0·4	0·2	—	—	17	15	13	11	14	15	14	15	15	—	18	19	19
Iran	10·4	10·7	9·3	7·8	6·6	8·4	8·5	9·6	12·8	13·0	15·6	18·5	16·1	17·8	10·7	3	3	3	4	4	3	5	5	3	3	3	3	3	1	5
Total Middle East and North Africa	85·8	84·2	84·2	91·0	88·9	86·0	83·4	82·0	85·0	82·4	80·8	94·1	80·3	73·9	66·4															

Sources: UN, Statistical Papers, 1968, 1972, 1974; Bundesministerium für Wirtschaft, 1977b, 1979a, 1980.

countries, like Morocco, which had not severed relations; lines were kept open to others. In September 1968 Hans-Jürgen Wischnewski, the Minister for Economic Co-operation, attended the celebrations for the relocation of the Abu Simbel temple in Egypt, and in November a delegation from the Federal Ministry for Economics was in Egypt for talks on German-Egyptian trade.

TOWARDS A NEW SPECIAL RELATIONSHIP?

By 1971 Germany imported 93·1 per cent of its oil, 83·4 per cent of which came from the Middle East and North Africa (Tables 8.3 and 8.5). Two years later the region was supplying 85 per cent of Germany's oil. It is not surprising, then, that by 1974 diplomatic relations had been restored with all ten countries that had closed their embassies in 1965.[3]

The SPD-FDP government publicly pursued a resumption of diplomatic relations with the Arab World as soon as it came to power in 1969.[4] The government insisted its policy was balanced in the Middle East and that Germany subscribed to UN Resolution 242. But the government was as sensitive to public Arab pressure as it had been sensitive to public pressure from Israel. It took the initiative to restore relations, but when pressed by Egypt to demand Israel's withdrawal from occupied territories, as a condition of diplomatic relations, the Federal government refused (*Deutschland-Berichte*, May 1971). A short time later Germany did endorse the Middle East paper of the EEC which supported Israeli withdrawal from all territory occupied in the 1967 war, but it would not define policy directly under conditions set by other countries.

The Arabs apparently did not mind that they got their way only indirectly. At the end of May 1971 Wischnewski, now leader of the SPD in the Bundestag, was welcomed in Algeria and Egypt as he pursued discussions on the resumption of diplomatic relations (*Le Monde*, June 5, 1971; *Süddeutsche Zeitung*, June 8 and 10, 1971; *Die Zeit*, June 11, 1971), and in June the deputy director of the Arab League office in Bonn observed: 'The Brandt-Scheel government no longer acts as though Germany were a captive of the past' (*Die Zeit*, June 11, 1971).

While Germany told Israel publicly that it conformed to the policy of the European Economic Community, it told the Arabs that its policies and Europe's were identical (*Süddeutsche Zeitung*, August 29 and September 10, 1971). The Arabs now were convinced that they had won their desired diplomatic conditions. By the end of 1971 Algeria and Sudan had renewed relations with the Federal Republic; in 1972 Egypt and Lebanon resumed and by the end of 1974 the rest of the countries had re-established diplomatic relations.[5]

Germany displayed its interest in its new friends immediately, sending Foreign Minister Scheel to Egypt, Lebanon and Jordan in May 1973.

During his visit Scheel emphasized Germany's neutral policy and denied that Germany had a privileged relationship with Israel.[6]

The acid-test for Germany's policy towards the Arabs came in 1973 with the Middle East war. Germany's actions – acceptance of the EEC's Resolution, prohibition of shipment from Germany of US arms to Israel – appear directly related to its need for oil. Libya, one of its main suppliers, had warned Germany and Europe, as had OAPEC, that oil would be cut off or limited if Israel were befriended (*International Herald Tribune*, November 2, 1973; *Guardian*, November 12, 1973; Lieber, 1976, pp. 12–13). Germany complied with Arab desires. When the embargo was announced on October 17, 1973, Germany was designated in the middle category (5 per cent per month reduction). Germany was apparently not as 'pro-Arab' as Britain and France, who were in the 'friendly' category (continuation of supplies); it was not, however, cut off for being 'friendly' towards Israel, as were Holland and the USA. And after signing the November EEC Resolution, the Arabs removed Germany from second-class treatment. During January 1974 Saudi Oil Minister Yamani and Algerian Industry Minister Abdessalam, in talks in Bonn, asked for technological knowhow in return for oil (*Guardian*, January 8, 1974; *Frankfurter Allgemeine Zeitung*, January 17 and 18, 1974; *Süddeutsche Zeitung*, January 18, 1974). Over a third of Germany's oil came from Algeria and Saudi Arabia (Table 8.5). In response, Chancellor Brandt sent an economic delegation to Saudi Arabia in February 1974.

In a letter to Yamani and Abdessalam, published by the Algerian newspaper *El Moudjahid* at the beginning of March 1974, Foreign Minister Scheel promised that the Federal Republic would not recognize territorial acquisition by force, and he agreed that peace in the Middle East could come about only through a return to the pre-1967 borders and a solution to the Palestinian problem (*Frankfurter Allgemeine Zeitung*, March 21, 1974; *Die Welt*, March 30, 1974; *Bonner Rundschau*, April 1, 1974; *Bayernkurier*, April 13, 1974; Deutscher Bundestag und Bundesrat, April 25, 1974, p. 6459). OAPEC promptly classified Germany in the most-favoured status, still leaving Holland labelled totally an enemy of the Arab World (*New York Times*, March 19, 1974).

The Federal Republic pursued public displays of friendship. In May 1974 Willy Brandt visited Algeria and Egypt, emphasizing Germany's traditional friendship with the Arab World, its neutral Middle East policy and the importance of the Middle East for Europe. He spoke to the Arabs equally as a European and a German.[7]

A POLICY OF PARTNERSHIP

The change in foreign policy leadership in 1974 brought West Germany from a burgeoning relationship with the Arab World to an economic and political partnership with key actors such as Egypt and Saudi Arabia. By 1975 94 per cent of Germany's oil consumption came from imports, of which the Middle East and North Africa supplied 80·8 per cent. Three years later imported oil had risen to 95 per cent of use and 73·9 per cent of imports still came from the Middle East and North Africa. Although imports were decreasing (in large part because of events in Iran), limited international alternatives (Alkazaz, 1980, p. 59) and a divisive domestic debate over nuclear energy assure continuing dependence on the Middle East.

The Middle East in the 1970s and 1980s also has been growing as an export market for German goods. Exports to the Middle East and North Africa climbed from 3·0 per cent of Germany's total in 1973 to 7·6 per cent in 1978. Despite a drop to 6·0 per cent in 1979, and a trade imbalance with the Arab World, there has been a decisive growth of German exports (255 per cent) compared to 1973.

GENERAL POLICY

The policies of Schmidt and Genscher after 1975 have reflected Germany's acute energy dependence and the needs of its export-oriented economy.[8] They have seen security of supply and market potential dependent on the existence and good-will of moderate Arab regimes upon which, with the exception of Libya, they have focused their policies. Together with Israel, according to Chancellor Schmidt, Egypt and Saudi Arabia constituted Germany's 'most important friends' in the area (*Der Spiegel*, February 23, 1981). The Federal Republic has sought stability for Egypt, and has viewed a stable Saudi regime, moderate within OPEC and OAPEC, as a guarantor of political and economic security in the Persian Gulf.

Diplomatic visits with the Arab World, a common occurrence in the Brandt–Scheel years, became a central feature of Middle East policy under Schmidt and Genscher. From 1975 until the spring of 1981 a year did not pass without at least one visit to an Arab capital or to Bonn by a high-level German or Arab official.[9] The familiar themes struck by Germany have been traditional friendship, economic interdependence and Germany's adherence to EEC policy on the Middle East, particularly to the dual commitments of Palestinian self-determination and Israel's security. Economic delegations have exchanged visits and there have been regular meetings of the Mixed Economic Commissions with Saudi Arabia, Egypt, Libya and Oman to co-ordinate the various aspects of economic relations (Federal Ministry for Economics correspondence, 1980).

ASSISTANCE FOR DEVELOPMENT

In addition to the general instruments of diplomatic visits and economic commissions, there have been three specific areas of German policy in the Middle East: development aid, trade and investment. With the re-establishment of diplomatic relations in the early 1970s, Germany officially resumed development aid to Arab countries, especially Egypt, Syria, Jordan, Tunisia and the Sudan (Table 8.6). The terms have varied according to category of development (see Chapter 4) and all five classifications can be found among Arab recipients. OPEC countries usually have received technical aid in exchange for repayment. Only Egypt has received more aid than Israel in the past few years; in 1977 and 1978 Egypt was second to India as a recipient of German largesse. Moreover, Germany has been committed to an increase in contributions to aid Egypt's economic development policies (Federal Ministry for Economic Co-operation interview, 1979).[10] Nevertheless, on a per capita basis aid to Israel has far outstripped aid to Egypt or India.

Table 8.6 *German Development Aid to Middle East and North African Countries, 1977–8*

Million DM	1977 Capital aid*	Technical aid	1978 Capital aid*	Technical aid	Development category†
Egypt	283·0	17·6	342·3	13·8	LDC/MSAC
Syria	101·6	10·0	122·1	9·5	TO
Lebanon‡	6·9	0	3·7	0	TO
Iraq§	0·9	0	0·8	0	OPEC
Saudi Arabia§	0·07	0	0·3	0	OPEC
Jordan	64·7¶	8·2	74·4	11·2	LDC
Kuwait	0	0	0	0	OPEC
Libya§	0·2	0	0·1	0	OPEC
Algeria	4·6	5·0	5·1	8·1	OPEC
Tunisia	160·5¶	8·0	156·2	22·0	TO
Morocco	55·4	8·5	168·9	17·4	LDC
United Arab Emirates§	0·02	0	0·02	0	OPEC
Iran§	0	0	0	0	OPEC
Sudan	27·6¶	22·1	92·0	46·6	LLDC/MSAC
South Yemen	1·3	0	0·3	0·005	LLDC/MSAC
North Yemen	18·5	10·7	20·1	15·5	LLDC/MSAC

*Includes special payments.
†LDC = less developed country;
  MSAC = most seriously affected country;
  TO = take-off or threshold;
  OPEC = Organization of Petroleum Exporting Countries;
  LLDC = least developed country.
‡Because of the civil war, the development situation is considered uncertain and since 1974 no regular aid contribution has been made.
§Technical aid in exchange for payment.
¶For 1976–7.
Source: Bundesministerium für wirtschaftliche Zusammenarbeit, 1978a, 1979c.

The Federal Republic contributed in 1974–80 approximately 15·5 million marks to scientific and technological projects in the Arab World (Federal Ministry for Research and Technology correspondence, 1980), a sum Israel has received per annum. Until 1980 Egypt was the key recipient (some 5·5 million marks since 1974) and projects have included physics, desalination, radiation technology, hydrology, reverse osmosis and solar energy. The Agreement on Co-operation in Scientific Research and Technological Development, signed by Egypt and the Federal Republic in April 1979, institutionalized future co-operation, and in 1980 the German government contributed 10 million marks (of a projected 40 million marks total) to a joint reverse osmosis project with Kuwait.

TRADE AND INVESTMENT

Trade and investment are largely private, but as with other Third World areas, the German government has offered special tax incentives to German investors in the Arab World, treaties with Arab governments for the encouragement and reciprocal protection of investments (with Egypt, Morocco, Tunisia, Syria and the Sudan), and guarantees to German exporters. In no Middle Eastern or North African country have Germans invested more than in Israel (585 million marks by 1978) (Table 8.7), but

Table 8.7 *German Investment in the Middle East and North Africa as a Percentage of Total German Investment, 1952–78*

	Million DM	Percentage
Egypt	169·4	0·29
Syria	10·5	0·02
Lebanon	12·8	0·02
Iraq	3·2	0·005
Saudi Arabia	39·7	0·07
Jordan	0·5	0·0009
Kuwait	2·8	0·005
Libya	359·0	0·61
Algeria	216·9	0·37
Tunisia	57·0	0·09
Morocco	50·3	0·086
UAE	46·8	0·08
Iran	528·3	0·90
Sudan	7·5	0·01
North Yemen	1·1	0·002
Qatar	2·9	0·005
Oman	12·5	0·02
All countries	58,192·6	

Source: Bundesministerium für Wirtschaft, 1979b.

investment does appear to be increasing steadily in the Arab World. Germany, among OECD countries, has been the chief architect of joint financing (domestic and foreign, government and private investors) that Egypt and Saudi Arabia find particularly attractive (Alkazaz, 1980, p. 70). Investment in Germany by Middle Eastern oil and Arab countries has remained small, only 1,542 million marks by 1978 or 2·9 per cent of total foreign investment (Bundesministerium für Wirtschaft, 1979e).

NEW TOOLS?

The West German government has tried to develop a reliable and mutually beneficial relationship with the Arab World, particularly with Egypt and Saudi Arabia. This effort, revolving around oil, may be leading towards the supply of military weapons. Since 1973 Germany has rejected Arab proposals for arms deals in exchange for oil (*Guardian*, November 12 and November 13, 1973, January 8, 1974; *Financial Times*, December 4, 1973), but during King Khaled's visit to Bonn in the summer of 1980 Germany did agree to train Saudi airforce personnel (*Saudi Arabia Newsletter*, June–July, 1980). According to *Der Spiegel*, discussion included the sale of Leopard-2 tanks and other military equipment.[11] Chancellor Schmidt asked the Saudi king to wait for the Bundestag election in October, and by the end of the year Schmidt had decided in favour of the sale. In exchange for the weapons, the Saudis allegedly promised to guarantee 40 per cent of Germany's oil requirements (*Der Spiegel*, January 5 and January 12, 1981; *Die Zeit*, February 6 and March 6, 1981).

In early 1981 the transaction was in doubt. A Cabinet committee would have to approve, and the guidelines on arms exports would have to be revised. Bundestag vice-president Annemarie Renger, an SPD deputy, spoke for many in challenging the deal's morality:

> We do not have the power [to prevent such weapons from being used against Israel]. However, it is not just a question of power but above all of moral quality. A delivery of German armaments to Arab countries, to Saudi Arabia, without doubt would bring with it not only a deterioration of relations with Israel, but also a justified impression in Israel that Germans are indifferent to Israel's security interests. (*Der Spiegel*, January 12, 1981)

Chancellor Schmidt subsequently denied any firm decision and called a link between the arms deal and Saudi economic concession 'mere journalistic speculation' (*Der Spiegel*, February 23, 1981).

During a visit to Saudi Arabia in April 1981 Schmidt announced that Bonn would not supply tanks to Saudi Arabia in the immediate future. He cited domestic political difficulties (*Der Spiegel*, April 27 and May 4, 1981; *Süddeutsche Zeitung*, April 29, 1981). Perhaps as compensation to Saudi Arabia, on returning to Bonn Schmidt made a statement particularly favourable to the Palestinians that drew the wrath of Israeli Prime Minister Begin (see Chapter 7), and he reiterated the centrality of Saudi Arabia for German foreign policy (Federal Republic of Germany Consulate-General, Boston, May 7, 1981).

Relations between Germany and the Arab World have flourished in the last few years. To a considerable degree the Arabs have deprived Israel of the political support it now wants and needs, and the Arab states enjoy benefits unknown when Germany depended less on imported oil. Nevertheless, Israel still enjoys preferential treatment in economic aid, in science and technology, in defence questions and in youth exchange programmes over its neighbours in the Middle East.

SOCIETAL LINKS BETWEEN GERMANY AND THE ARAB WORLD
The preponderance of policy relations in Israel's favour is also apparent across societies. Even without formal relations Germany and the Arab World always have maintained cultural relations. Historically relations are most established with Egypt, Lebanon and Tunisia. The Goethe Institute has been active in the Arab World; the German language is widely taught in Egyptian schools and universities; Arab students often attend German universities and joint archaeological activities thrive (Kramer, 1974, pp. 230–5; Abediseid, 1976, p. 103; Foreign Office interview, 1979).

The German government's growing youth exchange with the Arab World seeks to maintain these personal and informal contacts for the future. Government agreements for youth exchange exist with Egypt, Morocco, Sudan, Syria and Tunisia. The German government spent 891,000 marks (5·6 per cent of its total) in 1977 for youth exchanges with the Arab World, and 1,042,000 marks in 1978 (6·4 per cent of the total) (Federal Ministry for Youth, Family and Health correspondence, 1980). For the same years, however, the programmes with Israel amounted to 14·3 and 15·1 per cent.

The constant interaction between Israeli and German parliaments and between Israeli and German politicians is not possible between the Federal Republic and the very different Arab regimes. There were only three bilateral parliamentary friendship groups with Middle Eastern countries outside Israel during the 1976–80 legislative period of the Bundestag; their German membership was small: Egypt (37 members), Iran (39) and Tunisia (23). In contrast, the German-Israeli group recorded 114 members (Deutscher Bundestag Protokoll correspondence, 1980). German politicians do travel extensively in the Arab World, but the depth of contact cannot match the German-Israeli friendships that date from the early 1950s.

Personal ties in the Arab World through trade and investment are developing rapidly and have an historical base. Organizations like the Africa Association and the Near and Middle East Association, both founded in 1934, facilitate contacts for German businessmen with Arab private sectors and governments. There also still exist some of the strictly bilateral fora started after the First World War.

The more commercially oriented institutions are complemented by pure research organizations, such as the German Oriental Institute. The Institute's preoccupation is with Arab countries, but attention is also paid to Israel. However, these various information channels are not yet fully utilized. According to the *Middle East Economic Digest's* 1979 special report on German relations with the region, 'Apart from language difficulties, lack of information is supposed to be keeping West German businessmen shy of the Middle East' (p. 41).

Non-governmental relations between Germany and the Arab World cannot parallel in the near future those between groups and individuals in Germany and in Israel. The conditions that set German-Israeli relations apart do not exist. Historical peculiarities made German-Israeli relations special, and a similar special relationship between Germany and the Arab World probably will never exist. There may be preferences in individual policy areas; but they do not exist across a range of substantive policy sectors, nor are they buttressed by close and complex societal links. West Germany has worked hard to build bridges with the Arab World, but there are limits on the future. Relations with Israel are not the sole obstacle, although Germans plainly are concerned not to cashier Israel for the Arabs. More important is the fabric and history that brought the special relationship into being. No similar conditions have ever existed for German relations with any Arab country.

NOTES: CHAPTER 8

1. For details of the Arab reaction to the Luxembourg Agreement and of German efforts to mitigate the impact on the Arab World, see Deutschkron (1970a, ch. 4); Büren (1974); Abediseid (1976, pp. 68–83). Abediseid analyses in detail the various crises in German–Arab relations from 1952 until 1974. Kramer (1974) emphasizes Egypt and positive aspects of the relationship. For a chronological review of German-Egyptian relations from 1951 until 1972, see Deutsche Welle (March 29, 1972).
2. These figures are for capital and technical aid only; including commercial loans and trade guarantees Egypt received 1,158 million marks in the period 1958–65, while Israel received a total of 1,074 million marks in aid and commercial loans. The capital aid was, and is, considered the best financial arrangement because of the easy terms and Israel received much more than Egypt in the years 1958–65 (625 million vs 130 million marks).
3. For German–Arab economic relations in the period after 1970, see Bockmeyer (1974); on Germany's oil policy since the mid-1960s, see Lieser (1975). For comprehensive analyses of various aspects of the German–Arab relationship, see the contributions to the volume edited by Kaiser and Steinbach (1981).
4. See, for example, statements by Brandt, Scheel and the government spokesman Ahlers in *Deutschland-Berichte* (January 1970, April 1971, May 1971).
5. In March 1972 the Arab League decided that countries could determine for themselves whether to renew relations with Germany. Renewed relations came with Jordan, 1967; South Yemen, 1969; Algeria, 1971; Sudan, 1971; Lebanon, 1972; Egypt, 1972;

Kuwait, 1973; Saudi Arabia, 1973; Syria, 1974; North Yemen, 1974; Iraq, 1974; Libya, Tunisia and Morocco never severed relations.

6. For details of Scheel's visit, see *Deutschland-Berichte* (June 1973); *Vorwärts* (May 24 and 31, 1973); *Le Monde* (May 23, 1973); *Süddeutsche Zeitung* (May 21 and 26–27, 1973); *Frankfurter Allgemeine Zeitung* (May 24, 26, 28 and 29, 1973); *New York Times* (May 23, 1973); *Welt am Sonntag* (May 27, 1973); *Neue Zürcher Zeitung* (May 31, 1973).

7. For statements by Brandt during his visit, see *Deutschland-Berichte* (May 1974; June 1974); *Die Welt* (April 11 and 29, 1974); *Frankfurter Allgemeine Zeitung* (April 18, 19, 20, 22 and 23, 1974); *Süddeutsche Zeitung* (April 18, 22 and 24, 1974); *Le Monde* (April 19, 20 and 21–22, 1974); *Egyptian Gazette* (April 22, 23 and 25, 1974); *Financial Times* (April 18, 1974).

8. For details of Germany's economic relationship with the Arab World in the 1970s and 1980s, see the special issues of *Middle East Economic Digest* (November 1979, February 1982) and the article by Alkazaz (1980).

9. Genscher, Saudi Arabia and Egypt, April 1975; Schmidt, Saudi Arabia, May 1976; Schmidt, Egypt, December 1977; Genscher, Libya, Tunisia, Saudi Arabia and Iraq, June 1979; Genscher, Jordan, Syria, Lebanon and Egypt, August–September 1979; Genscher, Egypt, March 1980; Schmidt, Saudi Arabia, April 1981; Sadat, Germany, March 1976 (Egyptian president); Sadat, Germany, March 1977; Fahd, Germany, June 1978 (Saudi crown prince); Assad, Germany, September 1978 (Syrian president); Hussein, Germany, November 1978 (Jordanian king); Saud al Faisal, Germany, January 1979 (Saudi Foreign Minister); Sadat, Germany, March 1979; Hammadi, Germany, February 1980 (Iraqi Foreign Minister); Saud al Faisal, Germany, March 1980; Mubarak, Germany, May 1980 (Egyptian vice-president); and Khaled, Germany, June 1980 (Saudi king).

10. During Sadat's visit to Bonn in March 1979 he looked to Germany for massive aid contributions to finance his peace plan. Although the German government could not accommodate Sadat to the degree he desired, it did promise to make aid to Egypt a continuing central element of its aid policy (*Frankfurter Allgemeine Zeitung*, March 30, 1979; *Süddeutsche Zeitung*, March 30, 1979; *Der Spiegel*, March 26 and April 2, 1979).

11. There have been other incidents of allegations concerning German arms to Arab countries. For example, on various equipment to Syria, Libya and the Sudan, see *Frankfurter Allgemeine Zeitung* (January 2, 1974); *Guardian* (January 8, 1974). For press reports of armaments deliveries to Syria from the Franco-German joint production company Euromissile, see *Die Zeit* (February 10, 1978); *Le Monde* (June 29, 1978). Details of German supplies to various Arab countries can be found in the arms trade registers of the SIPRI yearbooks; information is contained also in United States Arms Control and Disarmament Agency (1979, p. 156).

Part Three

ENDURANCE

Not all bilateral relations persist, nor do they necessarily stay the same. Special relations, for example, do not always remain special, and the pressures of the international system suggest that the endurance of a relationship as special requires deliberate effort from the partners. They actively must maintain a special relationship. Otherwise, it would follow a life's course from creation to termination.

For a special relationship between two countries to last, there must be a constant psychological relationship. There must be a reason for the countries to persist in extending each other preferential treatment that surmounts common pressures and politics. The special relationship between West Germany and Israel has survived three decades, despite difficulties over diplomatic relations and the German scientists, threats regarding trade and oil, and even terrorism and assassination. It has survived because both Germany and Israel have perceived a need for its survival.

The special relationship has been a source of enormous frustration for the Arab World, and a useful measure of how and why the special relationship is maintained may lie in asking what Arab leaders surely have asked: what must one do to end the special relationship? What must be overcome? Arab leaders have raised moral as well as practical challenges to Germany, comparing the fate of the Palestinians to the fate of the Jews. They have given Germany considerable economic incentive, and they have succeeded in affecting German policy respecting arms and political support. But the special relationship still exists.

The complexity of German-Israeli relations is reflected in the networks of informal and non-institutional relations that complement formal and institutional ties. Whereas it may be possible to coax or coerce official German policy in areas such as technical assistance, trade, youth exchange, or aid, it is a different matter to overcome the extent and depth of relations that now bind Germany and Israel. For it is the non-institutional as well as the institutional, the informal as well as the formal, that has maintained the special relationship, underwritten by mutual feelings of guilt, respect and friendship.

9
The Maintenance of the Special Relationship

THE ROLE OF PROMINENT GERMANS

There are psychological forces within Germany potentially mobilized against the special relationship, and there are institutional and non-institutional forces in opposition as well. But the predominant German commitment has been to maintain special relations.

A number of prominent German politicians have been more committed to the Arab world than to Israel. Gerhard Schröder, former CDU–CSU Foreign Minister, had long been considered an opponent of Israel; his meeting with PLO chief Yassir Arafat in Damascus in 1974 was considered a virtual recognition of the PLO, an act explicitly hostile to Israel (*Die Welt*, December 18, 1974; *Der Spiegel*, December 23, 1974).

Although the SPD generally supports Israel, Hans-Jürgen Wischnewski, frequent government emissary to North Africa and the Arab World, has not. Since his involvement with the Algerian war, Wischnewski has been considered such a friend of the North Africans and the Arabs that he is popularly known in Germany as 'Ben Wisch'. In the early 1970s he was active in the re-establishment of diplomatic relations with the Arab World and more recently has been a fierce proponent of arms sales to Saudi Arabia (*Der Spiegel*, May 11, 1981).

In 1974 during a visit to Israel the then secretary-general of the FDP, Dr Martin Bangemann, insisted the term 'special relationship' was an empty formula. He said that he rejected relations based on the past and on moral obligation. In his position as a member of the European Parliament and as president of the Parliament's Liberal and Democratic Group, Bangemann continued to argue for an intensification of relations with the Arab World and the Palestinians and to criticize Israel (see, for example, FDP-Europe Spezial, 1980b).

Bangemann was joined in criticism of Israel and support of Palestinian self-determination and statehood by his FDP party colleague Jürgen

Möllemann (FDP-Tagesdienst, 1980d, 1980f, 1980g, 1980h), who met with Yassir Arafat in August 1979. Möllemann proposed to Arafat an eight-point peace plan that included mutual recognition by Israel and the PLO (*Jerusalem Post*, August 9 and August 12, 1979; *Deutschland-Berichte*, October 1979). In April 1980 Möllemann received a PLO representative in Bonn to continue discussion (FDP-Tagesdienst, 1980c). Although Möllemann, like Schröder, Wischnewski and Bangemann, denies being anti-Israel, he certainly is unconstrained by the past.

In contrast to these leaders of Germany's important political parties a host of prominent individuals, inside and outside politics, have expressed publicly, through statements and actions, their friendship for Israel. They include Konrad Adenauer, Theodor Heuss, Franz Böhm, Carlo Schmid and Willy Brandt, all singled out by David Ben-Gurion for their friendship (*Bulletin*, March 1, 1961; *Der Spiegel*, March 31, 1965). In addition, Ludwig Erhard and Eugen Gerstenmaier have been noted especially by Felix Shinnar (1967, p. 110); and others who have signed statements, delivered special public addresses, or written special articles, include Erich Lüth, Franz-Josef Strauss, Herbert Wehner, Heinz Kühn, Annemarie Renger, Klaus Schütz, Thomas Dehler, Walter Hesselbach, Günter Grass, Axel Springer, Ludwig Rosenberg, Erich Ollenhauer, Oskar Vetter and Gustav Heinemann – a veritable 'Who's who' in German public life. All these individuals, important shapers of German public opinion, openly and repeatedly have voiced personal and psychological commitments to the Jewish state.[1]

PUBLIC NON-INSTITUTIONAL DISPLAYS OF OPPOSITION TO ISRAEL AND TO JEWS

In addition to the few powerful politicians well placed institutionally to weaken the special relationship, there are non-institutional forces of antisemitism and anti-Zionism that exist politically on both the extreme right and the extreme left. The antisemitism and anti-Zionism of the extreme left, the New Left and Extra Parliamentary Opposition began to appear in the late 1960s in the statements and activities of groups such as the Baader–Meinhof terrorist organization.[2] Ulrike Meinhof and Horst Mahler were openly antisemitic.[3] The Socialist Student Federation demonstrated against the 'fascist' Israeli ambassador, Asher Ben-Natan, mixing anti-Israel sentiments with traditional antisemitic slogans (Krämer-Badoni, 1969; Ben-Natan, 1974, pp. 159–207). The 'Black Rats', part of the Extra Parliamentary Opposition and members of the Republic Club, appear to have been responsible in 1969 for the attempt to blow up the Jewish Community Centre in Berlin in an open display of antisemitism, and anti-Zionism was apparent in the Black Rats' propaganda leaflets praising the *Fedayeen* and proclaiming solidarity with guerilla efforts against the 'fascist' state of Israel (Krämer-Badoni, 1969).

Rightist antisemitism and anti-Zionism have been embodied in the newspaper *Deutsche National und Soldaten-Zeitung*. From the time of the Luxembourg Agreement this publication has been anti-Israel if not antisemitic.[4] The radical right grew in Germany in the 1960s, which was reflected in greater circulation for the *Deutsche National-Zeitung* and in increased popular support for the neo-Nazi National Democratic Party of Germany (NPD) (4·3 per cent of the vote in the 1969 Bundestag election).

According to the Federal Ministry of the Interior, the appeal of the right continued through the 1970s.[5] In 1978 the weekly circulation of the *Deutsche National-Zeitung* and its companion *Deutscher Anzeiger* stood at 100,000. Although the NPD received a bare 0·2 per cent of votes in the 1980 Bundestag election (0·3 per cent in 1976) and membership of right-wing groups declined in the late 1970s to an all-time low, the number of extremist incidents doubled in 1978 over 1977 (*Deutschland-Berichte*, November 1978). The murder of Shlomo Lewin, a leader of the north Bavarian Jewish community, at the end of 1980, and of Heinz Herbert Karry, the Jewish Minister of Economics in Hessen, in early 1981, raised questions about right-wing extremist involvement.

The traditional activities of swastika-daubing on synagogues and the desecration of Jewish cemeteries have continued in Germany, exacerbated by a new, virulent attack on the Holocaust as a myth that the Federal government ruled a criminal offence in August 1981. The Federal government was worried, too, by an incident in the officer corps at the Federal Armed Forces Academy in Munich (*Deutschland-Berichte*, November 1977, March 1978). There appears to be a strong relationship between right-wing behaviour and sympathy in Germany and antisemitism.

In addition to the concrete antisemitism of the right and the left, there was much controversy in the mid-1970s over latent antisemitism among a large section of the German public. Results of a study by the Mass Communications Department of the Research Institute for Sociology at Cologne University were first published in a scientific journal in June 1976. Based on answers to a twenty-question antisemitic scale only 23·6 per cent of respondents vigorously rejected antisemitic statements. 46·4 per cent mildly agreed, while 25·6 per cent agreed more vigorously and 4·5 per cent declared themselves in wholehearted agreement. The study's director, Professor Alphons Silbermann, has interpreted such results to conclude 'that about two-thirds of the population still retain some antisemitic attitudes while one third decidedly subscribes to antisemitic views' (1976). There has been considerable and significant methodological criticism; the attention given the study and subsequent polls have demonstrated at least an active sensitivity to the subject as well as possible validity in the suggestion that some *degree* (the central debate

218 *Endurance*

is over how much and its effects) of latent antisemitism persists in the Federal Republic.[6]

NON-INSTITUTIONAL SUPPORT FOR ISRAEL

There may be, whatever the analysis of the Cologne study, some degree of latent antisemitism in Germany. It is not, however, easily exploited, for there has been entrenched popular and emotional support for Israel. Germans have preferred Israel to the Arabs, and most have been more sympathetic than neutral. At times of acute crisis for Israel (June 1967, July–August 1967 and October 1973) more than 50 per cent of survey respondents expressed support for Israel (Table 9.1). Asked specifically about oil (and hence about their own pocketbooks) after the 1973 war, only 16 per cent of German respondents thought Israel should not be supported; 57 per cent thought Western Europe should stand firm against the Arabs even if they cut off oil (Institut für Demoskopie, 1974, p. 596).

Israel's greatest support has come from those born after the Second World War, contradicting the popular argument that a new generation free of association with the Third Reich would reduce public support for Israel.[7] Indeed, inspection of survey data by age suggests an enduring special relationship into the future. And as officially Germany tempered support for Israel during the decade after 1967, Israel won 25–69 per cent more adherents among Germans urging the closest possible co-operation between the two countries (Institut für Demoskopie, 1974, p. 533, 1976, p. 279).[8]

Public opinion surveys through the mid-1970s have shown, then, a hard core of support, larger than any popular opposition, for the State of Israel.[9] Public demonstrations – an open display of psychological and

Table 9.1 *Responses of Germans to Question of Whose Side They Would Take in Middle East War*

%	Attitude to question Pro-Israel	Pro-Arab	Neutral	No opinion	Age cohorts pro-Israel 16–29	30–44	45–59	60+
March 1965	10	—	75	15	14	9	8	10
May 1965	24	15	44	17	—	—	—	—
June 1967	55	6	27	12	—	—	—	—
July–August 1967	59	6	27	8	—	—	—	—
December 1968	16	4	63	17	—	—	—	—
May 1970	45	7	32	16	—	—	—	—
April 1971	43	8	29	20	—	—	—	—
April 1973	37	5	37	21	43	39	37	29
Mid-October 1973	57	8	25	12	61	63	54	49
December 1973–January 1974	23	5	59	13	34	23	21	21
December 1974	50	7	29	14	—	—	—	—

Sources: Institut für Demoskopie, 1965, 1967, 1973, 1974, 1976; Infas, 1974; Neumann and Noelle-Neumann, 1967.

emotional commitment – have given even greater testimony. Germans have been motivated to testify publicly by a feeling of special moral obligation due to the past.

When the German government refused to recognize Israel diplomatically, many prominent Germans publicly supported Israel's aspirations. In early 1965 435 university professors signed an open letter to the government condemning the absence of diplomatic relations and the presence of German scientists in Egypt (Seelbach, 1970, pp. 115–16; Deligdisch, 1974, pp. 90–1). In 1967 academics again showed solidarity with Israel during the Six-Day War (Vogel, 1969, pp. 305–11), and throughout Germany there were signs of support for Israel's position. German citizens offered to do civilian service in Israel, to raise funds and donate blood. From Aachen to Marburg to Würzburg, in at least thirty-six cities, Germans prayed and marched in emotional support for Israel (Vogel, 1969, pp. 305–11; Ben-Natan, 1974, p. 72; Deligdisch, 1974, pp. 137–9). Countless Germans were moved enough to write Israel's ambassador personally to express solidarity once Nasser had United Nations peace-keeping forces withdrawn in May 1967 (Ben-Natan, 1974, pp. 71–102).

Germany's major newspapers, having favoured reparations and diplomatic relations, also supported Israel during the war. In fact, according to a study of media in Germany, after 1952 the media made every effort 'to present Israel in a positive light and to gloss over any imperfections'. Israel ranked only behind Europe and the USA in media attention (Medzini, 1972–3). And although media support has declined since the end of the 1960s, certain major newspapers (such as Axel Springer's *Die Welt*) remain staunch, while others, such as *Die Zeit*, refuse, in their criticism, to turn completely against Israel.[10]

When public government support waned, popular support continued. During the 1973 war Ambassador Ben Horin reported that the 'Israeli embassy in Bonn had received letters, telegrams, and other demonstrations of solidarity from countless Germans of all ages, including many children' (interview with Bayerischer Rundfunk, October 11, 1973). Academics launched a 'Help for Israel' movement, declaring:

> We call on the Arab people to show understanding for a people who have found a home after centuries of persecution. We call on them to give Israel real guarantees of safety ...We call on Israel to conceive its problem of safety not only as one of borders. Regardless of the fact that peace in the Middle East requires compromise from Israel, too, Israel continues to need special moral and material support. Above all, Germans must stand by the Jews and Israel as they are increasingly isolated economically and politically by the Arab world and other countries. (*Frankfurter Allgemeine Zeitung*, November 14, 1973)

After 1967, Israel's German friends began to caution it on certain policies, as in this statement concerning borders. But the spirit of friendship dominated this move away from total avoidance of criticism, and public criticism has never acquired the tone of official objection to Israel policies. After the UN Palestinian debate in 1974, the divergence between public and official views became particularly clear, with groups denouncing both the United Nations debate and the German abstention (*Berliner Morgenpost*, December 29, 1974). And after the release of hostages at Entebbe in 1976, the Israeli embassy received more than 4,000 letters and telegrams expressing support for Israel. More than 500,000 marks were sent unsolicited by private citizens. In 1981 during the debate over German arms sales to Saudi Arabia the position of one of Israel's main defenders, Annemarie Renger, received massive public support (*Der Spiegel*, April 27, 1981).

MIXING PRIVATE AND PUBLIC COMMITMENT

Many personal friendships have developed between Germans and Israelis. Personal friendships among Shimon Peres, Franz-Josef Strauss and David Ben-Gurion were apparently essential in the arrangements for arms shipments to Israel (Vogel, 1969, pp. 122–3; Peres, 1970, p. 78). Both Ben-Gurion and Adenauer stressed the importance of their personal relations, as did Adenauer with Felix Shinnar (*Jerusalem Post*, October 14, 1963; Adenauer, 1968, p. 158; 1970, p. 34) and Yigal Allon with Hans-Dietrich Genscher (*Deutschland-Berichte*, July–August 1976, March 1977).

Personal friendships pervade all levels of German-Israeli relations, and references to these friendships constitute a good deal more than political rhetoric. They have great political consequence. Organizations and political parties with similar world views and missions have been the vehicle for warm individual ties, especially between members of the SPD and the Israel Labour Party and between the German Federation of Trade Unions (DGB) and the Histadrut. According to one Labour Party member, those friendships have been crucial at times, such as during the 1973 war when Israelis had channels to their friends in Germany to plead Israel's case (Melchior interview, 1975). Overcoming the special relationship would require retractions from these many important Germans and the renunciation of countless personal ties.

Many personal friendships are the product of institutional arrangements, and institutional arrangements often then endure because of personal friendships. Meetings between German and Israeli politicians have been frequent since 1952, and the most frequent and close ties have been between the SPD and Mapai (Israel Labour Party). Both are socialist parties and belong to the Socialist International, where they try to consult with one another and to synchronize positions; some Israeli socialists are old German socialists; some SPD members were victims of Nazism themselves. In 1957 SPD leader Erich Ollenhauer visited Israel and in 1958 Mapai sent a delegate to the SPD party conference, establishing a now well-entrenched tradition.[11] For many years there were exchanges between different levels of the SPD and Mapai. Since the early 1970s many of these arrangements have been formalized into agreements on exchanges between the party executives, the parliamentary parties and local party organizations in the two countries.[12] Links between the two parties have continued to intensify and increase in number (Dingels correspondence, 1980). David Melchior, an Israeli Labour Party spokesman on international relations, characterized SPD–Labour Party contacts as a 'solid relationship of friendship based on common views, concepts, and words': 'as part of the ongoing cooperation we discuss issues that arise from specific situations. At such times we discuss our differences, but reach conclusions together as friends would' (*Allgemeine Wochenzeitung der Juden in Deutschland*, December 14, 1973). Israel Gad, international secretary of the Labour Party, observed that,

> Our relationship means we have accessibility because of the hundreds and thousands of SPD and Labour Party members who know each other. With the CDU Israel's relationship with Germany has been through the embassies and the German Foreign Office. With the SPD we do not need the Foreign Office. We have contacts to different branches and levels of the government through people. (Interview, 1975)

The equivalent official in the SPD agreed with Gad's assessment (confidential interview, 1975).

In times of crisis transnational party solidarity has played an important role in German-Israeli relations. Up until 1966 the SPD, in opposition, exerted public and parliamentary pressure supporting Israel over both the scientists and diplomatic relations.[13] Later, during the Six-Day War, the Yom Kippur War and after the United Nations Palestinian debate, public and parliamentary support continued despite shifts in government policy, and these semi-private relations helped temper government statements (Melchior interview, 1975). Willy Brandt's references to 'no neutrality of the heart' and a commitment to 'Israel's right to exist' in 1967 and 1973 have been attributed to the influence of his socialism and to his solidarity with the Israel Labour Party,[14] and after his meeting with Arafat in July 1979, there were intensive discussions between the SPD and the Labour Party (Dingels correspondence, 1980).

Party contacts have been used also to iron out difficulties and misunderstandings between the governments, for example, over *Ostpolitik* in 1971 and over the 1972 release of the Munich terrorists. In both cases Brandt's personal emissaries discussed the problems with Golda Meir as socialists, even though she was, besides a socialist, the

Prime Minister.[15] As a result of the strain in relations after the 1972 incident, the SPD and the Labour Party installed a 'hot-line' for instant access to one another in times of crisis. This 'crisis-control mechanism' was employed during the 1973 Middle East war, and prominent SPD friends of Israel, including the Minister of Defence, apparently made the movement of American war matériel possible.[16]

The influence of the SPD on governmental policy affecting Israel has been displayed most vividly over the sale of German tanks to Saudi Arabia. Opposition from his own party seemed the decisive factor in Schmidt's decision to postpone plans. Socialists throughout the party – Annemarie Renger, Horst Ehmke, Egon Bahr, Hans Apel, Willy Brandt, Herbert Wehner and Karl-Heinz Hansen – advanced different arguments against the weapons sale, including fear of a confrontation with the USSR and a revival of German militarism, but a consistent theme of opposition was Israeli sensibilities and an obligation to history (*Der Spiegel*, January 12 and April 27, 1981; *Die Zeit*, March 6, 1981).

There are other notable examples of party influence. Voices within the SPD limited the declaration of the EEC's Venice Summit in June 1980 to a call for association, not full participation, for the PLO in the Middle East peace process (confidential interview, 1980). Herbert Wehner's spring 1980 resolution supporting the Camp David process was delivered before the EEC summit in the name of 'important Social Democrats' and a 'majority of the parliamentary party' (*Der Spiegel*, June 16, 1980). And a year earlier SPD lobbying was decisive in the positive debate over the statute of limitations, as it had been in the initial discussions in 1965.[17] The SPD enjoys close contacts with other socialist parties, especially in France and Holland, but relations with Israel's Labour Party are exceptionally numerous and close.

There have been party and private contacts also between the CDU and Likud and between the FDP and the Independent Liberal Party.[18] The CDU and Likud have had no formal links but there are regular visits; for example, in 1979 the Deputy Speaker of the Knesset, Moshe Meron, participated in the CDU party conference. CDU contacts with Likud rank far behind active and institutionalized ties with other Conservative or Christian Democratic parties, but they are improving and have increased since Likud entered office in 1977. CSU parliamentarians and dignatories also have been involved in visits; for example, Franz-Josef Strauss was in Israel in May 1980. The meetings of German and Israeli politicians include exchanges of information, explanations of positions on the Middle East conflict and general goodwill. Like the SPD, the CDU no longer automatically identifies with the Israeli government's position; none the less, significant segments in both parties are acutely aware of an obligation to the past. The survival of the State of Israel is a cardinal objective (Heck interview, 1975; Wohlrabe interview, 1975; *Deutschland-Berichte*, February 1976; Wegener correspondence, 1980; Meron correspondence, 1980; Skuler correspondence, 1980).

Ties between the FDP and Independent Liberal Party are more restricted than the arrangements of either the SPD or the CDU. Much of the relationship occurs, as with other Liberal parties, through the Liberal International. The FDP historically showed greater sympathy for the Arab World than for Israel, an attitude that continued through the 1960s and 1970s. FDP statements on the Middle East uniformly refer to the importance of Arab oil and of Arab markets; to the need for PLO participation in a resolution of the Middle East conflict; and to criticism of Israeli policy (for example, FDP – Tagesdienst, 1977, 1979, 1980a, 1980b, 1980c; FDP – Fraktion, 1978; FDP – Europa Spezial, Freie Demokratische Partei, 1980a). There remains, however, a core of German Free Democrats who are consistently supportive of Israel, including influential figures such as Hildegard Hamm-Brücher (*Der Spiegel*, June 16, 1980).

Members of all three parties have expressed their general support for Israel in the German-Israeli Parliamentary Association, formed at the end of 1972. By August 1979, with membership at 114, more German deputies subscribed to the friendship group with Israel than to any of the other twenty-five parliamentary groups (Deutscher Bundestag Protokoll correspondence, 1980).[19] At critical times, including the Yom Kippur War and the UN Palestinian debate, the Association has expressed solidarity with Israel. The Knesset's Israeli-German Parliamentary Group is essentially unique; an Israeli-Italian Parliamentary group was inaugurated in December 1979 but has remained inactive (Meron correspondence, 1980).

TRADE CONDUCTED BY PEOPLE: FRIENDLY BYPRODUCTS OF ECONOMIC CONTACT

Friendship forged from political activity is complemented in the special relationship by friendships emerging from economic activities. In 1967 the Israel–German Chamber of Commerce and the German Society for Economic Relations with Israel were set up with the aim of furthering trade relations between the two countries. The two organizations work closely together (*Deutschland-Berichte*, December 1979). The Society performs a public relations role, and growing German support for the Society and for trade with Israel has been visible in the establishment of branch offices in Berlin and in Düsseldorf and in the successful operation of three committees of experts (metals, textiles and fashions and foodstuffs) (Hess interview, 1975; Hesselbach, 1973; *Deutschland-Berichte*, 1977, December 1979). The Israel–German Chamber of Commerce has over 250 members and is one of the largest trade chambers in Israel (Moosberg, 1973; *Deutschland-Berichte*, 1977). The

German Society has lobbied successfully for Israel's interests in Germany respecting trade and investment and close contacts with the EEC.

Moshe Hess and Walter Hesselbach, in their capacities as director and president of the Bank für Gemeinwirtschaft, developed contacts with the Bank Hapoalim in Israel. Both are trade union banks that have funded common projects in Israel, including the creation of the Israel Continental Bank. In recent years Bank Hapoalim had no such joint projects with any other country (Levinsky interview, 1975), and Israel was one of only four countries to share such arrangements with the Bank für Gemeinwirtschaft (Hess interview, 1975). The German bank also has invested with other banks in Israeli economic projects and, on its own, is an important investor in the Israeli economy.

In addition to the more recent trade union-related contacts through the Bank für Gemeinwirtschaft and the Bank Hapoalim, there have been since 1950 relations between the German and Israeli umbrella union organizations, the DGB and the Histadrut. Annual exchanges of visits involving groups and individuals have taken place between various sections of the union organizations (executive, youth, adult and women) and between individual unions; in 1974 and 1975 partnership treaties were signed to expand formally the contacts between the union members in the two countries. And DGB has links with other Israeli organizations. For example, in the mid-1970s it installed a professorship for the social history of the German labour movement at Tel Aviv University (*Deutschland-Berichte*, January 1977). Union-owned construction companies, Neue Heimat and Shikun Ovdim, have invested jointly in housing projects in Israel. Frequent and varied links have existed between the Friedrich Ebert Stiftung and the Perez Naftali Stiftung, German and Israeli foundations concerned with socialism and labour movements (Frankfurter correspondence, 1975; Matthiesen correspondence, 1980).[20] According to the International Division of the Histadrut 'in the extent of contacts, in the frequency and size of the visits, from the Israeli perspective German-Israeli union relations are unparalleled' (Frankfurter correspondence, 1975).[21] According to Horst Becker of the Central Committee of the Socialist Education Organization, which has been an active participant in the union exchanges, Germany's relationship with unionists and socialists in Israel has been unique (interview, 1975). Heinz Matthiesen of the International Division of the DGB has outlined the unique features: 'The decisive difference between the DGB's relations with Histadrut and with union organizations in other countries lies in the fact that in the former case relations are multi-faceted, institutionalized and have a life of their own' (correspondence, 1980). The significance of these union ties is demonstrated in the existence of a social affairs counsellor at the German Embassy in Tel Aviv, part of whose work concerns 'the promotion of relations between German and Israeli trade union organizations' (*Deutschland-Berichte*, January 1978).

STUDENT AND ACADEMIC CONTACTS

Germans and Israelis recognize that the attitudes of present-day youth will shape future relations. In addition to government-sponsored youth exchange, the DGB and the Histadrut have managed their own programmes. Various student organizations have done likewise.

During 1956–7 students organized German-Israeli study groups at eleven universities in the Federal Republic. According to an Israeli founder, 'they were strictly a German organization, with only a few Israelis being members ...For some time they were the only, or at least the most important, link between Israel and an influential section of the German public' (Bloch correspondence, 1975). For many years the study group at the Free University in Berlin published a news magazine, *Diskussion*, which focused on questions of mutual importance to Germany and Israel. However, by the mid-1960s the pro-Israeli outlook of the magazine began to change into a decidedly left-wing and anti-Israel publication. Concern for German-Israeli relations, the original intention of the magazine, gave way to articles on Israeli social problems and Israeli 'imperialism'. The magazine's sponsor organized annual study trips to Israel, but the movement to the left of student organizations in the late 1960s and early 1970s stymied further efforts for co-operation between German and Israeli students. Among some students the special relationship has proved vulnerable (Müller, 1965; Kusche, 1967).

Despite successful challenge to German-Israeli friendship within some student organizations, student and academic contact continued through the 1970s. Organizations such as the German Academic Exchange and the Alexander von Humboldt Foundation have offered generous scholarships to study in Germany and in Israel and have attracted many scholars. The Friends of the Hebrew University and the Society for Scientific Co-operation with Tel Aviv University have guaranteed ongoing exchanges. The Volkswagen Foundation has funded joint scientific research and underwrote the Institute for German History at Tel Aviv University (Vogel, 1969, pp. 270–2; *Deutschland-Berichte*, May 1974; *DIG*, no. 3, 1971, no. 2, 1975) and the Department of German Studies at the Hebrew University (*Deutschland-Berichte*, June 1978). Since the end of 1973 there has been a general channel for scientific co-operation in the form of the German-Israeli Committee for Scientific and Technological Co-operation. Not all students, and not all academics, are on the far left or the far right; many of those who are not continue to make the special relationship prosper.

RELIGIOUS NETWORKS IN GERMANY

The Sign of Atonement Movement was founded in 1958 by the evangelical church to encourage young Germans, regardless of religious affiliation, to work as volunteers in countries that had suffered under Nazism. Volunteers first arrived in Israel in 1960 to work on kibbutzim and gradually turned more to social work. As many as fifty volunteers may work in Israel at any one time, financed largely by the Protestant Church. Since 1969 the Federal government has recognized the *Aktion Sühnezeichen* as legitimate alternative service for conscientious objectors (Krupp interview, 1975).[22] In recent years controversy has surrounded the organization as some of the volunteers have involved themselves in questions of Palestinian rights and have become critical of Israeli policy (*FrankfurterAllgemeine Zeitung*, February 7, 1975). For the most part, however, the group has been committed through work in Israel to the atonement of German crimes against Jews (*Frankfurter Allgemeine Zeitung*, December 23, 1978).

The Societies for Christian-Jewish Co-operation were first created in 1947 in Hamburg, Wiesbaden and Munich, modelled after the American World Brotherhood. By the early 1980s there were some fifty societies in the Federal Republic with approximately 6,000 members. The societies appeal to the German public at large and sponsor discussions on anti-semitism, on the relationship between Christianity and Judaism and on Israel. They publish *Emuna*, a journal favourable to Israel, and organize trips to Israel, seminars and various special demonstrations of support for the Jewish state. In May 1980 the general meeting of the societies passed a resolution condemning the 'appeasement policy' of the EEC on the Middle East and its preference for Middle East oil over the security of Israel. It noted that Germany's good relations with Israel were being endangered by the EEC and urged caution on the Federal Republic (*Deutschland-Berichte*, June 1980). These societies are financed principally through members' subscriptions the Ministry of the Interior has contributed approximately 90,000 marks per annum. The Federal Länder have added up to 10,000 marks per annum to the local societies, and local communities also have contributed (Eckert interview, 1975). The importance of the German societies was symbolized in April 1979 by the establishment at the Martin Buber House in Heppenheim of the headquarters of the International Council of Christians and Jews (*Deutschland-Berichte*, May 1979).

THE GERMAN-ISRAELI SOCIETY AND THE ISRAELI-GERMAN SOCIETY

The most general of all the societies involved in German-Jewish and German-Israeli relations is the German-Israeli Society. The society was founded in 1966 after the establishment of diplomatic relations in order to bring together people interested in the promotion of German-Israeli relations, and it emphasizes political, cultural and social links. It sponsors youth exchanges and, like other organizations, the German-Israeli

Society has disseminated its views through its own publications, *DIG* and *Israel-Berichte* and through lectures, seminars and trips to Israel.

The German-Israeli Society is not eligible for federal funding and for some time has operated at a deficit. Nevertheless, in the mid-1970s with some 1,500 individual and 100 corporate members all paying annual subscriptions, including Federal chancellors, ministers, and Bundestag and Ländertage deputies, the society was an important and effective lobbyist for Israeli interests and a powerful force in the continuous promotion of German-Israeli friendship.[23]

In 1976 the society clashed with the Israeli Embassy in Bonn, which considered critical discussions of Israel's internal politics inappropriate for a bilateral society committed to German-Israeli friendship (*Die Welt*, December 23, 1976). By 1977, however, some of the problems were resolved as reflected in a statement by the society's newly elected president, Erik Blumenfeld:

> We want first of all to concentrate on the true objectives of the DIG, which was established to foster solidarity with the Israeli people and the State of Israel on all levels of society. We have deleted the words 'critical solidarity' which some members of the DIG were keen to introduce because it has been misinterpreted. We have specifically reaffirmed that it cannot be the task of the DIG to comment publicly on official policy of the Israeli Government ... my aim will be to intensify the society's practical work, the youth work, with less political involvement and more personal contacts. (*Deutschland-Berichte*, July–August 1977)

Blumenfeld also expressed the hope that the German-Israeli Society could be revived through co-operation with its Israeli counterpart, the Israeli-German Society, an objective realized through several joint meetings of the two separate societies since 1977 (*Deutschland-Berichte*, October 1978, December 1979, January 1980).

The Israeli-German Society was founded in Tel Aviv in 1971 by prominent Israelis, including then Transport Minister Shimon Peres and Jerusalem mayor Teddy Kollek. In 1979 a Jerusalem section of the society was organized. There are now also branch offices in Haifa and in West Galilee, with plans for Beer Sheva and Natanya (Gluecksmann correspondence, 1980). The rector of Tel Aviv University was elected the society's first President, later followed by Knesset member Josef Tamir and in 1980 by Asher Ben-Natan, Israel's first ambassador to Germany. According to its charter, the Israeli Society seeks

> to foster and develop contacts between Germans and Israelis; to increase cultural contacts between the countries through lectures, exhibitions, seminars, concerts and theatre; to publish and disseminate literature on the theme of German-Israeli relations; to aid the

exchange of individuals and groups; to meet and entertain guests from Germany; to work with all other organizations to this end and to provide for the financial and other needs of the Society. (*DIG*, no. 3, 1971)

The Israeli-German Society is already an especially important non-official force within Israel sustaining friendship with Germany; it now has approximately 400 members.

OPPOSITION IN ISRAEL

The founding of the special relationship required overcoming fierce, even violent, popular opposition in Israel. To sustain the relationship it has been necessary to reduce progressively this opposition. Considerable anti-German feeling remains nevertheless, even after a quarter-century of German aid and help. Ironically, since German choices largely govern relations now, the special relationship probably remains most vulnerable where it least matters for its survival, inside Israel.

As in Germany, the political extremes are least favourable to the special relationship in Israel. However, the popular opposition galvanized in 1952 has been institutionalized since, and generally gone are the mass and violent demonstrations against Germany.

Achdut Haavoda, in December 1957, challenged relations with Germany by leaking Israel's planned military mission (*New York Times*, December 18, 1957). The Communist Party, supported by Herut, renewed opposition in June 1959, sponsoring a parliamentary no-confidence vote because of the German-Israeli arms trade; the vote failed. The government then introduced its own resolution opposing the cancellation of arms export to Germany; the resolution was adopted but the Communists, Herut, Achdut Haavoda and Mapam all voted against. The four opposition parties tried to bring down the government in 1963 and again in 1964 over the German scientists, and during this period their complaints were generally supported by the Israeli press (*Jerusalem Post*, April 2, 3, 8 and 11, 1963; *Die Welt*, October 21, 1964; *Neue Zürcher Zeitung*, October 14 and 21, 1964; November 5, 1964).

In 1965 when Levi Eshkol presented the German offer of diplomatic relations, Menachem Begin denounced Germany in 1952 terms. He accused Germans and members of the German government of involvement in Nazi activities during the Third Reich, and he accused the Federal government of complicity with postwar expressions of Nazism (Vogel, 1969, p. 169; *Jerusalem Post*, March 17, 1965). Rolf Pauls's arrival in Israel in August 1965 was met by protests comparable to the street fights in front of the Knesset in 1952. Pauls was accused of a Nazi background, and demonstrators insisted that Germany had not changed. Thousands marched in Tel Aviv to protest the establishment of diplomatic relations, carrying banners with statements like, 'Normal relations with murderers – a sin against history'. Hebrew University students demonstrated against Pauls and against Germany in Jerusalem. When Pauls presented his credentials, some 1,500 protesters nearly produced a riot in Jerusalem (*Jerusalem Post*, August 9, 13 and 20, 1965).

Some members of Gahal opposed Foreign Minister Eban's state visit to Germany in 1970 (Eban, 1977, p. 483). Young members of Betar, a group affiliated with Herut, demonstrated against Germany during the state visits of the Foreign Minister and the Chancellor in 1971 and 1973. Emotional placards denouncing the Germans as murderers were waved at both Scheel and Brandt; eggs were thrown and the German flag was burned (*Jerusalem Post*, July 8, 1971; *New York Times*, June 11, 1973; *Jedioth Chadashoth*, June 8, 1973). In all of the demonstrations since 1952 the 'Survivors of the Holocaust' and ex-partisan groups have shared anti-German views, most recently attacking the 'final payment' nature of the special reparations fund set up by the Federal government in the fall of 1980 (*Jerusalem Post*, September 2, and 24, 1980).

Whereas the Israeli government resisted these protests and defended the policy of improved political relations, the government was sympathetic with attacks on cultural programmes; Israel still has refused to sign a cultural agreement with Germany, even though the Labour Party had been interested in an agreement before the May 1977 elections ended its opportunity to continue negotiations. It is still politically inexpedient in Israel to promote ties with Germany which do not seem to promise pragmatic dividends. Indeed, public consensus banned most German music and the government banned screenings of German films until the late 1960s (Vogel, 1969, p. 275; Deutschkron, 1970a, p. 175).

The Israel Mission in Cologne and the West European division of the Israeli Ministry for Foreign Affairs granted permission to a German priest to address Israeli schoolchildren during a study trip in November 1961. He discussed German-Jewish relations with teachers and encouraged the children to write to pen-pals in the Federal Republic. Anti-German feeling throughout Israel erupted. Herut forced a Knesset debate that resulted in government guidelines, drawn up at Cabinet level, to restrict formally all cultural contact with Germany (Deutschkron, 1970a, pp. 175–7; Eban, 1962; Associated Press, January 11, 1962; Eban, 1977, p. 286). For the most part, German artists would not be allowed to perform in Israel nor Israelis in Germany; German societies, institutions, or associations (unless philanthropic) would not be permitted to open branch offices in Israel. Israelis could not accept German scholarships for study in Germany, thereby sharply limiting the possibility of young Israelis to be taught in German institutions. Education Minister Abba Eban summarized the guidelines: 'We stand between past and future. We are not free to ignore one or the other. The fact that certain restrictions exist means that we are nearer the past than the future' (1962).[24] Some private activities were to be allowed, but there would be no official cultural relations.

The Knesset Resolution of December 1961 retarded the development of German-Israeli cultural relations, although by the early 1970s attitudes and behaviour had begun to change. Still, a German Culture Week in November 1971 inadvertently fell on the anniversary of *Kristallnacht*. There were public demonstrations in opposition, re-affirmed in protests against a planned special concert of the Israel Philharmonic in June 1974. The orchestra scheduled works by Wagner and Strauss; public pressure forced cancellation of the performances for the fourth time in a decade, this time with a statement that, 'The Wagnerian concert has been postponed to safeguard the public in view of the threats of violence that have been made' (*Deutschland-Berichte*, July-August, 1974). A public opinion poll conducted after the concert cancellation showed 39 per cent of respondents rejecting the idea of a Wagner concert (*Deutschland-Berichte*, December 1974). Still today, there are restrictions on playing Wagner (*Jerusalem Post*, August 29, 1980), as the conductor of the Israel Philharmonic found out in October 1981 when he attempted to play Wagner as an encore (*New York Times*, October 17, 20, 24 and 27, 1981, November 1 and 2, 1981). There were physical disturbances from some members of the audience, but the majority of the orchestra, audience and public opinion agreed with Zubin Mehta's decision that Wagner should be part of the Israel Philharmonic's repertoire (*New York Times*, October 17 and November 2, 1981).

Menachem Begin and his followers, when in opposition, may have intensified German-Israeli relations in other, material areas as compensation for the crimes he kept in the public eye. Moreover, the radical behaviour of opponents to Germany inside Israel provoke Israelis sympathetic to Germany to come publicly to Germany's defence. Thus, in many ways even opposition has helped sustain the special relationship, for where indifference would surely terminate German-Israeli contact, the fever pitch of emotions sustained over such long periods of time have guaranteed preoccupation. And in any event, even within Israel – despite hard-core hostility – significant changes have taken place.

THE EMERGENCE OF FORCES THAT BIND: ISRAEL'S NON-OFFICIAL COMMITMENT TO THE SPECIAL RELATIONSHIP

If Germans have had guilt to assuage through emotional and symbolic organizations and activities, Israelis have been the wounded, not the healers. German activity discouraged public Israeli attacks on Germany, but it is all the more remarkable that by the 1980s Israelis, too, have become more engaged in the active promotion of German-Israeli friendship. The popular feelings and friendships expressed by Germans were confined more in Israel to elites, but the network of contact and association has resulted from initiatives on both sides.

Germany was never, of course, a popular subject in Israel and despite a country heavily committed to taking its own pulse in surveys, questions about Germany have been perceived generally as too sensitive for inclusion. Nevertheless, several polls have been conducted and they reflect support for the relationship with Germany.[25] In March 1970 Israelis were asked which people they considered Israel's friends: the Germans, the Americans, the French, or the British. Most, 42·9 per cent, opted for the USA with France second (4·7 per cent) and Britain and Germany third and fourth (2·4 and 1·7 per cent respectively). The results are consistent with the size of the Jewish community in each country. Moreover, although Germany came last, it was within the survey's margin of error for both Britain and France, and they did not have the Holocaust as a burden. Furthermore, in May 1970 Germany polled ahead of both Britain and France as a friendly government (2·3–2·1–0·6 per cent); the USA was considered the friendliest country by 50·7 per cent of the respondents.

As cultural and societal ties between Germany and Israel developed in the early 1970s, the Israeli public grew friendlier towards Germany. In March 1972 56·3 per cent of respondents favoured ties with Germany, while only 17·9 per cent opposed. By May 1973, at the time of Chancellor Willy Brandt's visit to Israel, 66·6 per cent favoured good relations (the number of those against had risen slightly to 19·7 per cent). Even at a low point in the relationship, the assassination of Israeli athletes in the Munich Olympics in 1972, 34·6 per cent of Israelis surveyed considered Germany a friend and only 9·4 per cent saw Germany as a foe. Symbolic evocations of the past, such as the prospect of a West German officer in military uniform stationed in Tel Aviv as military attaché, did not provoke the negative attitudes one might have anticipated: 56·7 per cent were not disturbed; only 30·5 per cent objected. And when the German government's policies were considered by Israelis as particularly harmful (just after the spring 1981 bitter verbal exchanges between Begin and Schmidt), 43·2 per cent of Israelis polled, a large plurality, still believed that today Germany constituted 'another Germany' and that Germans are different from those of the Second World War.

Israeli sympathy for Germany has grown steadily since the mid-1960s. Professor Gershom Sholem of the Hebrew University told a 1966 World Jewish Congress Conference on Germans and Jews:

> There are many Jews today who consider the German people a 'hopeless case' or, at most, a people with whom they would not like to have anything to do ... I am not one of them, for I simply do not believe that there ought to be a permanent state of war among nations. I deem it right and even important that Jews talk to Germans...in full

consciousness of what has happened ...To many of us, the German language, our mother tongue, has given unforgettable experiences which have determined the landscape of our youth. (Text in Vogel, 1969, pp. 212–22)

Sholem's views were echoed at the conference, and his appeal for greater contact has been answered. The German Cultural Centre and Hirsch Library were founded in the 1960s. The library nearly doubled its membership (from 3,710 to 6,571) in 1971–4 (Federal Foreign Office interview, 1975), and by the end of the 1970s it stood at around 10,000. More than 27,000 visitors used the library in 1974, and by 1978 when the Cultural Centre became officially a Goethe Institute (signifying its full relationship to Germany), visitors totalled 36,000. Of new members, 27 per cent were under 30 and only 46 per cent of all users originated from Germany or Austria (*Deutschland-Berichte*, June 1977, November 1978). An interest in Germany has reached deeply into the population of Israeli youth with various cultural backgrounds.

By 1975 the staff of the Institute for German History at Tel Aviv University funded only four years earlier, included six professors, one assistant and thirty-two doctoral candidates for whom one of the chief academic requirements is fluent German. The Institute has published in German the *Yearbook for German History* since 1972, and provides liaison for German academics visiting Tel Aviv University and for academics inside Germany (Wallach interview, 1975; Miller 1975).

The cultural and educational promotion of German-Israeli understanding reached Jerusalem's Hebrew University in 1974 when the Educational Committee of the Faculty of Arts agreed to the creation of a Department for German Language and Literature and to a special chair in German history. University officials explained:

During the...discussions the importance of training Israel's scholars in the field of German culture was repeatedly emphasized ...The need for continuity especially as regards German language and literature in Israel, was given special emphasis. Until only a few years ago Israel had many people, including a large number of scholars, who were of German origin and had a complete mastery of the German language and literature ...[Most] of these have retired or have died. It is therefore particularly important to ensure that the study of the German language and literature have a secure place at the Hebrew University.

The intensification of these studies also has a special significance for the close relationship between Israel and the European Community. Courses of study on European culture and literature must also embrace German language and literature. (*Deutschland-Berichte*, September 1975)

A growing interest in German literature and language among young Israelis, to which university officials now thought it proper to cater, emphasized a rationale for the new programme, but notably the university sounded like the government, echoing themes of relations with Europe.

Memories of Germany are painful for most Israelis. German culture, especially when associated in any way with antisemitism or the Third Reich, has been extremely limited, as we already have seen. However, since the foundation of the German Culture Centre there has been a steady increase in Israeli acceptance of things German. During German Culture Week in 1971 some events were sold out, and in 1974 the Israel Radio Orchestra did finally introduce Wagner into its repertoire, to be followed seven years later by the Israel Philharmonic's public performance.

Increased cultural exposure has been accompanied by other significant changes reflecting the expansion and complexity of relations. Israeli visa regulations strictly controlling German visitors were relaxed substantially in 1975.[26] Germany's friends include some of Israel's most prominent personalities, among them Shimon Peres, Abba Eban and Asher Ben-Natan. Attitudes have changed. Israelis drive and ride in German buses and cars, cook with German appliances, watch German televisions, wear German clothes and even eat German food. Contact between the societies has grown steadily with the encouragement of the two states in exchanging goods and people. The once wholly negative Israeli psychological response to Germany is now mixed and gradually displaying distinctly positive features (Tavor, 1976, pp. 5–7). With the great time and pain it has taken to reverse popular feeling, it would not be easy to reverse it again.

CONFRONTATION WITH THE PAST

HOLOCAUST

Germans and Israelis have been engaged continuously for thirty years in an effort to remember the past and make amends. They have built complex social, economic and political networks. These networks, complementing numerous institutional arrangements, have bonded the German and Israeli states and their peoples. They are the product of deliberate, self-conscious efforts to deal with the past. They have sustained a psychological response between peoples and a political response between states. They have maintained the special relationship and given it continuous meaning.

It has been argued, particularly by the left, that the process of reconciliation between Germans and Israelis has occurred at the expense of a true German confrontation with Nazism, fascism and antisemitism; that Israel provided a relatively painless outlet for feelings of guilt; that antisemitism has been replaced merely by an uncritical philosemitism and pro-Zionism (Geisel and Offenberg, 1977; Bier, 1980, p. 21; Diner, 1980; Rabinbach and Zipes, 1980, p. 5). It is true that until the telecast of *Holocaust* in 1979, various attempts through literature, film, theatre and scholarly treatises to touch a wide German audience with the reality of German history had proved unsuccessful.[27] But it is impossible to establish a causal link between this failure and the special relationship with Israel. Jews and Israelis generally welcomed the film, which made Germans reflect, but even an event with such widespread immediate impact as *Holocaust* cannot *guarantee* continued reckoning with the past. The roots of relations between German and Israeli societies are deep, contributing to Germany's ability to use *Holocaust* as a catharsis.

Holocaust's audience was large with 31 per cent of all German viewers for its first instalment and 35, 37 and 40 per cent (some 15 million viewers) for the subsequent three nights (Magnus, 1979, p. 221; Markovits and Hayden, 1980, p. 64). Approximately half the population above 14 years of age, 20·3 million people, saw one or more of the instalments, and their reaction was immediate.[28] Over 30,000 telephone calls to television stations were logged during the four programme days and the subsequent day (Schoeps, 1979, pp. 225–30; Markovits and Hayden, 1980, pp. 62–3). Letters to newspapers full of confessions, remorse and astonishment were also numerous, as were editorials (*Deutschland-Berichte*, March 1979).

In a survey conducted by the Institut für Demoskopie after the telecast 42 per cent of respondents were ashamed that Germany had perpetrated such crimes and only 11 per cent said they wanted to forget the whole thing; 47 per cent said the film taught them more about the persecution of Jews (*Deutschland-Berichte*, March 1979). Visits to Dachau's memorial museum increased 22 per cent over the same period the previous year and the number of school visits nearly doubled (*International Herald Tribune*, July 9, 1979). Scores of people contacted the Bundeszentrale für politische Bildung to request additional educational materials (Ernst, 1979), and various analysts and commentators considered the film, despite its problems with accuracy and its Hollywood style, an important window on to the past for many Germans (for example, Ernst, 1979; Kogon, 1979; Märthesheimer, 1979b; Schoeps, 1979; Schmidt's speech to the nation, January 24, 1979, quoted in *Deutschland-Berichte*, March 1979). Indirectly at least, by making Germans conscious of Jews on a regular basis (for which the postwar German-Jewish population of 29,000 was too small), the ties with Israel had prepared the ground for the German reception to *Holocaust*; a direct link between the relationship with Israel and confrontation with the past, the statute of limitations (*Verjährung*), had a subsequent impact on Germany.

STATUTE OF LIMITATIONS AND NAZI WAR CRIMES

Chancellor Schmidt used *Holocaust* in his January 1979 speech to the nation to link the introspection provoked by the film to the abolition of the statute of limitations on murder. By a majority of 255 to 222, the Bundestag then voted in July 1979 to repeal the statute. Before the showing of *Holocaust*, the majority of those polled were against such abolition, but after the film, those in favour of repeal rose by 15 per cent to 47 per cent (*New York Times*, July 4, 1979). Honouring the past appeared as the government's central argument for abolition, for in the words of then Justice Minister Vogel: 'How are we to explain to our youth that crimes without parallel in our history occurred when at the same time we decline to prosecute those who committed these crimes' (*Jerusalem Post*, July 4, 1979).

Holocaust was one of three forces that influenced the outcome of the debate on the statute of limitations on murder. The other two were the international campaign launched by world Jewry, spearheaded by the Simon Wiesenthal Center for Holocaust Studies in the USA and by Simon Wiesenthal himself in Europe,[29] and the efforts of the State of Israel, whose influence had been critical in 1964-5 when the issue had first arisen.[30]

According to German law, the statute of limitations on murder would go into effect on May 8, 1965, after which no German war criminal or crime still undetected could be prosecuted. In the fall of 1964 a debate ensued in Germany on whether the statute might be extended or abolished. Israeli officials, wary after Germany's reluctant performance dealing with German scientists in Egypt and diplomatic relations with Israel (see Chapter 7), publicly favoured, with other countries, abolition.[31] Although Chancellor Erhard personally supported an extension, the majority of his Cabinet did not, and in November 1964 the German government sustained the spring deadline (*Jerusalem Post*, November 12 and 13, 1964).

Extension or abolition was opposed both procedurally and substantively. The views of Erwin Schuele, head of the Ludwigsburg Central Office of Land Judicial Authorities for the Investigation of National Socialist Crimes, were representative. He argued that the Federal Republic should repudiate the Nazi tactic of special laws and, therefore, should adhere to Germany's penal tradition and the letter of the Basic Law. Schuele said that 'hardly any crime or criminal would remain in the dark after May 8, 1965' (Deutschkron, 1970a, pp. 248-9), and he emphasized that prosecution for known crimes could still commence after the statute would take effect. With some lingering doubt about detection, the government did appeal at home and abroad for new evidence of Nazi crimes.

Nahum Goldmann travelled to Bonn to lobby against application of the statute. The German ambassador in the USA was deluged with protests; the US Senate called for abolition. Deputy Prime Minister Eban, usually a temperate diplomat, expressed Israel's profound disappointment and indignation at the German government's decision. Israel viewed Nazi war crimes as a unique event requiring special legislative treatment; it was 'permissible, necessary and essential to extend the period of prescription...as a measure for the protection of morality and justice' (*Jerusalem Post*, November 19, 1964). Israel questioned Germany's contention that few criminals or crimes remained undetected and, in Germany, the Central Council of Jews lodged formal opposition.

The SPD, unanimously for abolition, finally persuaded the government to postpone its decision until March 1, 1965, the deadline for receiving new evidence on Nazi crimes. Despite firm opposition from some members of the Cabinet, such as the FDP Minister of Justice, Ewald Bucher, the government bowed to domestic and foreign pressure (Seelbach, 1970, pp. 121–2; Deutschkron, 1970a, pp. 25–7). The government announced in December that it would reconsider, and at the end of February with new evidence pouring in that could not be investigated before the March deadline, the government invited a legislative solution.

Proposals to abolish were supported in a preliminary Bundestag handvote on March 10 (Deutscher Bundestag und Bundesrat, March 10, 1965, pp. 8516–71; *Jerusalem Post*, March 11, 1965). Nevertheless, SPD and CDU floor leaders substituted a Bill extending the statute only to 1969, which passed easily on March 25 by 341–96 (with four abstentions) (Deutschkron, 1970a, pp. 243, 262–3; Deutscher Bundestag und Bundesrat, March 25, 1965, pp. 8760–90).[32] Israel protested (*Jerusalem Post*, March 26 and March 29, 1965; Birrenbach, 1972, p. 377; Seelbach, 1970, p. 138), and in the final exchange of letters on diplomatic relations Eshkol specified that the statute of limitations remained an outstanding issue (Shinnar, 1967, p. 169).

There are various explanations available for the decisions to let the statute of limitations take effect, then to abolish it and finally to extend it. During the Bundestag debate Kurt Birrenbach was negotiating with Israel to halt the flow of German arms and to establish diplomatic relations.[33] It is impossible to determine the degree of influence exerted by Israel compared to other foreign and domestic pressures, and Ernst Benda, author of one of the Bundestag motions for abolition (and later president of the German-Israeli Society), maintained that foreign influence should not and did not play a role (Deutscher Bundestag und Bundesrat, March 10, 1965, p. 8520). Nevertheless, Birrenbach and the Israelis did discuss the statute of limitations (*Jerusalem Post*, March 11, March 12 and March 14, 1965; Birrenbach, 1972, pp. 374–5), and it was alleged to be part of their final accord (*Jerusalem Post*, April 14, 1965). Prime Minister Eshkol, when advocating acceptance of Germany's offer of diplomatic relations (which was coincident with the Bundestag debate), suggested some link between the relationship with Israel and Germany's desire for direct confrontation with its own past (*Jerusalem Post*, March 15, 1965; Vogel, 1967, p. 170).

During the two weeks between the expression of support for abolition and the vote only to extend German politicians plainly detected the domestic public opinion that could effect pending elections. Their voters, including 64 per cent of German men and 76 per cent of German women, opposed any further prosecutions of Nazi crimes (*Diskussion*, 1965, p. 26). Israel may have influenced a change in German politics, from retention of the statute of limitations to its extension (ibid., 1965, p. 28), but it took another fifteen years for Israel's objective of abolition to be satisfied.

When the extension expired in 1969, the Bundestag voted (279–126 with 4 abstentions) an extension until December 31, 1979 (Deutscher Bundestag und Bundesrat, June 11, 1969, pp. 13053–69, June 26, pp. 13554–64). On the fortieth anniversary of *Kristallnacht*, in November 1978, Chancellor Schmidt called on Israel in particular to help resolve definitively the renewed debate Germans would face during the next year: 'We politicians and legislators shall listen to what our Jewish citizens, our friends in Israel and our neighbours have to tell us. Each of us will pray that his conscience may guide him in finding the right action in this question' (text in *Deutschland-Berichte*, December 1978). Israel again issued statements, passed Knesset resolutions and lobbied in Germany with the government, the parties and individual Bundestag deputies, trying to communicate as the German chancellor had requested.[34]

German opponents again argued the defence of legal tradition. They said evidence thirty-five years after the war could not be reliable, and they thought it time to forget. Advocates of abolition, such as Chancellor Schmidt and Justice Minister Hans-Jochen Vogel, said the issue was moral and individual. The passage of time could not undo the deliberate destruction of human life, Schmidt argued; it could not erase memories of horror and savagery, could not end the process of addressing the past. Confrontation with the past should be an ongoing process for which the permanent possibility of prosecuting Nazi criminals provided an appropriate mechanism (Deutscher Bundestag und Bundesrat, March 29, 1979, pp. 11579–80).[35] The telecast of *Holocaust* dramatized the significance of a continuing dialogue with history, and Israel's presence in the debate did not go unrecognized. According to the *Jerusalem Post*: 'Yochanan Meroz, the Ambassador of Israel, followed the full debate and voting from the diplomatic gallery, a silent reminder of the influence failure to repeal the statute of limitations would have had on Israeli-German relations' (July 4, 1979). The statute of limitations was abolished by a Bundestag vote in July 1979 (Deutscher Bundestag und Bundesrat, July 3, 1979, pp. 11561–651).

The immediate impact of *Holocaust* was incontrovertible, although some saw its energizing effect dissipating within the year after the film was shown (Herf, 1980, p. 51; Markovits and Hayden, 1980; Rabinbach and Zipes, 1980; Zielinski, 1980). The effect of the abolition of the

238 *Endurance*

statute of limitations is nevertheless more permanent. As long as they live Nazi criminals may be brought to trial, reminding the German people of its past.

The Israeli government now called for a more vigorous prosecution of criminals (*Jerusalem Post*, July 4, 1979). Between May 1945 and 1981 87,305 investigations for war crimes had been conducted, but only 6,450 individuals had been convicted. Twelve were sentenced to death (prior to the abolition of the death penalty) and 170 received sentences of life imprisonment. The majority was sentenced to various terms in prison (Institute of Jewish Affairs, 1981c, p. 4). The modest conviction rate has been attributed by German authorities to the death and migration of suspects, their lack of fitness to stand trial (because of old age or infirmity) and the shortage of evidence (Rückerl, 1979, pp. 118–19). Despite their inadequacies, trials remain useful, according to the Institute of Jewish Affairs:

> The implementation of justice may have been imperfect but the rule of law, on the whole, has been upheld. Germany has, perhaps, belatedly, tried 'to come to terms with the past' and has, to a certain extent, been cleansed of the causes of the Nazi period. Despite the shortcomings of the trials as an instrument of retribution, they touch on fundamental issues which are crucial to the moral fibre and democratic character of the Federal Republic, and therefore remain imperative. (Institute of Jewish Affairs, 1981c, p. 1)

In a variety of ways Germans have sought to confront their twentieth-century historical experiences, but the findings of Dieter Bossmann on the ignorance of German schoolchildren about Hitler and the Jews indicate they still have a long way to go (1977).[36] German schoolbooks have not helped, and since 1960 there have been efforts on the Land level to improve the political and civic education of German youth through more accurate and rounded treatment of the past. Despite these efforts, in a detailed study of textbooks published before and after 1960 Martin and Eva Kolinsky concluded that little had changed. Their main criticism centred on the depersonalized depiction of Hitler as an aberration, of Nazism as an elite phenomenon removed from the German people (Kolinsky and Kolinsky, 1974). A more recent study concurred with the Kolinskys' assessment but detected signs of improvement in the examination of types of Nazi criminals among the German masses (Schallenberger, 1978).

The German generation of the Holocaust, at least until 1979, largely detached itself from the past through psychological avoidance. Children of this generation were permitted to follow their parents' example through the omissions and orientations of their education. But for thirty years the relationship between Germans and Israelis has been cultivated among organizations and between governments. It has involved both parents and children and has educated Germans about Israelis and about Jews. This relationship may not fulfil the Mitscherlichs' sense of a mass need for psychological grappling with history, nor Adorno's requirement of an eradication of the structural causes of fascism and antisemitism, but its impact on international affairs has been of significance and its durability has been proven repeatedly.

CONCLUSION

The special relationship was created out of historical experience and conditions and out of mutual needs. Time has changed these needs. The need for a special military relationship, for example, faded in 1965. Germany's need for special diplomatic treatment faded in the 1970s. The relationship could not live on guilt alone, and although moral concerns and historical conscience remain vital, other mutual needs, and new reinforcements, have developed. The worn links gradually have been replaced, forged by numerous societies, political parties, trade and labour associations. The psychological response that embodied hostility in 1952 has been transformed into an emotional responsibility, and it is felt deeply enough, by a sufficient number of key actors, to assure the continued life of the special relationship.

The special relationship is above all based on public policy (although often secretly communicated and expressed). It is only possible, however, when peoples sustain it through personal commitments. Germany and Israel have developed networks of friendship and communication. Mutual resentments gradually have been replaced by mutual admiration. Institutions nurture positive feelings, and these positive feelings build new institutions to maintain them. The special relationship is remarkable above all because of its durability. The development of social and personal relationships has made it, below the visible surface, perhaps more durable than ever before.

NOTES: CHAPTER 9

1   Wehner has been considered by Israeli officials and Labour Party functionaries to be one of Israel's greatest friends. He was honoured by Israel in 1978 on the occasion of his seventieth birthday (*Deutschland-Berichte*, December 1978). Kühn, as deputy president of the SPD, persisted in visiting Israel in November 1973, despite efforts within the Cabinet to postpone his trip. Much of Hesselbach's work for Israel has been carried out within the framework of the Bank für Gemeinwirtschaft of which he is president. Hesselbach was recognized for his work on behalf of Israel in the granting of an honorary degree by Haifa University in May 1980 (*Deutschland-Berichte*, June 1980). For Günter Grass's views on Israel, see his article, 'Israel und Ich', *Süddeutsche Zeitung* (December 31, 1973–January 1, 1974). In addition to Axel Springer's publishing support, he has donated large sums of money for various projects in Israel, including the Jerusalem Museum. For his contributions to Israel, Springer has received

various Israeli and Jewish honours (*Deutschland-Berichte*, June 1977, November 1978). As president of the Deutscher Gewerkschaftsbund, Rosenberg made a number of trips to Israel in the 1960s and urged diplomatic relations; Vetter, as head of the DGB, was rewarded for his work for Israel with an honorary degree from the Technion. Heinemann was a founder of Aktion Sühnezeichen one of whose chief aims was reconciliation with the Jews and the State of Israel. Annemarie Renger, vice-president of the Bundestag, has been president ot the German-Israeli Parliamentary Association. The attitude towards Israel of an important segment of Germany's political and economic elite can be found in the special edition of *Tribüne* (1978) to commemorate Israel's thirtieth anniversary.

2   On the anti-Zionism and antisemitism of the New Left in Germany, see Herman Lewy's article in *Allgemeine Wochenzeitung der Juden in Deutschland* (July 30, 1971); Krämer-Badoni (1969); Kadritzke (1969); article by Hans Habe in *Welt am Sonntag* (January 24, 1971); Postone (1980); and Henryk Broder's 'open letter' criticizing the left (*Die Zeit*, February 17, 1981).

3   For an example of the Baader–Meinhof position, see *Frankfurter Allgemeine Zeitung* (October 10 and December 15, 1972).

4   See, for example, *Deutsche National- und Soldatenzeitung* (June 12, 1964) against diplomatic relations. Other examples of the paper's stand on Israel are quoted in Deligdisch (1974, p. 119). For the paper's stand on the 1967 war, see Ben-Natan (1974, p. 74). For later examples, see Vogt (1980) and Institute of Jewish Affairs (1980a).

5   For details of neo-Nazism, see Institute of Jewish Affairs (1980b, 1981a, 1981b).

6   The main criticism levelled against the survey was the absence of positive questions. See Rolf Vogel's interviews with Elisabeth Noelle-Neumann, the well-known German demographer, and with the president of the Deutsche Forschungsgemeinschaft which funded the study (*Deutschland-Berichte*, October 1976, March 1977). Both these criticisms also noted the absence of comparisons with other countries. For Vogel's own criticism of the study, see *Deutschland-Berichte*, (July–August 1976). For a more recent analysis of the Silbermann study and of other data, see Weil (1980); he argues that 'popular anti-Semitism has largely declined in West Germany since the war' and refers to the 'virtual disappearance of anti-Semitic political movements' (1980, p. 136). Elisabeth Noelle-Neumann had noted in 1976 that 'there is nothing to suggest to me that antisemitism is present to a serious degree in this country' (*Deutschland-Berichte*, October 1976). In 1981 her polling organization, the Allensbach Institut für Demoskopie reached similar conclusions on Nazism in Germany (*Jerusalem Post*, May 5, 1981). For examples of the questions the Institut für Demoskopie has asked about Jews and the results, see Neumann and Noelle-Neumann (1967, pp. 127, 189–91); Institut für Demoskopie (1967, pp. 174, 1974, p. 217, 1976, pp. 26–7, 66). In the yearbook for 1976–7 (1977) no questions were asked about Jews. For a more recent elaboration of Silbermann's views, see his book on antisemitism (1982).

7   This development may be related to the encouragement given to youth exchange with Israel by the general public. In addition to federal funding for youth programmes with Israel, major financial support comes from private sources. In the period 1976–8, 13-14 per cent of all non-federal monies for youth programmes with other countries went to exchanges with Israel (Federal Ministry for Youth, Family and Health correspondence, 1980).

8   When asked directly whether they support government decisions, respondents generally do approve of official policy; see the survey done by Allensbach on the question of German scientists, arms to Israel and diplomatic relations in Neumann and Noelle-Neumann (1967, pp. 569–71); also the survey on the 1973 arms embargo in Institut für Demoskopie (1974, p. 595).

9   For the period after 1975 through mid-1980, it is hard to assess the German public's views through surveys as the Federal government did not commission any polls on Germany-Israel or German–Arab relations or the Middle East (Press and Information Office correspondence, 1980). Nor did major polling organizations such as Emnid or

the Institut für Demoskopie undertake independent surveys on these relations. Their polls relate only indirectly to German-Israeli relations. For example, in 1977 the results of an Emnid survey revealed that 29 per cent of all Germans thought Israel was part of Europe. In 1978 52 per cent of respondents believed Israel's policy in the Middle East was balanced (correspondence, 1980). Only 23 per cent of Germans in a 1978 survey by the Institut für Demoskopie thought Sadat's 1977 initiatives would lead to a lasting Middle East peace, but 40 per cent of respondents in another 1978 poll thought Israel could maintain itself against the Arabs (only 20 per cent believed the Arabs were stronger) (correspondence, 1980). Other polls are in the yearbooks of the Institut für Demoskopie for 1974–6 and 1976–7 (1976, 1977).

10 The German media were critical of Prime Minister Begin's attack on Chancellor Schmidt in May 1981, but the Springer press stood out as an exception. For a review of media comments, see the publication of the Embassy of the Federal Republic of Germany, Washington (May 1981).
11 See, for example, the speech of Abba Eban to the SPD party conference in Berlin in December 1979 (*Deutschland-Berichte*, January 1980).
12 See the SPD *Pressemitteilungen* for the SPD visits to Israel in 1971, 1973 and 1975. The first visit of the Labour Party executive to Bonn occurred in June 1973.
13 The SPD together with other parliamentary parties called for legislation to recall the scientists in June 1963; on diplomatic relations, see the article by Fritz Sänger, SPD deputy, in *Tribüne* (1963).
14 Melchior interview. *Allgemeine Wochenzeitung der Juden in Deutschland* (December 14, 1973); on the importance of SPD–Labour Party ties at crucial points, see the article by Melchior (1973). Brandt's remarks to an SPD party conference in April 1973 are typical of SPD sentiment towards Israel: 'A German Socialist Democrat, whether young or old, must not place the right to life of the Jewish people or the State of Israel in question' (*Egyptian Gazette*, April 23, 1973). Brandt expressed the same view in July 1979 after his meeting with Arafat (*Jerusalem Post*, July 18, 1979).
15 Wehner acted as the emissary in May 1971 (*Süddeutsche Zeitung*, May 5, 1971; Melchior, 1973; Melchior interview, 1975). After the 1972 incident, Brandt sent Hans Koschnick, president of the Senate of Bremen, on a personal mission to Golda Meir (Melchior interview, 1975).
16 Israel Gad cites the friendship of Leber, then Minister of Defence, and Koschnick affecting Israeli interests during the 1973 war (interview, 1975).
17 Some Israelis have noted that support within the SPD for Israeli policies is not as firm as it was in the early 1970s when Labour governed Israel. See, for example, the article by Dov Ben Meir, secretary of the Tel Aviv Labour Council, reflecting his impressions gained during a trip to Germany and participation in a SPD regional conference (*Jerusalem Post*, September 21, 1980). It is the left of the SPD which has been critical of Israeli policies on the Palestinians, on settlements in the West Bank and on Lebanon.
18 The CDU has contacts with various parties in the Likud bloc (Wegener correspondence, 1980). Likud also has links with the FDP (Skuler correspondence, 1980).
19 The rank ordering of German parliamentary associations according to membership for the eighth electoral period (1976–80) was as follows: Israel (114), Latin America (96), France (93), USSR (92), Austria (87), Africa (77), Britain (75), Spain (54), Scandinavia (51), Japan (51), Yugoslavia (41), Italy (39), Iran (39), Egypt (37), Holland (36), Bulgaria (36), Portugal (34), Greece (34), Finland (33), Rumania (33), Turkey (31), Indonesia (31), India (29), Korea (25), Tunisia (23) and Benelux (20). For the Israel Association, there were fifty-nine members from the CDU–CSU, forty-four from the SPD and eleven from the FDP. In the ninth electoral period the Israel Association was outranked only by the newly formed parliamentary group with the USA (*Boston Globe*, May 15, 1982).
20 For this and other facets of the relationship between the two organizations, see *Sozialistische Bildungsgemeinschaft* (1974).

21 The Histadrut has relations with other countries including the USA and Scandinavia. Although the relationship with the USA is of longer standing, it is not as diverse or as institutionalized as Histadrut's ties with Germany.
22 General information on the movement is contained in its publication *Aktion: Berichte, Meinungen, Ausblicke* (1975).
23 Information on the *Deutsch-Israelische Gesellschaft* was gathered from Ernst Benda (interview, 1975), Heinz Westphal (interview, 1975) and Hartwig Bierhoff (interview, 1975). For a general article on the society, see Westphal (1973). On the financial difficulties of the society see *DIG* (no. 4, 1975); *Israel-Berichte* (May 1975).
24 The guidelines allowed participation of Israel in international events in Germany and vice versa and visits of German citizens, especially young people, to Israel. Public performances of German citizens in Israel or vice versa under the auspices of the Israeli government were disallowed. The acceptance by an Israeli group to perform in Germany was subject to government approval. Some education and technical training would be allowed if it were clearly to the benefit of Israel. A permanent Committee of Ministers was set up to decide on all questions of cultural relations with West Germany (Vogel, 1969, pp. 273–4). There is no longer strict adherence to the Knesset resolution (*DIG*, no. 4, 1971).
25 The polls cited here were conducted by Public Opinion Research of Israel, established in 1966. Its polls on German-Israeli relations began in 1970.
26 The visa restrictions were eased at the beginning of 1975, so that Germans could obtain one visa for multiple visits. By the end of 1975 Germans no longer needed visas if born after 1928.
27 Details of these efforts are to be found in *Deutschland-Berichte* (February, 1979); Bier (1980); Huyssen (1980); Postone (1980) and Zielinski (1980).
28 The impact of *Holocaust* on West Germany is reported by the Westdeutscher Rundfunk (1979), the television network that broadcast the film. For a sample of some of the immediate effects, see *New York Times* (January 21, 22, and 29, 1979); *International Herald Tribune* (January 23, 1979); *Die Zeit* (January 26 and February 2, 1979); *Neue Zürcher Zeitung* (January 27, 1979); *Süddeutsche Zeitung* (January 27–28, 1979).
29 For details of the Center's campaign, see its two publications on the question of the statute of limitations. In March 1979, on invitation of the German Ministry of Justice and the German Foreign Office, a delegation organized by the Center spent four days in Germany meeting with key politicians, including Helmut Schmidt and Franz-Josef Strauss, with the US ambassador and the Israeli ambassador (Cooper interview, 1982).
30 Details of the debate during this period can be found in *Diskussion* (April 1965); Deutschkron (1970a, ch. 14); and Deligdisch (1974, pp. 78–82). In 1960 after a full-scale parliamentary debate on extension, the statute of limitations on manslaughter did go into effect.
31 Expressions of Israel's position were a statement by Prime Minister Eshkol (*Jerusalem Post*, October 13, 1964), a Knesset resolution (*Jerusalem Post*, October 20, 1964) and a Note to the German government (Deutschkron, 1970a, p. 251).
32 The extension until 1969 was based on the argument that the twenty-year period of the statute of limitations should begin with the independent functioning of German justice when the Federal Republic was created in 1949.
33 The Cabinet decision to halt arms to Israel was announced on February 12, 1965 (Seelbach, 1970, p. 131). On February 24 the Cabinet concluded that a legislative solution must be found (Deutschkron, 1970a, p. 258).
34 In addition to the Israeli Embassy in Germany, the Israeli government mounted its campaign through the activity of the Israeli Nazi Documentation Centre which received a budget of one-half million Israeli pounds to fight for the abolition of the statute of limitations. The Centre's head, Tuwiah Friedman, was designated by Prime Minister Begin as 'Israel's delegate' in his travels to Germany and the USA on this question (Friedman interview, 1982). For the November 1978 Knesset resolution calling for abolition, see *Deutschland-Berichte* (January 1979). Representative

statements by the Israeli ambassador to Germany are in *Münchner Merkur* (December 1, 1978) and *Bild Zeitung* (January 31, 1979).
35 The main contours of the debate are treated in the *Jerusalem Post* (September 1, 1978); *Deutschland-Berichte* (January 1979, March 1979); *Frankfurter Allgemeine Zeitung* (February 8 and 17, 1979; March 30, 1979; June 20, 1979; July 3 and 5, 1979); *Die Zeit* (March 23, 1979); *Guardian* (March 30, 1979); *New York Times* (July 4, 1979); *Süddeutsche Zeitung* (July 4, 1979).
36 German Jews appear divided on whether Germany has come to terms with the past successfully and whether Germany, therefore, is an hospitable environment in which to live. For the two sides of the debate, see the interview with Henryk Broder and the article by Sibylle Krausse-Burger in *Der Spiegel* (April 20, 1981, May 11, 1981). Jewish and non-Jewish reactions to Broder's decision to leave Germany and live in Israel can be found in *Der Spiegel* (May 11, 1981).

Part Four

THEORY AND CONCLUSIONS

The collection of data for the case of German-Israeli relations was guided by a preliminary theoretical framework that facilitated distinctions among foundations, operation and endurance. This tentative construct derived from treatment of the concept of the special relationship in analyses of US relations with Britain, Canada and West Germany and from extant theories of international relations dealing with co-operation.

Neither separately nor in combination did the preliminary framework or the extant theories, or the case sketches, provide a comprehensive framework. Only after the detailed analysis of a specific case – German-Israeli relations – was it possible to articulate an elaborated framework for identifying and explaining special relationships. Thus, although the theory was present in preliminary form before the case was studied, it is more readily understood here, set against both other theories in international relations and other bilateral cases.

10
Special Relationships and International Relations Theory

The term 'special relationship' originated as a description of relations between Britain and the USA. Here, more than in any other case, the term has been used deliberately.

Four observers merit particular attention for characterizing Anglo-American relations as special: Winston Churchill, Henry Kissinger, Coral Bell and Arthur Campbell Turner. Unfortunately, each fails to develop the concept systematically and Kissinger and Turner equate 'special' with 'unique', defying wider generalization. None the less, their descriptions of the Anglo-American case provide a first step in identifying this category of bilateral international relations.

THE DEVELOPMENT OF THE CONCEPT

THE ANGLO—AMERICAN CASE
Winston Churchill Although it is now usually forgotten, the term 'special relationship' was first used in contemporary international relations by Winston Churchill. His March 1946 speech to Westminster College in Fulton, Missouri, is famous primarily because he there coined the term 'iron curtain'. On the same occasion however, Churchill called for a 'special relationship' between Great Britain and the USA:

> Neither the sure prevention of war, nor the continuous rise of world organisation will be gained without...the fraternal association of the English-speaking peoples. This means a special relationship between the British Commonwealth and Empire and the United States ... Fraternal association requires not only the growing friendship and mutual understanding between our two vast but kindred systems of society, but the continuance of the intimate relationship between our military advisers, leading to common study of potential dangers, the

248 *Theory and Conclusions*

>similarity of weapons and manuals of instructions, and to the interchange of officers and cadets at technical colleges. It should carry with it the continuance of the present facilities for mutual security by the joint use of all Naval and Air Force bases in the possession of either country all over the world ...The United States has already a Permanent Defence Agreement with the Dominion of Canada, which is so devotedly attached to the British Commonwealth and Empire. This Agreement is more effective than many of those which have often been made under formal alliances. This principle should be extended to all British Commonwealths with full reciprocity ...Eventually there may come...the principle of common citizenship ...I spoke earlier of the Temple of Peace. Workmen from all countries must build that temple. If two of the workmen know each other particularly well and are old friends, if their families are inter-mingled...why cannot they work together at the common task as friends and partners? (Churchill, 1948, pp. 98–9)

In the rest of his speech Churchill allowed for the possibility that there can be other bases and forms of special relationships. Special relationships can be military alliances directed against third countries, but they do not have to be. Special relationships can have common language as a base, but language is not a prerequisite (ibid., pp. 99, 104–5).

What is Churchill saying in general about special relationships? First, the basis of a special relationship is linked in some way to history and to a psychological relationship between people whose language may be the same and whose societies are kindred. Secondly, informality should characterize joint arrangements. Thirdly, in Churchill's conception the form of a special relationship seems like both an alliance (defence pact) and an integrated community (common citizenship). The form of a special relationship therefore can relate to defence, it can be an alliance, yet it does not have to be concerned with aggrandizement and can refer to co-operation in areas such as science and economics. Churchill's reference to more than one special relationship suggests its specialness does not originate from uniqueness.

Henry Kissinger Henry Kissinger's diplomacy was marked by the frequent use of the concept of special relations. He suggested that the USA has enjoyed special relations with at least Israel, Germany and Europe. In *The Troubled Partnership* he details his views on the special relationship between the USA and Britain.

Unlike most other analysts of the special relationship between Great Britain and the USA, Kissinger admits that the 'relationship is difficult to define' (1965, p. 77). He emphasizes the sentimental foundation of the relationship based on a common language and culture. These aspects, he claims, are unique and account for both specialness and the informality of ties (ibid., pp. 77–8).

Kissinger sees a co-ordination in policy as a product of the distinct perspectives of individual states. His suggestion of US preference towards Britain (in return for British acquiesence, or 'pliability', as Kissinger calls it), finds full expression in his discussion of the continued existence of the special relationship. Hence, despite opposition to the special relationship among some US government officials, it did exist in a number of fields, most importantly, according to Kissinger, in collaboration on matters of nuclear power (ibid., pp. 78–9).

Henry Kissinger sees decline in the Anglo-American special relationship, which he attributes above all to the depreciation by some American policy-makers of the historical tie. Also the psychological connections between the countries have not proved strong enough to maintain special relations: 'For one thing, the "special relationship" has never had the same psychological significance for the United States that it did for Britain. The memory of Britain's wartime effort, despite the very great prestige gained by it, has diminished with time' (ibid., p. 78). Kissinger's view supports Churchill's notion that a special relationship needs a strong psychological relationship between peoples to sustain it.

Kissinger's analysis of Anglo-American relations offers some insight into their special qualities. Again history, sentiment, psychology and policy preference are all understood as keys to making an international relationship special. But Kissinger in unsystematic in his analysis, and his confusion of unique with special remains an obstacle to general theory.

Coral Bell Unlike Henry Kissinger and some others, Coral Bell does not view the basis of the special relationship between the USA and Britain as unique, but she does see it as extraordinary. There is between the two powers an exceptional 'underlying common interest' (Bell, 1972, p. 103). Bell later mentions 'parallel strategic interests', whose unusual character seems the condition for making relations special.

Obviously, the existence of common or parallel interests is not out of the ordinary in bilateral international relations. Relationships must be special for other reasons. Perhaps Anglo-American interests are *especially* common, but Bell offers no guidelines by which to judge such gradations.

Bell notes some of the other ingredients of a special relationship between Britain and the USA, but she fails to emphasize or combine them. Her analysis nevertheless does include history, common traditions, psychology, policy and the active maintenance of relations. The historical and psychological relationships have a personal impact on elites who, in making policy, choose the USA over Europe.

Coral Bell sees the general preference for the USA expressed in specific policies. She stresses parallel strategic interests as perhaps the most important part of the relationship and emphasizes exchanges of information between the intelligence communities. She also appreciates preference outside security matters, particularly in economic considerations (Bell,

1972, p. 105). However, she emphasizes Britain's preference for the USA, whereas Churchill, at least, makes the relationship special through more mutual choices.

Bell recognizes that the Anglo-American special relationship survived both the Suez and Skybolt crises, but she attributes greatest importance for the maintenance of the relationship through crisis to personalities (ibid., pp. 111, 114). Despite the complexity of relations resulting from historical and psychological relationships, special qualities are maintained through institutions or intersocietal or transgovernmental forces.

Anglo-American relations also are maintained, according to Bell, through the constant psychological imprinting of crucial events, but above all in individuals and elites. The generation born after the Second World War does not share the wartime generation's common experience of the war itself or the subsequent Cold War; the decline of the special relationship is a consequence (ibid., pp. 117–18).

For Coral Bell, then, the special relationship between Great Britain and the USA, which she considers highly unusual in international affairs, is the product of common traditions and is sustained by a psychological mechanism. It is manifested in preferential policy in areas concerned not only with security. It survives crises, however, due to the strength and importance of personalities, not because of other forces the preconditions may foster. The future of special relations therefore depends on the continuing commitment, emotionally and psychologically, of postwar generations.

Arthur Campbell Turner In the literature on Anglo-American relations Arthur Campbell Turner's *The Unique Partnership: Britain and the United States* is the fullest statement on the composition of a special relationship. Yet, focusing on this lone case Turner sees Anglo-American relations as 'special' because they are unique (1971, p. 4).

It is possible for the features of Anglo-American relations to be unique and not replicated in other relationships. At first, Turner disputes this possibility himself by emphasizing that Britain has a similar relationship to all Commonwealth countries. Later, however, he contradicts this finding to suggest that common language and culture, brought about by immigration, are unique to Anglo-American relations (ibid., p. 13). Moreover, there is an element of 'significance', wherein the USA is more important to Britain than any of the Commonwealth countries.

Turner's elements of a special relationship are common language and culture, significance and co-operation, but he limits the wider application of the term by emphasizing uniqueness. Still, the main features are similar to those identified by Churchill, Kissinger and Bell.

OTHER SPECIAL RELATIONSHIPS

Uniqueness is a central emphasis of literature on Anglo-American relations. It is also a constant theme in analyses of relations between Canada and the USA. Analysts often refer to Canadian-US relations as unique; sometimes the relations are called special, but only rarely is the special quality of relations defined. One major exception to this rule in the literature is John Sloan Dickey's chapter 'The "special relationship": concept and prospect'.

Dickey informs us about the foundation of a special relationship, its maintenance, policy expressions and the needs that forged the policy links:

> This specialness, while rooted in geography and history, has also been manifested in the unimpeded...intermingling of peoples...in the unparalleled cultural and commercial integration of the two national societies, and of course, in a border that has been more 'undefended' in (and from) transnational rhetoric than any other boundary in human experience ...In the post-World War II era the concept of a special relationship found concrete expression as policy in various areas...in the North American Air Defense Command (NORAD) and the Defense Production Sharing arrangements, the exemption of Canada at Canada's request from United States restrictions on the outflow of United States capital in the 1960s, and the 1965 Automotive Agreement providing for free trade between the automobile industries of the two countries ...World War II had drawn them closer together in private activity and public policy than anyone, except perhaps the early American annexationists, had ever dared dream. Then came the Cold War with what seemed to be the first external security threat to North America in modern times. It was perceived in both countries as a common danger which could be countered only by close military collaboration. (Dickey, 1975, pp. 180–2)

Dickey here confirms the contours of a special relationship identified by analysts of Anglo-American relations, yet as with other observers of the phenomenon, his work is of limited theoretical utility because of the insistence on perceiving the case he is studying – in this instance the Canadian-US relationship – as unique and therefore special. In Dickey's view, 'The life force of the United States–Canada relationship flows from its unique potential for the symbiosis of "intimate living together of two dissimilar organisms in a mutually beneficial relationship"' (ibid., p. 195).

Not all analysts confine their use of the term 'special relationship' to just one case. Hans Gatzke, in a chapter entitled 'A "special relationship"?', suggests 'The term special relationship might as easily be applied to the entente between Bonn and Washington' and he notes that the term was 'hitherto reserved for American-British friendship'. For Gatzke, 'special relationship' as a general proposition means 'the two countries are each other's best friends', and three conditions are essential: '(1) common interests, political and economic; (2) identity of basic aims, ideals and values; and (3) personal acquaintance and empathy between the two peoples' (Gatzke, 1980, pp. 276–81). There is, too, a fourth requirement: 'For the relationship to be lasting...these ties must be firmly rooted in the past' (ibid.).

If Gatzke's 'special relationship' does not suffer from the complaint of uniqueness, has it a theoretical deficiency? Unfortunately, Gatzke expects relations to be permanently conflict-free; a special relationship implies 'eternal friendship'. Gatzke disqualifies US-German relations from the special relationship category because the countries were enemies in two world wars. Anglo-American relations were not so harmonious in the eighteenth and nineteenth centuries. Indeed, no bilateral relationship can meet this test.

Because of his narrow sense of history, Gatzke diminishes the importance of the close ties between Germany and the USA after 1945. For Gatzke, these relations represent a new departure, but they cannot be called special because of prior antagonism. Hence, Gatzke creates a category for which he offers logical examples, but he proceeds to enunciate criteria that effectively exclude even his own examples.

In characterizing special relationships all of the authors refer to relations rooted in history, psychology and societal ties and whose concrete expressions are policies of preference, co-operation and friendship in a range of substantive areas. One should note that all three cases that these authors examine – Anglo-American relations, Canadian-US relations and German-US relations – are of long standing. Endurance, the ability to weather crises, appears a hallmark. However, the existing literature cannot explain different cases of special relationships because special relations are viewed either as unique phenomena or as ideal types that can never be realized. None the less, if we borrow ideas from the analyses of the above concrete cases and combine them with concepts from those theories that generalize about co-operative bilateral relations, we will have a tentative framework for understanding special relationships.

INTERNATIONAL RELATIONS THEORY

Theories of integration, interdependence, attention, influence and alliance, all of which relate to co-operation, can help us understand bilateral relations that have been called special. Other theoretical developments concerning bilateral relations are inappropriate, such as realist theory, dependence theory and conflict theory, because they contradict the extensive preference and sentimental ties associated with special relationships.

INTEGRATION

Robert Keohane and Joseph Nye have argued persuasively the weaknesses of integration theory[1] for analysing a wider phenomenon of interdependence (1975). Integration theory's regional emphases and focus on institutional unity (Keohane and Nye, 1975, pp. 373, 389, 395) also limit application to special relationships that occur in diverse geographical settings and sometimes eschew the formality of institutions.

Despite these limitations, Keohane and Nye identify 'seven contributions of "integration theory" to the analysis of politics...in the contemporary world' (ibid., p. 395). If integration theory as a whole is inappropriate for analysing special relationships, these seven particular items may be more helpful.

Keohane and Nye on integration   One of the broader contributions of integration theory is its conclusion that 'patterns of decision making vary quite strikingly by issue area' (Keohane and Nye, 1975, p. 395). However, this observation requires a careful appreciation of 'patterns'. Partners in the Anglo-American and Canadian-American cases consistently showed each other preference across different issue areas, which may also be seen as a pattern. Similarly, integration theory distinguishes between 'high' and 'low' politics for agenda setting, but in the bilateral cases cited here the partners are not preoccupied with such distinctions.

Integration theory does not restrict important action to the decisions of central government politicians. Non-governmental actors in the private sector, and transgovernmental actors from respective bureaucracies, also shape relations. These observations are particularly useful with reference to Anglo-American and Canadian-American relations. The societal links are obvious and the bureaucratic contact plentiful. But in theories of integration and interdependence these actors may promote rival coalitions with or across countries; in the examples here they are more likely to promote harmony and co-operation.

Keohane and Nye identify 'linkage' as a central concept of integration theory. It, too, is a useful lens for identifiable phenomena in the cases here. The consistency of preference in policies acquires a sense of spillover from one issue area to another. Moreover, such linkage must be conscious and by design. Integration theorists emphasize planning for the creation and maintenance of a community, and the commentators on special relationships recognize a similar requirement.

Integration requires greater formal institutionalization than does an interdependent relationship. Keohane and Nye have observed that degrees of institutionalization can distinguish types of relations, but that international institutions are of consequence in all co-operative relationships. This observation certainly is true of the Anglo-American, Canadian-American and German-Israeli examples. Each is, of course, bilateral, but each must be understood in a multilateral framework, whether of NATO or of the European Economic Community or of some other institutional arrangement of the international system. Nevertheless, one of the distinguishing characteristics of these relationships is their bilateral informality.

There is useful application, then, for some of the seven contributions. The importance of transgovernmental and non-governmental actors, the linkage of issue areas, formal international institutionalization, and deliberate planning and political design all apply to descriptions of the examples here. But utility is limited. Concentration on decision-making by issue area can be misleading; distinctions between 'high' and 'low' politics are not salient; traditional actors – central governments – are more important than bureaucrats and private sector participants, and they emphasize harmony while resisting conflict. Institutionalization is important, but informality can dominate. Integration theory as presented by Keohane and Nye, therefore, applies only in limited fashion to bilateral relationships that have been called special.

Deutsch on integration There is a further element in integration theory of particular interest for the analysis of special relationships, Karl Deutsch's concept of 'security community', which is one of the oldest and most debated of the theory's terms (Nye, 1968, p. 873). Deutsch distinguishes between two forms of integration: the amalgamated security community, which involves formal union, and the pluralistic security community, which does not (Deutsch, *et al.*, 1957, p. 6). Special relationships obviously do not require the surrender of sovereignty; therefore, the pluralistic security community may be useful. Moreover, Deutsch's conclusions are derived from analyses of bilateral relations (among other combinations), whereas much of the other integration literature has been posited on the combination of two or more states.

Deutsch's 'sense of community', which he defines as 'a matter of mutual sympathy and loyalties; of "we feeling", trust, and mutual consideration; of partial identification in terms of self-images and interests' (ibid., p. 36), appears to relate to the history, psychology and societal ties identified by analysts of special relationships. However, the sense of community is the goal of a pluralistic security community; in a special relationship it appears more as a necessary condition. Furthermore, the second part of 'sense of community' – 'mutual successful predictions of behavior, and of cooperation in accordance with it...a perpetual dynamic process of mutual attention, communication, perception of needs, and responsiveness in the process of decision-making' (ibid.) – conforms more readily to the actual expression of a special relationship. What Deutsch calls the 'background conditions' for a pluralistic security community – 'compatibility of major values', 'the capacity of the participating...units...to respond to each other's needs, messages and actions quickly, adequately, and without resort to violence', 'mutual predictability of behavior' (ibid., pp. 66–7) – are the actual activities of a special relationship.

Features of Deutsch's pluralistic security community are similar to special relationships, but in the final analysis the emphases of the two arrangements are different. Deutsch focuses on attitudinal and psychological factors and mentions policy only briefly. In special relationships psychological and societal ties seem to be more conditions than outcomes; what analysts and actors call 'special' are policy relationships.

INTERDEPENDENCE

Keohane and Nye sought to narrow careless use of 'interdependence' by focusing on sensitivity and vulnerability (1975, pp. 368–70, 1977, pp. 11–19). In the special relationships described here countries are not only sensitive to developments in their partners; they monitor policy formation constantly. Similarly, special relationships appear to relate a high degree of vulnerability between the partners. Interdependence can refer to either positive or negative relationships, and they may be asymmetrical (Keohane and Nye, 1975, p. 367). Because of reciprocity, special relationships appear more symmetrical, but it would seem possible to consider them as a particularly intensive type of positive and symmetrical interdependence.

Complex interdependence Complex interdependence is an alternative ideal type to the traditional realist approach to international relations. It is characterized by multiple channels connecting societies (formal, informal, interstate, transnational and transgovernmental), multiple issues with an absence of hierarchy and the non-existence of military force (Keohane and Nye, 1977, pp. 24–9). All these features coincide with what analysts have identified as the heart of a special relationship. Keohane and Nye are particularly interested in the effect of complex interdependence on international organization, and its impact, in turn, on international regime change. This emphasis on consequences rather than contours or causes, however, means complex interdependence cannot detail what a special relationship is or how it comes into being. A generalization across cases for these features sets the special relationship apart from the definition of complex interdependence, for the latter makes inadequate reference to origins and conditions and therefore cannot guarantee that examples of special relationships will, indeed, be merely intensive cases of complex interdependence.

ATTRACTION AND INFLUENCE: BETWEEN INTEGRATION AND INTERDEPENDENCE

The work of Annette Baker Fox on 'attraction' between two countries falls between integration and complex interdependence.[2] Her findings relate to ties between the USA and four middle powers – Canada, Mexico, Brazil and Australia. The attempt to generalize beyond the four cases is restricted to other middle powers in their relations with major powers. Structural conditions are, then, the core determinant of participation in a relationship of attraction.

The background to a relationship of attraction is, in one respect, like the basis of a special relationship: similar economic and political systems, together with common language, facilitate close relations (Fox, 1977, ch. 2). Historical relations are also important but indifference is the main feature.

Common or collective needs are emphasized in relations of attraction. In Canadian-American and Anglo-American relations, however, needs appear more mutual than collective. Churchill certainly saw defence in collective terms, but Dickey's reference to symbiosis, for example, suggests that needs may be satisfied simultaneously for the partners across different issue areas.

Fox's concern for the non-pragmatic considerations in policy-making, the diversity of policy areas and the partners' expectation of special consideration are all relevant to the study of special relationships. She focuses on reciprocity in policy relations within the same issue area but also notes the existence of reciprocity across areas within her country cases (ibid., chs 5, 6, 7, 8 and 9). Preference, an essential element of the various special relationships, occasionally is acknowledged, but not as a critical condition.

Informality helps maintain relations of attraction as do the many governmental and transnational ties. Personal relations among key individuals in the executive and bureaucracy play a substantial role, too. Endurance of the relationship is connected to past co-operative experiences in the partnership, and the domestic and international environments clearly influence relations (ibid., pp. 5, 7, 91, 98, 297). All these characteristics may be found in special relations, and Fox even refers casually to attraction as a 'special relationship' (ibid., pp. 7-8). But attraction refers to a list of features within a deliberately restrictive category of middle power–great power relations. Hence, the concepts are limited for explaining relationships that occur between other kinds of powers, and their emphases plainly differ from the elements emphasized by observers of special relations.

Annette Fox acknowledges an intellectual debt to Kal Holsti's work on influence (1977, p. 4). Holsti, too, approximates aspects of the special relationship. According to Holsti, 'the successful wielding of influence varies with (1) the type of goals a state pursues, (2) the quality and quantity of capabilities at a state's disposal, (3) the skill in mobilizing these capabilities in support of these goals, (4) the credibility of threats and rewards, (5) the degree of need or dependence, and (6) the degree of responsiveness among the policy-makers of the target country'. Success also relates to the compatibility of objectives and the nature of the commitment of the partners to achieve them (Holsti, 1967, p. 204).

Holsti's influence model seems to come closest to the special relationship when assessing needs and action, which he calls 'responsiveness': 'Responsiveness can be seen as a disposition to receive another's requests with sympathy, even to the point where a government is willing to sacrifice some of its own values and interests in order to fulfil those requests; responsiveness is the willingness to be influenced' (ibid., pp. 202-3). 'Factors [such] as pride, traditional friendships and enmities, personality characteristics of policy makers, and unique circumstances' determine responsiveness (Holsti, 1977, p. 175). Holsti characterizes high mutual responsiveness between countries as 'relations of consensus'.

Despite its clear utility, there are two central difficulties with Holsti's theory. First, he sees only positive foundations leading to high responsiveness; each of the cases mentioned here, however, involves both negative and positive historical relations. Gatzke emphasizes such mixed history in German-US relations to disqualify them as 'special', thus agreeing essentially with Holsti; Canadian-US relations were marked by periods when the southern neighbour seemed poised to annex the north, and of course Anglo-American relations began with revolt of one country against the other. Secondly, Holsti's category of consensus relations includes both partners who are highly responsive and those with 'a very low level of interaction and involvement' (Holsti, 1977, p. 179). Special relationships would appear to exclude low levels of interaction and involvement.

ALLIANCE THEORY: SCHOLARLY DISAGREEMENTS

Alliance theory, like integration theory, is the subject of abundant intellectual effort and disagreement. A survey of more than 100 books and articles on alliances led Holsti, Hopmann and Sullivan to advance 347 propositions dealing with the causes and forms of alliance and 70 propositions relating to its effects (1973).[3] Application of a general theory of alliances to specific cases obviously is neither popular nor easy.

There are as many definitions of alliance as there are analysts. Holsti, et al. (1973) opt for a broad view of alliance as 'a formal agreement between two or more nations to collaborate on national security issues' (ibid., p. 4). The definition deliberately excludes 'the accidental or temporary coordination of foreign policy acts...[and] a broad range of formal agreements on trade, cultural affairs, and the like' (ibid.). Observers of alliances disagree whether informal arrangements should be embraced, but they generally concur that 'The predominant usage is restricted to military matters' (Russett, 1974, p. 301) and that non-security questions, therefore, must be excluded. The two principal components of an alliance, formality and a preoccupation with security issues, are generally absent from special relationships.

Unlike Keohane and Nye, theorists concerned with alliances do want to explain cause, but they differ over levels of analysis and over motives for actors. Alliance analysts look to either the international system or the domestic system, and they accentuate either pragmatic, short-term interests or longer-term sentimental ties 'arising from common ethnic, cultural, ideological or other attributes' (Holsti, et al., 1973, p. 4). They also disagree over whether benefits derived from an alliance are in proportion to capabilities, with the stronger power gaining more advantages, or whether weakness can be a source of strength.

The structure of the alliance itself, as opposed to the structure of each constituent, is also a source of disagreement for alliance theorists. The debate is over whether hierarchy and centralization or pluralism and decentralization is the source of cohesion in an alliance. In both structures alliance members' efforts centre on co-ordinated activity and common policies and are directed towards the outside actor against whom the alliance was first formed. In alliances performance depends essentially on military questions and the final weapon of an alliance is war. On the question of survivability, the disagreement is between 'the thesis that strains will develop within alliances of longer duration [and] the counter-argument that the longer an alliance endures, the greater its solidarity and legitimacy' (Holsti, *et al.*, 1973, p. 21). Hence, predictions of endurance within alliance theory seem wholly unreliable.

The causes of disintegration in alliances range from a surfeit of success to an insufficiency, from differences in values to inadequate resources, from the presence of nuclear weapons to the possibility of disarmament. The breakdown of an alliance also may have its roots in the international system and the international environment is a recurrent subject in alliances – in their formation, performance and continuation. The domestic environment, by contrast, is given little importance. Ole Holsti's survey of alliance studies concludes:

> The most obvious conclusion that emerges ... is that the literature on alliances is marked by competing explanations, none of which appears sufficient for a general theory, and contradictory findings: Whether discussing the formation, performance, termination, or effects of alliances, we have repeatedly cited propositions which allegedly explain some fundamental issue, only to find that its exact opposite has been proposed in another source. Indeed it is not impossible to find contradictory propositions coexisting in the same source. (Holsti, *et al.*, 1973, p. 41)

No one theory of alliance will explain a special relationship; parts of alliance theory, especially with reference to mutual accommodation and mutually beneficial enterprise, may contribute to our understanding of aspects of special relationships. Unfortunately, the limited scope of alliance theory, as well as its tendency to emphasize common over reciprocal activity, military over other considerations, international over domestic conditions, prevents its wider application. In some instances alliance theory may even inhibit our appreciation of the diverse range of activity characteristic of relations between nations, especially when analysts demand choices between pragmatism and sentiment, between structure and personal ties, between endurance through strength and through weakness. Yet despite the controversies in alliance literature, the concept of alliance has been employed more than any other theory for the study of specific bilateral relationships, including Anglo-American and German-American relations. Dependence on such ambiguity makes only more difficult the matching of theory to empirical observations.

SUMMARY

Relations between Britain and the USA when Winston Churchill went to Fulton included the essential elements of an alliance. But relations were more extensive. They were not restricted to military concerns, and they were not built solely on a common hostility towards a third party. Yet the common citizenship to which Churchill alluded, and which might have been a vital ingredient of integration, did not come to pass. The relationship was no mere attraction, involving as it did great, not middle, powers. It may have satisfied the criteria of complex interdependence, but the relationship influenced its partners more than the international system in the following decades. Anglo-American relations were more than some theories such as alliance allowed, and less than some others, such as integration, seemed to hope.

Anglo-American relations might have seemed unique for their partners, but the relations shared by the USA with other partners, including Canada and West Germany, bore similar characteristics. These relations, too, defied the categories identified by analysts of bilateral relations, and so explanations for their formations, and predictions of their directions, inevitably would depend on partial observations. No elaborated theory in international relations could account thoroughly for these cases.

Analysts of these particular bilateral relationships each identified similar features to distinguish their cases. Each emphasized background conditions of sentiment, sense of community, common language, kindred social systems, societal and individual ties, and mutual attention; each recognized a catalyst of concrete needs for the formation of relations, and each observed the expression of relations in policy preferences, common or reciprocal policies, and substantial linkage; each of the analysts witnessed the active maintenance of the special features of the bilateral relationship through personal ties and non-governmental actors, and each was concerned with the conditions under which maintenance efforts could or did fail.

These similar features identifiable in Anglo-American, German-American and Canadian-American relations can also be observed in relations between West Germany and Israel. Yet precisely because there is such similarity, no extant theory can be applied to the case. These four examples include a non-alliance; they include relations between major, middle and minor powers; they emphasize linkage but without distinction for high and low politics. They require, therefore, their own

260 *Theory and Conclusions*

elaborated theoretical framework where terms are defined and concepts articulated. Such a framework can enable the systematic collection of observations about bilateral relations, and can permit modest prediction about the dynamics of specific cases.

NOTES: CHAPTER 10

1 For comprehensive reviews of integration theory, see Nye (1968) and Harrison (1974).
2 Fox's discussion of integration (of the pluralistic security-community type) and interdependence may be found on pp. 2, 4, 7, 105, 290 and 297.
3 The propositions and the works surveyed are found in appendix C (1973). Some of the major works reviewed by Holsti and separately by this author include Liska (1962), Riker (1962), Olson and Zeckhauser (1966), Osgood (1968), Singer and Small (1968), Neustadt (1970) and Friedman, *et al.* (1970).

11
A Theoretical Framework for Special Relationships

Bilateral relationships can be friendly or hostile. Partners can be friendly on some questions and hostile on others. They can actively pursue friendship or hostility, or they can be indifferent. The degree of preference they express for one another, therefore, can measure their friendship or hostility. If bilateral relations are seen on a continuum, then the special relationship is at the friendly end. Partners actively pursue friendship on many issues.

Special relationships come into being, last for a time and sometimes terminate. This dynamic process in the creation, endurance and termination of bilateral relations is central to what a special relationship is, and essential to analysis of the impact the relationship has on partners and on the international system. The generalizations for this process are consistent here with limited observations of three diverse cases, relations between the USA and Great Britain, Canada and West Germany, and detailed analysis of relations between West Germany and Israel.

Formulation of a theoretical framework for special relationships has four main benefits. First, by comparing a specific bilateral relationship to the abstract criteria here we may determine whether the relationship is special. Secondly, by comparing the criteria for the creation of a special relationship to the conditions prevailing between specific bilateral partners, we may predict whether relations are likely to become special. On such bases, for example, we could have determined that US-Iranian relations were not special when the Shah claimed they were, and we could have predicted that they were not destined to become special.

The other two benefits from the formulation of a theoretical framework follow from the determination whether a relationship is special. We can predict that when a country is challenged to forsake its special partner on behalf of another, it will probably remain loyal despite crisis conditions. Such was the case, for example, when West Germany stood by Israel against various Arab demands in the 1970s. Moreover, when partners appear disloyal, as the British thought of the Americans over Suez, there is rapid healing in relations when they have been special. And finally, we can predict that when a special partner cannot satisfy a critical need, it will compensate in some other area. Special relationships in some circumstances can oblige the international system to adjust; the international system cannot always dictate the interaction of partners to a special relationship. The Arab countries have had to learn this lesson as they have tried to manipulate the international political economy to pressure changes in German policy, and in policies of the USA towards Israel.

The power of this theoretical framework, then, is in facilitating certain predictions about international behaviour in those cases of bilateral relations that qualify as special. The special forces in such relations can defy the traditional features of power in the international system, and the traditional predictions of behaviour in international relations theory. Such patterns may now be apparent from the discussion of West German-Israeli relations; in Chapter 12 we will consider the special relationship more in terms of other cases.

FOUNDATIONS

There are three essential foundations of a special relationship. The partners must share either significant historical relations over a long period (an 'historical intertwining'), or an exceptionally intense history of mutual preoccupation. They may share both. These historical or intense relations must be shared, moreover, by both the peoples of the two countries and by their governments. These conditions (historical intertwining or intensity, between both peoples and countries) constitute an essential background for the relationship's creation. Finally, the countries and their peoples must simultaneously perceive needs that only the specific partners can fulfil. The needs may be different for each partner, but they must be perceived at the same time, and each partner must be persuaded that no alternative partner exists for their satisfaction.

HISTORY

An historical relationship does not mean merely the existence of a relationship between two countries for a long period of time. A long time is required, but that time must be filled with a complicated historical intertwining of the countries whether in a positive or a negative sense. If the length of relations were the lone criterion of an historical relationship, as it applies to this framework, then the term special relationship could refer to many more relationships than would be useful. The USA and Italy, for example, do not have a special relationship, even though an Italian explorer, Cristoforo Colombo, is credited as the first foreign arrival on the continent named for and by his Italian compatriot, Amerigo Vespucci. Nor did Columbus's Spanish flag launch a special relationship between the United States and Spain. Time is important, but not enough to satisfy the criterion here.

What are the indicators, then, of historical intertwining? There are two principal possibilities, mutual awareness and common traditions. Mutual awareness involves the constant calculation of the other country, *over the long term*, in the formulation of foreign policy. In a negative sense this calculation suggests the recognition of the threat the other country poses or an incompatibility of interests. In a positive sense it implies general diplomatic support, a foreign policy compatible with the other country's interests; it might involve preference in a single policy area, such as economics or defence, but it does not include the consistent practice of policy preferences across a range of specific policy areas, which is the ultimate expression in a special relationship. A rough measure of this type of intertwining can be the amount of positive or negative attention devoted to the other country (in contrast to attention devoted to other actors in the international system) by national leaders; such attention may be expressed in speeches and policy statements.

Over a long period of time (by which is meant scores of years) relations should constitute something of a mutual preoccupation. Germany and France after 1860 would satisfy this criterion negatively; Anglo-American relations in the era of global conflict is a positive example. Canadian-American relations in the eighteenth and nineteenth centuries fluctuated between positive and negative relations, but preoccupation was a constant characteristic.

Mutual awareness usually will be affected by common traditions, which include common language, common culture, or common forms of government. Such influence is obvious within the English-speaking world, or among European nation states. It is not apparent in, for example, Japanese-American relations and, therefore, is more an important feature of historical intertwining than a necessary precondition of special relations. Language and cultural differences do not present insurmountable obstacles to the development of a special relationship, but their existence does necessitate increased efforts at mutual understanding.

INTENSITY

Two countries that have no record of an historical intertwining may still have the basis for a special relationship. Intensity can substitute for (or complement) historical intertwining. 'Intensity' involves a telescoping of mutual preoccupation into a period of time that makes the relationship obsessive. Intense common experience can also substitute for common traditions. Intensity must not be, however, the momentary or short-lived result of a brief crisis (as in, say, nineteenth-century German-African relations), but rather, must be established over a longer period of time. It is indicated, as historical intertwining can be, when both sides spend a good deal of time thinking and talking about each other. Should relations develop between the USA and Vietnam, for example, the intensity of previous historical association provides sufficient basis for the evolution of a special relationship.

There is much confusion in discussions of so-called special relationships between the terms 'unique' and 'special'; often they are used interchangeably as if synonymous. No two relationships are exactly alike, and in this sense all bilateral relationships are unique. Each such relationship is full of peculiar features and circumstances and conditions. However, when these peculiarities contribute consistently to the history or intensity (or both) of a relationship, then they contribute to the conditions necessary for the establishment of a special relationship.

West Germany and Israel share the unique experience of the Holocaust. It is notable that the testimony of Germans and Israelis alike with reference to the unique features and characteristics of German-Israeli relations is testimony that deals consistently with the history, tradition, and culture of the peoples involved, focusing on the unique foundations, both out of historical circumstance and out of intensity of involvement, which foster the special relationship. Anglo-American relations are rooted in the founding of the United States through a war against the mother country. Canada and the USA share, after the USSR and China, the world's longest border, one of the decisive geographical factors defining their relations. In every case of special relations there is some unique feature that binds the partners, but it is not the uniqueness *per se* that makes the relationship special.

PSYCHOLOGICAL RESONANCE BETWEEN PEOPLES
There is something tangibly different in the relationship between the peoples of the two countries that have a special relationship in contrast to relations between two nations that do not enjoy something special. This different relationship between two peoples predates policy relations.

The 'psychological' element takes the following form: for the 'average' person, and especially for elites, the special partner has a particular meaning that other countries do not share. When the citizen of country A hears, reads of, or comes into contact with country B, it touches off some association, whether positive or negative. This same citizen would not stop to think about similar information concerning other countries. There is a trigger-effect. The relationship between the two peoples is characterized by *Befangenheit*, a German term referring to psychological resonance, psychological embarrassment, prejudice, or conditioned response.* For example, if a German hears the words

* The adjective *befangen* translates loosely into English as prejudiced, biased, partial, passionate, interested, embarrassed, abashed, constrained, unnatural, affected, disingenuous.

'Israel' or 'France', those words strike chords that the word 'Madagascar' or even 'England', for that matter, would not. The same could be said of the American when hearing the word 'England' or the Frenchman when hearing 'Algeria'.

Resonance or *Befangenheit* is probably the result of the historical intertwining and/or intensity between the two countries. One measure of this psychological or emotional element could be the frequency with which the public opinion polls of a country inquire about the special partner, and the public's answers may be indicative. Newspaper editorials and letters to the editors of the national press may also reflect resonance.

History/intensity and psychology are both necessary conditions for the development of a special relationship; neither of them alone is sufficient. Both parts of this foundation for a special relationship can be negative, but the ultimate expression of a special relationship, the behaviour of the parties, must be positive.

The likelihood of a special relationship developing, therefore, increases when (1) states have a long, intertwined history or a short history of great mutual intensity; and (2) relations between the two peoples is characterized by *Befangenheit*.

SIMULTANEOUS NEEDS

A major catalyst for the creation of a special relationship is the existence, for both partners, of a specific need that both perceive only the other country capable of fulfilling. Special relationships are formed for specific purposes, although the objectives need not be stated formally. Countries do not slip into special relationships unintentionally. A mutual and simultaneous perception of need is necessary for the special relationship to develop; after the inception of the special relationship, mutuality remains essential but simultaneity does not. Whether before the special relationship develops or after, it is not essential that the two countries need the same thing, although commonality of interests can be the basis for a special relationship.

Exchanges in special relationships are not necessarily symmetrical, nor must relations develop between countries that are equal in economic, political, or military power. Rather, the mutuality of need involves merely the mutual and simultaneous perception that satisfaction – perceived as necessary – can be achieved only in relations with the other country, even when the things to be satisfied are different. The needs do not have to be common or even alike. They must, however, be compatible.

For need to be translated into relations of preference initiatives must be taken. Charismatic leadership, the presence of actors who can push and persuade, is necessary. Moreover, individual leaders require at least a simple majority of support from political elites who share in decision-making. When an historical relationship has been established, there is the mutual and simultaneous perception of a high degree of need and the belief that no alternative providers exist, and when there is an adequate degree of internal political support and forceful leadership, then a special relationship is likely to develop.

THE NATURE OF THE SPECIAL RELATIONSHIP

What makes a special relationship special? What gives evidence that a special relationship exists? Special relationships are expressed quintessentially in what countries do. For a relationship to be special, both countries must practise preferential treatment towards each other in more than one substantive policy area. It is not sufficient that a preferential economic agreement, for example, exists between two countries, or that they are close military allies. The partner must be extended priority in additional policy areas. It is impossible now to specify the number and the exact combination of preferential policy areas, for there is neither a finite number nor a specific order of importance. Economics and defence seem to be essential, but given their appearance in many bilateral relationships, at least one additional policy area appears necessary. Indeed, special relationships appear to be characterized by the involvement of most agencies of government in the two countries.

In all areas preference rarely will be stated or expressed formally. Special relationships thrive on informal *ad hoc* arrangements. Both the content and the form of the policy must be preferential. The content can be preferential quantitatively and/or qualitatively. For example, country A might supply more weapons to country B than to any other country; at the same time the quality of these weapons might be superior to those provided to other countries. To establish whether the form of a policy is preferential one can consider the enunciated rules or criteria a country applies in the conduct of its foreign relations in specific policy areas and then assess whether it deviates in a positive direction from these professed criteria, that is, the norm, in a particular case. For example, in 1963 President Kennedy introduced a 15 per cent interest equalization tax to limit foreign lending on US capital markets; an exception to this rule was made for Canada. In the case where no rules exist in a particular area and favourable rules are specified for a country, the form, again, could be said to be special.

The proof of a special relationship resides, then, in two comparisons: (1) with policy towards other individual countries, and (2) with the norm or the rule in a discrete policy area. The type of preference outlined so far is direct and obvious special treatment. One partner to the special relationship must be engaged in this type of activity. If direct preference is not reciprocal, the partner must offer indirect preference that also involves comparison. The behaviour of country B towards country A is more positive than it would be if country A were not granting preferences to B. In practice, the recipient of preferential treatment is, at least, neutralized from any inclination towards hostility or detrimental activity. Hence, the country that offers direct preference gets at least equanimity in return; equanimity, compared to outright hostility, may also be a demonstration of preference.

In a special relationship the questions of equality or symmetry of outcome through comparison of what each partner gives to the other is less relevant; the crucial measure of preference and, therefore, of symmetry is against an alternative, be it the alternative of another country or of another kind of behaviour. Country A may provide more apparent benefits than it receives from country B, but the relationship can be special if country A receives more than country B gives to any other country or more than country B might otherwise provide. Let us look at several possible policy areas separately to clarify this concept of preferential treatment.

DEFENCE

Both the content and the form of defence relations could be significant. Suppose country A has a restrictive policy with respect to military assistance. The very granting of military aid (whether in the form of weapons or training) in itself could be special. However, whether the policy is restrictive or liberal, a special relationship in military terms may be said to exist if (*a*) the quantity and quality of arms or training are superior to what is offered to other countries (content), and (*b*) if the normal procedures for granting military assistance are not followed (form). Suppose, for example, that a country's policy is to give military aid openly; if that country then sends arms to another country covertly, say, through third countries, a special military relationship apparently exists. Alternatively, a special military relationship may exist if normal policy consists of providing arms only through third countries but are delivered to a particular country directly.

Another expression of a special relationship in military terms would be a defence agreement, which might include consultations in the event of armed conflict involving one or both of the partners, the joint training of forces and the exchange of information on weapons technology. There is also the possibility of specific preferential purchasing agreements, whereby countries exchange particular weapons.

Finally, the absence of any perceived threat of armed conflict is part of a special relationship. As in all the policy areas, the greatest indicator of a special relationship is a positive departure from the normal way of conducting affairs, or from the normal content, level, or volume of bilateral relations. Defence is but one of many policy areas – and not necessarily a decisive one – through which a special relationship may be identified.

ECONOMIC AFFAIRS

The economic sphere includes trade and investment, but only to the extent that the state is involved. The focus is on trade agreements, export promotion and export licences, investment promotion and investment guarantees, that is, those areas where there is a state policy with respect to economic relations in addition to the private economic transactions between citizens of two countries. With respect to trade, investment and general economic issues, a special relationship can be demonstrated through unilateral economic preference, through the joint management of common economic problems or through co-operation, co-ordination and consultation.

For trade, the content of a relationship between two countries could be special in terms of quotas, both quantitatively and qualitatively. An agreement might exist for a stipulated amount of trade between the two countries during a given period; alternatively, one country could decide to buy all of a particular commodity from its special partner. The form of the trade relationship also may be special through preferential tariff arrangements.

Preference in investment guarantees, for example, could be shown in one of two ways. Let us suppose that country A's general policy is not to grant investment guarantees except in unusual circumstances. If country A's investors are accorded guarantees for investment in country B, then this grant could be an economic feature of a special relationship. Alternatively, let us suppose that a country generally gives its investors guarantees abroad because it doubts that the foreign nation will or can protect investment. It may then express a special relationship with a foreign country by withholding guarantees – by indicating confidence in the foreign country's ability and willingness to protect investment,

The content of development aid could be quantitatively or qualitatively superior to aid given to other countries. The form may also be special. Let us imagine that a country normally requires a prospective recipient of development aid to submit for approval by the donor government the projects that it would like funded. Waiving that rule, donating unrestricted funds to be allocated by the recipient for projects of a recipient's own choosing, indicates a special relationship. Content and form are often both special, but the two do not have to be special simultaneously.

SCIENCE AND TECHNOLOGY

Nations normally pool resources for joint research in their scientific relations. The granting of financial aid to a foreign country for scientific research, with no strings attached, exemplifies a special relationship in this policy area. If the exchange of scientists is a normal activity between countries, then the numbers and ranks involved may also indicate, in content, a special relationship.

CULTURE

Cultural exchange is a normal feature of bilateral relations, but marked deviation from normal exchange, whether in the number or in the quality, indicates special relations. Youth exchange is an important feature of cultural ties.

DIPLOMATIC SUPPORT

Countries enunciate general attitudes, and general lines of policy, towards other countries. Such expressions, when special, include diplomatic support through statements and speeches at home as well as in international fora, as at the United Nations. Special relationships are characterized by pronouncements that are generally favourable in tone.

Diplomatic support also may be demonstrated in visits by government leaders, particularly heads of state and foreign ministers, and through the speeches and statements they make on such trips. When one actor in the special relationship is under verbal assault from the international community, silence or abstention from voting by the partner could signify support. Consultation, co-ordination, or collaboration in diplomatic activities also can denote the existence of a special relationship. As in other policy areas, however, diplomatic support alone (or its

Table 11.1 *A Comparison of 'Special' Relationships with 'Normal' and 'Abnormal' Relationships*

Abnormal (negative)	Normal (average)	Abnormal (positive-special)
Hostile, unfriendly	Not hostile, benign indifference	Special, very friendly
Discrimination	Treat like others	Policy preferences in multiple areas
Open conflict, verbal or physical	Occasional verbal conflict, not always overcome	Occasional verbal conflict, with ability to overcome
Very few governmental contacts	Governmental contacts	Network of governmental contacts
Very few societal contacts	Societal relations exist	Close societal relations
USA–China until 1970	USA–New Zealand	USA–Britain until early 1970s
USA–Cuba after 1959	West Germany–Switzerland	USA–Canada
West Germany–East Germany until mid-1970s	Israel–Australia	West Germany–Israel
Israel–USSR after 1950	France–India	USA–Israel
Israel–Egypt, 1948–77	Britain–Austria	France–Germany

absence) cannot determine the presence of special relations. Anglo-American relations remained special for a time despite American criticism during Suez, for example, as did Canadian-American relations despite the Canadian diplomatic position during the war in Vietnam.

A special relationship exists only when the governments of both countries involved at some point acknowledge that relations are special. Recognition occurs either in public statements or in discussions between policy-makers of the two countries. When the actors are not mutually committed to the notion that the relationship between them is special, in all likelihood there is nothing special about it. However, merely saying something is special does not make it so, and public denial of special relations does not necessarily mean they do not exist (Table 11.1).

ENDURANCE

Just as disagreement in an uninspired marriage may prompt divorce, conflicts or threats between participants in a non-special relationship may be permanently damaging. Depending on the importance of a particular issue tension could lead to indifference or even a rupture of relations. The hallmark of special relations is their ability to endure crises in which the interests of the two partners seem opposed.

One of the most common examples of 'endurance' is the survival of Anglo-American relations, despite the overt disagreement during the 1956 Suez invasion. No such accommodation was possible in the non-special relationship between the USA and France. A more recent example of endurance is offered by the way in which Canada and the USA restored (and one could argue improved) the friendship that had undergone severe attack in the early 1970s. Another such attack in the early 1980s promises also to be overcome. There may be periods of coolness in a special relationship, but because of the very foundation of the relationship and the previous experience of specialness the two countries share, there is the capacity to come together again for mutual advantage.

Whether a special relationship can be sustained after a crisis in relations depends on the extent of policy preferences, the commitment of political leadership to the relationship and the magnitude of societal networks. There must be a continuous flow of needs, and the partner must provide either satisfaction, better treatment than would be offered to others, or compensation through special treatment in an alternative area of policy.

Maintenance of a special relationship does not necessarily depend on charismatic leaders, but it does require well-known government officials working actively on its behalf. Relations between personalities are, as Coral Bell suggested, of vital importance not only among political leaders, but also among bureaucrats who facilitate the extension of mutual preference through informal transactions.

For a special relationship to endure, the psychological resonance present at the founding must have become positive and continuous. Such psychological relations develop from the interactions of individuals. Interest groups become preoccupied with their counterparts in the special partner. Groups that engage in such bilateral activity may include cultural societies, chambers of commerce, trade unions and political parties.

TERMINATION

It is difficult to discern precisely when a special relationship is over. The German-Israeli special relationship continues and, therefore, provides no real clues. Even past special relationships, such as those between France and Israel or between Britain and the USA, offer no definitive answers, for vestiges of these special relationships remain. It does seem, however, that the weakening of all the conditions that led to the creation of the special relationship – psychological factors, need and domestic political support – herald its disappearance, but the order or intensity of decline in these factors is unclear.

From the Anglo-American case it appears that a conflict between bilateralism and multilateralism may provide further explanation. The more that one of the partners sees the resolution of its problems through multilateral arrangements, the less importance it will accord bilateral commitments. For example, Britain's entry into the European Economic Community reduced the significance of relations with the USA. The priority West Germany gives its membership in the European Economic Community certainly has been a factor in the reduction of close relations with the USA, and it appears to be an irritant in West Germany's relations with Israel. In neither case, however, is it a sufficient condition for the disappearance of the special relationship. Canada tried to diversify its foreign relations through a contractual link with the EEC, but the arrangements offered a weak alternative to relations with the USA; the improvement in Canadian-US relations after 1975 was, in part, attributable to the absence of multilateral choice for Canada. The choice of a multilateral strategy means the pursuit of arrangements similar to those that exist with a special partner. This strategy obviously requires much time and effort. Multilateral arrangements, nevertheless, offer opportunities to deal with several countries over a variety of functional issues.

There is another factor which at first appears to affect termination: the international environment. It does not necessarily prevent the continued demonstration of preference, but a negative international environment can affect the form of a special relationship. If a special relationship evokes hostility or jealousy on the part of other members of the international system, it may go underground or behind closed doors. Termination in this case is only apparent, not real.

CONCLUSION

Many bilateral relations exhibit some of the features suggested here but to be special a relationship must be expressed consistently in terms of preference; it must be recognized as special by the partners and be able to endure crises. A special relationship comes about only under certain conditions of history, psychology, need and domestic support, and it fades when the influence of these factors declines.

Special relationships are special not merely because they deviate from the norm of a country's foreign relations. They deviate through positive expression. They are a category of co-operative bilateral international relations, but their characteristics distinguish them from other co-operative bilateral relations identified in the literature of international relations.

The criteria set out here for determining whether a relationship is special, and the conditions under which such a special relationship may come into being, correspond to the available descriptions of four bilateral examples. However, only the description of West German-Israeli relations was assembled systematically and deliberately as a test of an analytical category. West German-Israeli relations satisfy the criteria here and are special. They are not uniquely so.

12
Conclusion

This book has concentrated on two main concerns – the relationship between West Germany and Israel, and the concept of the special relationship in international affairs. General conclusions can be drawn for both, and the concept can be examined in other cases.

GERMAN-ISRAELI RELATIONS

A SUMMARY

West Germany and Israel as states, and Germans and Jews as peoples, share a history simultaneously antagonistic and mutually admiring. West German and Israeli societies interpenetrate at many levels and the states interact in many fields. No two states, and no two societies, have a shared history quite like theirs, and no two states have treated each other quite as they have. Since 1952 West Germany has played a crucial role in the economic development of Israel and Israeli co-operation has proved essential for German political rehabilitation and self-respect. The states have needed each other, and both have responded to the need.

Although relations between West Germany and Israel have not always been friendly in all fields, at all times there has been great co-operation and mutual sympathy in one field or another. Behind the political decisions to pursue good relations at all times stands the interwoven history of the peoples and the psychology of mutual responsiveness that has sustained and perpetuated the special relationship. The two states have not necessarily acted in concert with the immediately prevalent attitudes of their peoples, but their constant concern for one another appears to reflect a perpetual concern of their peoples.

The special relationship between West Germany and Israel has been characterized by a governmental display of preference in a wide range of public policies. West Germany has given Israel exceptional sums of money and other aid; it has risked relations with other nations on behalf of Israel more than for any other nation; it has sought contact in unusual ways, and its whole government has been involved with the State of Israel. Israel, in turn, has helped Germans expiate sins unparalleled in human history. Israel gave West Germany moral approval when Germany was universally doubted and Israel was widely accepted. At a time when only Germany could or would pay, and only Israel could absolve, each fulfilled the other's most dire needs. Moreover, the unusual tasks were accomplished in unusual ways, with each state doing for the other what it would not normally do for anyone else.

The mutual preferences experienced since 1952 persist and the relationship, because of its foundations and its sustaining features, is still special. West Germany and Israel still do for each other what they do for no one else. Whether in making research monies available or in guiding young people through their countries, whether in loaning money at favourable rates or in guiding rhetoric down friendly paths, West Germany and Israel do not treat each other as they treat other countries.

The determinants of West German and Israeli policy are complex and multiple, but often chief among them is a perception of morality. That certain choices do not necessarily serve an immediate national interest is demonstrable and decision-makers are fully aware of the potential consequences of such choices, but when German or Israeli leaders explain choices in terms of 'right' and 'wrong', their explanations are not mere rhetoric. Important preferences are exercised in the international arena because leaders perceive the necessity to behave according to moral responsibilities. The overall experience of West German-Israeli relations since 1952 bears witness to the impressive role of morality in international affairs.

West Germany and Israel have recognized that relations are special. The external environment can affect the form of such binding ties, but not the content, and recognition went underground, spoken in whispers because of the Hallstein Doctrine and relations with the Arab World. In one area of policy after another officials acknowledge privately what they may no longer say publicly – that relations between West Germany and Israel are special.

As a changing environment can affect the form of the relationship, so it can impose an enormous challenge on the relationship's durability. The relationship is special, in part, because it can survive crisis. Just as Anglo-American relations were in some respects even stronger after their public opposition over the Suez Canal in 1956, so German-Israeli relations have strengthened in some policy areas when Arab challenges have seemed most powerful.

There are limits, of course, on what Israel and West Germany will do for each other in the international arena, and it is possible to identify those limits, particularly in the realm of public political support. Those limits are the focus of the greatest controversy in the relationship, and they are also apparently the source of compensatory arrangements. Thus, even in the areas of non-cooperation something special emerges.

ASSESSMENT

Seven main points emerge from the analysis of German-Israeli relations, as follows.

(1) The bilateral relationship between West Germany and Israel has been special since 1952 and continues as a special relationship today.
(2) The relationship was built on a long history of mutual awareness between Germans and Jews dating from the existence of a Jewish community in Germany. The relationship was shaped by the wholly negative psychological trauma of the Holocaust and by the positive symbiosis of German and Jewish cultures prior to 1933. Psychological factors on both sides have been expressed frequently in terms of morality.
(3) Pragmatism catalysed the policy relationship. Israel needed economic rejuvenation, while Germany sought political rehabilitation. After attempts to meet their requirements elsewhere, each perceived the other actor as uniquely capable of satisfying needs. And as original needs seemed fulfilled, new needs have arisen and have been satisfied throughout the history of the relationship.
(4) Preference has been shown in defence, economics, science and technology, and culture. West Germany has pursued direct preferential treatment by offering Israel more, of better quality, more frequently and on better terms than it has offered to other partners. Israel's preferences for West Germany have been indirect, consisting of behaviour much more positive than the past might have predicted. When requirements could not be accommodated in a given area, compensation was offered in other vital areas.
(5) West Germany has special relationships with other countries such as France and the USA, but in general they do not conflict with West Germany's relationship with Israel. In the one area where the relationship with France has contradicted German policy towards Israel (on the Middle East conflict where France favoured the Arab and Palestinian positions from 1967 until at least the first year of François Mitterrand's presidency) West Germany has modified its public attitude towards Israel. However, this attitude has been by no means identical with that of France; the special relationship with Israel circumscribes West Germany's diplomatic behaviour.
(6) The relationship challenging German-Israeli ties most is between West Germany and certain Arab countries such as Saudi Arabia. Some German political figures (for example, Scheel, Schröder, Wischnewski, Bangemann and Möllemann) might have liked to frame German-Saudi relations as special, but they do not possess the necessary psychological roots, and need is confined to the specific areas of defence and science and technology for Saudi Arabia, and oil and markets for the Germans. The West German government has withstood pressures to dismantle the special relationship, and in the final analysis relations with the Arab World simply cannot rival the complex ties between West Germany and Israel. The Arabs or Palestinians fail to comprehend the binding character of the special relationship at their peril.

(7) German-Israeli relations have endured crises over policy towards the Arab World; the absence of diplomatic relations in the 1950s; the German scientists in Egypt and the cessation of arms shipments in the 1960s; Germany's public adherence to EEC Middle East policy in the 1970s; and Schmidt's statements on the Palestinians in the 1980s. Relations have survived because of the basic goodwill of policy-makers on both sides and because of the intricate network between individuals and groups in both societies. Past experience and institutional ties involving the post-Holocaust generations give the special relationship a strong probability of endurance in the future.

OTHER CASES

German-Israel relations are special, but not unique. The Holocaust was unique yet the type of relationship to which it gave rise can be found in other nation-state pairs; they, too, have some unique historical features that have helped to create a similar bilateral relationship. But each case must be tested against available theories in international relations so that we see, as with the detailed German-Israeli case, the utility of a theory of special relationships.[1]

CANADIAN-US RELATIONS

Canadian-US relations have been tested as a case of alliance, integration and complex interdependence. The existence of the alliance is obvious, and no analyst has attempted to confine the relationship in these terms. The other characterizations, however, merit further consideration.

Integration Of the four different theoretical frameworks presented in the first section of *Continental Community? Independence and Integration in North America* Charles Pentland's is the most useful for analysing Canadian-American relations.[2] Pentland outlines five dimensions for assessing integration, yet only one applies effectively to Canadian-US relations.

Pentland himself questions the usefulness of the first dimension, coercive power:

> Does...the ratio (over 40:1) of American to Canadian defence budgets mean the inevitable elimination (at least in the NATO–NORAD context) of distinctive Canadian command structures, procurement patterns and, ultimately, defence capabilities? Or does the increased visibility of such discrepancies have counter-effects akin to those of the massive, victorious Union army of 1865 on the will to federate British North America? (Pentland, 1974, pp. 48–9)

In other words, does integration, especially with asymmetric units, weaken or strengthen their autonomy? Pentland does not answer his own question. In a detailed analysis of the consequences of integration in the case of the defence production sharing agreements between Canada and the USA John Kirton also leaves the question unanswered. He remains sceptical about the ability of integration theory to get to one of the essential issues, 'the multiplicity of actors, at various levels and of differing organizational form' (1974, p. 133).

The second dimension, after coercive power, refers to decision-making. Whereas it affords a distinction between joint and autonomous decision-making, it says nothing about preferential treatment. How would this dimension, for example, facilitate explanation of the autonomous US decision to grant Canada preference through exemption from the interest equalization tax, or the autonomous Canadian decision in 1965 to grant the USA preference by excluding *Time* and *Reader's Digest* from an amendment to the Canadian Income Tax Act that prevented tax deductions for advertising in non-Canadian journals?

In the third dimension of integration, functional administration, 'the important point of reference is the system's success in meeting collective needs' (Pentland, 1974, p. 52). But what if needs are not common? What if the US government needs to move hydrocarbons from Alaska, and Canada needs to protect its own resources and its environment? Of course, there are collective needs in the Canadian-US case, such as environmental matters. In integration theory the 'community... possesses the institutional capacity to solve [such] functional problems in an economically and administratively rational manner' (ibid., p. 51). Maureen Molot, however, writes in 'The role of institutions in Canada–United States relations', that the Canadian-American dyad 'has little in the way of formal structures' (1974, p. 165). Even where such structures do exist, decision-makers usually prefer personal contact and informal meetings. She questions 'the conceptualization of interstate integration principally in terms of shared institutions and common processes of decision making' (ibid., p. 164). The functional dimension of integration theory, preoccupied with formal institutions, cannot capture the extent, diversity and central importance of non-institutional ties in a special relationship.

The informality and personal style of relations appear to be embraced by Pentland's fourth dimension, socio-political communication. Yet by differentiating among social acts (communication, transaction and interaction) instead of actors, the often crucial distinction (especially in the Canadian-US case) between personal relations in the private sector and personal relations among policy-makers is lost.

The final dimension, attitudes, relates to a psychological relationship that is useful for understanding the Canadian-US example. However, as the lone accurate dimension it does not salvage the application of integration theory for a comprehensive assessment of the particular case.

Indeed, some of the authors of this attempt to apply integration doubt themselves, in the end, the merit of the enterprise (Axline, 1974, p. 87). Naomi Black (1974, p. 100) and Gerald Wright (1974, p. 152) call the relationship special.[3]

Complex interdependence   Canadian-US relations surely are a case of complex interdependence. However, the framework of complex interdependence is limited in several critical areas. Most importantly, it offers no explanation for why the relationship comes about in its particular form. History before 1920, and psychology, generally find no place with Keohane and Nye in explaining a foundation for the relationship.

The emergence and negotiation of interstate conflict, integral to complex interdependence, are central in special relationships. The criteria employed by Keohane and Nye to chart interstate conflict in Canadian-US relations remain useful for understanding this case in 1980 and 1981. None the less, this analytical strength of complex interdependence is also the framework's weakness. Resolution of high-level interstate conflict is its only focus. Complex interdependence tells us little about the relative harmony in Canadian-US relations during 1976–9, and it does not predict the content of future relations of harmony once the temporary interstate conflict has been resolved. The framework of the special relationship affords explanation and prediction for periods of harmony and of conflict.

ANGLO-AMERICAN RELATIONS

Anglo-American relations have been characterized most often as a case of either integration or alliance. Again, the theorists themselves have doubted the wisdom of their own choices.

Integration   Bruce Russett studies Anglo-American relations the same way that the authors of *Continental Community?* viewed Canadian-US relations. He refers in *Community and Contention* to the need for both partners to nurture 'the roots of the "special relationship" ' (1963, p. ix), but he chooses the pluralistic security community as an explanatory model. The Anglo-American, like the Canadian-US case, does not fit the mould its analyst has chosen.

Russett's purpose is to examine 'the present and past state of relations between the United States and Great Britain, and to contribute something to the explanation of why those relations are as they are' (ibid., p. vii). His analytical framework has three main variables: (1) the loads, burdens, or demands made upon the political unit; (2) the capabilities to meet those needs (this capacity contains two features: the 'capability for action' or the wherewithal of power – military strength, size, population, and so on – and the 'capability for responsiveness' or the desire to act – attention, communication and mutual identification); and (3) mutual responsiveness, which is a function of the ratio of the capabilities for responsiveness over the loads.

Analysis of variables 1 and 2 explain why relations have been close historically between Britain and the USA. They focus on concrete needs and the reasons they might be satisfied: the networks of cultural, social and political ties between masses and elites emanating from historical links, migration, family ties, common language, cultural similarities, common political heritage, and political and educational socialization.

The capacity to respond to a demand is not the same as the response. Russett may reveal whether two countries have the ability and the desire to aid one another, but he does not show whether they in fact do. He admits that 'responsiveness is the *probability* that the demands of one party will be met with indulgence rather than with deprivation by the other party. Responsiveness is a general term giving us, in the specific case, only a probability statement' (ibid., p. 30). He does distinguish between responsiveness (the inclination to act) and response (action) but then ignores the action; similarly, he differentiates between attention (the awareness of a need) and indulgence (its satisfaction), but again he fails to explore the action. Probabilities may be statistically attractive yet divorced from reality. The relationship between countries must be defined in the end not by what might happen, but by what in fact does happen.

Russett defines integration for Anglo-American relations as 'the process of building capabilities for responsiveness relative to the loads put on the capabilities' (ibid., p. 39). The substantive chapters of his work neglect governmental policy. Trade, investment, invisible income and transport are all seen as capabilities for responsiveness involving private individuals. Economic relations appear important only because of rivalry between Britain and the USA over trade and investment in third countries. He compares present capability in Anglo-American relations to the past when it would be more useful to assess how the two governments actually deal with each other.[4]

Near the end of *Community and Contention* there is a faint recognition that governmental policy is the key to relations between Britain and the USA: 'One serious gap remains ... we must show that the decline in capabilities is relevant to the making of political decisions' (ibid., p. 144). He then examines voting patterns in the US Senate and statements in the British House of Commons. Cabinet, presidential and bureaucratic decisions are omitted, as is the still more important question of their implementation.[5]

Alliance Is alliance theory more instructive than integration theory for Anglo-American relations? Will it explain observable phenomena better than a theory of special relationships? Raymond Dawson and Richard Rosecrance, in 'Theory and reality in the Anglo-American alliance', address both questions (1966). They recognize that conventional alliance theory is inadequate for understanding Anglo-American relations, but they fashion no other conceptual lens for viewing what they sometimes call – but never define or understand – a special relationship.[6]

Citing George Liska, Dawson and Rosecrance note that 'Conventional alliance theory asserts that calculation, not sentiment, determines original combinations'. They rely on Hans Morgenthau to point out the theory's assertion that 'an alliance armed with nuclear weapons...is "obsolescent"' for, according to Morgenthau, 'either it cannot be relied on when the chips are down, or it gives one member power over the life and death of another member' (ibid., p. 21). Dawson and Rosecrance argue that sentiment plays an important role in Anglo-American relations, and that despite the possession of nuclear weapons, the alliance has survived. But whereas Dawson and Rosecrance are dissatisfied with available theory – 'from 1949 on...the relationship began to develop in ways not explicable in terms of conventional alliance theory' (ibid., p. 48) – they remain committed to looking at Anglo-American relations as an alliance: 'That alliance is ordinarily set apart as a "special relationship", as indeed it is, but it is still an alliance, the most durable and most influential of the nuclear age' (ibid., pp. 21–2).

Many of the features that make the Anglo-American relationship special are the features Dawson and Rosecrance hold responsible for the inadequacy of conventional theory. In addition to sentiment, for example, they note the ability of the relationship to surmount crises:

> The Suez crisis created another imponderable for traditional explanations of alliance politics. If any conflict of interests ever seemed certain to destroy the bases of alliance, that over Suez might have been expected to do so...Traditional theory would have us believe that where interests are contradictory, alliance must give way. In the Suez instance, since the alliance was primary, British interests had to yield. (Dawson and Rosecrance, 1966, p. 49)

They expose other 'special' features: complementary and simultaneous needs, mutual benefits, forceful leadership, the importance of personalities, cultural, linguistic and political affinities, collaboration and preference in several policy areas. They reaffirm the importance of sentiment in their conclusion: 'History, tradition, affinity have been crucial to the alliance, rather than peripheral' (ibid., p. 51).

The incremental theory-building of Dawson and Rosecrance prevents them from appreciating that Anglo-American relations do not constitute a mere alliance. They reject available theory to explain special relationships, but their effort to comprehend through some variation of traditional theory fails to improve significantly our understanding.

The dissatisfaction of Dawson and Rosecrance with traditional theory is blunt; their commitment to some variation of it, however, is persistent. They view the relationship as 'special' *because* alliance theory offers no explanation for it: 'The relationship is special in one notable sense: the theory of alliances does not explain it' (ibid.). Their proposition is backwards. Given that the relationship is special, alliance theory will not explain it. 'Specialness' does not derive from or depend upon a lack of explanation; it originates from features that can be identified, understood and organized into a model. That model does not depend on what we understand about alliances. Dawson and Rosecrance did not seek out – and so do not discover – an alternative explanation for Anglo-American relations. A critique of available theory, as they demonstrate very well, is simply not enough.

US RELATIONS WITH GERMANY, JAPAN AND ISRAEL, AND FRANCO-ISRAELI RELATIONS

Several co-operative bilateral relationships have been subjected to detailed studies as alliances. In every instance the application of alliance theory has proven flawed and an assessment as special relationships would be more accurate.

Alliance theory is ambiguous and often contradictory, yet there are modest areas of consensus among its practitioners. The analysts of the following cases, however, found it necessary to extend even the modest consensus, and in every instance they confessed they were not describing alliances even when they did not know what to call their particular bilateral relationship. Although they inclined to describe their cases as unique variants of alliance, the unique conditions, in varying degrees, described a consistent and recognizable pattern that seems, like the German-Israeli case, to satisfy the criteria of the special relationship.

German-US relations Observers of German-US relations also have contributed to the theoretical literature on alliances and special relationships. Hans Gatzke developed the concept of a special relationship despite deficiencies in application, and before him Roger Morgan detailed the close ties between the two countries in *The United States and West Germany, 1945–1973: A Study in Alliance Politics* (1974a). Morgan's analysis of German-US relations does not consider in any detail three areas – non-military policy relations (particularly economic ties), the role of transnational actors and the historical relationship. The analytical framework of alliances appears to have discouraged such an examination.

Morgan emphasizes several key elements of the German-US 'alliance' commonly ignored or discounted by alliance theory. He consistently considers the internal politics of the two countries and sets as a criterion of friendship domestic support. He finds the personal ties between principal individuals to be highly influential, both positively (for instance, Adenauer and Dulles) and negatively (for instance, Kennedy and Grewe), thereby reducing the impact of structural determinants. He observes frequent tensions between governments and consequently emphasizes their ability to overcome crises in their relations. And in his final analysis he sees this basic harmony as unusual, warranting consideration of an alternative appellation he regrettably does not pursue:

> The most striking theme running through...more than a quarter of a century [after 1945] is the high degree of harmony established between two nations which during the previous generation had twice been enemies in war. Despite the frequent incidents involving disagreement or friction...the partnership as a whole showed a degree of mutual confidence rare in the history of relations between two major states, to the point where the American Ambassador in...1973 could refer without exaggeration to a 'special relationship' uniting them for more than twenty years. (Morgan, 1974a, p. 247)

Japanese-US relations Roger Morgan's 'lasting' and 'remarkable' rapprochement between two 'ex-enemies' is not unique. The authors of *Managing an Alliance. The Politics of United States-Japanese Relations* write: 'the prospects for a close, mutually beneficial relationship between two bitter wartime enemies were not exactly encouraging. Yet such a relationship emerged and has persisted' (Destler, *et al.*, 1976, p. 1). Destler and his colleagues employ alliance theory also, but with different emphases. They give equal attention to economic and military relations, they feature transnational actors and judge domestic politics as a cause of problems in a relationship in which domestic political support is crucial for the continuation of ties (ibid., chs 2, 3 and 5). They say the relationship has endured, despite profound problems, in large part because of the 'sustained effort' of individual leaders and officials. Some of these emphases, of course, fall outside the more characteristic models of alliances, but they are chosen wisely as critical factors in assessing Japanese-US relations.

Destler and his colleagues see patterns in the relations between Japan and the USA that are recognizable in other cases: 'In fundamental respects, Japan is typical of the major countries with whom the United States has developed alliance relationships since World War II.' Yet Japan must be treated as a 'special case' (ibid., p. 184) because of the significant linguistic and cultural differences with the USA. Destler calls upon the USA to apply 'the same sort of effort that [it] should devote to Anglo-American or German-American relations' (ibid., p. 190), that is, Japan, like Germany and Britain, should receive preferential treatment. Thus, the Japanese-US relationship is seen as a special kind of 'major alliance'.

This study of Japanese-US relations describes many of the characteristics of a special relationship, despite an unfortunate neglect of history and explanation for the forces that founded postwar friendship. The description is permitted to distort conventional concepts of alliance instead of acknowledging the need for an alternative basis for analysis. The product is unnecessarily, and unfortunately, atheoretical.

US-Israeli relations American relations with Israel, like relations with Britain, Germany and Japan, frequently are examined as an alliance with unique characteristics. Nadav Safran describes the case in *Israel: The Embattled Ally:*

> The relationship between the United States and Israel has been exceptional among the respective relationships of the two countries and a most unusual one in the annals of international relations altogether. Formally, this relationship never attained the status of a contractual alliance, yet in practice, it has been as strong as any alliance, written or unwritten, in which either country has been involved, and it has permeated the societies as well as the governments of the two countries as no relationship of theirs has, with the possible exception of American-British relations. (Safran, 1978, p. 332)

The exceptional elements adduced by Safran in the section 'America's special connection with Israel' constitute the very areas on which alliance theory indeed sheds little light. History is paramount; so are the transnational links forged and nurtured by American Jews and which maintain the 'organic' and 'special connection' between the two countries. Policy preferences at different stages have covered diplomatic support, military relations and economic aid. Safran summarizes US preference for Israel before 1967 in non-diplomatic and non-strategic activities by noting that 'any benefit the United States granted to other countries was extended to Israel promptly and on a generous scale' (ibid., p. 576). After 1967, the same generosity characterized diplomatic and strategic relations.

American Jews have promoted close governmental relations between the USA and Israel, and they have been supported more broadly by the American people who feel a moral responsibility to help redress the historical persecution of the Jews. This psychological relationship has guaranteed domestic support which, in turn, has enabled the relationship to endure crises and disagreements; it has 'cushioned the shock when America and Israel fell out on particulars of perceived interests and facilitated the resolution of the differences' (ibid., p. 571). These factors clearly are not features of an alliance, but Safran offers no alternative framework for understanding US-Israeli relations. The elements vital, in his estimation, to understanding these relations are in fact the characteristics of a special relationship.

Franco-Israeli relations Franco-Israeli relations until 1967 bore many of the characteristics of US-Israeli relations after the Six-Day War. And Franco-Israeli relations have been assessed as an example of an unusual alliance remarkably similar to the allegedly unique examples discussed above. Sylvia Kowitt Crosbie concluded in *A Tacit Alliance: France and Israel from Suez to the Six-Day War:*

> The tacit alliance between France and Israel was a peculiar arrangement between two states whose interests ran parallel for a time, then

diverged. While it reflected some of the principal aspects of an alliance, in many respects it differed from the normal patterns of international politics. (Crosbie, 1974, p. 215)

How did it differ? Crosbie's study emphasizes the informality of the relationship, its tacit, exclusive and secret nature, the pervasiveness of bureaucratic interaction down to the smallest units of government, the personal ties and the sentimental links. The policy relationship began in the military sphere but spilled over into the economic field and into science and technology. From the beginning it was 'no ordinary diplomatic relationship', no 'orthodox' relationship, for 'by the time of the Suez crisis in 1956, when Israel and France embarked on the joint invasion of Egypt, it was apparent that a special relationship had indeed been forged between the two powers' (ibid., p. 3).

FRANCO-GERMAN RELATIONS

France's special relationship with Israel was short-lived, but relations with Germany after 1945 proved more durable. Indeed, the link to France is Germany's third special relationship, alongside relations with the USA and Israel.

Like German-Israeli relations, the background to Franco-German postwar relations is often discussed in terms of congenital hatred (*Erbfeindschaft*). As German-Israeli relations resulted from individual and societal friendships, so did the Franco-German rapprochement, and some Germans, including Carlo Schmid and Erich Lüth, participated centrally in both partnerships. German-Israeli and Franco-German relations ostensibly began to develop in different directions in the 1960s. Germany emphasized informal ties to Israel, while formalizing in 1963 a friendship treaty with France. Despite such institutional difference, however, Franco-German and German-Israeli relations were true to their origins and retained fundamentally similar characteristics.

Integration Some observers have said that the Franco-German Friendship Treaty was designed to produce an integrated community (see, for example, Bondy and Abelein, 1973, p. 218; Picht, 1978, p. 354; Loch, 1981). Whatever the intention, Franco-German relations must be measured according to the same criteria applicable in other bilateral cases. Have France and Germany integrated or have they forged mutually preferential policies between sovereign states? Joseph Rovan, one of the primary architects of the Franco-German rapprochement (Grosser, 1975, p. 35), concludes in 1978 that as an 'instrument to speed the achievement of a real political community...the treaty has failed rapidly'. 'There is a long way', Rovan wrote, 'before real integration or a fusion of the two peoples' (1978, pp. 37, 39).

Even though the Franco-German relationship amounts to 'much less than a federation', it is also '*de facto* something more than alliance' (ibid., p. 38). Rovan's description of Franco-German relations fifteen years after the treaty signature includes many of the features of a special relationship. He writes of myriad connections across all levels of society: between religious leaders, students, professors, journalists, lawyers, banks and industrial concerns. He identifies intense personal links, exemplified in the Franco-German organization, the Society for Transnational Co-operation. Frenchmen and Germans have become so well acquainted that they 'today know more about one another than any other two peoples who do not speak the same language' (ibid., p. 35). France and Germany share a high degree of mutual consciousness not experienced by other European countries; the German public, for example, reacts 'with particular sensitivity to French attacks, much more intensely than to criticism from England or Italy' (ibid., p. 36).

The intimacy of individual and societal relations extends to government. Rovan refers to a 'thick net of permanent consultation' in both the political and economic arenas. He notes that a French bureaucrat can be engaged in more frequent contact with his German counterpart than with members of his own ministry or with bureaucrats in other French ministries (ibid., pp. 31–8). Private and governmental activities come together and symbolize the relationship in Franco-German youth exchange (for figures, see Chapter 6), which represents in Rovan's view 'the largest organized free exchange of people not inspired by poverty, persecution or religion' (ibid., p. 39).

For Rovan, Franco-German relations clearly stand apart as unusual in magnitude and design, at a level of relations that he identifies between alliance and integration, a 'symbiosis' or *convivance* (ibid., p. 39). Although Rovan does not refer to a 'special relationship', he characterizes France and Germany as being 'drawn to one another and dependent on one another in a special way' (ibid., p. 36). This 'special way', marked by mutual preference in policy and psychological resonance between peoples, seems by any other name to be indeed a special relationship.

ARE ALL RELATIONSHIPS SPECIAL?

This book began with references to many special relationships, including several of those reviewed above. The analytical criteria for special relationships obviously exclude some cases. Saudi Arabia and the USA share no long or intense history. Their peoples have no dominating psychological tie. The governments of the two countries have extended to each other preference in defence and in some economic affairs, but Saudi Arabia had alternative arms-suppliers and the USA could purchase oil elsewhere. Neither the necessary founding conditions nor the essential policy preferences have been present to justify qualifying this bilateral case as special.

Relations between the USA and Iran were more extensive in the mid-1970s than between the USA and Saudi Arabia, but again relations centred on defence. The necessary conditions for the creation of a special relationship again were conspicuously absent, as were societal links. Consequently, relations plainly did not survive the crisis of the Iranian revolution.

The historical relations between France and the Arab World are well established, and there has been considerable preference expressed in defence, economics and, to a lesser extent, in science and technology. But when French relations are differentiated among Arab countries, it is more difficult to discern which bilateral ties will qualify as special. The most likely is Algeria. Other candidates include Iraq, where a range of policy preference has been expressed, and Syria, where the historical foundations are sturdier. Each pair would require systematic investigation.

Many countries have at least one special relationship, and some enjoy several. Nevertheless, the number is restricted by definition: preferential relations cannot exist with all parties. Country A may say it has a special relationship with country B, but mere pronouncement does not make it so. Special relationships share common features, but undoubtedly within the category countries also have different kinds of special relations. Analyses of further cases will make it possible to distinguish among special relationships and will facilitate a general theory of bilateral relations by applying consistent criteria to relationships that are not special.

CONCLUSION

Identification and categorization of bilateral relations are essential steps in predicting the direction of these relations in the international arena. Special relationships are more secure than others. Hence, Anglo-American friendship could not be destroyed by Suez or Skybolt. Special relationships can be identified, in part, through historical evidence of such durability, and once they exist as special relationships, they are especially capable of enduring further crisis. Even in an era of public coolness, and even with some of the foundations of recent memories and guilt eroding, West German-Israeli relations are likely to remain particularly friendly for a long time to come. Bilateral relations that do not bear special characteristics are far more unstable and incapable of surviving crisis.

The existence of special relationships has important implications for the international system. There is a bonding between nation states that is far more difficult to break than the ties of other co-operative relations. Whereas theorists of international relations stress the influence of either the international system or domestic systems as constraints on choice and freedom of action, the special relationship often is a condition defined by two nation states that constrains the international system. The international system cannot change the geographical bedrock of Canadian-US relations, for example, nor can it erase the impact of the Holocaust on West Germany and Israel. These unique features, when they have fostered special relations, contribute to bilateral relations that can defy international politics.

International actors often have failed to appreciate the significance of the special relationship. The Arab states, and the Palestinians, repeatedly have underestimated the task of altering German policy in the Middle East because they oversimplified the bond between West Germany and Israel. The European Economic Community, in similar fashion, has failed to comprehend the source of German resistance to parts of the common Middle Eastern policy. Until the Arabs, the Palestinians, and the European Economic Community accept the Holocaust and its consequences, they will never see a fundamentally altered relationship between Europe and the Arab World. No other theory of international relations has a similar power to explain the complex dynamic of these inter-regional relations. The particular case of West German-Israeli relations in the framework of a special relationship is the key to understanding relations between Western Europe and the Middle East.

'Traditional' relations of friendship are as important as ever in bilateral relations. Special relationships show that the fabric of mutual experience insulates bilateral activities from outside pressures and shifting international goals. Tradition, which for the social scientist means historical analysis, remains a useful tool for prediction, but the concept of the special relationship places tradition in a new analytical framework.

The special relationship, then, contributes to prediction in international relations. The bond between states in such a relationship is so strong that endurance can be predicted in most circumstances. The endurance can defy the desires of powerful states whose behaviour may be modified because of the relationship's strength. Furthermore, when a partner sacrifices preferential treatment in a policy area, it is probable that compensation will be offered in another area. Decline in diplomatic support thus does not signal, as many analysts mistakenly have supposed, decline in overall friendship. Observers must be more sensitive to the full array of policy relations.

These generalizations apply with equal force to a limited number of bilateral relations. These relations define a specific analytical category representing one type of co-operative bilateral international relationship. The research agenda now summons refinement not only for variants of the special relationship, but for other kinds of bilateral relations. For as all co-operative relations are not special, they also are not all alliances or examples of integration or complex interdependence, or any of the other extant theories. The more we understand what cases are truly examples of, the more we will understand the components of the international system and the range of possibility for international accommodation. And the more we understand the co-operative relations between nation-state pairs, the more we will comprehend the prospects for friendship and peace.

NOTES: CHAPTER 12

1 Authors have been selected on the basis of three criteria: (*a*) the application of a theoretical concept (integration, alliance, interdependence) to a specific case of bilateral relations; (*b*) the characterization of the relationship as unusually close; and (*c*) their expertise regarding the particular case. No attempt is made to be comprehensive with respect to the literature on the various cases or their details.
2 H. Edward English's definition of integration is so general as to offer no meaningful distinctions among types of bilateral relations (1974, p. 20). The other two theoretical attempts by Black (1974) and Axline (1974) labour under an assumption of asymmetry. The disparity in natural attributes between Canada and the USA does not make inevitable an asymmetry of benefits. Black is less conclusive on this point, but shares with Axline a focus on the effects of disparity. For a critical analysis of integration and other theoretical approaches to Canadian-US relations, see Redekop (1976). Redekop's alternative framework of 'continental systemic dominance' overemphasizes non-governmental actors almost to the exclusion of central governments. As Redekop admits, 'the vast array of Canadian-American relations includes conventional bilateral interaction' (ibid., p. 242), yet he provides no tools for analysing that part of the relationship.
3 For an initial application of the special relationship framework to Canadian-US relations, see Feldman and Gardner Feldman (1980).
4 Russett does compare US and British behaviour towards each other with their behaviour towards all other countries combined, or with their average behaviour. Rarely is there comparison, however, with individual countries. It is, therefore, impossible to identify preference (1963, pp. 227–40), but for two exceptions: (*a*) the number of agreements that the USA signed with Russia is a control for the number of agreements it signed with Britain; and (*b*) comparative trade figures. The statistical measures, however, say little about governmental policies. This absence of specific comparisons or disaggregation is part of the transactional school of analysis in international relations. Qualitative measures are almost non-existent.
5 Russett persists in his neglect of action. He refers to military actions, such as strategic planning and co-operation, but prefers to regard these as capabilities for integration (Russett, 1963, ch. 10). In an appendix he lists major government actions affecting Anglo-American relations in the period 1890–1961 but fails to integrate them into his theory or his analysis of the bilateral relationship (ibid., pp. 223–6).
6 Neustadt (1970) also calls the relationship 'special', yet analyses it within an alliance framework.

List of Interviews

GERMAN REPRESENTATIVES

Abs, Joseph Hermann, former economic adviser to Adenauer. Bonn, June 25, 1975.
Bangemann, Martin, secretary-general of FDP. Bonn, May 16 and July 25, 1975.
Barzel, Rainer, CDU deputy; Minister for All-German Affairs, 1962–3. Bonn, June 16, 1975.
Becker, Horst, leading figure in Sozialistische Bildungsgemeinschaft. Bonn, August 15, 1975.
Benda, Ernst, former president of German-Israeli Society. Karlsruhe, June 3, 1975.
Bierhoff, Hartwig, assistant in German-Israeli Society. Bonn, May 23 and 25, 1975.
Birrenbach, Kurt, emissary of Chancellor Erhard in negotiations over diplomatic relations with Israel, 1965. Düsseldorf, July 17, 1975.
Blumenfeld, Erik, CDU deputy; president of German-Israeli Society (as of May 1977). Bonn, February 27, 1975.
Böhm, Franz, head of German delegation to Wassenaar reparations negotiations. Butzbach, May 12, 1975.
Büren, Rainer, director of Orient-Institut. Hamburg, June 29, 1975.
Eckert, Pater Willehad Paul, leading figure in Gesellschaften für christlich-jüdische Zusammenarbeit. Cologne, August 14, 1975.
Ehmke, Horst, Minister for Research and Technology, 1972–4. Bonn, May 21, 1975.
Erhard, Ludwig, Chancellor, 1963–6. Bonn, June 16, 1965.
Gessner, Manfred, SPD deputy; member of German-Israeli Parliamentary Association. Bonn, May 16, 1975.
Heck, Bruno, CDU deputy; former Minister for Youth, Family and Health. Bonn, June 2, 1975.
Hess, Moshe, executive officer of the German Society for Economic Relations with Israel; director of Bank für Gemeinwirtschaft. Frankfurt, May 20, 1975.
Hohmann, Karl, aide to Ludwig Erhard. Bonn, June 18, 1975.
Hupka, Herbert, CDU deputy; member of German-Israeli Parliamentary Association. Bonn, May 21, 1975.
Isenberg, Veronika, staff member in International Relations Section, SPD. Bonn, May 30, 1975.
Jaeger, Richard, CSU deputy; member of parliamentary oversight committee on arms to Israel. Bonn, June 25, 1975.
Jahn, Gerhard, first president of German-Israeli Society. Bonn, June 18, 1975.
Jansen, Thomas, aide to Rainer Barzel. Bonn, July 28, 1975.
Dr Jung, aide to Gerhard Schröder. Bonn, July 28, 1975.
Kleinert, Detlef, FDP deputy; member of German-Israeli Parliamentary Association. Bonn, June 20, 1975.
Kliesing, Werner, CDU deputy; member of oversight committee on arms to Israel. Bonn, May 23, 1975.

Knieper, Werner, head of Armaments Section of German Ministry of Defence, 1951–66. Bonn, September 4, 1975.
Knoke, Karl Hermann, ambassador to Israel, 1968–71. Bonn, July 23, 1975.
Krupp, Michael, spiritual leader of Aktion Sühnezeichen in Israel. Jerusalem, April 15, 1975.
Küster, Otto, deputy head of German delegation to Wassenaar reparations negotiations. Stuttgart, June 3, 1975.
Küstermeier, Rudolf, co-founder of Peace with Israel Movement. Berlin, May 1, 1975.
Lieser, Peter, academic. Hamburg, June 27, 1975.
Lüth, Erich, co-founder of Peace with Israel Movement. Hamburg, June 28, 1975.
Mattick, Kurt, SPD deputy; member of German-Israeli Parliamentary Association. Bonn, February 20, 1975.
Mende, Erich, president of Free Democratic Party (FDP), 1960–8; Minister for All-German Affairs and Deputy Chancellor, 1963–6. Bonn, May 15, 1975.
Mertes, Dr Alois, CDU deputy. Bonn, May 27, 1975.
Metzger, Günther, SPD deputy; founding-member of German-Israeli Parliamentary Association. Bonn, May 13, 1975.
von Puttkamer, Jesco, ambassador to Israel, 1971–5. Bonn, February 4, 1975.
Schmid, Carlo, SPD deputy. Bonn, June 16, 1975.
Scholtz, Edeltraut, head of Section on Antisemitism, Bundeszentrale für politische Bildung. Bonn, May 21, June 19 and August 21, 1975.
Westphal, Heinz, former president of German-Israeli Society and former state secretary in Ministry for Youth, Family and Health. Bonn, May 7, 1975.
Westrick, Ludger, state secretary, German Ministry for Economics, 1951–63; Adenauer's emissary to Egypt for discussions over Luxembourg Agreement, 1953. Bonn, July 24, 1975.
Wohlrabe, Jürgen, CDU deputy; founding-member of German-Israeli Parliamentary Association. Bonn, June 18, 1975.

CONFIDENTIAL INTERVIEWS, GERMAN REPRESENTATIVES

Foreign Office, Bonn, February 26, June 2 and 13, July 2, 21, 22 and 30, August 19 and 27, September 9 and 11, 1975; September 3 and 5, 1979.
Foreign Office, Cultural Division, Bonn, June 19 and August 25, 1975; September 3, 1979.
German Embassy, Paris, June 10, 1975.
German Embassy, Tel Aviv, April 15 and 18, 1975.
Ministry of Defence, Bonn, July 18, 1975.
Ministry for Economic Co-operation, Bonn, June 23 and August 1, 1975; September 4, 1979.
Ministry for Economics, Bonn, June 24, 1975; September 4, 1979.
Ministry of Finance, Bonn, September 4, 1975; September 5, 1979.
Ministry for Research and Technology, Bonn, June 23, 1975; September 5, 1979.
Ministry for Youth, Family and Health, Bonn, July 1 and August 20, 1975; September 5, 1979.

Press and Information Office of the Federal Government, Bonn, June 16, 1975.
Protocol Office, Bundestag, Bonn, July, 1975.

ISRAELI AND JEWISH REPRESENTATIVES

Arad, David, former economic counsellor, 1971–3, Israeli Embassy in Bonn. Jerusalem, April 9, 1975.

Aronson, Shlomo, academic and former Israeli radio correspondent in Germany. Jerusalem, March 17, 1975.

Avner, Gershon, head of West European Division of Israeli Ministry for Foreign Affairs at time of Wassenaar reparations negotiations. Jerusalem, April 10, 1975.

Baruch, Ewald, member of Israeli Independent Liberal Party. Tel Aviv, April 17, 1975.

Bauer, Yehuda, academic. Jerusalem, April 7, 1975.

Begin, Menachem, leader of the Herut Party. Tel Aviv, April 20, 1975.

Ben-Natan, Asher, ambassador to the Federal Republic of Germany, 1965–9. Paris, June 10 and 12, 1975.

Ben-Yaacov, Ariad, former head of Consular Section, Israel Mission in Cologne. Jerusalem, March 21, 1975.

Bloch, Charles, academic. Tel Aviv, April 15, 1975.

Cohn, Josef, former personal secretary to Chaim Weizmann and Weizmann Institute's 'ambassador'. New York, September 27, 1980.

Cooper, Rabbi Abraham, project co-ordinator for International Statute of Limitations Effort; director of Operation Outreach, Simon Wiesenthal Center, Los Angeles, California. Los Angeles (telephone), June 29, 1982.

Deligdisch, Jekutiel, author of book on German-Israeli relations. Stuttgart, June 3, 1975.

Deutschkron, Inge, former *Maariv* correspondent in Bonn. Tel Aviv, March 25, 1975.

Eytan, Walter, director-general of Israeli Ministry for Foreign Affairs at time of Wassenaar reparations negotiations. Jerusalem, April 9, 1975.

Feldman, Nira, academic. Tel Aviv, April 6, 1975.

Friedländer, Saul, academic. Jerusalem, March 31, 1975.

Friedman, Tuwiah, head of Institute of Documentation in Israel. Boston, April 18, 1982.

Gad, Israel, Israeli Labour Party international secretary. Tel Aviv, April 17, 1975.

Galinski, Heinz, head of Jewish Community in Berlin. Berlin, April 29, 1975.

Ginor, Fanny, assistant to David Horowitz at time of Wassenaar reparations negotiations. Tel Aviv, April 20, 1975.

Gluecksmann, Hanna, member of Israeli Independent Liberal Party. Tel Aviv, April 17, 1975.

Golan, Yona, secretary for International Relations, Mapam. Tel Aviv, April 15, 1975.

Goldmann, Nahum, representative of world Jewry to the Wassenaar reparations. Paris, June 9, 1975.

Harel, Isser, head of Israeli Secret Service at time of the German scientists in Egypt. Tel Aviv, April 23, 1975.

Hausner, Gideon, chief prosecutor at Eichmann trial. Jerusalem, April 21, 1975.
Horowitz, David, former director-general, Israeli Ministry of Finance. Jerusalem, March 30, 1975.
Ilsar, Yehiel, former head of German desk, Israeli Ministry for Foreign Affairs. Jerusalem, April 13, 1975.
Katzenstein, E., representative of the Conference on Material Claims against Germany. Bonn, February 25, 1975.
Levinsky, Akiva, leading figure in Bank Hapoalim and the Histadrut. Tel Aviv, April 20, 1975.
Melchior, David, Israeli Labour Party spokesman on international relations. Jerusalem, April 9, 1975.
Meroz, Yochanan, ambassador to the Federal Republic of Germany, 1974–81. Bonn, June 13 and September 9, 1975.
Mushkat, Marion, academic. Tel Aviv, April 6, 1975.
Naor, Uri, former information officer, Israel Mission in Cologne. Jerusalem, April 16, 1975.
Rothschild, Eli, staff member, Irgun Oleh Merkas Europa. April 17, 1975.
Savir, Leo, deputy head, Israel Mission in Cologne, 1960–5. Jerusalem, April 8, 1975.
Scheck, Ze'ev, political secretary to Foreign Minister Sharett, 1953–6. Jerusalem, April 7, 1975.
Schweitzer, Avraham, journalist. Tel Aviv, April 20, 1975.
Sharef, Ze'ev, secretary to the government, 1951. Jerusalem, March 23, 1975.
Shinnar, Felix, joint head of Israeli delegation to Wassenaar reparations negotiations; head of Israel Mission in Cologne. Tel Ganim, March 24 and April 15, 1975.
Tavor, Moshe, former press officer, Israel Mission in Cologne. Jerusalem, April 8, 1975.
Wallach, Yehuda, member of Institute for German History, Tel Aviv University. Tel Aviv, March 24, 1975.
Weismann, Ernest, Conference on Material Claims against Germany, New York. New York (telephone), December 18, 1980.
Yahil, Leni, wife of Chaim Yahil, deputy chief of Israel Mission in Cologne. Jerusalem, April 22, 1975.

CONFIDENTIAL INTERVIEWS: ISRAELI REPRESENTATIVES

Israeli Embassy, Bonn, July 25 and 29, 1975; September 6, 1979.
Ministry for Foreign Affairs, Jerusalem, April 7, 8, 14 and 21, 1975.
Ministry for Foreign Affairs, Economics Division, Jerusalem, April 8, 1975.

List of Correspondence

GERMAN REPRESENTATIVES

Dingels, Hans-Eberhard, International Division, SPD, July 8, 1980.
Emnid, public opinion research organization, November 1980.
Hess, Moshe, August 18, 1975.
Hopf, Volkmar, former German Ministry of Defence official involved in arms deal with Israel, June 30, 1975.
Institut für Demoskopie, public opinion research organization, June 1980.
Küstermeier, Rudolf, November 13, 1975.
Matthiesen, Heinz, International Division, DGB, July 2, 1980.
Pauls, Rolf, ambassador to Israel, 1965–8, February 23, 1976.
Raichle, Gerhart, International Division, FDP, August 19, 1980.
Wegener, Henning, International Division, CDU, June 4, 1980.

CONFIDENTIAL CORRESPONDENCE, GERMAN REPRESENTATIVES

Foreign Office, Cultural Division, September 3, 1975.
Franco-German Youth Office, May 12, 1980.
German Embassy, Tel Aviv, June 5, 1980.
German Consulate-General, Boston, July 29, 1981.
Ministry of Defence, September 10, 1975; May 18, 1976; July 3, 1980.
Ministry for Economic Co-operation, May 6, 1976.
Ministry for Economics, June 9, 1976; April 25 and July 22, 1980.
Ministry for Finance, August 7, 1980.
Ministry for Research and Technology, October 25, 1979; April 11, 1980.
Ministry for Youth, Family and Health, May 12, 1980.
Ministry of Transport, May 17, 1976.
Press and Information Office of the Federal Government, June 18, 1980.
Protocol Office, Bundestag, June 11, 1980.
Statistical Office, September 4, 1975; May 12 and June 10, 1976.

ISRAELI AND JEWISH REPRESENTATIVES

Alon, Abraham, International Development, Histadrut, July 3, 1980.
Ben-Natan, Asher, May 25, 1980.
Bloch, Jochanan, founder of German-Israeli Study Groups, August 13, 1975.
Chaikin, Karen, executive director, American Histadrut Cultural Exchange Institute, June 20, 1980.
Frankfurter, David, International Department, Histadrut, September 28, 1975.
Gluecksmann, Hanna, honorary secretary-general Israeli-German Society, June 30, 1980.

Hill, Harold, executive vice-president, American Committee of the Weizmann Institute of Science, June 4, 1980.
Melchior, David, August 29, 1975.
Meron, Moshe, Deputy Speaker of Knesset, May 4, 1980.
Noah, Sammy, office of the deputy governor, Bank of Israel, May 16, 1980.
Public Opinion Research of Israel, June 28, 1980.
Skuler, Anat, director, Foreign Affairs Department, Likud, June 28, 1980.

CONFIDENTIAL CORRESPONDENCE, ISRAELI REPRESENTATIVES

Israeli Embassy, Bonn, May 8 and June 24, 1980.
Israeli Embassy, Washington, DC, June 24, 1980.
Ministry of Defence, August 10 and September 11 and 19, 1975; May 24, 1976; June 24, 1980.
Ministry of Finance, April 27, and June 17, 1980.
Ministry for Foreign Affairs, July 13, 1980.

Bibliography

Abdel Hadi, H., El-Labadi, M., Paech, N., Sommer, B. A., and Weingartz, H. (1973), *BRD, Israel und die Palästinenser. Eine Fallstudie zur Ausländerpolitik* (Cologne: Paul-Rugenstein Verlag).
Abediseid, Mohammad (1976), *Die deutsch-arabischen Beziehungen − Probleme und Krisen* (Zeitpolitische Schriftenreihe 15) (Stuttgart: Seewald).
Adenauer, Konrad (1966), 'Bilanz einer Reise: Deutschlands Verhältnis zu Israel', *Die Politische Meinung*, vol. 11, no. 115, pp. 15–19.
Adenauer, Konrad (1967), *Erinnerungen 1945–1953* (Frankfurt-am-Main: Fischer Bücherei).
Adenauer, Konrad (1968), *Erinnerungen 1953–1955* (Frankfurt-am-Main: Fischer Bücherei).
Adenauer, Konrad (1969), *Erinnerungen 1955–1959* (Frankfurt-am-Main: Fischer Bücherei).
Adenauer, Konrad (1970), *Erinnerungen 1959–1963. Fragmente* (Frankfurt-am-Main: Fischer Bücherei).
Adler, H. G. (1969), *The Jews in Germany. From the Enlightenment to National Socialism* (Notre Dame, Ind.: University of Notre Dame Press).
Adorno, Theodor W. (1970), *Erziehung zur Mündigkeit. Vorträge und Gespräche mit Hellmut Becker 1959–1969* (Frankfurt-am-Main: Suhrkamp Verlag).
Adorno, Theodor W. (1977a), 'Was bedeutet Aufarbeitung der Vergangenheit', in *Gesammelte Schriften Band 10.2* (Frankfurt-am-Main: Suhrkamp Verlag), pp. 555–72.
Adorno, Theodor W. (1977b), 'Einleitung zum Vortrag "Was bedeutet: Aufarbeitung der Vergangenheit"', in *Gesammelte Schriften Band 10.2* (Frankfurt-am-Main: Suhrkamp Verlag), pp. 816–17.
Adorno, Theodor W. (1977c), *Gesammelte Schriften Band 10.2. Kulturkritik und Gesellschaft II. Eingriffe. Stichworte. Anhang* (Frankfurt-am-Main: Suhrkamp Verlag).
Aeikens, H. O., and Guth, E. (1980), 'Implications of the second enlargement for the Mediterranean and "ACP" policies of the European Community', paper given at Annual Conference of Association for Economic and Social Science of Agriculture, Hanover, October 1980; reprinted by Commission of the European Communities, *Europe Information: Development*, X/235/80-EN.
Aktion 'Friede mit Israel' (1951), *Wir bitten Israel um Frieden!* (Hamburg: Aktion 'Friede mit Israel').
Aktion Sühnezeichen (1975), *Aktion, Berichte, Meinungen, Ausblicke* (Berlin: Aktion Sühnezeichen Friedensdienste).
Albrecht, Ulrich (1972), *Politik und Waffengeschäfte. Rüstungsexport in der BRD* (Munich: Carl Hanser Verlag).
Albrecht, Ulrich, and Sommer, Birgit A. (1972), *Die deutsche Waffen für die dritte Welt. Militärhilfe und Entwicklungspolitik* (Rheinbek bei Hamburg: Rowohlt Verlag).
Alkazaz, Aziz (1980), 'Die deutsch-arabischen Wirtschaftsbeziehungen.

Bisherige Entwicklung und Zukunftsperspektiven', *Orient,* vol. 21, no. 1, pp. 58–76.

Allen, D. J. (1978a), 'Foreign policy at the European level: beyond the nation state?', in W. Paterson and W. Wallace (eds), *Foreign Policy Making in Western Europe. A Comparative Approach* (New York: Praeger), pp. 135–54.

Allen, D. J. (1978b), 'The Euro-Arab Dialogue', *Journal of Common Market Studies,* vol. 16, no. 4, pp. 323–42.

Angress, Werner T. (1971), 'Juden im politischen Leben der Revolutionszeit', in Werner E. Mosse and Arnold Paucker (eds), *Deutsches Judentum in Krieg und Revolution 1916–1923,* (Tübingen: J. C. B. Mohr), pp. 137–315.

Arendt, Hannah (1966), *The Origins of Totalitarianism* (New York: Harcourt Brace Jovanovitch).

Artner, Stephen J. (1980), 'Europe's last chance in the Middle East', *International Affairs,* vol. 56, no. 3, pp. 420–42.

Asad, Abdul-Rahman (1966), *United States and West German Aid to Israel* (Beirut: Palestine Liberation Organization Research Centre).

Association of National Research Centres of the Federal Republic of Germany (1979), *Scientific and Technological Cooperation with Developing Nations* (Bonn: Association of National Research Centres of the Federal Republic of Germany).

Auerbach, Yehudith (1980), 'Foreign policy decisions and changing attitudes: Israel–Germany, 1950–1965', dissertation, Hebrew University, Jerusalem.

Auswärtiges Amt (1970), *Guidelines for a Foreign Cultural Policy* (Bonn: Auswärtiges Amt).

Auswärtiges Amt (1972), *Die Auswärtige Politik der Bundesrepublik Deutschland* (Cologne: Verlag Wissenschaft und Politik).

Auswärtiges Amt (1978), *Zweijahresbericht 1976/1977* (Bonn: Auswärtiges Amt. Abteilung für auswärtige Kulturpolitik).

Axline, W. Andrew (1974), 'Integration and inequality: notes on the study of integrative hegemony', in W. Andrew Axline, *et al.* (eds), *Continental Community? Independence and Integration in North America* (Toronto: McClelland & Stewart), pp. 67–91.

Axline, W. Andrew, Hyndman, James E., Lyon, Peyton V., and Molot, Maureen A. (eds) (1974), *Continental Community? Independence and Integration in North America* (Toronto: McClelland & Stewart).

Baade, Fritz (1965), 'Neugestaltung unserer Politik in Nah- und Mittelost', *Aussenpolitik,* vol. 16, no. 4, pp. 243–51.

Bacharach, Walter Zwi (1980), 'Jews in confrontation with racist antisemitism, 1879–1933', *Leo Baeck Institute Year Book,* Vol. XXV, pp. 197–219.

Balabkins, Nicholas (1967), 'West Germany and the Jews. Bonn's "moral comeback"', *Orbis,* vol. XI, no. 3, pp. 897–902.

Balabkins, Nicholas (1971), *West German Reparations to Israel* (New Brunswick, NJ: Rutgers University Press).

Bank of Israel (1974), *Annual Report 1973* (Jerusalem: Bank of Israel).

Bank of Israel (1976), *Annual Report 1975* (Jerusalem: Bank of Israel).

Bank of Israel (1979), *Annual Report 1978* (Jerusalem: Bank of Israel).

Bank Leumi Le-Israel (1962), 'Reparations in retrospect', *Review of Economic Conditions in Israel,* no. 36–7 (May), pp. 8–10.

Barbu, Z. (1966), 'Die sozialpsychologische Struktur des nationalsozialistischen Antisemitismus', in Werner E. Mosse and Arnold Paucker (eds), *Ent-*

scheidungsjahr 1932. Zur Judenfrage in der Endphase der Weimarer Republik (Tübingen: J. C. B. Mohr), pp. 157–81.

Baring, Arnulf (1969), *Aussenpolitik in Adenauers Kanzlerdemokratie. Bonns Beitrag zur Europäischen Verteidigungsgemeinschaft* (Munich: Oldenbourg Verlag).

Barou, Noah (1952), 'Origin of the German agreement', *Congress Weekly*, vol. 19, no. 24 (October 13), pp. 6–8.

Bartur, Moshe (1961), 'Israel und die europäische Integration', *Europäische Wirtschaft*, no. 18, pp. 449–50.

Bator, Angelika (1970), 'Bilanz des westdeutsch-israelischen Bündnisses 1969/70', *Dokumentation der Zeit*, no. 16, pp. 18–22.

Beer, Francis A. (ed.) (1970), *Alliances: Latent War Communities in the Contemporary World* (New York: Holt, Rinehart & Winston).

Bell, Coral (1972), 'The "special relationship"' in Michael Leifer (ed.), *Constraints and Adjustments in British Foreign Policy* (London: Allen & Unwin), pp. 103–19.

Ben-Gurion, David (1959), *Rede des Ministerpräsidenten David Ben-Gurion in der Knesset am 1. Juli 1959* (Cologne: Informationsabteilung der Israel Mission, July).

Ben-Gurion, David (1971), *Israel. A Personal History* (New York: Funk & Wagnalls/Sabra Books).

Ben-Gurion, David (1973), *Israel. Die Geschichte eines Staates* (Frankfurt-am-Main: S. Fischer Verlag).

Ben-Natan, Asher (1966), 'Die Chancen der Normalisierung – Interview', *Diskussion*, vol. 7, no. 18, pp. 3–4.

Ben-Natan, Asher (1974), *Dialogue avec des Allemands* (Paris: Librarie Plon).

Bennathan, Esra (1966), 'Die demographische und wirtschaftliche Struktur der Juden', in Werner E. Mosse and Arnold Paucker (eds), *Entscheidungsjahr 1932. Zur Judenfrage in der Endphase der Weimarer Republik* (Tübingen: J. C. B. Mohr), pp. 87–131.

Bentwich, Norman (1955), *URO. The United Restitution Office* (London: United Restitution Office).

Bentwich, Norman (1965), 'Nazi spoliation and German restitution – the work of the United Restitution Office', *Leo Baeck Institute Year Book*, Vol. X, pp. 204–24.

Bentwich, Norman (1969), *The United Restitution Organization, 1948–1968. The Work of Restitution and Compensation of Victims of Nazi Oppression* (London: Vallentine, Mitchell).

Ben-Vered, Amos (1965), 'Israel und Deutschland. Die Bedeutung der Aufnahme diplomatischer Beziehungen für den jüdischen Staat', *Europa-Archiv*, vol. 20, no. 13, pp. 481–9.

Besson, Waldemar (1970), *Die Aussenpolitik der Bundesrepublik. Erfahrungen und Massstäbe* (Munich: Piper Verlag).

Bier, Jean-Paul (1980), 'The Holocaust and West Germany: strategies of oblivion 1947–1979', *New German Critique*, no. 19 (Winter), pp. 9–29.

Bierhoff, Hartwig (1973a), 'Ueberlegungen zur Praxis des deutsch-israelischen Jugendaustausches', *DIG*, vol. 3, no. 3, p. 2.

Bierhoff, Hartwig (1973b), 'Ueberlegungen zur Praxis des deutsch-israelischen Jugendaustausches', *DIG*, vol. 3, no. 4, pp. 2, 11–12.

Bierhoff, Hartwig (1974), 'Ueberlegungen zur Praxis des deutsch-israelischen Jugendaustausches', *DIG*, vol. 4, no. 1, pp. 1–2.

Bierhoff, Hartwig (1979), 'Der deutsch-israelische Jugendaustausch. Erfahrungen im internationalen Jugendaustausch', *Deutsche Jugend*, no. 8, pp. 362–70.

Birrenbach, Kurt (1972), 'Die Aufnahme der diplomatischen Beziehungen zwischen der Bundesrepublik Deutschland und Israel', in Gerhard Schröder, *et al.* (eds), *Ludwig Erhard. Beiträge zu einer politischen Biographie. Festschrift zum fünfundsiebzigsten Geburtstag* (Frankfurt-am-Main: Ullstein Verlag), pp. 363-82.

Bissell, Richard E. (1980), 'The West in concert: a very complex score', *Orbis*, vol. 23, no. 4, pp. 825–43.

Black, Naomi (1974), 'Absorptive systems are impossible: the Canadian-American relationship as a disparate dyad', in W. Andrew Axline, *et al.* (eds), *Continental Community? Independence and Integration in North America* (Toronto: McClelland & Stewart), pp. 92–108.

Blitzer, Wolf (1979), 'Comrades and arms', *Jerusalem Post Magazine* (August 3), p. 9.

Bockmeyer, Martin (1974), 'Die Wirtschaftsbeziehungen zwischen der Bundesrepublik Deutschland und der arabischen Welt', *Zeitschrift für Kulturaustausch*, vol. 24, no. 2, pp. 35–40.

Böhm, Anton (1973), 'Neutralität-doppelbödig. Ueber "Beziehungen besonderer Art"', *Die Politische Meinung*, vol. 18, no. 151, pp. 6–8.

Böhm, Franz (1965), 'Die deutsch-israelischen Beziehungen', *Frankfurter Hefte*, vol. 20, no. 9, pp. 601–25.

Bolkosky, Sidney M. (1975), *The Distorted Image. German-Jewish Perceptions of Germans and Germany, 1918–1935* (New York: Elsevier).

Bondy, François, and Abelein, Manfred (1973), *Deutschland und Frankreich. Geschichte einer wechselvollen Beziehung* (Düsseldorf: Econ Verlag).

Bossmann, Dieter (ed.) (1977), *'Was ich über Adolf Hitler gehört habe...' Folgen eines Tabus. Auszüge aus Schüler Aufsätzen von heute* (Frankfurt-am-Main: Fischer Taschenbuch Verlag).

Bracher, Karl Dietrich (1970), *The German Dictatorship. The Origins, Structure, and Effects of National Socialism* (New York: Praeger).

Braun, Ursula (1977), 'Der Europäisch-Arabische Dialog – Entwicklung und Zwischenbilanz', *Orient*, vol. 18, no. 1, pp. 30–56.

Braunthal, Gerard (1965), *The Federation of German Industry in Politics* (Ithaca, NY: Cornell University Press).

Brecher, Michael (1972), *The Foreign Policy System of Israel. Setting, Images, Process* (London: Oxford University Press).

Brecher, Michael (1973), 'Images, process and feedback in foreign policy: Israel's decisions on German reparations', *American Political Science Review*, vol. 67, no. 1, pp. 73–102.

Brecher, Michael (1975), *Decisions in Israel's Foreign Policy* (New Haven, Conn.: Yale University Press).

Bretholz, Wolfgang (1963), 'Klarheit zwischen Deutschland und Israel', *Die Politische Meinung*, vol. 8, no. 86, pp. 33–44.

Broder, Henryk M., and Lang, Michel R. (1979a), *Fremd im eigenen Land. Juden in der Bundesrepublik* (Frankfurt-am-Main: Fischer Taschenbuch Verlag).

Broder, Henryk M. (ed.) (1979b), *Deutschland erwacht. Die neuen Nazis. Aktionen und Provokationen* (Bornheim-Merten: Lamuv Verlag).
Bronsen, David (ed.) (1979), *Jews and Germans from 1860 to 1933: The Problematic Symbiosis* (Heidelberg: Carl Winter Universitätsverlag).
Büren, Rainer (1974), 'Bemerkungen zum Stellenwert der arabischen Staaten in der aussenpolitischen Konzeption der Bundesrepublik Deutschland', *Zeitschrift für Kulturaustausch,* vol. 24, no. 2, pp. 41–8.
Bundesministerium der Finanzen (1975), *Bundesrepublik Deutschland. Wiedergutmachung früheren Unrechts. Tatsachen und Zahlen* (Bonn: Bundesministerium der Finanzen).
Bundesministerium der Finanzen (1979a), *Uebersicht über die Wiedergutmachungsregelungen* (Bonn: Bundesministerium der Finanzen).
Bundesministerium der Finanzen (1979b), *Uebersicht über die wahrscheinlich nach Israel geflossenen Wiedergutmachungsleistungen* (Bonn: Bundesministerium der Finanzen).
Bundesministerium der Finanzen (1979c), *Leistungen der öffentlichen Hand auf dem Gebiet der Wiedergutmachung* (Bonn: Bundesministerium der Finanzen).
Bundesministerium für Forschung und Technologie (1979), *Bundesbericht Forschung VI. Reihe: Berichte und Dokumentationen, Band 4* (Bonn: Bundesministerium für Forschung und Technologie).
Bundesministerium für Jugend, Familie und Gesundheit (1975), *Informationen des Bundesministeriums für Jugend, Familie und Gesundheit* (Bonn: Pressereferat des Bundesministeriums für Jugend, Familie und Gesundheit, July 11).
Bundesministerium der Justiz (1980), *Bundesanzeiger,* vol. 32, no. 192 (October 14).
Bundesministerium für Wirtschaft (1973), *Allgemeine Bedingungen für die Uebernahme von Burgschaften* (Bonn: Bundesministerium für Wirtschaft, December).
Bundesministerium für Wirtschaft (1976), *Merkblatt über die Gewährung von Ausfuhrgarantien und Ausfuhrburgschaften* (Bonn: Bundesministerium für Wirtschaft, September 20).
Bundesministerium für Wirtschaft (1977a), *Merkblatt. Ausfuhrgarantien und Ausfuhrburgschaften der Bundesrepublik Deutschland* (Bonn: Bundesministerium für Wirtschaft, March 3).
Bundesministerium für Wirtschaft (1977b), *Gesamtübersicht des Warenverkehrs der Bundesrepublik Deutschland mit den Ländern der arabischen Welt 1972–1976* (Bonn: Bundesministerium für Wirtschaft).
Bundesministerium für Wirtschaft (1979a), *Tagesnachrichten Nr 7710* (Bonn: Bundesministerium für Wirtschaft).
Bundesministerium für Wirtschaft (1979b), *Runderlass Aussenwirtschaft Nr 7* (Bonn: Bundesministerium für Wirtschaft).
Bundesministerium für Wirtschaft (1979c), *Tagesnachrichten Nr 7792* (Bonn: Bundesministerium für Wirtschaft).
Bundesministerium für Wirtschaft (1979d), *Daten zur Entwicklung der Energiewirtschaft in der Bundesrepublik Deutschland im Jahre 1978* (Bonn: Bundesministerium für Wirtschaft).
Bundesministerium für Wirtschaft (1979e), *Runderlass Aussenwirtschaft Nr 6* (Bonn: Bundesministerium für Wirtschaft).

Bundesministerium für Wirtschaft (1980), *Tagesnachrichten Nr 7882* (Bonn: Bundesministerium für Wirtschaft).
Bundesministerium für wirtschaftliche Zusammenarbeit (1974), *Grundsätze für technische Hilfe vom 2. 1. 1974* (Bonn: Bundesministerium für wirtschaftliche Zusammenarbeit).
Bundesministerium für wirtschaftliche Zusammenarbeit (1975a), *Die entwicklungspolitische Konzeption der Bundesrepublik Deutschland vom 6. 11. 1975* (Bonn: Bundesministerium für wirtschaftliche Zusammenarbeit).
Bundesministerium für wirtschaftliche Zusammenarbeit (1975b), *Richtlinien für die deutsche bilaterale Kapitalhilfe vom 9. Juni 1975* (Bonn: Bundesministerium für wirtschaftliche Zusammenarbeit).
Bundesministerium für wirtschaftliche Zusammenarbeit (1977), *Dritter Bericht zur Entwicklungspolitik der Bundesregierung* (Bonn: Bundesministerium für wirtschaftliche Zusammenarbeit).
Bundesministerium für wirtschaftliche Zusammenarbeit (1978a), *Politik der Partner. Aufgaben, Bilanz und Chancen der deutschen Entwicklungspolitik* (Bonn: Bundesministerium für wirtschaftliche Zusammenarbeit).
Bundesministerium für wirtschaftliche Zusammenarbeit (1978b), *Zusammenarbeit mit Schwellenländern* (Bonn: Bundesministerium für wirtschaftliche Zusammenarbeit).
Bundesministerium für wirtschaftliche Zusammenarbeit (1979a), *Vierter Bericht zur Entwicklungspolitik der Bundesregierung* (Bonn: Bundesministerium für wirtschaftliche Zusammenarbeit).
Bundesministerium für wirtschaftliche Zusammenarbeit (1979b), *The Federal Republic of Germany and the Third World. Cooperation in Development*, trans. Press and Information Office of the Federal Government (Bonn: Bundesministerium für wirtschaftliche Zusammenarbeit).
Bundesministerium für wirtschaftliche Zusammenarbeit (1979c), *Journalisten-Handbuch. Entwicklungspolitik 1979* (Bonn: Bundesministerium für wirtschaftliche Zusammenarbeit).
Cahnmann, Werner J. (1969), 'The three regions of German-Jewish history', in Herbert A. Strauss and Hanns G. Reissner (eds), *Jubilee Volume Dedicated to Curt C. Silberman* (New York: American Federation of Jews from Central Europe), pp. 1–14.
Churchill, Randolph S. (ed.) (1948), *The Sinews of Peace, Post-War Speeches by Winston S. Churchill* (London: Cassell).
Coburger, D. (1964), 'Die Beziehungen zwischen der westdeutschen Bundesrepublik und Israel von 1949 bis 1961 unter besonderer Berücksichtigung des sogenannten Wiedergutmachungsabkommen', dissertation, Karl Marx University, Leipzig.
Cohen, Gerson D. (1975), 'German Jewry as mirror of modernity. Introduction to the twentieth volume', *Leo Baeck Institute Year Book*, Vol. XX, pp. ix–xxxi.
Cohen, Yaacov (1979), *Israel and the EEC. Israel's Integration in the Economic Structure of the European Community* (Jerusalem: Ministry of Industry, Trade and Tourism).
Cohen, Yaacov (1980), 'Israel and the EEC, 1958–1978: economic and political relations', in Herbert Giersch (ed.), *The Economic Integration of Israel in the EEC* (Tübingen: J. C. B. Mohr), pp. 13–37.
Commission of the European Communities (1977), 'Israel and the EEC', *Information: Cooperation and Development*, 145/77E.

Commission of the European Communities (1979a), *Recommendation for a Council Decision Supplementing the Directives for Negotiations with Israel* (Brussels: Commission of the European Communities, May 31).

Commission of the European Communities (1979b), *Recommendation for a Council Regulation concerning Conclusion of a Second Additional Protocol to the Agreement between the European Economic Community and the State of Israel* (Strasbourg: Commission of the European Communities, December 11).

Commission of the European Communities (1980), *Bulletin of the European Communities,* vol. 13, no. 10, pp. 1–106.

Commission of the European Communities (1981), *Fourteenth General Report on the Activities of the European Communities* (Brussels: Commission of the European Communities).

Commission of the European Communities (1982a), *Fifteenth General Report on the Activities of the European Communities in 1981* (Brussels: Commission of the European Communities).

Commission of the European Communities (1982b), *Bulletin of the European Communities*, vol. 15, no. 6, pp. 1–109.

Commission of the European Communities (1982c), *Bulletin of the European Communities*, vol. 15, no. 9, pp. 1–80.

Congressional Quarterly (1979), *The Middle East. U.S. Policy, Israel, Oil and the Arabs* (Washington, DC: Congressional Quarterly).

Congressional Quarterly (1980), *U.S. Defense Policy. Weapons, Strategy and Commitments* (Washington, DC: Congressional Quarterly).

Crosbie, Sylvia K. (1974), *A Tacit Alliance: France and Israel from Suez to the Six-Day War* (Princeton, NJ: Princeton University Press).

Dahl, Robert (ed.) (1966), *Political Oppositions in Western Democracies* (New Haven, Conn.: Yale University Press).

Dahrendorf, Ralf (1971), 'Possibilities and limits of a European Communities foreign policy', *World Today,* vol. 27, no. 4, pp. 148–61.

Dahrendorf, Ralf (1973), 'The foreign policy of the EEC', *World Today,* vol. 29, no. 2, pp. 47–57.

van Dam, Hendrik G. (1963a), 'Reparation in the Federal Republic', in Walter Stahl (ed.), *The Politics of Postwar Germany* (New York: Praeger).

van Dam, Hendrik G. (1963b), 'Israel und die Bundesrepublik', *Tribüne*, vol. 2, no. 5, pp. 470–2.

Dawidowicz, Lucy S. (1975), *The War against the Jews 1933–1945* (New York: Holt, Rinehart & Winston).

Dawson, Raymond, and Rosecrance, Richard N. (1966), 'Theory and reality in the Anglo-American alliance', *World Politics,* vol. 19, no. 1, pp. 21–51.

Deligdisch, Jekutiel (1974), *Die Einstellung der Bundesrepublik Deutschland zum Staate Israel. Eine Zusammenfassung der Entwicklung seit 1949* (Bonn-Bad Godesberg: Verlag Neue Gesellschaft).

Department of State Bulletin (1975), 'U.S.-Iran relations: cooperation and shared interests: address by Alfred L. Atherton, Jr', *Department of State Bulletin,* vol. LXXIII, no. 1903 (December 15), pp. 862–4.

Destler, I. M., Sato, Hideo, Clapp, Priscilla, and Fukui, Haruhiro (1976), *Managing an Alliance. The Politics of United States-Japanese Relations* (Washington, DC: The Brookings Institution).

Deutsch, Karl W. et al. (1957), *Political Community and the North Atlantic Area. International Organization in the Light of Historical Experience* (Princeton, NJ: Princeton University Press).

Deutsch-Französisches Jugendwerk (1980), *Das Deutsch-Französische Jugendwerk 1980* (Bad Honnef: Deutsch-Französisches Jugendwerk).
Deutsche Welle (Dokumentation-Archivdienst) (1971), *Die deutsch-israelischen Beziehungen* (Cologne: Abteilung Dokumentation, Deutsche Welle, June 30).
Deutsche Welle (Dokumentation-Archivdienst) (1972), *Die deutsch-ägyptischen Beziehungen* (Cologne: Abteilung Dokumentation, Deutsche Welle, March 29).
Deutscher Bundestag und Bundesrat (1949), *Verhandlungen des Deutschen Bundestages. Stenographische Berichte. 1. Wahlperiode,* Vol. 1 (September 7–December 16).
Deutscher Bundestag und Bundesrat (1953), *Verhandlungen des Deutschen Bundestages. Stenographische Berichte. 1. Wahlperiode,* Vol. 15 (February 25–April 29).
Deutscher Bundestag und Bundesrat (1965), *Verhandlungen des Deutschen Bundestages. Stenographische Berichte. 4. Wahlperiode,* Vol. 57 (January 20–March 12).
Deutscher Bundestag und Bundesrat (1967), *Verhandlungen des Deutschen Bundestages. Stenographische Berichte. 5. Wahlperiode,* Vol. 63 (December 8, 1966–April 13, 1967).
Deutscher Bundestag und Bundesrat (1969), *Verhandlungen des Deutschen Bundestages. Stenographische Berichte. 5. Wahlperiode,* Vol. 69 (February 5–April 25).
Deutscher Bundestag und Bundesrat (1970a), *Verhandlungen des Deutschen Bundestages. Stenographische Berichte. 6. Wahlperiode,* Vol. 71 (October 20, 1969–February 18, 1970).
Deutscher Bundestag und Bundesrat (1970b), *Verhandlungen des Deutschen Bundestages. Stenographische Berichte. 6. Wahlperiode,* Vol. 73 (June 2–October 9).
Deutscher Bundestag und Bundesrat (1971a), *Verhandlungen des Deutschen Bundestages. Stenographische Berichte. 6. Wahlperiode,* Vol. 74 (October 14, 1970–January 29, 1971).
Deutscher Bundestag und Bundesrat (1971b), *Verhandlungen des Deutschen Bundestages. Stenographische Berichte. 6. Wahlperiode,* Vol. 75 (February 2–March 26).
Deutscher Bundestag und Bundesrat (1971c), *Verhandlungen des Deutschen Bundestages. Stenographische Berichte. 6. Wahlperiode,* Vol. 76 (March 31–July 19).
Deutscher Bundestag und Bundesrat (1973), *Verhandlungen des Deutschen Bundestages. Stenographische Berichte. 7. Wahlperiode,* Vol. 81 (December 13, 1972–February 16, 1973).
Deutscher Bundestag und Bundesrat (1974), *Verhandlungen des Deutschen Bundestages. Stenographische Berichte. 7. Wahlperiode,* Vol. 87 (March 13–April 25).
Deutscher Bundestag und Bundesrat (1980), *Verhandlungen des Deutschen Bundestages. Drucksachen. 8. Wahlperiode,* Vol. 258 *(Drucksachen 8/3461–8/3580)* (December 4, 1979–January 21, 1980).
Deutscher Bundestag und Bundesrat (1983), *Verhandlungen des Deutschen Bundestages. Stenographische Berichte. 9. Wahlperiode*, Vol. 123 (November 24, 1982–January 20, 1983).
Deutschkron, Inge (1970a), *Bonn and Jerusalem. The Strange Coalition* (Philadelphia, Pa: Chilton Book Co.).

Deutschkron, Inge (1970b), *Israel und die Deutschen. Zwischen Ressentiment und Ratio* (Cologne: Verlag Wissenschaft und Politik).
Dickey, John Sloan (1975), *Canada and the American Presence. The United States Interest in an Independent Canada* (New York: New York University Press).
DIG (1971a), vol. 1, no. 3.
DIG (1971b), vol. 1, no. 4.
DIG (1975), vol. 5, no. 4.
Diner, Dany (1980), 'Fragments of an uncompleted journey: on Jewish socialization and political identity in West Germany', *New German Critique*, no. 20 (Spring–Summer), pp. 57–70.
Dippmann, Klaus (1970), 'Die Aussenpolitik des Staates Israel 1948–1970', dissertation, Universität Braunschweig, Berlin.
Diskussion (1965), 'Die Diskussion über die Verlängerung der Verjährungsfrist für NS-Morde', *Diskussion*, vol. 6, no. 16 (April), pp. 25–9.
Eban, Abba (1962), *Erklärung des israelischen Kultusminister Abba Eban vor dem Knesset am 9. Januar 1962* (Cologne: Informationsabteilung der Israel Mission, January).
Eban, Abba (1977), *An Autobiography* (New York: Random House).
Ebeling, Joachim (1966), *Die Durchführung des Abkommens vom 10. September 1952 zwischen der Bundesrepublik Deutschland und dem Staate Israel in den Jahren 1952–1962* (Frankfurt-am-Main: Bundesamt für gewirbliche Wirtschaft).
von Eckardt, Felix (1967), *Ein unordentliches Leben. Lebenserinnerungen* (Düsseldorf: Econ Verlag).
Eckstein, Harry (1975), 'Case study and theory in political science', in Fred I. Greenstein and Nelson W. Polsby (eds), *The Handbook of Political Science* (Reading, Mass.: Addison-Wesley), Vol. 7, pp. 79–137.
The Economist (1979), 'West Germany: who wants to sell arms?', *The Economist*, vol. 270, no. 7063 (January 13), pp. 42–4.
The Economist (1982), 'German arms sales. Even for the tense', *The Economist*, vol. 283, no. 7236 (May 8), p. 63.
English, H. Edward (1974), 'The political economy of international economic integration: a brief synthesis', in W. Andrew Axline, *et al.* (eds), *Continental Community? Independence and Integration in North America* (Toronto: McClelland & Stewart), pp. 19–41.
Ernst, Tilman (1979), 'Anfragen an die Bundeszentrale für politische Bildung', in Peter Märthesheimer and Ivo Frenzel (eds), *Im Kreuzfeuer. Der Fernsehfilm 'Holocaust'. Eine Nation ist betroffen* (Frankfurt-am-Main: Fischer Taschenbuch Verlag), pp. 297–8.
Eschwege, Helmut (1970), 'Resistance of German Jews against the Nazi regime', *Leo Baeck Institute Year Book*, Vol. XV, pp. 143–80.
Eshkol, Levi (1962), *Erklärung des Finanzministers von Israel zur Eröffnung der Verhandlungen zwischen Israel und der Europäischen Wirtschaftsgemeinschaft, Brüssel 26. November 1962* (Cologne: Informationsabteilung der Israel Mission, November).
Europe (1979), 'EEC–Israel: several questions remain open', Europe (Agence Internationale d'Information pour la Presse), No. 2758 (September 29).
Europe (1980a), 'Middle East: Mr Thorn in Israel – differences persist', Europe (Agence Internationale d'Information pour la Presse), No. 2962 (August 2).
Europe (1980b), 'EEC–Israel: cooperation and prospects for development

described as generally positive – some Israeli demands met', Europe (Agence Internationale d'Information pour la Presse), No. 2994 (October 8).

Europe (1980c), 'EEC–Israel: results and prospects for cooperation looking good – views differ on trade and "enlargement" consultations', Europe (Agence Internationale d'Information pour la Presse), No. 2995 (October 9).

Europe (1981a), 'EEC–Israel: enlargement at centre of talks of Israeli farm minister', Europe (Agence Internationale d'Information pour la Presse), No. 820 (November 10).

Europe (1981b), 'EEC–Israel: new dialogue', Europe (Agence Internationale d'Information pour la Presse), No. 828 (December 8).

European Communities (1975), *Euro-Arab Dialogue. Joint Communiqué Cairo, June 14, 1975* (Brussels: European Communities, June).

European Community Information Service (1980), 'Gaston Thorn: Europe's view of world affairs', *European Community News*, no. 27 (October 6), pp. 2–3.

European Report (1980), 'Euro-Arab Dialogue. Meeting at political level. Luxembourg, 12 and 13 November, 1980. Joint communiqué', *European Report*, no. 728 (November 15), pp. 1–4.

Eyck, Erich (1970a), *A History of the Weimar Republic. Vol. 1, From the Collapse of the Empire to Hindenburg's Election* (New York: Atheneum).

Eyck, Erich (1970b), *A History of the Weimar Republic. Vol. 2, From the Locarno Conference to Hitler's Seizure of Power* (New York: Atheneum).

Federal Ministry for Research and Technology (1979a), *Contribution by Science and Technology in the Federal Republic of Germany to the Solution of Socio-Economic Development Problems* (Bonn: Federal Ministry for Research and Technology).

Federal Ministry for Research and Technology (1979b), *Science and Technology for Development. Contributions by the Federal Republic of Germany* (Eschborn: German Agency for Technical Co-operation/Federal Ministry for Research and Technology).

Federal Republic of Germany Consulate-General, Boston (1981), *Text of Statement by Chancellor Schmidt to the Bundestag on May 7, 1981* (Boston, Mass.: Consulate-General of the Federal Republic of Germany, May).

Federal Republic of Germany Embassy, Washington, DC (1981), *German Press Review*, no. 18 (May 6).

Feldman, Elliot, and Gardner Feldman, Lily (1980), 'The special relationship between Canada and the United States', *Jerusalem Journal of International Relations*, vol. 4, no. 4, pp. 56–85.

Ferencz, Benjamin B. (1979), *Less than Slaves: Jewish Forced Labor and the Quest for Compensation* (Cambridge, Mass.: Harvard University Press).

Fichtner, Otto (1977), 'Vorwort', in *Gemeinsame Bestimmungen für die Durchführung des deutsch-israelischen Jugendaustausches* (Bonn: Internationaler Jugendaustausch- und Besucherdienst der Bundesrepublik Deutschland im Auftrage des Bundesministers für Jugend, Familie und Gesundheit, May).

Forsyth, Frederick (1972), *The Odessa File* (New York: Viking Press).

Fox, Annette Baker (1977), *The Politics of Attraction. Four Middle Powers and the United States* (New York: Columbia University Press).

Fraenkel, Josef (1962), 'Noah Barou, the man from Poltava', in Henrik F. Infield (ed.), *Essays in Jewish Sociology, Labour and Co-operation in Memory of Dr Noah Barou, 1889–1955* (London: Thomas Yoseloff/World Jewish Congress), pp. 3–8.

Freie Demokratische Partei (1980a), *Stichworte zur Aussen-, Deutschland-, Entwicklungs-, Europa-, Ost- und Sicherheitspolitik* (Bonn: FDP-Bundestagsfraktion).

Freie Demokratische Partei – Europa Spezial (1980b), 'Bangemann verteidigt Nahost-Erklärung der EG', No. 475 (June 19).

Freie Demokratische Partei – Fraktion (1978), *Positionspapier – Arabische Länder* (Bonn: FDP-Fraktion im Deutschen Bundestag/Europa – Büro, September 26).

Freie Demokratische Partei – Tagesdienst (1977), 'Bangemann: Kontakte zur arabischen Welt auf allen Ebenen ausbauen', No. 35 (January 24).

Freie Demokratische Partei – Tagesdienst (1979), 'Schäfer zur Lage im Nahen Osten', No. 1001 (November 27).

Freie Demokratische Partei – Tagesdienst (1980a), 'Möllemann fordert neue EG-Initiativen in Nahost und im südlichen Afrika', No. 260 (April 3).

Freie Demokratische Partei – Tagesdienst (1980b), 'Möllemann: Durch Gewaltverzicht Klima des Vertrauens schaffen', No. 266 (April 14).

Freie Demokratische Partei – Tagesdienst (1980c), 'PLO Delegation zu einem Meinungsaustausch empfangen', No. 267 (April 15).

Freie Demokratische Partei – Tagesdienst (1980d), 'Möllemann fordert beherzte europäische Friedensinitiative', No. 340 (May 6).

Freie Demokratische Partei – Tagesdienst (1980e), 'Schäfer: Gemeinsame Initiative der EG in der Nahost-Frage notwendig', No. 430 (June 3).

Freie Demokratische Partei – Tagesdienst (1980f) 'Möllemann: Haltung der USA unverständlich', No. 435 (June 4).

Freie Demokratische Partei – Tagesdienst (1980g), 'Möllemann: Die Friedensbemühungen der EG tatkräftig unterstützen', No. 459 (June 16).

Freie Demokratische Partei – Tagesdienst (1980h), 'Möllemann sieht neue Hindernisse für eine Friedensregelung', No. 599 (July 24).

Friedländer, Saul (1971), 'Die politischen Veränderungen der Kriegszeit und ihre Auswirkungen auf die Judenfrage', in Werner E. Mosse and Arnold Paucker (eds), *Deutsches Judentum in Krieg und Revolution 1916–1923* (Tübingen: J. C. B. Mohr), pp. 27–65.

Friedman, Julian R., Bladen, Christopher, and Rosen, Steven (eds) (1970), *Alliance in International Politics* (Boston, Mass.: Allyn & Bacon).

Fürstenau, J. (1969), *Entnazifizierung. Ein Kapitel deutscher Nachkriegspolitik* (Neuwied: Luchterhand Verlag).

Gatzke, Hans (1980), *Germany and the United States. A 'Special Relationship'?* (Cambridge, Mass.: Harvard University Press).

Gay, Peter (1968), *Weimar Culture. The Outsider as Insider* (New York: Harper & Row).

Gay, Peter (1978), *Freud, Jews and Other Germans. Masters and Victims in Modernist Culture* (New York: Oxford University Press).

Geisel, Eike, and Offenberg, Mario (1977), 'Die gegenwärtige Vergangenheit – Zur Aktualität von Isaac Deutschers Schriften zur jüdischen Frage', postscript to Isaac Deutscher, *Die ungelöste Judenfrage. Zur Dialektik von Antisemitismus und Zionismus* (Berlin: Rotbuch Verlag), pp. 105–42.

George, Alexander L. (1979), 'Case studies and theory development: the method of structured, focused comparison', in Paul Gordon Lauren (ed.), *Diplomacy:*

New Approaches in History, Theory, and Policy (New York: The Free Press), pp. 43–68.

Giersch, Herbert (ed.) (1980), *The Economic Integration of Israel in the EEC* (Tübingen: J. C. B. Mohr).

Ginor, Fanny (1972–3), 'The impact of German reparations and restitution payments on the Israeli economy', *Wiener Library Bulletin,* vol. XXVI, no. 3–4, pp. 38–45.

Ginor, Fanny, and Tishler, J. (1965), *Reparations and their Impact on the Israeli Economy* (Hebrew) (Tel Aviv: Bank of Israel).

von Gizycki, Horst, and Baethge, Martin (eds) (1972), *Jugendreisen nach Israel* (Munich: Juventa Verlag).

Golan, Yitzhak (1976), 'Common Market trade: opportunity and risk', *New Outlook,* vol. 19, no. 7 (170), pp. 27–9, 35.

Goldmann, Nahum (1952), 'Why I favour direct Israel–German negotiations', *Jewish Observer and Middle East Review,* vol. 1, no. 3 (February 22), pp. 9–11.

Goldmann, Nahum (1962), 'A noble son of Jewry', in Henrik F. Infield (ed.), *Essays in Jewish Sociology, Labour and Co-operation in Memory of Dr Noah Barou, 1889–1955* (London: Thomas Yoseloff/World Jewish Congress), pp. 9–13.

Goldmann, Nahum (1969), *The Autobiography of Nahum Goldmann. Sixty Years of Jewish Life* (New York: Holt, Rinehart & Winston).

Goldmann, Nahum (1978), *The Jewish Paradox* (London: Weidenfeld & Nicolson).

Goodman, Hirsh (1980), 'Friends in need', *Jerusalem Post Magazine* (October 10), pp. 4–5.

Grieve, Hermann (1975), 'On Jewish self-identification. Religion and political orientation', *Leo Baeck Institute Year Book,* Vol. XX, pp. 35–46.

Greive, Hermann (1980), 'Zionism and Jewish orthodoxy', *Leo Baeck Institute Year Book,* Vol. XXV, pp. 173–95.

Grewe, Wilhelm (1960), *Deutsche Aussenpolitik der Nachkriegszeit* (Stuttgart: Deutsche Verlagsanstalt).

Gröner, Helmut (1975), 'Die westdeutsche Aussenhandelspolitik', in Hans-Peter Schwarz (ed.), *Handbuch der deutschen Aussenpolitik* (Munich: Piper Verlag), pp. 405–35.

Grosser, Alfred (1975), *Gegen den Strom. Aufklärung als Friedenspolitik* (Munich: Carl Hanser Verlag).

Grossmann, Kurt R. (1954), *Germany's Moral Debt. The German–Israel Agreement* (Washington, DC: Public Affairs Press).

Grossmann, Kurt R. (1958), *Germany and Israel: Six Years Luxemburg Agreement,* Herzl Institute Pamphlet No. 11 (New York: Theodor Herzl Foundation).

Grunfeld, Frederic V. (1979), *Prophets without Honour. A Background to Freud, Kafka, Einstein and their World* (New York: Holt, Rinehart & Winston).

Haftendorn, Helga (1971), *Militärhilfe und Rüstungsexporte der BRD* (Düsseldorf: Bertelsmann Universitätsverlag).

Halevi, Nadav, and Klinov-Malul, Ruth (1968), *The Economic Development of Israel* (New York: Praeger).

Halpern, Ben, and Wurm, Shalom (eds) (1966), *The Responsible Attitude: The Life and Times of Giora Josephtal* (New York: Schocken Books).

Hamburger, Ernest (1968), *Juden im öffentlichen Leben Deutschlands. Regierungsmitglieder, Beamte und Parlamentarier in der monarchischen Zeit 1848–1918* (Tübingen: J. C. B. Mohr).
Hamburger, Ernest (1975), 'Hugo Preuss: scholar and statesman', *Leo Baeck Institute Year Book,* Vol. XX, pp. 179–206.
Hanrieder, Wolfram F. (1967), *West German Foreign Policy 1949–1963: International Pressure and Domestic Response* (Stanford, Calif.: Stanford University Press).
Hanrieder, Wolfram F. (1970), *The Stable Crisis. Two Decades of German Foreign Policy* (New York: Harper & Row).
Hanrieder, Wolfram F. (ed.) (1980), *West German Foreign Policy: 1949–1979* (Boulder, Colo.: Westview Press).
Hanrieder, Wolfram F., and Auton, Graeme P. (1980), *The Foreign Policies of West Germany, France and Britain* (Englewood Cliffs, NJ: Prentice-Hall).
ul Haq, Mahbub (1980), 'Negotiating the future', *Foreign Affairs,* vol. 59, no. 2, pp. 398–417.
Harris, James F. (1975), 'Eduard Lasker: the Jew as national German politician', *Leo Baeck Institute Year Book,* Vol. XX, pp. 151–77.
Harrison, Reginald J. (1974), *Europe in Question. Theories of Regional International Integration* (London: Allen & Unwin).
Hauff, Volker, and Haunschild, Hans-Hilger (eds) (1978), *Forschung in der Bundesrepublik* (Stuttgart: Kohlhammer Verlag, zweite Auflage).
Henig, Stanley (1971), *External Relations of the European Community. Associations and Trade Agreements* (London: Chatham House/PEP).
Henkys, Reinhard (1966), 'Oeffentliche Meinung und NS-Prozesse', *Diskussion,* vol. 7, no. 18 (February), pp. 13–17.
Herf, Jeffrey (1980), 'The *Holocaust* reception in West Germany: right, center and left', *New German Critique,* no. 19 (Winter), pp. 30–52.
Hesse, Kurt (1969), *Das System der Entwicklungshilfen* (Berlin: Duncker und Humblot).
Hesselbach, Walter (1973), 'Die Deutsche Gesellschaft zur Förderung der Wirtschaftsbeziehungen mit Israel und die Entwicklung des deutsch-israelischen Handels', *Israels Aussenhandel,* vol. 7, no. 5–6, pp. 7–8.
Hoffmann, Stanley (1974), 'Toward a common European foreign policy?', in Wolfram F. Hanrieder (ed.), *The United States and Western Europe. Political, Economic and Strategic Perspectives* (Cambridge: Winthrop), pp. 79–105.
Holbik, Karel, and Myers, Henry Allen (1968), *West German Foreign Aid 1956–1966. Its Economic and Political Aspects* (Boston, Mass.: Boston University Press).
Holsti, Kal J. (1967), *International Politics. A Framework for Analysis,* 1st edn (Englewood Cliffs, NJ: Prentice-Hall).
Holsti, Kal J. (1977), *International Politics. A Framework for Analysis,* 3rd edn (Englewood Cliffs, NJ: Prentice-Hall).
Holsti, Ole R., Hopmann, P. Terrence, and Sullivan, John D. (1973), *Unity and Disintegration in International Alliances: Comparative Studies* (New York: Wiley).
Hottinger, Arnold (1965), 'Die Hintergründe der Einladung Ulbrichts nach Kairo', *Europa–Archiv,* vol. 20, no. 4, pp. 107–14.
Huntington, Samuel P. (1973), 'Transnational organizations in world politics', *World Politics,* vol. XXV, no. 3, pp. 333–68.

Huyssen, Andreas (1980), 'The politics of identification: *Holocaust* and West German drama', *New German Critique,* no. 19 (Winter), pp. 117–36.
von Imhoff, Christoph (1965a), 'Aufmarsch im östlichen Mittelmeer', *Aussenpolitik,* vol. 16, no. 5, pp. 326–38.
von Imhoff, Christoph (1965b), 'Die Araber-Liga nach der Nahostkrise', *Aussenpolitik,* vol. 16, no. 7, pp. 466–76.
von Imhoff, Christoph (1971), 'Germans and Arabs: prospects and limitations on Bonn's Middle Eastern policies', *Wiener Library Bulletin,* vol. XXV, no. 1–2, pp. 17–23.
Infas (1974), *Infas Report für die Presse* (December 12).
Institut für Demoskopie (1956), *Jahrbuch der öffentlichen Meinung 1947–1955. Band I* (Allensbach: Verlag für Demoskopie).
Institut für Demoskopie (1957), *Jahrbuch der öffentlichen Meinung 1957. Band II* (Allensbach: Verlag für Demoskopie).
Institut für Demoskopie (1965), *Jahrbuch der öffentlichen Meinung 1958–1964. Band III* (Allensbach: Verlag für Demoskopie).
Institut für Demoskopie (1967), *Jahrbuch der öffentlichen Meinung 1965–1967. Band IV* (Allensbach: Verlag für Demoskopie).
Institut für Demoskopie (1973), *Allensbacher Berichte,* No. 41.
Institut für Demoskopie (1974), *Jahrbuch der öffentlichen Meinung 1968–1973. Band V* (Allensbach: Verlag für Demoskopie).
Institut für Demoskopie (1976), *Allensbacher Jahrbuch der Demoskopie 1974–1976. Band VI* (Vienna: Verlag Fritz Molden).
Institut für Demoskopie (1977), *Allensbacher Jahrbuch der Demoskopie 1976–1977. Band VII* (Vienna: Verlag Fritz Molden).
Institut für Demoskopie (1983), *Allensbacher Jahrbuch der Demoskopie 1978–1983. Band VIII* (Munich: K. G. Saur).
Institute of Jewish Affairs (1980a), 'Anti-Zionism and the extreme right', *Research Report,* No. 14 (September).
Institute of Jewish Affairs (1980b), 'The neo-Nazi campaign in Germany', *Research Report,* No. 24 (December).
Institute of Jewish Affairs (1981a), 'How popular is neo-Nazism in Germany?', *Research Report,* No. 6 (May).
Institute of Jewish Affairs (1981b), 'Antisemitism in the Western world today', *Research Report,* No. 7 (June).
Institute of Jewish Affairs (1981c), 'Trials of Nazi war criminals: has justice been done?' *Research Report,* No. 12 (August).
Institute of Jewish Affairs (1982), 'Making the denial of the Holocaust a crime in law', *Research Report,* no. 8 (March).
International Defense Review (1978), 'German arms exports', *International Defense Review,* vol. 11, no. 9, p. 1374.
International Defense Review (1979), 'Israeli ammunition for German army', *International Defense Review,* vol. 12, no. 2, p. 158.
International Monetary Fund (1951), *International Financial Statistics,* vol. IV, no. 10 (October).
International Monetary Fund (1952), *International Financial Statistics,* vol. V, no. 7 (July).
International Monetary Fund (1959), *International Financial Statistics,* vol. XII, no. 4 (April).
Internationaler Jugendaustausch- und Besucherdienst der Bundesrepublik

Deutschland (IJAB) (1977), *Gemeinsame Bestimmungen für die Durchführung und Förderung des deutsch-israelischen Jugendaustausches* (Bonn: IJAB im Auftrage des Bundesministers für Jugend, Familie und Gesundheit, May).

Israel-Berichte (1975), 'Demokratischer Bürgersinn darf nicht sterben – Zur finanziellen Situation der DIG', *Israel-Berichte*, vol. 2, no. 5 (May), pp. 2–4.

Jacobsen, Walter (1963), 'Have the Germans changed?', in Walter Stahl (ed.), *The Politics of Postwar Germany* (New York: Praeger), pp. 171–92.

Jaspers, Karl (1946), *Die Schuldfrage. Ein Beitrag zur deutschen Frage* (Zürich: Artemis Verlag).

Jochmann, Werner (1971), 'Die Ausbreitung des Antisemitismus', in Werner E. Mosse and Arnold Paucker (eds), *Deutsches Judentum in Krieg und Revolution 1916–1923* (Tübingen: J. C. B. Mohr), pp. 409–510.

Jochmann, Werner (1976), 'Struktur und Funktion des deutschen Antisemitismus', in Werner E. Mosse and Arnold Paucker (eds), *Juden im Wilhelminischen Deutschland 1890–1914* (Tübingen: J. C. B. Mohr), pp. 389–477.

Jochum, Herbert, and Kremers, Heinz (eds) (1980), *Juden, Judentum und Staat Israel im christlichen Religionsunterricht in der Bundesrepublik Deutschland* (Paderborn: Ferdinand Schöningh Verlag).

Kadritzke, Niels (1969), 'Die deutsche Linke und der Nahost-Konflikt – Solidarität mit wem?', *Diskussion*, vol. 10, no. 27, pp. 9–13.

Kahn, Lothar (1975), 'Moritz Gottlieb Saphir', *Leo Baeck Institute Year Book*, Vol. XX, pp. 247–57.

Kaiser, Karl, and Steinbach, Udo (eds) (1981), *Deutsch-arabische Beziehungen* (Munich: Piper Verlag).

Keesing's Contemporary Archives (1950–2), Vol. VIII.

Keohane, Robert O., and Nye, Joseph S. Jr (1975), 'International interdependence and integration', in Fred I. Greenstein and Nelson W. Polsby (eds), *The Handbook of Political Science* (Reading, Mass.: Addison-Wesley), Vol. 8, pp. 363–414.

Keohane, Robert O., and Nye, Joseph S. Jr (1977), *Power and Interdependence. World Politics in Transition* (Boston, Mass.: Little, Brown).

Kesten, Hermann (1975), 'Heinrich Heine and Joseph Roth', *Leo Baeck Institute Year Book*, Vol. XX, pp. 259–73.

Kirton, John J. (1974), 'The consequences of integration: the case of the defence production sharing agreements', in W. Andrew Axline, *et al.* (eds), *Continental Community? Independence and Integration in North America* (Toronto: McClelland & Stewart), pp. 116–36.

Kissinger, Henry (1965), *The Troubled Partnership: A Re-Appraisal of the Atlantic Alliance* (New York: McGraw-Hill).

Klein, Dennis (1980), 'Assimilation and dissimilation: Peter Gay's *Freud, Jews and Other Germans. Masters and Victims in Modernist Culture*', *New German Critique*, no. 19 (Winter), pp. 151–65.

Klein, Manfred (1978), 'Studienfahrten nach Israel. Eindrücke und Begegnungen', *Tribüne*, vol. 17, no. 66, pp. 64–6.

Knauss, Gerhard (1960), 'Der Staat Israel, die Araber und die Bundesrepublik', *Frankfurter Hefte*, vol. 15, no. 9, pp. 609–19.

Knusel, Jack L. (1968), *West German Aid to Developing Nations* (New York: Praeger).

Kogon, Eugen (1979), 'Ueber die innere Wahrheit des Fernsehfilms *Holocaust*', in Peter Märthesheimer and Ivo Frenzell (eds), *Im Kreuzfeuer. Der Fernsehfilm 'Holocaust'. Eine Nation ist betroffen* (Frankfurt-am-Main: Fischer Taschenbuch Verlag), pp. 66–9.

Kolinsky, Martin, and Kolinsky, Eva (1974), 'The treatment of the Holocaust in West German textbooks', in Livia Rothkirchen (ed.), *Yad Vashem Studies on the European Jewish Catastrophe and Resistance* (Jerusalem: Yad Vashem), pp. 149–216.

Kossoy, Edward (1971), 'Deutsche Wiedergutmachung aus israelischer Sicht. Geschichte, Auswirkung, Gesetzgebung und Rechtsprechung', dissertation, Universität zu Köln, Cologne.

Krämer-Badoni, Rudolf (1969), 'Answering the German anti-Zionist New Left', *Wiener Library Bulletin,* vol. XXIII, no. 4, pp. 21–5.

Kramer, Thomas W. (1974), *Deutsch-ägyptische Beziehungen in Vergangenheit und Gegenwart* (Tübingen: Horst Erdmann Verlag).

Kreysler, Joachim, and Jungfer, Klaus (1965), *Deutsche Israel-Politik* (Diessen-Ammersee: Wolf von Tucher Verlag).

Kühnl, Reinhard (1971), 'Die Auseinandersetzung mit dem Faschismus in BRD und DDR', in Gerhard Hess (ed.), *BRD-DDR. Vergleich der Gesellschaftssysteme* (Cologne: Paul Rugenstein Verlag), pp. 248–71.

Küster, Otto (1952), *Mitteilung an die Presse. Wortlaut seines Rücktrittschreibens vom 7. Mai 1952,* statement to press, Stuttgart, May 23.

Küster, Otto (1967), 'Erfahrungen in der deutschen Wiedergutmachung', in *Recht und Staat in Geschichte und Gegenwart. Eine Sammlung von Vorträgen und Schriften aus dem Gebiet der gesamten Staatswissenschaften,* No. 346/347 (Tübingen: J.C.B. Mohr), pp. 3–35.

Kusche, Ulrich (1967), 'Die deutsch-israelischen Studentenbeziehungen. Bilanz, Chancen, Aufgaben', *Diskussion,* vol. 8, no. 21, pp. 10–12.

Lamberti, Marjorie (1980), 'Liberals, socialists and the defence against anti-semitism in the Wilhelminian period', *Leo Baeck Institute Year Book,* Vol. XXV, pp. 147–62.

Landmann, Michael (1971), *Das Israelpseudos der Pseudolinken* (Berlin: Colloquium Verlag Otto Hess).

Laqueur, Walter (1974), *Confrontation: The Middle East and World Politics* (New York: Bantam Books).

Lehrman, Hal (1951), 'Foreign-trade gap imposes austerity on Israel', *Foreign Policy Bulletin,* vol. XXX, no. 32 (May 18), pp. 3–4.

Levin, Nora (1968), *The Destruction of European Jewry, 1933–1945* (New York: Thomas Y. Crowell).

Levy, Richard S. (1975), *The Downfall of the Anti-Semitic Political Parties in Imperial Germany* (New Haven, Conn.: Yale University Press).

Levy, Walter J. (1980), 'Oil and the decline of the West', *Foreign Affairs,* vol. 58, no. 5, pp. 999–1015.

Lewan, Kenneth M. (1975), 'How West Germany helped to build Israel', *Journal of Palestine Studies,* vol. IV, no. 4, pp. 41–64.

Lieber, Robert J. (1976), *Oil and the Middle East War: Europe in the Energy Crisis* (Cambridge, Mass.: Harvard University Center for International Affairs).

Lieber, Robert J. (1979), 'Europe and America in the world energy crisis', *International Affairs,* vol. 55, no. 4, pp. 531–45.

Lieber, Robert J. (1979–80), 'The European Community and the Middle East', in Colin Legum (ed.), *Middle East Contemporary Survey* (New York: Holmes & Meier), Vol. 4, pp. 70–6.

Liebeschütz, Hans (1970), *Von Georg Simmel zu Franz Rosenzweig. Studien zum jüdischen Denken im deutschen Kulturbereich* (Tübingen: J. C. B. Mohr).

Liebeschütz, Hans, and Paucker, Arnold (eds) (1977), *Das Judentum in der deutschen Umwelt 1800–1850* (Tübingen: J. C. B. Mohr).

Lieser, Peter (1975), 'Zur Genesis der Energiekrise. Der vierte Nahostkrieg, Erdölpolitik und internationale Beziehungen', *Orient*, vol. 16, no. 2, pp. 21–56.

Liska, George (1962), *Nations in Alliance: The Limits of Interdependence* (Baltimore, Md: Johns Hopkins University Press).

Liviatan, Oded (1980), 'Israel's external debt', *Bank of Israel Economic Review*, no. 48–9 (May), pp. 1–44.

Loch, Theo M. (1981), 'Bonn and Paris share key role in Europe', *Atlantic Community Quarterly*, vol. 19, no. 1, pp. 13–17.

Lönnendonker, Siegward (1964), 'Die deutschen Wissenschaftler in Aegypten. Eine Zusammenstellung der Fakten', *Diskussion*, vol. 5, no. 14, pp. 9–11.

Loewenberg, Peter (1979), 'Insiders and outsiders', *Partisan Review*, vol. XLVI, no. 3, pp. 461–70.

Loewenstein, Kurt (1966), 'Die innerjüdische Reaktion auf die Krise der deutschen Demokratie', in Werner E. Mosse and Arnold Paucker (eds), *Entscheidungsjahr 1932. Zur Judenfrage in der Endphase der Weimarer Republik* (Tübingen: J. C. B. Mohr), pp. 349–403.

Löwenthal, Richard, and Schwarz, Hans-Peter (1974), *Die zweite Republik. 25 Jahre Bundesrepublik Deutschland – eine Bilanz* (Stuttgart: Seewald Verlag).

Low, Alfred D. (1979), *Jews in the Eyes of the Germans. From the Enlightenment to Imperial Germany* (Philadelphia, Pa: Institute for the Study of Human Issues).

Lownethal, E. G. (1966), 'Die Juden im öffentlichen Leben', in Werner E. Mosse and Arnold Paucker (eds), *Entscheidungsjahr 1932. Zur Judenfrage in der Endphase der Weimarer Republik* (Tübingen: J. C. B. Mohr), pp. 51–85.

Lüth, Erich (1952), *Through Truth to Peace* (Hamburg: Gesellschaft für christlich-jüdische Zusammenarbeit in Hamburg e. V.).

Lüth, Erich (1966), *Viele Steine lagen am Weg. Ein Querkopf berichtet* (Hamburg: Marion von Schröder Verlag).

Lüth, Erich (ed.)(1976), *Die Friedensbitte an Israel 1951. Eine Hamburger Initiative* (Hamburg: Hans Christians Verlag).

MacGuigan, Mark (1981), 'Address to the Empire Club of Canada in Toronto', *Canada Weekly*, vol. 9, no. 8 (February 25), pp. 1–2, 8.

Märthesheimer, Peter (1979a), 'Vorbemerkungen der Herausgeber', in Peter Märthesheimer and Ivo Frenzel (eds), *Im Kreuzfeuer. Der Fernsehfilm 'Holocaust'. Eine Nation ist betroffen* (Frankfurt-am-Main: Fischer Taschenbuch Verlag), pp. 11–18.

Märthesheimer, Peter (1979b), 'Das muss er schon selbst vertreten', in Peter Märthesheimer and Ivo Frenzel (eds), *Im Kreuzfeuer. Der Fernsehfilm 'Holocaust'. Eine Nation ist betroffen* (Frankfurt-am-Main: Fischer Taschenbuch Verlag), pp. 49–50.

Märthesheimer, Peter, and Frenzel, Ivo (eds) (1979), *Im Kreuzfeuer. Der Fern-*

sehfilm 'Holocaust'. Eine Nation ist betroffen (Frankfurt-am-Main: Fischer Taschenbuch Verlag).
Magnus, Uwe (1979), 'Die Einschaltungsquoten und Sehbeteiligung', in Peter Märthesheimer and Ivo Frenzel (eds), *Im Kreuzfeuer. Der Fernsehfilm 'Holocaust'. Eine Nation ist betroffen* (Frankfurt-am-Main: Fischer Taschenbuch Verlag), pp. 221–4.
Majonica, Ernst (1965), *Deutsche Aussenpolitik. Probleme und Entscheidungen* (Stuttgart: Kohlhammer Verlag).
Majonica, Ernst (1969), *Möglichkeiten und Grenzen der deutschen Aussenpolitik* (Stuttgart: Kohlhammer Verlag).
Markovits, Andrei S., and Hayden, Rebecca S. (1980), '"Holocaust" before and after the event: reactions in West Germany and Austria', *New German Critique*, no.19 (Winter), pp. 53–80.
Massing, Paul W. (1949), *Rehearsal for Destruction. A Study of Political Anti-Semitism in Imperial Germany* (New York: Harper).
Matenko, Percy (1975), 'Ludwig Tieck and Rahel Varnhagen: a re-examination', *Leo Baeck Institute Year Book,* Vol. XX, pp. 225–46.
Maull, Hanns W. (1980a), *Europe and World Energy* (London: Butterworths).
Maull, Hanns W. (1980b), 'Western Europe: a fragmented response to a fragmenting order', *Orbis,* vol. 23, no. 4, pp. 803–24.
Max-Planck-Gesellschaft (1979), 'Weizmann Institut: Wissenschaft im Dienst des Friedens', *Max-Planck-Gesellschaft Spiegel. Aktuelle Information für Mitarbeiter und Freunde der Max-Planck-Gesellschaft*, No. 1/79, pp. 15–17.
Max-Planck-Gesellschaft (1980), 'Ueber zwanzig Jahre Zusammenarbeit zwischen MPG und Weizmann Institut', *Max-Planck-Gesellschaft Spiegel. Aktuelle Informationen für Mitarbeiter und Freunde der Max-Planck-Gesellschaft,* No. 3/80, pp. 16–17.
Medzini, Meron (1972–3), 'Israel's changing image in the German mass media', *Wiener Library Bulletin,* vol, XXVI, no. 3–4, pp. 8–13.
Meir, Golda (1975), *My Life* (New York: Putnam).
Melchior, David (1973), 'Die SPD und die Israelische Arbeiterpartei', *Die Neue Gesellschaft,* vol. 20, no. 9, pp. 719–22.
Mendes-Flohr, Paul R., and Reinharz, Jehuda (eds) (1980), *The Jew in the Modern World. A Documentary History* (New York: Oxford University Press).
Merritt, Anna J., and Merritt, Richard L. (eds)(1970), *Public Opinion in Occupied Germany. The OMGUS Surveys, 1945–1949* (Urbana, Ill.: University of Illinois Press).
Merritt, Anna J., and Merritt, Richard L. (eds) (1980), *Public Opinion in Semisovereign Germany. The HICOG Surveys, 1949–1955* (Urbana, Ill.: University of Illinois Press).
Middle East Economic Digest (1979), 'West Germany and the Middle East' (special report), *Middle East Economic Digest* (November), pp. 3–54.
Middle East Economic Digest (1982), 'West Germany and the Middle East' (special report), *Middle East Economic Digest* (February), pp. 1–97.
Miller, Susanne (1975), 'Das "Institut für deutsche Geschichte" in Tel Aviv', DIG, vol. 5, no. 2, pp. 1–2, 13.
Mineralölwirtschaftsverband (1978), *Mineralöl-Zahlen 1978* (Hamburg: Mineralölwirtschaftsverband e.V.).
Mitscherlich, Alexander, and Mitscherlich, Margarete (1975), *The Inability to Mourn. Principles of Collective Behavior* (New York: Grove Press).

Molot, Maureen A. (1974), 'The role of institutions in Canada–United States relations: the case of North American financial ties', in W. Andrew Axline, *et al.* (eds), *Continental Community? Independence and Integration in North America* (Toronto: McClelland & Stewart), pp. 164–93.

Moosberg, K. A. (1973), 'Neue Wege zur Förderung der wirtschaftlichen Zusammenarbeit', *Israels Aussenhandel,* vol. 7, no. 5–6, p. 12.

Morgan, Roger (1974a), *The United States and West Germany, 1945–1973: A Study in Alliance Politics* (London: Oxford University Press).

Morgan, Roger (1974b), 'Can Europe have a foreign policy'?, *World Today,* vol. 30, no. 2, pp. 43–50.

Mosse, George L. (1964), *The Crisis of German Ideology. Intellectual Origins of the Third Reich* (New York: Grosset & Dunlap).

Mosse, George L. (1970), *Germans and Jews. The Right, the Left, and the Search for a 'Third Force' in Pre-Nazi Germany* (New York: Howard Fertig).

Mosse, George L. (1977), *The Jews and the German War Experience 1914–1948. The Leo Baeck Memorial Lecture 21* (New York: Leo Baeck Institute).

Mosse, Werner E. (1966), 'Der Niedergang der Weimarer Republik und die Juden', in Werner E. Mosse and Arnold Paucker (eds), *Entscheidungsjahr 1932. Zur Judenfrage in der Endphase der Weimarer Republik* (Tübingen: J. C. B. Mohr), pp. 3–49.

Mosse, Werner E. (1971), 'Die Krise der europäischen Bourgeoisie und das deutsche Judentum', in Werner E. Mosse and Arnold Paucker (eds), *Deutsches Judentum in Krieg und Revolution 1916–1923* (Tübingen: J. C. B. Mohr), pp. 1–26.

Mosse, Werner E. (1976), 'Die Juden in Wirtschaft und Gesellschaft', in Werner E. Mosse and Arnold Paucker (eds), *Juden im Wilhelminischen Deutschland 1890–1914* (Tübingen: J. C. B. Mohr), pp. 57–113.

Mosse, Werner E., and Paucker, Arnold (eds) (1966), *Entscheidungsjahr 1932. Zur Judenfrage in der Endphase der Weimarer Republik* (Tübingen: J. C. B. Mohr).

Mosse, Werner E., and Paucker, Arnold (eds) (1971), *Deutsches Judentum in Krieg und Revolution 1916–1923* (Tübingen: J. C. B. Mohr).

Mosse, Werner E., and Paucker, Arnold (eds) (1976), *Juden im Wilhelminischen Deutschland 1890–1914* (Tübingen: J. C. B. Mohr).

Bill Moyers' Journal (1975), *International Report* (New York: WNET/13 for Public Broadcasting Service, January 23).

Müller, Peter (1965), 'Waffenhilfe an Israel und deutsche Demokratie. Verfassungspolitische Aspekte der Krise der deutschen Nahostpolitik', *Diskussion,* vol. 6, no. 17, pp. 6–10.

Mushkat, M. (1980), 'Israel and the Common Market', *The Israel Year Book, 1980,* pp. 133–7.

Nachmansohn, David (1979), *German-Jewish Pioneers in Science 1900–1933. Highlights in Atomic Physics, Chemistry and Biochemistry* (New York: Springer-Verlag).

Nasmyth, Jenny (1954), 'Israel's distorted economy', *Middle East Journal,* vol. 8, no. 4, pp. 391–402.

National Council for Research and Development (Israel) (1977), *Scientific Ties with the Federal Republic of Germany* (Hebrew) (Jerusalem: National Council for Research and Development).

National Council for Research and Development (Israel) (1978), *Science and*

Technology in Israel 1975/76 (Jerusalem: National Council for Research and Development).
Neumann, Peter, and Noelle-Neumann, Elisabeth (eds) (1967), *The Germans. Public Opinion Polls, 1947–1966* (Allensbach: Verlag für Demoskopie).
Neustadt, Richard E. (1970), *Alliance Politics* (New York: Columbia University Press).
Newsweek (1974), 'Arabia's Faisal gets impatient', *Newsweek* (September 30), p. 41.
Nicosia, Francis R. J. (1979), 'Weimar Germany and the Palestine question', *Leo Baeck Institute Year Book,* Vol. XXIV, pp. 321–45.
Nye, Joseph S. Jr (1968), 'Comparative regional integration: concept and measurement', *International Organization,* vol. 22, no. 4, pp. 855–80.
Olson, Mancur Jr, and Zeckhauser, Richard (1966), 'An economic theory of alliances', *Review of Economics and Statistics,* vol. XLVIII, no. 3, pp. 266–79.
Oppermann, Thomas (1980), *'Israel und Pälastina-Reifeprüfung der Bonner Aussenpolitik',* *Europa-Archiv,* vol. 35, no. 14, pp. 435–47.
Osgood, Robert E. (1968), *Alliances and American Foreign Policy* (Baltimore, Md: Johns Hopkins University Press).
Ott, Hanns (1972), 'Jugend überwindet die Vergangenheit', *Das Parlament,* vol. 22, no. 45 (November 4), p. 10.
Palmer, Michael (1976), 'EEC: the road to better political co-operation', *World Today,* vol. 32, no. 1, pp. 25–30.
Patinkin, Don (1960), *The Israel Economy* (Jerusalem: Falk Project).
Paucker, Arnold (1966), 'Der jüdische Abwehrkampf', in Werner E. Mosse and Arnold Paucker (eds), *Entscheidungsjahr 1932. Zur Judenfrage in der Endphase der Weimarer Republik* (Tübingen: J. C. B. Mohr), pp. 405–99.
Pearlman, Moshe (1965), *Ben Gurion Looks Back in Talks with Moshe Pearlman* (New York: Simon & Schuster).
Pentland, Charles (1974), 'Political integration: a multidimensional perspective', in W. Andrew Axline, *et al.* (eds), *Continental Community? Independence and Integration in North America* (Toronto: McClelland & Stewart), pp. 42–66.
Peres, Shimon (1970), *David's Sling: The Arming of Israel* (London: Weidenfeld & Nicolson).
Philipp, Udo (1982), 'German government continues restrictive arms export policy', *International Defense Review,* vol. 15, no. 3, p. 260.
Picht, Robert (1978a), 'Ergebnisse und offene Fragen', in Robert Picht (ed.), *Deutschland, Frankreich, Europa. Bilanz einer schwierigen Partnerschaft* (Munich: Piper Verlag), pp. 351–9.
Picht, Robert (ed.) (1978b), *Deutschland Frankreich, Europa. Bilanz einer schwierigen Partnerschaft* (Munich: Piper Verlag).
Pinder, John (1977), 'The reform of international economic policy: weak and strong countries', *International Affairs,* vol. 53, no. 3, pp. 345–63.
Pomfret, Richard W. T., and Toren, Benjamin (1980), *Israel and the European Common Market. An Appraisal of the 1975 Free Trade Agreement* (Tübingen: J. C. B. Mohr).
Pomfret, Richard W. T., and Tovias, Alfred (1980), 'The global Mediterranean policy of the EEC', in Herbert Giersch (ed.), *The Economic Integration of Israel in the EEC* (Tübingen: J. C. B. Mohr), pp. 41–67.
Popp, Manfred (1972), 'Gute Zusammenarbeit in der naturwissenschaftlichen Forschung', *Das Parlament,* vol. 22, no. 45 (November 4), p. 11.

Poppel, Stephen M. (1977), *Zionism in Germany, 1897–1933. The Shaping of a Jewish Identity* (Philadelphia, Pa: Jewish Publication Society of America).
Postone, Moishe (1980), 'Anti-Semitism and National Socialism: notes on the German reaction to "Holocaust"', *New German Critique,* no. 19 (Winter), pp. 98–115.
Prowe-Isenbörger, Ina (1962), *Deutsche Juden* (Hangelar bei Bonn: Verlag Heinrich Warnecke).
Pulzer, Peter G. J. (1964), *The Rise of Political Anti-Semitism in Germany and Austria* (New York: Wiley).
Pulzer, Peter G. J. (1976), 'Die jüdische Beteiligung an der Politik', in Werner E. Mosse and Arnold Paucker (eds), *Juden im Wilhelminischen Deutschland 1890–1914* (Tübingen: J. C. B. Mohr), pp. 143–239.
Pulzer, Peter G. J. (1980), 'Why was there a Jewish Question in Imperial Germany?', *Leo Baeck Institute Year Book,* Vol. XXV, pp. 133–46.
Rabinbach, Anson G., and Zipes, Jack (1980), 'Lessons of the Holocaust', *New German Critique,* no. 19 (Winter) pp. 3–7.
Ragins, Sanford (1980), *Jewish Responses to Anti-Semitism in Germany, 1870–1914* (Cincinnati, Ohio: Hebrew Union College Press).
Ramazani, Rouhollah K. (1964), *The Middle East and the European Common Market* (Charlottesville, Va: University of Virginia Press).
Rathmann, Lothar (1966), 'Die Vereinigte Arabische Republik und die beiden deutschen Staaten im Jahre 1965', *Rat für Asien-, Afrika- und Lateinamerikawissenschaften an der Karl Marx Universität Leipzig.*
Redekop, John H. (1976), 'A reinterpretation of Canadian-American relations', *Canadian Journal of Political Science,* vol. IX, no. 2, pp. 227–43.
Reichmann, Eva G. (1966), 'Diskussionen über die Judenfrage 1930–1932, in Werner E. Mosse and Arnold Paucker (eds), *Entscheidungsjahr 1932. Zur Judenfrage in der Endphase der Weimarer Republik* (Tübingen: J. C. B. Mohr), pp. 503–31.
Reichmann, Eva G. (1971), 'Der Bewusstseinswandel der deutschen Juden', in Werner E. Mosse and Arnold Paucker (eds), *Deutsches Judentum in Krieg und Revolution 1916–1923* (Tübingen: J. C. B. Mohr), pp. 511–612.
Reinharz, Jehuda (1975), *Fatherland or Promised Land. The Dilemma of the German Jew, 1893–1914* (Ann Arbor, Mich.: University of Michigan Press).
Rheins, Carl J. (1980), 'The *Verband nationaldeutscher Juden* 1921–1933', *Leo Baeck Institute Year Book,* Vol. XXV, pp. 243–68.
Richarz, Monika (1974), *Der Eintritt der Juden in die akademischen Berufe. Jüdische Studenten und Akademiker in Deutschland 1678–1848* (Tübingen: J. C. B. Mohr).
Richarz, Monika (1975), 'Jewish social mobility in Germany during the time of emancipation (1790–1871)', *Leo Baeck Institute Year Book,* Vol. XX, pp. 69–77.
Richarz, Monika (ed.)(1976), *Jüdisches Leben in Deutschland. Selbstzeugnisse zur Sozialgeschichte 1780–1871* (Stuttgart: Deutsche Verlagsanstalt).
Richarz, Monika (ed.)(1979), *Jüdisches Leben in Deutschland. Zweiter Band. Selbstzeugnisse zur Sozialgeschichte im Kaiserreich* (Stuttgart: Deutsche Verlagsanstalt).
Riker, William H. (1962), *The Theory of Political Coalitions* (New Haven, Conn.: Yale University Press).
Robinson, Nehemiah (1964), *Ten Years of German Indemnification* (New York: Conference on Jewish Material Claims against Germany).

Rovan, Joseph (1978), 'Zwischenbilanz auf dem Wege zu einem deutsch-französischen Bund', *Frankfurter Hefte*, vol. 33, no. 2, pp. 34–41.
Rosenberg, Arthur (1964), *Imperial Germany. The Birth of the German Republic 1871–1918* (Boston, Mass.: Beacon Press).
Rosenblüth, Pinchas E. (1976), 'Die geistigen und religiösen Strömungen in der deutschen Judenheit', in Werner E. Mosse and Arnold Paucker (eds), *Juden im Wilhelminischen Deutschland 1890–1914* (Tübingen: J. C. B. Mohr), pp. 549–98.
Rückerl, Adalbert (1979), *The Investigation of Nazi Crimes 1945–1978. A Documentation* (Heidelberg: C. F. Müller).
Rürup, Reinhard (1975), 'Emancipation and crisis – the "Jewish question" in Germany 1850–1890', *Leo Baeck Institute Year Book,* Vol. XX, pp. 13–25.
Rumpf, Helmut (1973), 'Die deutsche Frage und die Reparationen', *Zeitschrift für ausländisches öffentliches Recht und Völkerrecht,* vol. 33, no. 2, pp. 344–71.
Russett, Bruce M. (1963), *Community and Contention. Britain and America in the Twentieth Century* (Cambridge, Mass.: MIT Press).
Russett, Bruce M. (1974), *Power and Community in World Politics* (San Francisco, Calif.: W. H. Freeman).
Sachar, Howard M. (1979), *A History of Israel. From the Rise of Zionism to Our Time* (New York: Knopf).
Sänger, Fritz (1963), 'Aus Gründen der Vernunft', *Tribüne*, vol. 2, no. 5, pp. 464–5.
Safran, Nadav (1978), *Israel: The Embattled Ally* (Cambridge, Mass.: Belknap Press of Harvard University).
Sagi, Nana (1980), *German Reparations. A History of the Negotiations* (Jerusalem: Magnes Press).
Saudi Arabia Newsletter (1980), 'Khaled's visit a snub to US', *Saudi Arabia Newsletter,* no. 27 (June 30–July 13), p. 3.
Schallenberger, E. Horst (1978), 'Deutsches Schulbuch der Gegenwart', *Tribüne*, vol. 17, no. 67, pp. 33–58.
Scheel, Walter (1973), 'Interview mit Bundesaussenminister Walter Scheel', *Tribüne*, vol. 12, no. 46, pp. 5166–9.
Schoeps, Julius H. (1979), 'Angst vor der Vergangenheit. Notizen zu den Reaktionen auf "Holocaust"', in Peter Märthesheimer and Ivo Frenzel (eds), *Im Kreuzfeuer. Der Fernsehfilm 'Holocaust'. Eine Nation ist betroffen* (Frankfurt-am-Main: Fischer Taschenbuch Verlag), pp. 225–30.
Schoeps, Julius H. (1980), 'Neonazismus und Wurzeln des Antisemitismus', *Tribüne*, vol. 19, no. 73, pp. 20–33.
Scholem, Gershom (1976), *On Jews and Judaism in Crisis. Selected Essays,* ed. Werner J. Dannhauser (New York: Schocken Books).
Scholem, Gershom (1979), 'On the social psychology of the Jews in Germany: 1900–1933', in David Bronsen (ed.), *Jews and Germans from 1860 to 1933: The Problematic Symbiosis* (Heidelberg: Carl Winter Universitätsverlag).
Schorsch, Ismar (1972), *Jewish Reactions to German Anit-Semitism, 1870–1914* (New York: Columbia University Press).
Schürholz, Franz (1968), *Ergebnisse der deutschen Wiedergutmachungsleistungen in Israel* (Bonn: Bundeszentrale für politische Bildung).
Schulin, Ernst (1976), 'Die Rathenaus – Zwei Generationen jüdischen Anteils an der industriellen Entwicklung Deutschlands', in Werner E. Mosse and

Arnold Paucker (eds), *Juden im Wilhelminischen Deutschland 1890–1914* (Tübingen: J. C. B. Mohr), pp. 115–42.

Schultheiss, Franklin (1976), 'Studienfahrten nach Israel. Eine "Bilanz" nach 12 Jahren', *Tribüne,* vol. 15, no. 60, pp. 7162–8.

Schwarz, Hans-Peter (1966), *Vom Reich zur Bundesrepublik. Deutschland im Widerstreit der aussenpolitischen Konzeptionen in den Jahren der Besatzungsherrschaft 1945–1949* (Neuwied: Luchterhand Verlag).

Schwarz, Hans-Peter (1975), 'Die westdeutsche Entwicklungshilfe', in Hans-Peter Schwarz (ed.), *Handbuch der deutschen Aussenpolitik* (Munich: Piper Verlag), pp. 723–39.

Schwerin, Kurt (1972), 'German compensation for victims of Nazi persecution', *Northwestern University Law Review,* vol. 67, no. 4, pp. 479–527.

Seelbach, Jörg (1970), *Die Aufnahme der diplomatischen Beziehungen zu Israel als Problem der deutschen Politik seit 1955 (Marburger Abhandlungen zur Politischen Wissenschaft, Band 19)* (Meisenheim am Glan: Verlag Antoin Hain).

Sharett, Moshe (1950), 'International pooling of efforts', *United Nations Bulletin,* vol. IX, no. 8 (October 15), pp. 393–4.

Sharett, Moshe (1952a), *Staatsprobleme. Nach einer Rede gehalten in der Knesseth am 9. Januar 1952* (Jerusalem: Informationsdienst des Staates Israel, May).

Sharett, Moshe (1952b), 'Statesmanship needed', *Jewish Frontier,* vol. XIX, no. 3(203), pp. 14–16.

Shinnar, Felix (1967), *Bericht eines Beauftragten. Die deutsch-israelischen Beziehungen 1951–1966* (Tübingen: Rainer Wunderlich Verlag).

Shlaim, Avi, and Yannopoulos, George N. (eds)(1976), *The EEC and the Mediterranean Countries* (Cambridge: Cambridge University Press).

Sicherman, Harvey (1980), 'Politics of dependence: Western Europe and the Arab-Israeli conflict', *Orbis,* vol. 23, no. 4, pp. 845–57.

Sicron, Moshe (1957), *Immigration to Israel, 1948–1953* (Jerusalem: Falk Project/CBS).

Silbermann, Alphons (1976), 'Antisemitismus in der Bundesrepublik Deutschland', *Bild der Wissenschaft,* vol. 13, no. 6 (June), pp. 68–74.

Silbermann, Alphons (1982), *Sind wir Antisemiten? Ausmass und Wirkung eines sozialen Vorurteils in der Bundesrepublik Deutschland* (Cologne: Verlag Wissenschaft und Politik Berend von Nottbeck).

Simon Wiesenthal Center for Holocaust Studies (1979a), 'Statute of Limitations', Simon Wiesenthal Center for Holocaust Studies.

Simon Wiesenthal Center for Holocaust Studies (1979b), 'This murderer has not been found!', Simon Wiesenthal Center for Holocaust Studies.

Singer, J. David, and Small, Melvin (1968), 'Alliance aggregation and the onset of war, 1815–1945', in J. David Singer (ed.), *Quantitative International Politics: Insights and Evidence* (New York: The Free Press), pp. 247–86.

SIPRI (Stockholm International Peace Research Institute)(1969–80), *World Armaments and Disarmament,* SIPRI Yearbooks, 1968–9 through 1977 (Stockholm: Almqvist & Wiksell); SIPRI Yearbooks, 1978–80 (London: Taylor & Francis).

SIPRI (1971), *The Arms Trade with the Third World* (Stockholm: Almqvist & Wiksell).

SIPRI (1975), *The Arms Trade with the Third World,* rev. abridged edn (New York: Holmes & Meier).

318 Bibliography

Sohn, Karl-Heinz (1972), *Entwicklungspolitik. Theorie und Praxis der deutschen Entwicklungshilfe* (Munich: Piper Verlag).
Sozialdemokratische Partei Deutschlands, *Pressemitteilungen und Informationen* (Bonn: SPD).
Sozialistische Bildungsgemeinschaft (1974), *Wir und Israel* (Bonn: Zentralausschuss Sozialistischer Bildungsgemeinschaften).
State of Israel Central Bureau of Statistics (1964), *Statistical Abstract of Israel 1964*, No. 15 (Jerusalem: Central Bureau of Statistics).
State of Israel Central Bureau of Statistics (1966), *Statistical Abstract of Israel 1966*, No. 17 (Jerusalem: Central Bureau of Statistics).
State of Israel Central Bureau of Statistics (1968), *Statistical Abstract of Israel 1968*, No. 19 (Jerusalem: Central Bureau of Statistics).
State of Israel Central Bureau of Statistics (1971), *Israel's Balance of Payments 1952–70*, special series, No. 365 (Jerusalem: Central Bureau of Statistics).
State of Israel Central Bureau of Statistics (1972), *Statistical Abstract of Israel 1972*, No. 23 (Jerusalem: Central Bureau of Statistics).
State of Israel Central Bureau of Statistics (1973), *Statistical Abstract of Israel 1973*, No. 24 (Jerusalem: Central Bureau of Statistics).
State of Israel Central Bureau of Statistics (1974), *Statistical Abstract of Israel 1974*, No. 25 (Jerusalem: Central Bureau of Statistics).
State of Israel Central Bureau of Statistics (1975), *Statistical Abstract of Israel 1975*, No. 26 (Jerusalem: Central Bureau of Statistics).
State of Israel Central Bureau of Statistics (1976), *Statistical Abstract of Israel 1976*, No. 27 (Jerusalem: Central Bureau of Statistics).
State of Israel Central Bureau of Statistics (1977a), *Statistical Abstract of Israel 1977*, No. 28 (Jerusalem: Central Bureau of Statistics).
State of Israel Central Bureau of Statistics (1977b), *Israel's Balance of Payments 1966–1976*, special series, No. 549 (Jerusalem: Central Bureau of Statistics).
State of Israel Central Bureau of Statistics (1980), *Statistical Abstract of Israel 1979*, No. 30 (Jerusalem: Central Bureau of Statistics).
State of Israel Ministry for Foreign Affairs (1953), *Documents Relating to the Agreement between the Government of Israel and the Government of the Federal Republic of Germany (Signed on 10 September, 1952, at Luxembourg)* (Jerusalem: Government Printer).
State of Israel Ministry for Foreign Affairs (1965), *Text of Statement by Asher Ben-Natan on the Occasion of the Presentation of his Credentials as Ambassador, August 24, 1965* (Jerusalem: Ministry for Foreign Affairs, August).
Statistisches Bundesamt (1964), *Statistisches Jahrbuch für die Bundesrepublik Deutschland 1964* (Wiesbaden: Statistisches Bundesamt).
Statistisches Bundesamt (1965), *Statistisches Jahrbuch für die Bundesrepublik Deutschland 1965* (Wiesbaden: Statistisches Bundesamt).
Statistisches Bundesamt (1968), *Statistisches Jahrbuch für die Bundesrepublik Deutschland 1968* (Wiesbaden: Statistisches Bundesamt).
Statistisches Bundesamt (1972), *Statistisches Jahrbuch für die Bundesrepublik Deutschland 1972* (Wiesbaden: Statistisches Bundesamt).
Statistisches Bundesamt (1973), *Statistisches Jahrbuch für die Bundesrepublik Deutschland 1973* (Wiesbaden: Statistisches Bundesamt).
Statistisches Bundesamt (1974a), *Statistisches Jahrbuch für die Bundesrepublik Deutschland 1974* (Wiesbaden: Statistisches Bundesamt).

Statistisches Bundesamt (1974b), *Fachserie G, Aussenhandel Reihe 1* (Wiesbaden: Statistisches Bundesamt).
Statistisches Bundesamt (1976), *Statistisches Jahrbuch für die Bundesrepublik Deutschland 1976* (Wiesbaden: Statistisches Bundesamt).
Statistisches Bundesamt (1980), *Statistisches Jahrbuch für die Bundesrepublik Deutschland 1980* (Wiesbaden: Statistisches Bundesamt).
Steinbach, Udo (ed.)(1979a), *Europäisch-arabische Zusammenarbeit. Arbeitspapiere zur internationalen Politik 11* (Bonn: Forschungsinstitut der Deutschen Gesellschaft für Auswärtige Politik e.V.).
Steinbach, Udo (1979b), 'Western European and EEC policies towards Mediterranean and Middle Eastern countries', in Colin Legum (ed.), *Middle East Contemporary Survey* (New York: Holmes & Meier), Vol. 2, 1977–8, pp. 40–8.
Steinbach, Udo (1981), 'German policy on the Middle East', *Aussenpolitik,* vol. 32, no. 4, pp. 315–31.
Stephens, John (1950), 'Israel's economic progress', *Foreign Commerce Weekly* (September 25), pp. 3–6.
Stern, Fritz (1963), *The Politics of Cultural Despair* (Berkeley and Los Angeles, Calif.: University of California Press).
Stern, Fritz (1975), 'The integration of Jews in nineteenth-century Germany', *Leo Baeck Institute Year Book,* Vol. XX, pp. 79–83.
Stern, Fritz (1977a), 'The burden of success: reflections on German Jewry', in Quentin Anderson, Stephen Donadio and Steven Marcus (eds), *Art, Politics and Will; Essays in Honor of Lionel Trilling* (New York: Basic Books), pp. 124–44.
Stern, Fritz (1977b), *Gold and Iron: Bismarck and the Building of the German Empire* (New York: Knopf).
Stern-Taeubler, Selma (1970), 'The first generation of emancipated Jews', *Leo Baeck Institute Year Book,* Vol. XV, pp. 3–40.
Tal, Uriel (1975), *Christians and Jews in Germany. Religion, Politics and Ideology in the Second Reich, 1870–1914* (Ithaca, NY: Cornell University Press).
Tavor, Moshe (1976), 'Aus israelischer Sicht. Ein Geleitwort', in Erich Lüth (ed.), *Die Friedensbitte an Israel 1951. Eine Hamburger Initiative* (Hamburg: Hans Christians Verlag), pp. 5–7.
Taylor, Alan R. (1978), 'The Euro-Arab Dialogue: quest for an interregional partnership', *Middle East Journal,* vol. 32, no. 4, pp. 429–43.
Taylor, Robert (1980), 'Implications for the Southern Mediterranean countries of the second enlargement of the European Community', in Commission of the European Communities, *Europe Information: Development,* X/225/80-EN.
Tern, Jürgen (1972), 'Normalisierung in der deutschen Orientpolitik', *Tribüne,* vol. 11, no. 41, pp. 4480–85.
Toury, Jacob (1966a), *Die politischen Orientierungen der Juden in Deutschland. Von Jena bis Weimar* (Tübingen: J. C. B. Mohr).
Toury, Jacob (1966b), ' "The Jewish Question" – a semantic approach', *Leo Baeck Institute Year Book,* Vol. XI, pp. 85–106.
Tovias, Alfred (1980), 'Israel and a community of twelve: challenges ahead', in Herbert Giersch (ed.), *The Economic Integration of Israel in the EEC* (Tübingen: J. C. B. Mohr), pp. 69–87.

Tramer, Hans (1971), 'Der Beitrag der Juden zu Geist und Kultur', in Werner E. Mosse and Arnold Paucker (eds), *Deutsches Judentum in Krieg und Revolution 1916–1923* (Tübingen: J. C. B. Mohr), pp. 317–85.

Tribüne (1978) '30 Jahre Israel', *Tribüne*, vol. 17, no. 66, pp. 4–151.

Tribüne (1980), 'Diskussion über Neonazismus', *Tribüne,* vol. 19, no. 73, pp. 61–86.

Tsoukalis, Loukas (1978), 'A community of twelve in search of an identity', *International Affairs,* vol. 54, no. 3, pp. 437–51.

Turner, Arthur Campbell (1971), *The Unique Partnership. Britain and the United States* (New York: Pegasus).

Union Interparlementaire (1950), *Compte Rendu de la XXXIXe Conférence Tenue à Dublin du 8 au 13 Septembre 1950* (Geneva: Bureau Interparlementaire).

Union Interparlementaire (1952), *Compte Rendu de la XLe Conférence Tenue à Istanbul du 31 août au 6 Septembre 1951* (Geneva: Bureau Interparlementaire).

United Nations (1953), *Statistical Yearbook 1953* (New York: Statistical Office of the United Nations Department of Economic Affairs).

United Nations (1954), *Statistical Yearbook 1954* (New York: Statistical Office of the United Nations Department of Economic Affairs).

United Nations (1968), *Statistical Papers. Series J. No. 11. World Energy Supplies 1963–1966* (New York: Statistical Office of the United Nations Department of Economic and Social Affairs).

United Nations (1972), *Statistical Papers. Series J. No. 15. World Energy Supplies 1961–1970* (New York: Statistical Office of the United Nations Department of Economic and Social Affairs).

United Nations (1974), *Statistical Papers. Series J. No. 17. World Energy Supplies 1969–1972* (New York: Statistical Office of the United Nations Department of Economic and Social Affairs).

United Nations (1979), *Demographic Yearbook 1978* (New York: Statistical Office of the United Nations Department of International Economic and Social Affairs).

United States Arms Control and Disarmament Agency (1979), *World Military Expenditures and Arms Transfers 1968–1977* (Washington, DC: United States Arms Control and Disarmament Agency).

United States Information Service (1975), *Daily Wireless File* (Rome: Embassy of the United States of America, February 26).

Vernon, Raymond (1979), 'The fragile foundations of East–West trade', *Foreign Affairs,* vol. 57, no. 5, pp. 1035–51.

Vogel, Rolf (ed.)(1967), *Deutschlands Weg nach Israel* (Stuttgart: Seewald Verlag).

Vogel, Rolf (ed.)(1969), *The German Path to Israel. A Documentation* (London: Oswald Wolff).

Vogt, Hannah (1980), 'Rechtsradikale Propaganda in der Bundesrepublik', *Tribüne,* vol. 19, no. 73, pp. 45–60.

Wagner, Wolfgang (1965a), 'Ueberprufung des deutschen Instrumentariums. Die Hallstein-Doktrin nach Ulbrichts Besuch in Aegypten', *Europa-Archiv,* vol. 20, no. 5, pp. 157–65.

Wagner, Wolfgang (1965b), 'Der Rückschlag der Bonner Politik in den arabischen Staaten', *Europa-Archiv,* vol. 20, no. 10, pp. 359–70.

Walichnowski, Tadeusz (1968), *The Tel-Aviv – Bonn Axis and Poland* (Warsaw: Interpress Publishers).

Wallace, Wiliam, and Allen, D. J. (1977), 'Political cooperation: procedure as substitute for policy', in H. Wallace, W. Wallace and C. Webb (eds), *Policy-Making in the European Communities* (Chichester: Wiley), pp. 227–47.

Wallich, Henry C. (1955), *Mainsprings of the German Revival* (New Haven, Conn.: Yale University Press).

Ward, Barbara (1980), 'Another chance for the North?', *Foreign Affairs,* vol. 59, no. 2, pp. 386–97.

Wasser, Hartmut (1966), 'Israel, die arabische Welt und die Bundesrepublik Deutschland', *Schweizerische Monatshefte,* vol. 46, no. 2.

von Wechmar, Rüdiger (1972), 'Besonnenheit statt Emotionen', *Tribüne,* vol. 11, no. 44, pp. 4913–16.

Weekly Compilation of Presidential Documents (1977), 'The President's news conference of May 12, 1977', *Weekly Compilation of Presidential Documents,* vol. 13, no. 20 (May), pp. 705–13.

Weil, Frederick (1980), 'The imperfectly mastered past: anti-semitism in West Germany since the Holocaust', *New German Critique,* no. 20 (Spring–Summer), pp. 135–53.

The Weizmann Institute of Science (1979), *Report for 1978* (Rehovot: The Weizmann Institute of Science).

Weltsch, Robert (1966), 'Entscheidungsjahr 1932', in Werner E. Mosse and Arnold Paucker (eds), *Entscheidungsjahr 1932. Zur Judenfrage in der Endphase der Weimarer Republik* (Tübingen: J. C. B. Mohr), pp. 535–62.

Weltsch, Robert (1970), 'Prefatory remarks', *Leo Baeck Institute Year Book,* Vol. XV, pp. 143–4.

Weltsch, Robert (1971), 'Schlusswort', in Werner E. Mosse and Arnold Paucker (eds), *Deutsches Judentum in Krieg und Revolution 1916–1923* (Tübingen: J. C. B. Mohr), pp. 613–34.

Weltsch, Robert (1972), *An der Wende des modernen Judentums. Betrachtungen aus fünf Jahrzehnten* (Tübingen: J. C. B. Mohr).

Weltsch, Robert (1976), 'Die schleichende Krise der jüdischen Identität – Ein Nachwort', in Werner E. Mosse and Arnold Paucker (eds), *Juden im Wilhelminischen Deutschland 1890–1914* (Tübingen: J. C. B. Mohr), pp. 689–702.

Westdeutscher Rundfunk (1979), *Holocaust – Analysen und Dokumente* (Cologne: Westdeutscher Rundfunk).

Westphal, Heinz (1973), 'Die Arbeit der Deutsch-Israelischen Gesellschaft', *Israels Aussenhandel,* vol. 7, no. 5–6, p. 8.

Wewer, Heinz (1963), 'Die deutsch-israelischen Beziehungen: Ende oder Neubeginn?', *Frankfurter Hefte,* vol. 18, no. 7, pp. 455–64.

Weymar, Paul (1955), *Konrad Adenauer. Der autorisierte Biographie* (Munich: Kindler Verlag).

Weymar, Paul (1957), *Adenauer. His Authorized Biography* (New York: Dutton).

White, John (1965), *German Aid. A Survey of the Sources, Policy and Structure of German Aid* (London: Overseas Development Institute).

The White House (1977), *Exchange of Remarks between the President and Yitzhak Rabin, Prime Minister of Israel* (Washington, DC: Office of the White House Press Secretary, March 7).

The Wiener Library (1951), *From Weimar to Hitler. Germany 1918–1933*, catalogue series, No. 2 (London: The Wiener Library).
The Wiener Library (1953), *Books on Persecution, Terror and Resistance in Nazi Germany*, 2nd edn with supplement, catalogue series, No. 1 (London: The Wiener Library).
The Wiener Library (1958), *German Jewry. Its History, Life and Culture*, catalogue series, No. 3 (London: Vallentine, Mitchell).
The Wiener Library (1963), *After Hitler. Germany 1945–1963*, catalogue series, No. 4 (London: Vallentine, Mitchell).
The Wiener Library (1964), *From Weimar to Hitler. Germany, 1918–1923*, 2nd rev. edn., catalogue series, No. 2 (London: Vallentine, Mitchell).
The Wiener Library (1971), *Prejudice. Racist-Religious-Nationalist*, catalogue series, No. 5 (London: Vallentine, Mitchell).
The Wiener Library (1978a), *German Jewry. Part II, Additions and Amendments to Catalogue Number 3, 1959–1972*, catalogue series, No. 6 (London: Institute of Contemporary History).
The Wiener Library (1978b), *Persecution and Resistance under the Nazis. Part I, Reprint of Catalogue Number 1*, 2nd edn; *Part II, New Material and Amendments*, catalogue series, No. 7 (London: Institute of Contemporary History).
Williamson, David Graham (1975), 'Walther Rathenau: patron saint of the German liberal establishment (1922–1972)', *Leo Baeck Institute Year Book*, Vol. XX, pp. 207–22.
World Today (1950), 'Austerity and enterprise in Israel', vol. VI, no. 1, pp. 6–15.
Wormann, Curt D. (1970), 'German Jews in Israel: their cultural situation since 1933', *Leo Baeck Institute Year Book*, Vol. XV, pp. 73–103.
Wright, Gerald (1974), 'Persuasive influence: the case of the interest equalization tax', in W. Andrew Axline, *et al.* (eds), *Continental Community? Independence and Integration in North America* (Toronto: McClelland & Stewart), pp. 137–63.
Yaniv, Avner (1976), 'The French connection: a review of French policy toward Israel', *Jerusalem Journal of International Relations*, vol. 1, no. 3, pp. 115–30.
Yisrael, Yitzhak (1971), 'Les relations Germano-Israeliennes de 1949 à 1965', dissertation, Fondation National des Sciences Politiques, Paris.
Zielinski, Siegfried (1980), 'History as entertainment: the TV series "Holocaust" in West Germany', *New German Critique*, no. 19 (Winter), pp. 81–96.

Index

Abs, Josef Hermann 40, 53, 61–4, 77–8, 83, 86, 90, 93, 101, 120, 289
Achdut Haavoda 129, 228
Act for the Control of Weapons of War xiii, 137, 141, 208
Adenauer, Konrad 37, 39–42, 47–65, 67, 74–5, 77–9, 83–6, 90–2, 101, 110–11, 120, 128, 131, 133–6, 143, 155–63, 168, 177, 180, 191–2, 194, 196, 198–9, 216, 220
Allon, Yigal 115, 152, 155, 173–4, 186
Altmaier, Jakob 55, 60, 84
antisemitism 13–27, 30, 35–8, 42, 47–8, 58–9, 111, 134, 154, 216–18, 226, 233–4, 239–40
Arab World
  relations with Europe xi, 2, 3, 82
  relations with France 3, 286
  relations with West Germany xi, xii, xiii, 3, 8, 82, 88, 103, 120, 128, 157–76, 180, 184, 194–211, 213, 223, 240, 261–2, 274–6, 287
  relations with West Germany, economic aid, see economic relations
  relations with West Germany, diplomatic 122, 128, 162–3, 199–201, 203, 206, 210–11, 215
  relations with West Germany, investment 205, 207–8
  relations with West Germany, military, see military relations
  relations with West Germany, oil 167, 171, 176, 190, 194, 198–205, 208, 213, 218, 223
  relations with West Germany, parliamentary 209
  relations with West Germany, political support, see political support
  relations with West Germany, science and technology 207
  relations with West Germany, societal 210
  relations with West Germany, trade 194–8, 203, 205, 207, 210–11
  relations with West Germany, youth exchange see youth exchange
  view on arms to Israel, see military relations
  view on reparations 78–9, 86, 92, 95, 99, 120, 194, 196, 210

Arafat, Yassir 175, 188, 215, 221, 241
'areas of tension' xiii, 137, 141, 182
arms, see military relations
assimilation 18–21, 24, 31

balanced policy in the Middle East 87, 164–8, 170, 186, 191–2, 194, 201, 203–4, 221, 241
Barou, Noah 60, 70, 84
Barzel, Rainer 162, 191, 289
Befangenheit, see psychological factors
Begin, Menachem 2, 41, 45–6, 48, 174–5, 187–9, 193, 228, 230–1, 241–2, 291
Benda, Ernst 236, 289
Ben-Gurion, David 37–8, 42, 44, 57, 69, 70, 72, 74, 76, 80, 101, 110–11, 118, 120, 127, 129–31, 134–5, 139–40, 143, 155, 158, 160, 165, 178–81, 183, 186, 189, 192, 216, 220
Ben–Natan, Asher 102, 104, 111, 133–4, 136, 183–4, 192–3, 216, 219, 227, 233, 240, 291, 293
bilateral relations 2–3, 5–9, 51, 87–8, 172, 174, 187, 189, 213, 245, 249, 252–4, 259–62, 266–7, 269, 271–2, 276, 281, 284–8
Birrenbach, Kurt 121, 140, 162, 190–1, 236, 289
Blankenhorn, Herbert 52–3, 55, 60, 78, 83, 84
Blumenfeld, Erik 227, 289
Böhm, Franz 52–3, 60–5, 77–8, 83, 85–6, 90, 216, 289
Brandt, Willy 121, 163, 165–6, 168–71, 175, 184–5, 188, 191, 193, 200–5, 210–11, 216, 221–2, 229, 231, 241
von Brentano, Heinrich 57, 158

Canada 6
  relations with USA, see USA
Carter, James E. 4
Central Association of German Citizens of Jewish Faith xvii, 19–22, 24, 26, 31
Central Council of Jews in Germany xvii, 33, 43, 71, 95, 236
CDU xii, xvii, 40–1, 55, 86, 95, 140, 159, 161, 191, 198, 221–3, 236, 241
CSU xvii, 77, 79, 86, 95, 140, 161, 191, 222

Index

Churchill, Winston S. 247–50, 256, 259
Cohn, Josef 48, 142–3, 146, 155–6, 291
collective shame 39, 47
common traditions 28, 32, 146, 232, 275
   in general 263
   in other cases 248–51, 256–9, 279
Conference on Jewish Material Claims against Germany 61, 76, 89–90, 93, 95
'confrontation with the past' 233–8, 242
co-operative international relations, *see* bilateral relations
cultural relations 142, 147, 155, 229–33, 242, 275
   in general 269, 271

van Dam, Hendrik 43, 71
Dayan, Moshe 174, 178, 187, 193
defence, *see* military relations
denazification 36, 48
development aid, *see* economic relations
diplomacy, *see* political support
diplomatic relations 48, 82, 102, 105, 110–11, 122–3, 133, 136, 157–67, 177–84, 189–91, 198–201, 213, 219, 221, 226, 228–9, 235–6, 240–1, 276
   in general 269–70, 287
domestic environment
   in general 266, 271–2, 286
   in other cases 256–8, 281–3
   Israel 80–2, 129, 178, 180, 187–8
   West Germany 76–9, 82, 237

Eban, Abba 167, 184–5, 229, 233, 235–6, 241
economic conditions, Israel 67–75, 85, 97–9, 120, 129, 273
economic necessity, Israel 1, 43, 49, 54, 65–76, 81, 110–11, 118, 145
economic relations 1, 87–120, 164, 166,
   aid 1, 89, 100–11, 121, 123, 182, 190–1, 200–1, 206, 209–10, 273–4
   aid, 1960, 'agreement' 101–4, 110–11, 120 128, 134, 160, 192
   aid, 1965 agreement 101–4, 110–11, 121
   aid, from other countries to Israel 1–2, 68–9, 81, 96–7, 108–10
   aid, from West Germany to other countries 102–9, 206
   aid, from world Jewry to Israel 69, 96–7
   aid, to Arab World 107–9, 161–2,198–9, 200–1, 205–6, 210–11
   banking 224
   in general 266, 268

investment 1, 89, 117–18
trade 1, 89, 112–17, 223–4
trade, with other countries 112–13, 121, 194–8, 205
trade unions 220, 224–5, 239, 242, 271
Egypt 79, 158, 161, 168, 173, 190, 192, 194–9, 202–3, 205–11 *see also* Arab World and German scientists
   peace treaty with Israel 172, 174–6, 211
Eichmann, Adolf 132, 134, 160–1, 179
emancipation of Jews 11, 13, 15–16, 18, 23–5, 30
endurance 7, 8, 213, 245, 274, 276
   in general 261, 270–2, 286–7
   in other cases 252, 256, 258, 280–1
energy 144, *see also* Arab World and oil
   West German use and requirements 198, 200
Erhard, Ludwig 40, 64, 78, 86, 101–2, 111, 121, 123, 133, 138, 140, 157, 159–63, 168, 183, 191, 198–9, 216, 235, 289
Eshkol, Levi 103, 111, 118, 121, 131, 155, 160, 162, 177–8, 181–3, 189, 228, 236, 242
EEC xii, 1–2, 82, 190–1, 253, 271 *see also* oil
   Euro-Arab Dialogue 3, 172–3, 192
   relations with Arab World 191
   relations with Arab World, trade 115
   relations with Israel 89, 130, 145, 155, 181, 191–2, 200, 232
   relations with Israel, trade xi, 1, 114–16, 118–19, 121, 224
   relations with Middle East 9
   trade agreements 1, 114–5, 121
   view on Middle East conflict xi, xii, 2, 157, 167, 169–76, 181, 184–8, 191–2, 203–5, 222, 226, 276, 287
even-handed policy in the Middle East, *see* balanced policy
Extra-Parliamentary Opposition 216

fascism 25, 28, 35–6, 234, 239
Federal Indemnification Law xviii, 90, 94–5, 119
   'post-1953' cases 94
   'post-1965' cases 95
   'special fund' 95–7, 229
Federal Restitution Law xviii, 90, 94–7, 119
Federation of the German Jews xviii, 21
'Final Solution' 27–8, 49
First World War 21–3, 31
Fischer, Maurice 60, 67, 83
foreign currency 67–8, 71, 74

Index

Foreign Office (West Germany) xviii, 84, 121, 137, 145, 158, 170, 176–7, 221, 242, 290, 293
Foreign Trade Act xviii, 137
Foreign Trade Ordinance xviii, 141
foundations 7, 11, 32, 127, 245, 274, 286
 in general 262–5
 in other cases 257, 285–6
France
 policy in EEC on Israel 114–15, 119
 policy in EEC on Middle East conflict 169–70, 172, 175, 177, 187
 relations with Arab World 34, 265, 286
 relations with Israel 189, 231, 271, 283–4
 relations with Israel, military 1, 126–7, 130, 136
 relations with West Germany 4, 130–1, 144, 148–51, 156, 169, 187, 222, 263, 265, 269, 275, 284–5
 role in reparations 42, 55
 view on Middle East conflict xi, 2, 191, 204, 275
FDP xii, xviii, 79, 86, 95, 140, 159, 162, 166, 175, 191, 198–9, 203, 215–16, 222–3, 236, 241

Gahal 229
General Zionists 76, 80
genocide 49
Genscher, Hans-Dietrich xi, 115, 117, 121, 154, 173–6, 186–7, 205, 211
German Academic Exchange xviii, 222
GDR 50, 85, 92–4, 158, 161–2, 190–1, 198–9, 209
 relations with FRG 4
German Federation of Trade Unions xviii, 220, 224–5
German–Israeli Committee for Scientific and Technological Co-operation xviii, 144, 225
German–Israeli Parliamentary Association xii, xviii, 209, 222, 240–1
German–Israeli Society xviii, 226–8, 236, 242
German Oriental Institute xviii, 210
German Party xviii, 58–9, 79, 97
German scientists in Egypt 82, 135, 157, 159–61, 177, 180–3, 186, 190, 213, 219, 221, 228, 235, 240–1, 276
German Society for Economic Relations with Israel xviii, 114, 222–3
Gerstenmaier, Eugen 161, 216
Ginor, Fanny 66, 70, 74–5, 97–100, 120, 291

Globke, Hans 134, 177
Goldmann, Nahum 33, 40, 43–4, 48, 60, 62–3, 65, 70, 74, 77, 84, 90, 93, 95, 235, 291
Grass, Günter 216, 239
guilt 32–3, 35–6, 38–40, 46–8, 56, 58–9, 83, 133, 146, 175, 213, 230, 234, 239, 286

Hallstein, Walter 64, 78–9, 158, 178
 Hallstein Doctrine 158–9, 161, 274
Harel, Isser, 180, 192, 291
Heinemann, Gustav 216, 239
Herut 41, 45, 48, 80, 129, 228–9
Heuss, Theodor 39, 47, 216
Histadrut 220, 224–5, 242
historical intertwining xiii, 7–8, 11, 13–28, 32, 39, 46, 222, 229, 239, 273, 275
 in general 262–5, 272
 in other cases 248–50, 252, 254, 256–9, 283–6
Hitler, Adolf 28, 34–5, 37, 42, 54, 130, 154, 175, 181, 238
Holland
 policy in EEC on Israel 114–15, 171, 204
 relations with West Germany 222
Holocaust 1–2, 27–30, 43, 47, 49, 130–2, 172, 180, 183, 187–8, 192, 217, 229, 231, 238, 264, 275–6, 287
'Holocaust' 33, 36, 47, 233–5, 237, 242
Horowitz, David 44, 48, 55, 60, 66–7, 70–5, 83–5, 100, 292

integration of German Jews 18–19, 22–3
Independent Liberal Party 222–3
informality 284
 in general 266
 in other cases 248, 253–7, 277, 284
intensity 7, 11, 27–8, 32, 39, 46
 in general 262–5
 in other cases 285
international system 3, 8–9, 50–1, 83, 213, 261–2, 287–8
 in general 269, 271–2, 274, 286–7
 in other cases 256–8
investment, see economic relations
Iraq 175–6, see also Arab World
Israel–German Chamber of Commerce and Industry 114, 222
Israeli–German Parliamentary Group 223
Israeli–German Society 226–8
Israel Labour Party, see Mapai
Israel Mission 90, 119, 229
Israel Philharmonic Orchestra 230, 233

'Jewish question' 13–15, 18, 23–5
Jordan 173, *see also* Arab World
Josephtal, Giora 70, 83, 100

Kiesinger, Kurt Georg 121, 166, 199–200
Kissinger, Henry 4, 248–50
Knoke, Karl Hermann 165, 191, 290
Kohl, Helmut xii, xiii
Kristallnacht 25–6, 230, 237
Kühn, Heinz 148, 216, 239
Küster, Otto 61–4, 77–8, 83, 85, 290
Küstermeier, Rudolf 37–9, 48, 53, 58, 119, 290, 293

Lebanon xi, xii, 192, 241
Libya 171, 175, *see also* Arab World
Likud 188, 222, 241
Livneh, Eliyahu 60, 84
London Debt Conference 53, 61–4, 77–8, 85, 91–2
Lüth, Erich 32–3, 37–9, 47–8, 55–6, 58–9, 216, 284, 290
Luxembourg Agreement, *see* reparations

maintenance 11, 213, 215–43, 273–4
  in general 270–1
Maki 80, 228
Mapai 80, 187, 220–2, 229, 239, 241
Mapam 45–6, 48, 80, 129, 135, 228
'mastering the past' 33–5, 47, 165, 167, 234, 238, 243
Max Planck Society 143
McCloy, John 51, 54, 56, 58, 63, 65, 84
Meir, Golda 70, 80, 178, 180, 183, 185, 189, 221, 241
Mende, Erich 191, 290
Meroz, Yochanan xiii, 187, 193, 237, 292
Middle East 2, 5, 50, 137, 161, 240
  views on conflict, *see* EEC; France; UK and USA
  West German view on conflict 2–3, 219, 222, 240–1
  see also Arab World and political support
Minerva Foundation 143–4
military relations xiii, 122–41, 231, 266–7, 275
  agreements 123–35, 140–1. 161, 190
  aid 1, 104, 123–38, 161–3, 169, 181, 188, 201, 209, 220
  aid, from other countries to Israel 1, 126–7, 130, 136
  aid, from West Germany to other countries 123–6, 135, 139
  aid, opposition in Israel 129, 186, 228
  arms, termination 1965 121, 135, 161–2, 177, 182–3, 191, 201, 213, 236, 239, 240, 242, 276
  arms, to Jordan 124, 139
  arms, to Libya 211
  arms, to Saudi Arabia xiii, 138–9, 208, 215, 220, 222
  arms, to Sudan 124, 211
  arms, to Syria 187, 211
  training of armed forces 127, 136–9
  weapons technology 1, 127, 136–7
Ministry of Defence
  Israel 122, 136–8, 294
  West Germany xvii, 122, 126, 129, 137–8, 141, 222, 290, 293
Ministry for Economic Co-operation (West Germany) xiii, 100–1, 103, 105, 121, 290, 293
Ministry for Economics (West Germany) xiii, 64, 102, 111, 121, 171, 174, 290, 293
Ministry for Education
  Israel 229–30
  West Germany xiii, 143
Ministry of Finance
  Israel 66, 68, 70–1, 85, 120–1, 294
  West Germany xvii, 63, 71, 77, 86, 98, 120, 290, 293
Ministry for Foreign Affairs (Israel) xiii, 64, 69, 71–2, 74, 83, 137, 152, 188, 191, 292, 294
Ministry for Research and Technology (West Germany) xvii, 143–4, 155, 290, 293
Ministry for Youth, Family and Health (West Germany) xvii, 147–8, 154, 290, 293
Mizrachi 80
morality xiii, 1, 11, 40–1, 43–9, 51–4, 58, 60–1, 63–6, 71–4, 78, 80–1, 83, 91, 93, 95, 100, 110–11, 119, 128–33, 135, 140, 146, 153, 161–2, 165, 172, 183, 186, 188–9, 191, 208, 213, 215, 219, 236–9, 273–5, 283
multilateral relations 5–6, 253, 271

National Council for Research and Development 143–6, 155
NDP xviii, 217
national socialism 13–14, 17–18, 24–8, 31–8, 40, 46–8, 50, 56, 134–5, 153, 164, 169, 175, 179–81, 183, 188, 192, 220, 226, 228, 234, 242
  crimes 27, 37–40, 42, 44, 46–7, 49, 52–3, 55, 57–9, 63, 66, 72–3, 76, 90, 95, 99, 110, 119, 146, 168–9, 179, 189, 226, 235–9

neo-Nazism 217, 240
Near and Middle East Association xix, 209
need 2, 8, 11, 46, 49–85, 99–100, 110–11, 118–19, 127, 129–36, 145–6, 153–5, 157, 189, 213, 239, 273–5
  in general 262, 265–6, 270–1
  in other cases 249, 254–6, 259, 277–8, 280
  with Arab World 275
New Left 99–100, 216, 240
normal relations xiii, 87, 104–5, 108, 114, 124, 137–8, 144, 148–50, 158, 163–5, 167–9, 173, 176, 178–9, 183–5, 193, 198, 200–1, 229, 274, 284
  in general 267–9, 272
NATO 124, 131, 133, 135, 253
Nuremburg laws 25–6

obsession 11, 18, 28, 32
  in general 263
occupation authorities 50, 54–5, 72, 84
Occupational Statute 50, 55–6, 60, 84, 90
oil
  embargo 170, 201, 204
  European dependence on Arabs 2, 81, 167, 191
  West German dependence on Arabs, *see* Arab World
Olympic Games Munich 82, 185, 221, 231
operation 7–8, 87–8, 245
opposition to relations, *see* domestic environment
OAPEC 170, 204–5
OECD 105, 208
OPEC 109, 205–6
orthodox Jews 18–19, 23, 30–1
Ostpolitik 166, 168, 21

PLO b, 82, 172–3, 175–6, 188, 215–16, 222–3
Palestinian question xii, 2, 81, 171–6, 185–8, 190, 192, 200, 204–5, 209, 213, 215, 220–1, 223, 226, 241, 275–6, 287
parliamentary relations 209, 222–3, 240–1
  with Arab World *see* Arab World
  with other countries 209, 223, 241
Pauls, Rolf 163–6, 169, 228–9, 293
Peace with Israel Movement xix, 32, 37–9, 57, 60
perception 41, 43, 54, 65–6, 73, 81, 114, 128, 157, 274
  in general 262, 265–7

in other cases 254
Peres, Shimon 118, 122, 124, 126–8, 131, 133–5, 139, 178–9, 220, 227, 233
philosemitism 234
political parties 271, *see also* individual parties
Poland 4, 93, 95, 120
political support xi, xii, xiii, 2, 157–93, 213, 274–5
  in general 269–70
'post-1953' cases, *see* Federal Indemnification Law
'post-1965' cases *see* Federal Indemnification Law
power 4, 252, 255–6, 259, 262
pragmatism xiii, 39, 41, 43, 49–54, 57, 60–5, 75–6, 81–3, 91, 110–11, 119, 129–35, 140, 155, 165, 169, 178–9, 186–9, 192, 198, 201, 213, 229, 273–5, *see also* economic necessity
  in other cases 257–8, 280
preference xii, 4, 46–7, 88, 90–2, 94, 100–1, 104–5, 112, 114, 118, 123, 126–8, 135, 137–8, 155, 157–60, 163, 168–9, 186, 194, 209–11, 226, 273–5
  in general 261, 263, 265–7, 269–72
  in other cases 249–53, 256, 259, 277, 280, 282–7
preoccupation 11, 32, 82, 230
  in general 262–3
psychological factors 7, 8, 11, 28, 32–47, 213, 215–6, 218, 228–30, 233–43, 264–5, 273, 275, 277
  Befangenheit 264–5
  in general 264, 271–2
  in other cases 248–50, 252–5, 278, 283, 285
Public Council for Youth and Young Adult Exchange 148, 156
public opinion xi, 33, 39, 47–8, 216–43
  polls xi, 32, 34–5, 45, 47–8, 217–18, 230–1, 234–5, 237, 240–2, 265

Rabin, Yitzhak 4, 154, 175, 186
reform Jews 19–20
rehabilitation 49–57, 64–5, 75, 81–2, 85, 111, 134, 140, 163–4, 166, 189–90, 239, 273–5
religious associations 225–6
reparations 1, 42–5, 47, 51, 53–5, 57–9, 62, 64–7, 71–2, 88–9, 91–3, 99, 104, 111, 120, 128, 131–2, *see also* Federal Indemnification Law, Federal Restitution Law and restitution

Adenauer speech, September 1951 39–40, 42, 49, 54, 58–60, 63–4, 74, 78, 83–4
direct negotiations 42–6, 48–9, 53–4, 58, 60–5, 67, 70–1, 73–7, 80, 83, 85, 129, 194
Israeli claim 42, 45, 49, 55, 57, 59–62, 64, 67, 72–4, 77–8, 84–5, 94
Luxembourg Agreement 54–5, 57–60, 70–1, 73–6, 78, 80–1, 83–6, 89–94, 96–100, 110–12, 114, 119–20, 129, 158, 160, 177, 181–2, 195–6
opposition in Arab World, *see* Arab World
opposition in Israel 80–1, 186
opposition in West Germany 76–9, 86
Paris meeting 55, 59–60, 67, 83, 85
to other countries 92
unofficial talks 54–60, 70–1, 73–4, 83–5
restitution 1, 39–40, 42–3, 52, 59, 71–2, 75, 77, 85, 89, 94, 98–9, 146, *see also* Federal Indemnification Law and Federal Restitution Law
Richtlinienkompetenz 162

Saudia Arabia 3–4, 174, 176, 188, 192, *see also* Arab World
arms to, *see* military relations
Schäffer, Fritz 61–3, 77, 83, 86, 90
Scheel, Walter 3, 121, 146, 166–71, 184, 191, 198, 203–5, 210–11, 229, 275
Schmid, Carlo 41, 53, 57–8, 216, 284, 290
Schmidt, Helmut xi, xii, 2, 109, 163, 173–6, 187–9, 192–3, 205, 208–9, 222, 231, 234–5, 237, 241–2, 276
schoolbooks 238
Schröder, Gerhard 127, 162, 191, 215–16, 275, 289
Schütz, Klaus 121, 154, 174, 176, 192–3, 216
Schumacher, Kurt 47, 59
science and technology 1, 82, 142–6, 155, 209, 274–5
with other countries 144–5, 207

Second Reich 11, 13–21, 29–30
Second World War 1, 27–30, 93, 231, 250
sentiment, *see* morality
in other cases 257–8
Shamir, Yitzhak 187–8
Sharett, Moshe 44–5, 56–7, 64, 69–71, 76, 83, 90, 155, 178, 181

Shinnar, Felix 41, 44, 48, 55, 62, 69–70, 74, 84, 93, 97, 99, 101–2, 104, 110, 112, 120–1, 128, 131, 133, 139–40, 158, 160–1, 177–8, 190–1, 216, 220, 236, 292
Sign of Atonement Movement xix, 225–6, 240, 242
Six-Day War 81, 114, 126, 163, 166, 199, 201, 218–19, 221, 240
SPD xii, xiii, xix, 23, 41, 47, 55, 59–60, 64, 86, 95, 133, 137, 159, 203, 208, 215, 220–3, 236, 241
societal relations xii, 2, 213–33, 239, 273, 276
in general 269–70
in other cases 252–4, 259, 284–6
Societies for Christian-Jewish Co-operation xix, 47, 226
special relationships 3–8, 11, 13, 28, 30, 32, 41, 46, 48, 75–6, 82, 87–8
and theories of international relations 213, 245, 247, 251–59, 276–86
Anglo–American, *see* USA
Canadian–American, *see* USA
definition 4, 272
EEC–Arab, *See* Arab World
Franco–Arab, *see* France
Franco–German, *see* France
Franco–Israeli, *see* France
German–American, *see* USA
German–Arab, *see* Arab World
German–Israeli xi, xii, xiii, 3, 6–9, 11, 13, 28, 32, 41, 46, 49, 75–6, 81–2, 87–9, 101, 103–5, 109, 114–5, 119–20, 122–9, 133, 136, 138, 140, 142, 144, 146–8, 151, 153, 155, 157–8, 160, 163–9, 171, 173, 175–7, 181, 183–7, 189–91, 193, 198, 201, 204, 210, 213, 215–16, 219–20, 223, 225, 228, 230, 233–4, 239, 259, 261–2, 264–5, 269, 271–6, 281, 284, 286–7
measurement 7, 88, 266–7
origin of term 247–8
Soviet–Cuban, *see* USSR
theory 261–72
US–Iranian, *see* USA
US–Israeli, *see* USA
US–Japanese, *see* USA
US–Saudi, *see* USA
West German–East German, *see* GDR
West German–Polish, *see* Poland
Springer, Axel 216, 239, 241
Statute of Limitations 82, 222, 234–8, 242–3
Strauss, Franz-Josef 79, 128, 131–4, 140,

191, 216, 220, 222, 242
students 225, *see also* youth exchange
Syria 161, 173–5, 187, *see also* Arab World

termination 271–2
theory
  definition 7–9
  international relations 2–4 245–60, 286
  alliance 257–60, 276, 279–80, 281–4, 287
  attraction 255–6, 259
  influence 255–6, 259
  integration 4–5, 252–5, 259–60, 276–9, 284–5, 287
  interdependence 5, 252–3, 255, 259–60, 276, 278, 287
  linkage 4–5
  realism 4–5, 252, 255
  special relationships, *see* special relationships
  transnationalism 5
Third Reich 13–14, 25–7, 39, 52, 68, 93, 159, 177, 180, 218, 228, 233
trade, *see* economic relations

uniqueness 2, 3, 6, 49, 65, 88, 90, 100, 127–8, 135, 144, 148, 182, 184, 224, 236, 275–6
  in other cases 247–52, 257, 259, 264, 272, 281, 287
United Kingdom
  relations with Israel 231
  relations with Israel, trade 112–13, 121
  relations with USA, *see* USA
  role in reparations 42, 55, 65
  view on Middle East conflict 2, 169–70, 191, 201, 204
UN 56, 82, 159, 172–3, 181, 186, 191–2, 200, 220–1, 223, 269
  Resolution 168–9, 174, 191, 203
USSR 4, 6, 42, 50–1, 65, 69, 93, 129, 132–3, 136, 158, 160–2, 166, 190, 198, 222
  relations with Cuba 4
USA
  relations with Australia 255
  relations with Brazil 255
  relations with Canada 7, 245, 251–3, 256–7, 259, 261, 264, 266, 269–71, 276–8, 287
  relations with Iran 3, 261, 286
  relations with Israel 4, 51, 81, 99, 129, 159, 187, 204, 231, 248, 269, 282–3
  relations with Israel, economic aid 1, 2, 68–9, 81, 96–7, 110, 127

  relations with Israel, investment 117
  relations with Israel, military 1, 81, 122, 126, 138, 141, 170–1
  relations with Israel, science and technology 144
  relations with Israel, trade 112–13
  relations with Israel, trade unions 242
  relations with Italy 62
  relations with Japan 4, 263 282
  relations with Mexico 255
  relations with Saudi Arabia 3–4, 285–6
  relations with UK 7, 245, 247–53, 256–7, 259, 261–2, 264–5, 269–71, 274, 278–81, 286
  relations with USSR 50–1, 129, 166, 198
  relations with Vietnam 264
  relations with West Germany xi, xii, 4, 7, 144, 159, 191, 204, 240, 245, 248, 251–2, 257, 259, 261, 275, 281–2, 284
  role in diplomatic relations 162, 191
  role in military relations 129, 135, 140–1, 161
  role in reparations 50–1, 54–6, 58, 63, 65, 80, 83–5, 99–100, 111
  role in statute of limitations abolition 235, 242
  view on Middle East conflict xi, xii, 170–2, 201, 204

Volkswagen foundation 143, 225

Waldorf Astoria meeting, *see* economic relations
Wassenaar negotiations, *see* reparations
Wehner, Herbert 216, 222, 239, 241
Weimar Republic 23–5, 29, 31
Weizmann Institute 143–5, 156
West Bank settlements 169–72, 174, 191–2, 241
Western Allies 36, 42, 50, 52–6, 58, 60, 63–5, 71, 77, 84, 90, 158, *see also* occupation authorities
Western Europe 50, 59, *see also* EEC
Wischnewski, Hans-Jürgen, 203, 215–16, 275
world Jewry, *see* Conference on Jewish Material Claims against Germany
  aid to Israel, *see* economic relations
  role in reparations 38, 43, 59, 62–4, 70–1, 97
  role in statute of limitations abolition 235

Yom Kippur War 2, 4, 81, 144, 170–2, 185, 204, 218–23, 240–1
youth exchange 142, 146–56, 209, 225–6, 240, 274
 in general 269
 with Arab World 150–1, 209
 with France, *see* France
 with other countries 148–53, 285

Zionism 18, 20, 24, 26, 172
 anti-Zionism 216–17, 240
 pro-Zionism 234